BRITISH FASCISM
1918–39

MANCHESTER STUDIES IN MODERN HISTORY
General editor Jeremy Black

BRITISH FASCISM
1918–39

PARTIES, IDEOLOGY
AND CULTURE

Thomas Linehan

MANCHESTER
UNIVERSITY PRESS
Manchester and New York

Copyright © Thomas Linehan 2000

The right of Thomas Linehan to be identified as the author of this work has been asserted by him in accordance with the Copyright, Designs and Patents Act 1988.

Published by Manchester University Press
Oxford Road, Manchester M13 9NR, UK
and Room 400, 175 Fifth Avenue, New York, NY 10010, USA
www.manchesteruniversitypress.co.uk

Distributed exclusively in the USA by
Palgrave, 175 Fifth Avenue, New York NY 10010, USA

Distributed exclusively in Canada by
UBC Press, University of British Columbia, 2029 West Mall, Vancouver, BC, Canada V6T 1Z2

British Library Cataloguing-in-Publication Data
A catalogue record for this book is available from the British Library

Library of Congress Cataloging-in-Publication Data
A catalog record for this book is available from the Library of Congress

ISBN-10: 0 7190 5024 3

ISBN-13: 978 0 7190 5024 4

First published 2000 by Manchester University Press

First digital, on-demand edition produced by Lightning Source 2006

For my father,
Daniel Christopher Linehan

CONTENTS

Preface and acknowledgements—*page ix*
List of abbreviations—*xii*

Introduction: the historiography of fascist studies—*1*

One—*13*
Origins and progenitors

Two—*38*
The early postwar context and the
pre-fascist groups: incipient fascism?

Three—*61*
The arrival of fascism: the British Fascisti
and the Imperial Fascist League

Four—*84*
The British Union of Fascists

Five—*124*
The minor parties, 'one-man bands'
and some fellow-travellers

Six—*150*
The membership

Seven—*176*
British fascism and anti-semitism

Eight—*201*
Defining culture

NINE—*222*
A host of 'decadent' phenomena

TEN—*245*
The city, the countryside and the machine

ELEVEN—*269*
Responding to the visual arts:
British fascism and artistic modernism

SELECT BIBLIOGRAPHY—*288*

INDEX—*299*

PREFACE AND ACKNOWLEDGEMENTS

It is important at the outset to explain the focus of this book. It is pre-eminently a survey of the development of British fascism between the World Wars. The book has two main strands. Firstly, it provides a clear and accessible guide to the essential features of interwar British fascism. Here, there is a particular stress on the various fascist parties, fascist personalities and fascist ideologies. This first strand of the book also familiarises the reader with the historiography of this subject. The second feature of the book looks at British fascism and culture, hitherto an under-researched area in this field. In the first instance, then, the book will develop the knowledge of undergraduate students by providing a solid source of background material on this important area of interwar British history. In the second respect, the focus on fascist culture throws new light on the character of native fascism and suggests a potentially rich vein of new enquiry for scholars of British fascism.

It is also necessary at the outset to explain the scope of this book. Inevitably, because of restrictions of space imposed on the author by the nature of the book, in that it is both textbook and monograph, it was impossible to cover all aspects of British fascist culture. There is no extensive treatment of topics such as theatre or music, for example. This wider focus on British fascist culture will form the basis of a new project to be undertaken at a later date. In addition, the book does not follow the trail of the fascists through the war years. This represents another story and one that is adequately covered in works such as T. Kushner, *The Persistence of Prejudice. Antisemitism in British Society During the Second World War* (Manchester, Manchester University Press, 1989); A. W. B. Simpson, *In the Highest Degree Odious. Detention Without Trial in Wartime Britain* (Oxford, Oxford University Press, 1992);

Preface and acknowledgements

R. Thurlow, *Fascism in Britain. A History, 1918–1985* (Oxford, Blackwell, 1987); R. Griffiths, *Patriotism Perverted. Captain Ramsay, the Right Club and British Anti-Semitism 1939–40* (London, Constable, 1998) and T. Linehan, *East London for Mosley. The British Union of Fascists in East London and South-West Essex 1933–40* (London, Frank Cass, 1996). To do justice to such a vast topic as the war years would have required the writing of another book.

I should like to express my gratitude to the following individuals and members of staff at various institutions, who have helped in some way in the preparation and completion of this book. To begin with, may I express my sincere thanks to the editorial staff at Manchester University Press, who have provided me with due guidance and patience throughout this project.

This book contains a small proportion of material from my first book, *East London for Mosley. The British Union of Fascists in East London and South-West Essex 1933–40* (London, Frank Cass, 1996). I would like to thank Frank Cass & Co. Ltd for kindly granting me permission to reproduce this material.

It is also a pleasure to acknowledge the assistance of archivists and librarians who generally assisted me during my visits and some of whom granted me permission to consult material. My thanks go to those at the Public Record Office, British Library, British Newspaper Library, British Library of Political and Economic Science, the Board of Deputies of British Jews, the Wiener Library and Cambridge University Library. I should also like to express my gratitude to staff at Brunel University Library for their help in procuring copies of various theses for consultation.

Additionally, I would like to extend my thanks to a number of scholars whose work on various areas associated with fascist studies and related fields such as anti-semitism has provided much inspiration over the years. Special mention here must be made to Roger Griffin, Colin Holmes, Richard Thurlow and Geoffrey Alderman. The works of those non-British scholars of generic fascism, George Mosse, Stanley Payne and Zeev Sternhell, too, have helped to stimulate my thinking. Other historians and political theorists have been helpful in giving an understanding of aspects of the background to this book. These scholars include David Baker, Michael Biddiss, Hilary Blume, Philip Coupland, Mike Cronin, Stephen Cullen, Martin Durham, Roger Eatwell, Barbara Farr, Julie Gottlieb, Richard Griffiths, Tony Kushner, Gisela Lebzelter, D. S. Lewis,

Preface and acknowledgements

Kenneth Lunn, Andrew Mitchell, Robert Skidelsky, David Turner, G. C. Webber, Larry Witherell and Stephen Woodbridge.

I would also like to thank the following individuals who have expressed interest in this project and who have offered much-appreciated support and encouragement. Many thanks to some very valued friends including David Scott, Clare Nairn, and John and Marian March for their friendship, support and interest in this project. Carol Potter at Durham University has provided valuable technical support as well as interest and encouragement. Thanks are due also to Chris Whittaker, also at Durham University, who provided valuable comments on parts of the manuscript in its formative stages. I would also like to acknowledge Professor Maureen Moran, Dean of the Faculty of Arts at Brunel University, for her support during my time at Brunel. She has consistently encouraged and supported my research work. Grateful thanks, too, are extended to Professor Geoffrey Alderman at Middlesex University and Professor Colin Holmes at the University of Sheffield. Professor Alderman supervised my Ph.D. degree and both he and Professor Holmes were enthusiastic about the undertaking of this book. Thanks are also due to Mr J. Wallder for the loan of some very useful primary source material.

Finally, I would like to thank my immediate family, my mother and father and my two sisters, Kathleen and Julie, and their families, for their encouragement and interest. I would particularly like to thank my father, Daniel Linehan, whose unstinting support has been invaluable for this book and whose interest in my work has never wavered since I first entered that inspirational centre of learning, Ruskin College, Oxford, in 1981. I would also like to take this opportunity to give a special mention to my uncle, an East End Jewish tailor, who was present at the 'Battle of Cable Street' on 4 October 1936. My wife Janet, too, is deserving of a very special mention. She was responsible for much of the final arrangement of the book manuscript. Her hard work and technical expertise in these trying final stages have been greatly appreciated. Indeed, her patience, unswerving support and love have proved invaluable throughout this project. Finally, I would like to thank my lovely two-year-old daughter, Ciara, for just being Ciara.

ABBREVIATIONS

ASU	Anti-Socialist Union
BBL	British Brothers' League
BCCSE	British Council for Christian Settlement in Europe
BCU	British Commonwealth Union
BEFP	British Empire Fascist Party
BEU	British Empire Union
BF	British Fascisti, British Fascists Ltd
BPP	British People's Party
BUF	British Union of Fascists
BWL	British Workers' League
CINEF	Centre International d'Études sur la Fascisme (International Centre of Fascist Studies)
CPGB	Communist Party of Great Britain
EL	Economic League
IFL	Imperial Fascist League
ILP	Independent Labour Party
LCC	London County Council
MCP	Militant Christian Patriots
NCCL	National Council for Civil Liberties
NCU	National Citizens' Union
NF	National Fascisti
NL	Nordic League
NP	National Party
NPL	National Political League
NSDAP	Nationalsocialistische Deutsche Arbeiterpartei (National Socialist German Workers' Party)
NSL	National Service League
NSL	National Socialist League
NWP	National Workers' Party

Abbreviations

PEP	Political and Economic Planning
PNF	Partito Nazionale Fascista (Italian Fascist Party)
UBP	United British Party

Abbreviations used in the notes

BD	Board of Deputies of British Jews, Woburn House, London
BUQ	*British Union Quarterly*
FQ	*Fascist Quarterly*
HO	Home Office
JPC	Jewish People's Council Against Fascism and Anti-Semitism
MEPOL	Metropolitan Police
NCCL	National Council for Civil Liberties Archive, Brynmor Jones Library, University of Hull
PRO	Public Record Office

INTRODUCTION: THE HISTORIOGRAPHY OF FASCIST STUDIES

It is appropriate to begin this study of fascism in one of its national contexts with a consideration of the historiography of fascist studies, in order to comprehend more clearly the principal theoretical characteristics of the phenomenon under investigation. The preceding decades have been marked by a welter of scholarly attempts to define the nature of fascism and identify its quintessential features. This process has been marked by intense scholarly disagreement as historians, political theorists and social scientists groped towards an understanding of this novel orientation in twentieth-century ideology and politics. A degree of intellectual confusion would mark the earliest attempts to comprehend fascism, particularly in those interpretations that emerged contemporaneous with its initial appearance during the interwar period, as well as in the scholarship of the immediate postwar period. Confronted more immediately by its barbarism and brutality, these accounts, both liberal and leftist, tended to view fascism as an aberrant phenomenon, an irrational descent into savagery, which temporarily ruptured Europe's evolutionary development. For liberals like Benedetto Croce and Friedrich Meinecke it was Europe's evolutionary *moral* and *cultural* development that had been punctured by fascist barbarism, a line of ethical continuity that had remained broadly intact since the Enlightenment.[1] The contemporary Marxist view of fascism as a secondary phenomenon shared many of these historicist and teleological assumptions. Prompted by the line of the Third International, Marxists writers asserted that the 'terroristic dictatorship' of fascism was the reactionary arm of finance capital in crisis. Fascism, so ran the argument, had been summoned forth to prevent the revolutionary European working-class movement from continuing its inexorable historical ascent to its goal of socialism.[2] The assumption here was that a fault line appeared in capitalism which ultimately led to the emergence of fascism, capitalism's darker, reactionary alter ego.

While both the early Marxist and liberal 'moral disease' perspectives correctly highlighted fascism's demonological and terroristic aspects, particularly the depravity of the German National Socialist regime, such models have limited usage as tools of historical analysis. The high moral tone, polemical nature and sweeping generalisations of many of the observations, the tendency to view fascism as a 'parenthesis' and the preoccupation with its terroristic dimensions to the detriment of a consideration of other areas of its ideology and political agenda, seriously hampered scholarship of this type. The 'classical' Marxist view of fascism as an epiphenomenon of capitalism, an anti-proletarian instrument of 'ruling-class' reaction, for example, disseminated in Britain during the 1930s by the polemical writings of John Strachey and Rajani Palme Dutt, ignored fascism's anti-capitalist and even anti-establishment leanings.[3] Absent from a classical Marxist analysis, too, was an awareness of fascism's potential for political radicalism and the independently generated character of many of its ideas and motivations. Fascism was not a sub-text of other ideologies, a derivative of capitalism. It is important to recognise that fascism possessed an ideology in its own right, however offensive and objectionable this ideology was. In the same vein, the tendency by some practitioners of the school of 'vulgar Marxism' to view fascists as essentially reflections of economic categories simplified the complex question of fascist motivation. Marxist writers tended to underestimate also the complex dynamic of circumstances from which fascism emerged in any given national context.

The liberal perspective also ignored the complicated accumulation of factors that produced fascism. The notion of fascism as a temporary lapse into insanity, a moral and cultural deviation that drove a wedge into European history and diverted it from its path to reason and enlightenment, failed to appreciate the distinct lines of *continuity* between fascism and the European society and culture that spawned it. As Zeev Sternhell noted, fascism needs to be viewed as an 'integral part of the history of European culture'.[4] Sternhell thus saw fascism as an aspect of the intellectual and cultural revolt against the principles of the Enlightenment and French Revolution 'which swept across Europe at the end of the nineteenth century and the beginning of the twentieth'.[5] The same was true with continental fascism's British counterpart. In order to comprehend more accurately the essence of British fascism, it must be viewed as an organic element of this *fin-de-siècle* intellectual and cultural revolt. This powerful intellectual and cultural paradigm would provide British fascism, particularly in its more developed variants, with a substantial body of ideas to draw on and a measure of intellectual coherence.

Another early view of fascism that found common ground with the Marxist and liberal 'moral and cultural collapse' interpretations was the socio-psychological account of fascist mobilisation. Drawing on Marxist concepts and Freudian psychological and personality theory, these accounts suggested that the origins of fascism could be located in the pathological-psychological disposition of individuals.[6] In these models, there was a stress on personality disturbance, prejudice, the 'authoritarian personality', aggression projection and the repressive nature of bourgeois society.[7] Essentially, fascism was defined here as a form of displaced aggression that emanated from personal failures in interpersonal relations, particularly pertaining to child–parent relationships, as well as a reluctance on the part of disturbed individuals to confront their underlying neuroses. Aggression-projection therefore served a vital function in that it resolved inner emotional conflicts within psychologically disturbed individuals. In this revamped Freudian model, fascism was thus assumed to have links with the primary drives, such as envy, cruelty and wanton lust. In some variants of the psychological theory of fascism, particular attention was given to the primary drive of lasciviousness. Here it was supposed that there were links between people's sexual behaviour and their political preferences. This supposition had its basis in the Freudian idea that people's sexual behaviour provided vital clues to their inner personality and character. Wilhelm Reich, in *The Mass Psychology of Fascism* (1933), contended that in fascism, individuals found a compensatory outlet for their sadomasochistic and aggressive behaviour that was rooted, in turn, in bourgeois sexual repression.[8] Erich Fromm's *Escape From Freedom* (1941), too, argued that people fled from bourgeois alienation and found refuge in the regimented conformity and 'sadomasochistic authoritarianism' of fascism.[9]

The socio-psychological approach to fascism, however, had obvious drawbacks, not least the speculative nature of its concepts and its dependence on hypotheses that are too often unsupported by empirical evidence. It would be unwise to dismiss this method out of hand, though, for the psychoanalytical approach highlighted the importance for the analyst of 'the style and methods of fascism: the unshackling of primitive instincts, the denial of reason, the spellbinding of the senses by pageantry and parades'.[10] In the hands of a sophisticated historical analyst, the psychoanalytical method can yield valuable insights into the more opaque workings of the fascist subconscious and the inner compulsions which motivated the fascist 'joiner'. Theweleit's research into the *Freikorps*, for example, claimed to have exposed the misogynous undercurrent lurking in the far-right activist's subconscious.[11] The *Freikorps* male activist, as with his fascist successor, had a pathological terror of the 'flabbiness' and 'softness' of contemporary political reality, which he associated with female flux or the 'morass of femaleness'. The remedy for encroaching inner and outer dissolution was the *Freikorps* 'armoured body'. By transforming his body into a firm, erect instrument, or 'machine', the male *Freikorps* warrior would be safeguarded from the waves of 'softness' that threatened to engulf him. Fascists, too, would favour the masculine warrior ethic of hard lines and athletic muscularity, the symbol of personal invulnerability.

In the main, however, later scholars became dissatisfied with the classical Marxist, liberal and psychological theories of fascism that came out of the contemporary and early postwar period. Motivated by a desire for greater analytical rigour, they began the task of producing the array of concepts that were required to comprehend more closely fascism's complex and contradictory character. During this phase of scholarship, some of fascism's core characteristics and features would be identified and the main lines of controversy and debate established. Moreover, these areas of convergence and disagreement continue to define the field of fascist scholarship.[12] It was principally the desire to discover the existence of *generic* features that would place fascist studies on a more solid theoretical foundation. The identification of these core generic features, or set of 'underlying commonalities', would henceforth serve as standard points of reference for the study of the fascist phenomenon across a range of national boundaries. This process of categorisation is most adeptly articulated in the scholarship of Ernst Nolte, Stanley Payne and more recently Roger Griffin.[13] There are clear analytical advantages to be derived from a generic approach, as Stanley Payne has recently noted. He stated that like 'all general types and concepts in political analysis, generic fascism is an abstraction which never existed in pure empirical form but constitutes a conceptual device which serves to clarify the analysis of individual political phenomena'.[14]

The generic approach has enabled historians to identify a number of core elements associated with fascism's political style, as well as its ideological and organisational structure. These would include fascism's extreme nationalism, whether of an organic, tribal or populist type, its rejection of models of ideological class conflict and its preference for consensus and corporatist solutions. A variant of this latter feature, particularly in the case of Oswald Mosley's British Union of Fascists (BUF), would be the favouring of meritocratic norms in the ordering of administrative, business and industrial relations. A stress on elite or charismatic leadership, an emphasis on youth, a militaristic and authoritarian ethos, and a predilection for political violence are other basic components of fascism. Innovative propaganda techniques, particularly the deliberate choreographing of fascist gatherings which drew on secular liturgical symbols and rituals, pointing to a distinct fascist aesthetic, were another salient feature of the fascist political style. This unique fascist aesthetic, the attempt to create what Payne has referred to as a novel visual framework for public and political life, sought to ensnare the 'participant in a mystique and community of ritual that appealed to the aesthetic and spiritual sense'.[15]

Stanley Payne's ground-breaking scholarship on generic fascism, moreover, has aimed at a *synthetic* definition of fascism, in order to avoid the limitations inherent in the generic approach of the lengthy 'check-list type'.[16] The synthetic definition of fascism sought to weld the various generic 'parts' into a sense-making, coherent whole by way of emphasising that fascism had a distinct, internally coherent political ideology in its own right. Roger Griffin, too, has crafted a highly sophisticated synthetic definition of fascism, seeing fascism, in its various permutations, as essentially a form of 'palingenetic populist ultra-nationalism'.[17] Griffin's treatment of the generic fascism topic, with its stress on the regenerative urge at the heart of fascist doctrine as well its highlighting of fascism's intensely pessimistic preoccupation with decadence and national decline, has proved particularly valuable for this book.

The generic validity of certain 'anti-' features of fascism's ideology beyond anti-decadence cannot be disputed either, such as its anti-Marxism, anti-liberalism, anti-conservatism, anti-rationalism, anti-positivism and anti-materialism. In other respects, though, the 'anti-' model of fascism, with its overemphasis on fascism's reactionary and negative dimension, has analytical drawbacks.[18] It does not give due account to the 'positive', even revolutionary, content of much of fascism's ideology and programme. We are grateful to the observations of A. James Gregor and Eugen Weber, amongst others, for uncovering this aspect of fascist ideology.[19] Nonetheless, the 'anti-' model of fascism at least serves as a useful analytical device to probe the reactionary, negative and imprecisely formulated pronouncements of 1920s manifestations of fascist ideology in Britain, particularly Rotha Lintorn-Orman's British Fascists (BF). Its application is of limited use, however, when applied to Mosley's BUF, which had a highly developed fascist programme containing both negative and positive elements.

The dispute amongst historians concerning fascism's 'negative' or 'positive' nature overlaps with another contentious area of scholarship, the question of whether fascism was an ideology of the *right*, *left* or *centre*. A more recent statement of the former position was provided by R. Soucy, who stated that interwar fascism sought to 'mobilise the masses for right-wing ends', defining it as 'a new variety of authoritarian conservatism and right-wing nationalism'.[20] There are weaknesses in this contention, too. While correctly identifying the points at which fascist and authoritarian conservative policy intersect, and indeed the extent to which fascist movements were prepared to enter alliances with established conservative elites, this position understated the leftist content in fascist ideology.[21] A. James Gregor and David D. Roberts, for example, traced some of the origins of Italian fascist productivism to revolutionary syndicalism.[22] Sternhell also pointed to fascism's radical aspects and its leftist origins, particularly its intellectual debt to Sorelian revolutionary syndicalism, but in a more qualified manner. Although fascism 'expressed a revolutionary aspiration' which rejected the prevailing intellectual and political heritage of liberalism and Marxism, notably the Hegelian determinism and historicism of the latter, it was a novel departure in political doctrine that was neither left nor right.[23] Other historians saw fascism as a centrist movement. In the British context, D. S. Lewis's work falls into this category. He defined Mosley's BUF as a movement of the 'centre' that sought to appeal to elements across the political spectrum.[24]

Closely related to this issue of whether fascism leaned to the left, right or centre, was the question of whether it was pre-eminently the expression of the sectional interests of one particular social-class group, namely the middle class. This is another of the postwar era's 'classic' paradigmatic theories of fascism. Analysts like Seymour

Introduction

Lipset held that fascism was essentially rooted in the fears of this specific social stratum.[25] The middle classes stampeded towards fascism, so ran the argument, because they felt that their status and economic security were being imperilled by an impersonal and uncontrollable modernisation process, and socialism, with its egalitarian rhetoric and anti-middle-class bias.[26] Marxist historians, too, assumed a link between the middle class and fascism. The Marxist argument that fascism was essentially a 'terroristic', anti-proletarian and anti-socialist instrument of bourgeois reaction by implication assumed middle-class support for this reactionary enterprise. The 'middle-class fascism' thesis has evident weaknesses. It is reductionist, in that it resorts to defining fascism, particularly its recruitment profile, in terms of a single stereotype. Additionally, it is a hypothesis that was initially constructed without recourse to the empirical evidence. Recent research on fascist mobilisations and membership profiles, including those in interwar Britain, have demonstrated that fascism was not rooted in one specific social class. Rather, it attracted a diverse range of social-class and occupational types who were motivated to join for a variety of reasons that were not necessarily related to their socio-economic position in society.[27]

There is another aspect of fascist doctrine that has divided historians. In an influential article published in 1975, Alan Cassels stated that fascist ideas 'constituted a vague *Weltanschauung*', fascist movements being motivated not by a 'precise ideology', but 'loosely formulated aspirations and inchoate impulses'.[28] Such assessments, which suggested that fascist ideology lacked precision and coherence primarily because it could not be traced to a distinct intellectual genealogy, as with the Marxism of Marx and Lenin and the liberalism of Hobbes, Locke and Mill amongst others, have quite correctly been challenged by other scholars. According to these critics of the Cassels approach, fascist doctrine was logically coherent despite its evident eclecticism. We have already seen above that those historians, like Stanley Payne and Roger Griffin, who aimed at a synthetic definition of generic fascism implicitly recognised that fascism had a distinct and relatively internally coherent political ideology. This school of thought argued, therefore, that fascism, though it was composed of a conglomerate of ideas culled from a number of diverse sources, was able to merge these ideas into a novel intellectual synthesis. Zeev Sternhell was another who subscribed to this point of view. For Sternhell, fascism's political ideology, with its synthesis of organic tribal nationalism with the

Sorelian revision of Marxism, 'represented a coherent, logical and well-structured totality', while the 'absence of a common source comparable with that of Marxism need not be taken as a sign of incoherence'.[29] Britain's fascist movements, with varying degrees of sophistication and success, would also strive for logical coherence in doctrinal matters during the interwar period.

A generic concept that has proved particularly rewarding for fascist studies is the notion of fascism as an *anti-modern* phenomenon. The 'anti-modern' perspective would illuminate some of the novel features of the fascist *Weltanschauung*. These included fascism's neo-romantic fascination with the land, its anti-urbanism and its apparent aversion to many facets of modernity, including the ethos of technological progress.[30] Initially, this aspect of fascism tended to be overstated by historians. According to Wolfgang Sauer, for example, fascism 'turned against technological progress and economic growth', attempting 'to stop or even to reverse the trend toward industrialisation and to return to the earlier, "natural" ways of life'.[31] H. A. Turner Jnr also placed too great an emphasis on fascist anti-modernism. In relation to the German Nazis, for example, Turner claimed that what they 'proposed was an escape from the modern world by means of a desperate backward leap toward a romanticised vision of the harmony, community, simplicity, and order of a world long lost'.[32] This view of fascist, and Nazi, movements as backward-looking, atavistic and anti-modern further reinforced the idea of fascism as a negative, 'anti-' phenomenon.

Some historians, on the other hand, preferred to see fascism as essentially a *modernising* movement. One of the earliest and most forceful statements of this position was that given by A. James Gregor in relation to Italian Fascism. Gregor held that Italian Fascism enthusiastically embraced the ideas of technological Futurism and productivism, and in so doing aimed at the creation of a new industrial society.[33] Gregor also stated, more generally, that paradigmatic fascism 'displayed all the principal properties of a developmental nationalism'.[34] He thus likened fascism to the mass-mobilising modernisation movements of various ideological persuasions that had appeared in the underdeveloped world during the twentieth century, including Stalinist and Cuban communism. Writing later, Payne, too, pointed to the modernist content in fascist doctrine. 'Fascism was nothing if not modernist, despite its high quotient of archaic or anachronistic warrior culture', he noted.[35] However, on the question of whether fascism was exclusively and unambiguously modernist as Gregor was implying, Payne appeared to hestitate. He concluded that fascism's 'primary concern was neither antimodernism nor modernisation per se, for it promoted many new aspects of modernisation while combating or seeking fundamentally to readjust others'.[36]

Some historians have attempted to find a way out of the labyrinth of the fascist modernist/anti-modernist dichotomy by suggesting that fascism sought to articulate an alternative modernity, of a fundamentally different type from that of liberal capitalism's or communism's modernising agenda. Certainly, by way of summarising his analysis of the fascist modernist/anti-modernist debate, Stanley Payne took this view when he stated that fascism strove for 'a distinctive kind of modernity, apart from traditionalism, liberal capitalism, or Communist materialism'.[37] Roger Griffin has argued also for a greater appreciation of the modernising impulse within fascist and Nazi doctrine.[38] It is argued in this book, too, that domestic fascism, or at least its most influential and vocal representative, the BUF, advocated a distinct variant of modernity, an agenda that it pursued while simultaneously displaying an aggressive hostility towards many aspects of liberal capitalist modernity.[39] Oswald Mosley's fascism, for example, was characterised by Faustian restlessness and an unwavering belief in the potential benefits to humankind of science. He believed in technology's Faustian mission to subdue the world of inanimate nature and create a world 'reborn through science'. Nonetheless, even in the BUF there was a constituency that appeared to be unable to reconcile itself to the modernising impulse within the movement's political project, a disparate group of individuals that included romantic back-to-the-soil enthusiasts and technophobes who hankered nostalgically after a return to a pre-industrial past.[40]

Similarly, Zeev Sternhell has correctly given due weight to those currents in fascism's thought and political programme that were unequivocally modern, though he is careful to retain certain of the assumptions of the anti-modern perspective. For Sternhell, fascism did indeed represent a form of reaction to modernisation but of a distinct kind. Though fascism, he asserted, was repelled by the human fall-out from the modernisation process, he recognised that it never advocated a return to a mythical golden age, but sought to retain the benefits of liberal capitalist wealth creation.[41] Put another way, fascism 'wished to reap all the benefits of the modern age, to exploit all the technological achievements of capitalism'.[42] The feature of modernity that fascism repudiated, according to Sternhell, was its intellectual and moral heritage, the philosophical principles that underpinned it, not its economic or technological aspect.

Indeed, Sternhell's research into fascism's origins made much of its intense antipathy to philosophical liberalism, such as liberal rationalism, positivism, 'intellectualism' and materialism, a mood that had its genesis in ideas that initially surfaced in the intellectual foment of *fin-de-siècle* Europe. Along with the many scholars who have been mentioned in this introduction, Sternhell has made a number of very important contributions to fascist studies, this notion that fascism was a cultural and philosophical phenomenon prior to it becoming a political movement not least among them. By inviting historians to avert their gaze to the *fin de siècle* when they thought about the origins of fascism, he made another valuable contribution too. By shifting the chronological focus back almost a generation, he convincingly dispelled the notion that fascism was exclusively a child of the Great War, or even of the immediate post-1918 economic and political dislocation in Europe, an assumption that tended to prevail in much of the historiography of fascist studies.

Notes

1 R. De Felice, *Interpretations of Fascism* (Cambridge, MA, Harvard University Press, 1977), pp. 14–15.
2 On the Marxist view of fascism, see, for example, D. Beetham, *Marxists in the Face of Fascism. Writings by Marxists on Fascism from the Inter-War Period* (Manchester, Manchester University Press, 1983); G. Botz, 'Austro-Marxist Interpretations of Fascism', *Journal of Contemporary History*, 11 (October 1976), pp. 129–56; and J. M. Cammett, 'Communist Theories of Fascism, 1920–1935', *Science and Society*, 31 (Winter 1967), pp. 149–63.
3 J. Strachey, *The Menace of Fascism* (London, Gollancz, 1933); R. P. Dutt, *Fascism and Social Revolution* (London, Lawrence, 1934).
4 Z. Sternhell, *The Birth of Fascist Ideology* (Princeton, Princeton University Press, 1994), p. 3.
5 Ibid.
6 The principal advocates of this approach were Wilhelm Reich, Erich Fromm and Theodor Adorno.
7 L. Hoffman, 'Psychoanalytical Interpretations of Political Movements, 1900–1950', *Psychohistory Review*, 13 (1984), pp. 16–29.

Introduction

See also J. Milfull (ed.), *The Attractions of Fascism. Social Psychology and Aesthetics of the 'Triumph of the Right'* (Oxford, Berg, 1990).
8   S. G. Payne, *A History of Fascism 1914–45* (London, UCL Press, 1995), pp. 452–3; W. Reich, *The Mass Psychology of Fascism* (London, Souvenir Press, 1972; first German edition published in 1933).
9   B. Hagtvet and R. Kuhnl, 'Contemporary Approaches to Fascism: A Survey of Paradigms', in S. U. Larsen, B. Hagtvet and J. P. Myklebust (eds), *Who Were the Fascists? Social Roots of European Fascism* (Oslo, Universitetsforlaget, 1980), p. 32. See also E. Fromm, *Escape from Freedom* (New York, Farrar and Reinhart, 1941).
10 E. Nolte, *Three Faces of Fascism* (New York, Mentor, 1969), p. 39.
11 K. Theweleit, *Male Fantasies. Vol. 1: Women, Floods, Bodies, History* (Cambridge, Polity Press, 1987); K. Theweleit, *Male Fantasies. Vol. 2: Male Bodies: Psychoanalysing the White Terror* (Cambridge, Polity Press, 1989).
12 R. Griffin (ed.), *International Fascism. Theories, Causes and the New Consensus* (London, Arnold, 1998) is a recent, eloquent summary of this ongoing debate.
13 Nolte, *Three Faces of Fascism*; S. Payne, 'The Concept of Fascism', in Larsen *et al.* (eds), *Who Were the Fascists?*; R. Griffin, *The Nature of Fascism* (London, Routledge, 1991).
14 Payne, *A History of Fascism*, p. 4.
15 Ibid., p. 12.
16 Griffin (ed.), *International Fascism*, pp. 9–10, on generic fascism of the 'check-list' variety.
17 Ibid., p. 13.
18 Scholars who more fully embraced this model include Ernst Nolte and Alan Cassels in relation to Nazi Germany. See Nolte, *Three Faces of Fascism;* and A. Cassels, 'Janus: The Two Faces of Fascism', in H. A. Turner Jnr (ed.), *Reappraisals of Fascism* (New York, Franklin Watts, 1975), pp. 69–92.
19 A. J. Gregor, *The Fascist Persuasion in Radical Politics* (Princeton, Princeton University Press, 1974), pp. 16 and 430; E. Weber, *Varieties of Fascism* (New York, D. Van Nostrand, 1964), p. 17.
20 R. Soucy, *French Fascism. The Second Wave, 1933–1939* (New Haven, Yale University Press, 1995), pp. 17–18. Other historians who subscribed to the notion of fascism as essentially a movement of the right include Denis Mack Smith, William Sheridan Allen, Michael Kater, William Irvine and Arno J. Mayer.
21 On the 'alliance' theory of fascism, see Hagtvet and Kuhnl, 'Contemporary Approaches', pp. 36–8.
22 A. J. Gregor, *Italian Fascism and Developmental Dictatorship* (Princeton, Princeton University Press, 1979); David D. Roberts, *The Syndicalist Tradition and Italian Fascism* (Manchester University

Press, Manchester, 1979).
23 Sternhell, *The Birth of Fascist Ideology*, p. 6.
24 D. S. Lewis, *Illusions of Grandeur. Mosley, Fascism and British Society, 1931–81* (Manchester, Manchester University Press, 1987), pp. 7–8.
25 S. M. Lipset, '"Fascism" – Left, Right and Centre', in S. M. Lipset, *Political Man* (London, Heinemann, 1983), pp. 131–7.
26 Griffin (ed.), *International Fascism*, pp. 45–8.
27 On the socio-economic and occupational profile of Britain's fascists, see below, Chapter Six.
28 Cassels, 'Janus', p. 70.
29 Sternhell, *The Birth of Fascist Ideology*, pp. 8–9.
30 See below, Chapter Ten, on this.
31 W. Sauer, 'National Socialism: Totalitarianism or Fascism?', in Turner Jnr (ed.), *Reappraisals*, p. 107.
32 H. A. Turner Jnr, 'Fascism and Modernization', in Turner Jnr (ed.), *Reappraisals*, p. 120.
33 A. J. Gregor, 'Fascism and Modernization: Some Addenda', *World Politics*, 26 (1974), pp. 370–84.
34 Gregor, *The Fascist Persuasion*, p. 272.
35 Payne, *A History of Fascism*, p. 485.
36 Ibid.
37 Ibid., p. 486.
38 R. Griffin, 'Totalitarian Art and the Nemesis of Modernity', *Oxford Art Journal*, 19, 2 (1996), pp. 122–4.
39 See below, Chapter Ten.
40 See below, Chapter Ten.
41 Sternhell, *The Birth of Fascist Ideology*, pp. 6–7.
42 Ibid., p. 7.

CHAPTER ONE

ORIGINS AND PROGENITORS

As with their continental counterparts, the British fascist parties did not have a distinct and easily discernible intellectual genealogy. Their doctrines were forged from a complex amalgamation of ideas of varying degrees of sophistication and crudity that emanated from a range of sources. The domestic context is crucial to an understanding of this intellectual lineage, though it should be recognised that British fascism drew on ideas from a variety of both native and continental European sources. In stating this, it should also be stressed that at no time were the British fascist parties simply a pale imitation of continental fascist movements. In its more developed forms, British fascism was able to reconcile apparent contradictions, domestic and continental ideas merging in a series of novel dialectical syntheses. The origins of British fascism should not only be sought in ideas and intellectual currents, however. Other forces and tendencies in society, of a social, economic, technological, political and cultural nature, contributed to its emergence, nourished its growth and shaped its subsequent development.

An antipathy to economic and political liberalism was one of the most distinctive features of British fascist doctrine. For many fascists, the decline of British power after 1918 could be traced to the continuing national attachment to *laissez-faire* economics and the principles of parliamentary democracy. While the former was considered to be an outmoded doctrine, the latter was accused of fomenting party factionalism, class egoism, and bureaucratic excess and inefficiency. According to its propagandists, the fascist opposition to economic and political liberalism was solidly rooted in native traditions and influences. This attempt to give prominence to the domestic context was partly motivated by a desire to deflect allegations that the British fascists were simply mimicking the anti-liberal diatribes of their continental cousins. In another respect, it sprang from a naive belief that an authentic fascist tradition did indeed exist in British history. According to the propagandists of fascism, its anti-capitalist, anti-liberal, socio-political and economic programme had numerous antecedents in the policies followed by past English monarchs and statesmen. The search to uncover this anti-liberal and anti-capitalist pre-fascist lineage would become a highly subjective exercise in invention and take the fascists on an imaginative journey deep into the British past.

For A. L. Glasfurd of the BUF, fascism's revolutionary programme was fully in accordance with British political and economic traditions. He cited the medieval English guilds, with their enlightened regulation of wages, prices and conditions of labour, as a precursor of the fascist corporate system.[1] Fascism's opposition to the 'anarchy of uncontrolled capitalism' and sectional interests within the nation also followed a deep-rooted tradition of English statecraft, according to Glasfurd. The statutes of 'enlightened' English monarchs were mentioned, including Henry II's termination of the 'feudal anarchy that had arisen in Stephen's reign'. Fascism's desire for national integration and its suppression of self-interested sectional interests through the mechanism of the regulatory state found a precedent, too, in laws introduced during Henry III's reign, according to another Mosleyite, Mary Richardson, most notably a statute that defined a profiteer as an 'enemy of the State and a conspirator'.[2] Richardson also cited another statute written during the same reign, prohibiting merchants from importing foreign goods which could be produced by the home market, as reminiscent of Oswald Mosley's emphasis on the importance of the domestic market within a national economic recovery programme.

Interwar fascists idealised the economic and political model embodied in the Tudor State, in particular. The Tudor State's hostility to party factions and self-interested sectional interests, and its objective of national integration through authoritarian centralised government, were collectively held up as a prototype of fascist government and the modern fascist rational state. A. L. Glasfurd praised Henry VII's subjugation of the 'lawless barons who had brought about the Wars of the Roses', and the subsequent 'Tudor dictatorship's' introduction of national policies and restrictions on the export of English capital by self-serving private speculators.[3] Glasfurd also viewed the attempts at constructing a planned economic system by the authoritarian Tudor State as a forerunner of the 'scientific' national economic planning of fascism. Another Mosleyite, W. E. D. Allen, also expressed admiration for the Tudors' economic planning, as well as their attempts to regulate capital and exercise state control over the emerging financial-capitalist class.[4] In this alternative history, other characteristics of the Tudor period were cited as precursors of British fascism. The Mosleyites pointed to the apparent similarities between the purposeful heroic spirit of the Elizabethan age, the 'vital spirit of endeavour' that produced a national cultural renaissance and the epic voyages of global discovery, and their own attempt at national revival. The 'paternalistic' aspects of the Tudor dictatorships, with their 'advanced social conscience' and attempts at poor relief, were also viewed as forerunners of fascism. For Mary Richardson, Elizabeth I's attempt to relieve the poverty of her most distressed subjects mirrored the fascist ideal of 'social justice'.[5]

British fascists lamented the subsequent demise of Tudor national-state authority and the rise to ascendancy of the 'bourgeois' financial-capitalist class, which, for them, led to the 'legalised anarchy of group interests' and ushered in the hated era of individualism, 'class egotism' and free-trade *laissez-faire* internationalism. They also bemoaned the 'reappearance of party faction' following Elizabeth's death, with its corresponding dissipation of national strength.[6] According to the fascist perspective, this new historical departure was precipitated by the weak rule of the Stuarts and the democratic revolutions of the seventeenth century. For William Allen, 'the struggle for "the freedom of the Englishman" in the Parliamentary Wars was in great degree a rather sordid struggle for the "Freedom of the Market"'. The victory of the Parliamentarian armies, 'financed by the City of London', was pivotal in Allen's opinion. 'From the scaffold of King Charles the victorious Whigs', the political expression of free-trade capitalism, 'marched in triumph into the nineteenth century'.[7] The Puritan revolution was also thought to have assisted in this historical triumph of bourgeois commercial capital. According to William Joyce, the Puritans, whose exposure to Old Testament Jewish philosophy indicated that 'the materialism of the Jews' had 'bittten deeply into their souls', found common ideological cause with the 'new Plutocracy', represented by the aspiring merchant classes, in its struggle with the Crown.[8]

Despite the passing of the authoritarian national-monarchies of Tudor England and the triumphant entry of economic and political liberalism into the modern period, the fascists continued to scour the later centuries for evidence of the fascist historical tradition. E. D. Hart of the BUF believed that a strand of anti-free-trade 'fascism' survived into the nineteenth century in the personages of Charles Western, a Knight of the Shire for Essex who played a prominent role in devising the Corn Laws of 1815, and the Birmingham banker Thomas Attwood, a leader of the Parliamentary Reform movement of the early 1830s. Hart asserted that the protectionist impulse behind Western's 1815 Corn Laws, with its ideal of a self-supporting British agriculture and its goal of stimulating domestic production, was in accordance with fascist principles.[9] So too, apparently, was Attwood's opposition to efforts on the part of his contemporaries to restore the gold standard and his advocacy of a managed currency. Attwood's political methods during the Reform phase also excited Hart. The 'semi-military assemblies and processions' of Attwood's extra-parliamentary bodies, such as the Birmingham Political Union, for example, anticipated the massed paramilitary rallies of modern fascism.

The nineteenth-century figure most consistently cited by the fascists as the personal embodiment of the anti-liberal anti-capitalist ideal that they cherished was Thomas Carlyle. According to William Joyce, Carlyle ranked 'first amongst British heralds of the Fascist Revolution'.[10] Although Carlyle was celebrated as a principled opponent of the *laissez-faire* economics of the Manchester School and its 'sordid' materialist philosophy, it was his ideas on authoritarian leadership that excited the most interest amongst interwar fascists.[11] The BUF interpreted Carlyle's notion of the heroic, aristocratic leader-figure, the 'Hero-King' who 'stands in the van of men fronting the peril which frightens back all others', as a vindication of the fascist Leadership principle and the heroic-vitalist 'will-to-achievement' ethos that informed their own philosophical outlook. In the elitist model of political representation favoured by the BUF, the incorruptible fascist Leader, the modern equivalent of Carlyle's 'Hero-King', would revive the old aristocratic virtues of duty, responsibility and service and thus provide an alternative to the contemporary parliamentary 'age of government by mediocrities'. The aristocratic sense of life, with its celebration of heroic struggle, 'manly' virtues and gaiety, would also be resurrected through the charismatic personage of the fascist Leader-figure.

In much of the historiography of British fascism, it is similarly recognised that the fascists' opposition to economic and political liberalism was solidly rooted in native traditions and influences. However, scholars of British fascism quite correctly suggest that the roots of this antipathy reside in traditions and influences beyond those identified by the fascist propagandists. It is the decades that immediately preceded the Great War which are given prominence in the historiographical perspective, rather than the medieval or Tudor periods, or the nineteenth century. This reorientation of perspective has enabled us to discern more accurately the authentic roots of native fascism's hostility towards economic and political liberalism, and thus move beyond the more fanciful conjectures of the fascist propagandists.

During the decades in question, namely the late Victorian and Edwardian years, the foundations of the dominant liberal order were rocked by a series of crises. The most marked of these crises were suffragette agitation, the constitutional crisis that culminated in the 1911 Parliament Act, Ulster loyalist opposition to Home Rule which raised the spectre of civil war in Ireland, and the industrial unrest that was sparked by the heightened trade union militancy of the period.[12] It was in the context of these dislocations that a distinct vocabulary of protest began to take shape that would later find an echo in many of the anti-liberal arguments formulated by the fascists. This vocabulary was both iconoclastic and radical, and reflected the fact that a significant realignment in British politics and political discourse was under way. The novelty of this new political and ideological configuration renders it difficult to categorise in terms of conventional party-political labels, though historians have tended to describe it as a movement of the radical nationalist right. Besides identifying distinct lines of continuity between the vocabulary of the prewar radical right and many of the anti-liberal sentiments expressed by the fascists, native fascism would also inherit a tradition of extra-parliamentary political activism from this period. In certain respects, too, the propaganda style of British fascism found a precedent in the campaigning strategies and techniques developed by the various organisational manifestations of the radical right.

Many of the pivotal economic and political ideas of British fascism, then, were to germinate in this pre-First World War period. Oswald Mosley, for example, took up many of the intellectual arguments of the Edwardian radical right. Many of his proposals to restructure the British economy in the 1930s along fascist lines had their intellectual antecedents in the influential prewar anti-

Cobdenite protectionist tradition of social-imperialism. Mosley's advocacy of the 'scientific' protection of domestic industries against cheap foreign imports, and the boosting of the home market to offset the negative effect of Britain's diminishing foreign export outlets, can be traced to this anti-Cobdenite tradition. So, too, can his attempts to construct a self-contained imperial trading zone to insulate the domestic economy and the colonies against the vicissitudes of the international economy. A seminal figure in this prewar revolt against *laissez-faire* orthodoxy was the Birmingham MP and Colonial Secretary, Joseph Chamberlain. For one historian, Mosley would become 'the intellectual heir of the most extreme wing of Chamberlainism, of protectionist social-imperialism'.[13] In 1903 Chamberlain proclaimed his support for Tariff Reform, a radical new fiscal policy that called for the implementation of an import duty system that would insulate the British economy against cheap foreign competition. A system of imperial preference, with the mother country and the dominions absolved from paying duties on home-produced goods entering their respective markets, would complement the domestic programme of Tariff Reform protection. Tariff Reform activists also hoped that by strengthening the economic ties of Empire, the system of reciprocal preference would serve to reinvigorate the imperial spirit, both at home and within the Empire.[14] A vigorous campaign to win adherents to the new economic approach would later be conducted by the influential Tariff Reform League, which was formed in 1903.

Tariff Reform protectionists were motivated in their desire to construct their alternative fiscal doctrine by a perception that British commercial and industrial power was on the wane. Foreign rivals, in particular, were thought to be undermining Britain's economic position. Interwar British fascists would share many such perceptions and anxieties. During the period 1870–1914, economic competition from Germany and the United States began to erode Britain's share of the global market. Diminishing export outlets and a slower growth rate relative to these two main trading rivals caused many contemporary observers seriously to question the viability of liberal free-trade doctrine and the efficacy of the market mechanism. For the Edwardian anti-Cobdenites, the doctrine of *laissez-faire* was a fossilised nineteenth-century idea that was no longer relevant to the requirements of the twentieth-century international economic order. They noted wryly that the spectacular expansion of German and US industry was achieved behind a barrier of protectionist tariffs, in 1879 and 1885 in Germany, and in 1891 and 1897 in America with the McKinley tariff and the Dingley tariff respectively.[15]

Pessimistic anti-Cobdenites also warned that a deteriorating economic situation could have dire implications for imperial defence. Passionate enthusiasts for Empire, they thought that imperial commitments could not be sustained on a contracting economic base. The question of Germany was again to the fore in these imperial defence calculations. There was growing evidence that Germany's recent industrial achievements, with its economy excelling in the production of chemicals, steel and optics, sectors crucial to a military offensive capability, were fuelling an expansionist programme that endangered Empire security.[16] Underwritten by an expansive naval construction programme, Germany's 'New Course' *Weltpolitik* that it embarked on in the 1890s threatened to bring about a further erosion of British power.[17] These imperial concerns were brought into even sharper focus by events in southern Africa. Kaiser Wilhelm II's gesture of support for Kruger in January 1896, in the wake of the abortive Jameson Raid, appeared to many as a further indication of Germany's anti-British agenda. Even more alarmingly, the defects in Britain's military machine were glaringly exposed to potential imperial rivals as a result of the poor performance of British arms during the Boer War (1899–1902).[18] The military reversals of the Boer War also introduced a social dimension into the imperial equation. The poor physical quality of volunteers from working-class urban centres (the army recruiting station at Manchester, for example, rejecting 40 per cent of applicants) led many to wonder whether Britain possessed the human resources to conduct an effective imperial defence.[19]

Enthusiastic Tariff Reform protectionists included the editor of the *National Review*, the die-hard Tory Leopold James Maxse, a Germanophobe obsessed with the German threat to the Empire, and Leopold Amery, whose experience as a correspondent for *The Times* during the Boer War led him to promote the cause of army reform. Henry Page Croft, an energetic young MP and businessman, and Viscount Alfred Milner, the British High Commissioner in South Africa during the Boer War who, like Chamberlain, severed links with Gladstonian Liberalism and embraced the ideal of protection and imperial unity, were others.[20] There was also Rudyard Kipling, who requires no introduction, Field Marshall Lord Roberts, an advocate of army reform and national conscription, and the distinguished geographer Halford J. Mackinder. Mackinder converted to protectionist social-imperialism in 1903, following an earlier sojourn as a free-trade Liberal-Imperialist supporter of Lord Rosebery.[21]

British fascists and the more radical social-imperialists also held similar views on the political aspects of liberalism, including the liberal state and democracy. For radical social-imperialists, the goal of preserving Britain's economic and imperial pre-eminence was dependent on strengthening the institutional framework of the state. Lord Milner was highly critical of parliamentary government and democracy, as were F. S. Oliver and George Wyndham, members of his 'kindergarten' of young radical social-imperialists, the forerunner of the later influential Round Table group.[22] Leopold Maxse was also disapproving, condemning the corruption he believed was rife in British public administration, the convention of parliamentary compromise, and the apparent double standards and self-indulgence of wealthy cosmopolitan Cobdenite ministers.[23] Even Halford Mackinder harboured reservations about democracy, wondering whether parliamentary institutions were compatible with an efficiently organised state system and an imperialist disposition.[24] Like Leo Maxse, Lord Milner was contemptuous of parliamentary posturing and the 'collusion' between the opposition front benches, convinced that a politics based on allegiance to parties was an enterprise devoid of principle. Democracy itself, he thought, was an inefficient form of government, lacking in consistency and cohesion. Milner's views on Cabinet government in parliamentary democracies, 'huge' cumbersome bodies composed of mediocre individuals, were also reminiscent of Oswald Mosley's later antipathy to democratic committees and his New Party scheme to limit Cabinet representation to five working members. Milner's belief that secondary 'temporary' issues would often be given precedence over matters of national importance during Cabinet deliberations was similar, too, to Mosley's conviction that parliamentary government was unresponsive and indecisive during periods of national crisis.[25]

The prewar debate on the efficacy of democracy was not confined to these individuals. Even the free-trade Liberal-Imperialist Lord Rosebery thought that parliamentary institutions needed to be made more efficient. The Liberal MP (1906–10) and novelist Hilaire Belloc was another who frequently attacked the system of parliament, parties and democratic elections. Belloc's views were aired in *The Party System*, which he co-wrote in 1911 with Cecil

Chesterton, in the columns of the journal *The Eye Witness* which he edited on its launch in 1911, and *The New Witness*, with which he was closely involved along with the Chesterton brothers, Cecil and Gilbert.[26] For Belloc, as for Milner, the parliamentary party system lent itself to expedient compromises that overrode matters of political principle and the aspirations of the electorate, and as such could not truly represent the 'general will' of the people.

Radical social-imperialists and fascists also held similar convictions with regard to their perception of the ideal state and the essence of efficient government. Both endorsed the concept of the interventionist state, in that they favoured a more vigorous role for public bodies in national affairs. The ideal of a non-partisan government that would transcend the politics of party and party strife, embraced by radical rightists such as Milner, was another area of overlap between social-imperialist and later fascist thought. In addition, despite the fact that they were highly critical of democracy, it is important not to understate the rational or modernist elements in both the Milnerite and Mosleyite fascist view of the nature of government. Both groups, for example, identified with the goal of bureaucratic efficiency as well as sharing a meritocratic view of public administration. Both promoted the idea of technocratic efficiency, endorsing the notion of an administrative elite to undertake the functions of government, disinterested professional 'technicians' and 'experts', rather than the obstructive amateurs and sophists whom they believed thrived in a democratic system.

The antipathy of radical social-imperialists and fascists towards economic and political liberalism was not the only point of ideological convergence between the two. National regeneration for both groups was dependent on forging a spirit of national harmony, an arrangement that would unite all strata of society in a common patriotic front against the perceived forces of internal disintegration. This vision of a classless national community, Milner's 'nobler socialism' or the integral, organic, ultra-nationalism of the fascists, represented a repudiation of free-market liberalism and orthodox socialism, both of which were condemned as confrontational and divisive 'internationalist' doctrines which worked against the national interest. The socialist class-war doctrine which supposedly contaminated the minds of the urban proletariat was particularly reviled. The ideal of national unity would only be effectively realised by instilling new values in them based on deference and reciprocal obligation, detaching the workers from their traditional allegiance to free-trade liberalism and socialism and converting them, respectively, to the cause of Tariff Reform imperialism and fascism. Both groups thus advocated a positive approach to social reform as a means of eliminating the perceived causes of class animosity and pulling the proletariat into the respective imperial and fascist consensus. Indeed, Tariff Reform imperialists hoped that revenues accrued from import tariffs would help fund social projects. Despite the anti-German predilection of many social-imperialists, the Wilhelmine social welfare programme was held up as a successful model of social and class integration.

The nation's regeneration also meant fostering a spirit of national discipline for many social-imperialists, another prominent fascist theme. To the social-imperialist, resolution and dedication to duty, combined with an appreciation of fundamental national and imperial aspirations, were essential prerequisites for national survival. A cross-class emphasis was again in evidence, with the regime of discipline encompassing all social-class categories, including the working classes. The cultivation of a spirit of militarism was viewed as an effective means of advancing the goal of national discipline. The prewar period would witness a proliferation of organisations dedicated to the task of promoting this militaristic ethic. The National Service League (NSL), for example, formed in 1901, advocated universal adult male conscription. The NSL included amongst its members Viscount Milner, Lord Roberts and Rudyard Kipling. The Navy League, too, founded in 1895, sought the implementation of a voluntary national system of naval training, a scheme that it hoped would prove attractive to all social groups.[27] As a further device to inculcate in the working masses the imperial ideal and a reverence for martial values, the Navy League emphasised the importance of Britain's naval heritage as a crucial factor making for national unity and cohesion. By engaging in a ritual annual commemoration of Nelson's Trafalgar victory, Navy League activists invited the masses to forge an association with the heroic spirit of the national past, a common heritage that apparently superseded considerations of class difference.[28] British fascists in a later period would similarly engage in solemn ritual commemorations of dead national heroes, particularly the dead of the First World War generation. The National Defence Association, which boasted the editor of the *Morning Post*, H. A. Gwynne, and the *Daily Express* publisher, C. Arthur Pearson, on its committee, was another such organisation, as were the National Maritime League and the Imperial Maritime League.[29] Promoting themselves as authentic defenders of the higher national interest, these organisations professed to be truly national non-partisan entities, supra-class and 'above party'. Indeed for Navy League propagandists, Lord Nelson was the embodiment of the ideal of the national hero, the sincere, self-made patriot who defied convention and ultimately experienced a heroic death.[30] The attempt to cultivate martial values went beyond the issue of military preparedness as a response to potential external threats. Neither was it simply a manipulative exercise in social control by reactionary elites seeking to dampen working-class militancy. While it did have both these objectives in mind, there was more to it than this. It was assumed that nurturing a spirit of militarism would foster feelings of comradeship amongst the classes, inculcate a sense of high patriotism and self-sacrifice, improve the moral character of young working-class males, and enhance the physical quality of the population.[31] It would be left to the fascists in later years to attempt the task of fostering a spirit of national discipline via the medium of martial values and paramilitarism in a more systematic fashion.

It should be noted, too, that the attempt to cultivate popular support for imperialist goals, the techniques of manipulation developed by the various organisational manifestations of the Edwardian radical right, were reminiscent of the propaganda style of later British fascism. The social-imperialist orchestration of popular sentiments through extra-parliamentary political leagues, pressure groups and voluntary associations, with their objective of generating a groundswell of popular extra-parliamentary opinion for change, would anticipate fascism's later attempt at domestic political mobilisation.

Advocates of social-imperialism and national efficiency who ascribed to Social-Darwinist principles would also prove important to the development of British fascist ideas. The most influential spokesmen in this tradition were Benjamin Kidd and Karl Pearson. Kidd, a fervent anti-Marxist and anti-socialist of firm religious convictions, put forward his sociological perspectives on evolution and efficiency in his influential book *Social Evolution* (1894).[32] Of Quaker origin, Karl Pearson was a Professor of Applied Mathematics and Mechanics at University College London during the 1880s. Pearson would employ his considerable skills in mathematics to establish the subject of statistical biology or biometrics, a discipline he dedicated to the service of defending the science of evolution according to Darwinian principles.[33] Unlike Benjamin Kidd,

Pearson combined his interest in Darwinism with an enthusiasm for socialism and Marxist economics. His socialism, however, acquired an increasingly authoritarian and reactionary character by the early 1900s, as he endeavoured to apply evolutionary concepts and statistical methods to the contemporary debate on race. Besides being a positivist and a progenitor of national socialism, Pearson was a eugenicist, who in 1911 became the first Galton Professor of Eugenics at the University of London.[34]

At the more general level, British fascism bequeathed from Social-Darwinism the notion of evolutionary development and ascent to more advanced modes of biological existence. In one of the numerous examples of the vulgarisation of Darwin's thought, which involved the indiscriminate application of biological concepts to the human context, interwar fascists believed that fascism stood for a more advanced form of political arrangement that would elevate society to a higher stage of socio-economic development. As a Mosleyite optimistically asserted, fascism was 'the next step in civilisation'.[35] There were other areas of convergence. For Social-Darwinists, the nation was a biological organism similar to other organic life forms in nature. According to Darwinists, in the incessant competitive struggle for existence those species in the plant and animal kingdoms that had proved most capable of adapting to a hostile environment would be capable of survival and reproduction according to the laws of 'natural selection'. The same evolutionary mechanisms governed the relationship between nation-states, for imperialist Social-Darwinists. This meant that the British nation was locked into an unavoidable and fiercely competitive struggle for supremacy with rival nations. Struggle and hardship, therefore, had to be endured by all social classes to ensure survival and the nation's evolutionary progress.[36] This emphasis on the severity of the environment and the competitive struggle for life would be mirrored in fascism's pessimistic preoccupation with the question of national decline and renewal and the stress on the moral grandeur of struggle. 'We welcome the fiery ordeals through which we shall have to pass', a Mosleyite solemnly declared.[37] Another BUF member proclaimed that, 'we must not grudge the struggle, however hard it may sometime seem, against opposition, or the sacrifices that have to be made'.[38] There was a strong focus on discipline, service and duty, core fascist themes as we have seen, in this forbidding Social-Darwinist vista. For Benjamin Kidd such values were essential ingredients in the evolutionary life struggle. Imperial

Germany of the 'Teutons' was again admired. A paradigm of an efficient national organism, Imperial Germany's iron discipline and dedication to duty ensured national cohesion and provided strength in a hostile world.

Social-Darwinists such as Benjamin Kidd also deified the state, as did the fascists. In the international competition for life, survival was dependent on the technical and military efficiency of the state. Efficiency could only be attained if the individual recognised the state as the supreme authority. The doctrine of individualism, even the Spencerian Social-Darwinist variety, was as 'anti-social' as Marxism for Kidd, and as such, hindered the task of state efficiency and consequently impeded the struggle for existence. The subordination of the individual unit to the corporate whole was apparently in tune with the laws of evolutionary development.[39] The Social-Darwinist Kidd, therefore, promoted an instrumentalist model of the state, sanctifying the state's role as the interpreter of the peoples' will, and the guarantor of their welfare. This idea of the state guiding the fortunes of the national collective represented a further vulgarisation of Darwin's theories, in that the conscious intervention of an external force would now replace the random operations of 'natural selection'. According to Darwinist doctrine, humans had been elevated from primitive organisms to the pinnacle of the evolutionary scale via an impersonal process in nature that did not involve, nor was it reliant on, mediation by a guiding external agency. Other organic life forms in nature were similarly thought to be subject to the laws of 'natural selection'. Many interwar fascists would also find the principle of random 'natural selection' unsatisfactory as a guide to interpreting the national destiny. They would turn to vitalism in their search for a more efficient method, as we shall see below.

The national socialist Karl Pearson also revered the state. However, he would introduce sinister racial concepts into the equation. The state's role, for Pearson, was to enhance the nation's racial character in order to improve its prospects of survival in a hostile world. This concept of the state as an instrument of racial improvement had its roots in Pearson's views on the importance of heredity in determining individual characteristics and conduct. These views were influenced by Francis Galton's eugenicist fantasies on genetic health care and August Weismann's speculations on the cellular mechanism of heredity and his theory of the immutable 'germ plasm'.[40] These theories would challenge the influential Lamarckian model of evolution, which stressed the inheritance of environmentally acquired characteristics. For Pearson and Galton, on the other hand, individual characteristics were determined by heredity, or genetic factors, rather than environment, which only played a limited or marginal role. The investigations of August Weismann, a German biologist writing at the end of the nineteenth century, led to the adoption of a more extreme position. He claimed that in every life form there was an autonomous 'germ plasm', a hereditary substance that is transmitted from generation to generation, a theory he expounded in his influential book *The Germ-Plasm: A Theory of Heredity* (1892). This hereditary substance was exempt from environmental change, according to Weismann, which served virtually to deny the idea of environmental adaptation and the possibility of change through individual self-exertion.

The significance of the theory of heredity for imperialist Social-Darwinists, such as Karl Pearson, concerned the methods that were proposed to ensure survival in an inhospitable world. Convinced of the predeterminedness of individual characteristics and of the limitations of environmentally induced factors, they advocated a regulatory system of 'racial-selective breeding' to stimulate reproduction of the supposedly physically and mentally healthier elements in society and inhibit the procreation of 'less healthy' strains. In these sinister eugenicist fantasies, the adjustment of the relative fertility rates of the stronger and weaker strains would be achieved by both 'positive' and 'negative' eugenic measures. Included amongst the former was the proposal to urge 'healthy parents' to have large families, for which they would be granted certificates of hereditary fitness or 'eugenic certificates', as Francis Galton advocated. Karl Pearson's suggestion that the provision of state aid to the unfit should be limited was an example of the latter.[41] Pearson's 'negative' eugenics did not stop there. Emigration, the closure of casual wards and the curbing of progressive welfare reforms were other remedies he put forward to deter procreation amongst supposedly inferior categories. All such remedies would help redress the perceived imbalance in fertility levels between the higher (healthier) and the lower (unfit) social orders and thus check the process of 'race deterioration'. In this bleak, dispassionate, positivist vision of an efficient British 'race' and biologically healthy national organism, the supposed benefits of health provision for certain categories of 'degenerate' stock were also called into question. According to Pearson, the preservation of the allegedly weaker strains by modern medical science via such means as the general raising of life-expectancy levels contravened the laws of Nature and 'race betterment', by interfering with the selective 'purifying force' of 'natural selection'.[42] Pearson's chilling eugenic frame of mind led him inexorably towards an anti-immigration and anti-semitic stance. He believed that immigration, particularly Jewish immigration, needed to be discouraged on racial lines because it violated the laws of racial health and patriotism.[43]

The ideas of racial Social-Darwinism influenced British fascism in a number of ways. To begin with, hereditarian ideas and biological determinist models contributed to the emergence of racial theories of anti-semitism. As Richard Thurlow noted, the theory of fixed inborn characteristics, or genetic endowment, was a feature of the crude racial philosophy of the Imperial Fascist League (IFL). According to Thurlow, Arnold Leese of the IFL was convinced that different groups of individuals had 'fixed and immutable types of character', which led him to the conclusion that race determined behaviour and cultural attainment.[44] This stress on the predeterminedness of individual characteristics, and its consequent emphasis on fixed racial categories, would distinguish the racial fascists of the IFL from the 'neo-Lamarckians' of the BUF, who believed that 'culture rather than race determined behaviour'.[45] The racial fascist notion of predetermined mental, physical and behavioural traits, with its assumption that different groups of individuals constituted accumulations of healthy or degenerate biological entities, invariably encouraged the development and propagation of vulgar anti-semitic doctrines. Viewed as having exclusively negative characteristics, Jews were depicted by racial fascists as the incarnation of pure evil and the subverters of supposed 'Aryan' race purity and cultural values.

Eugenicist Social-Darwinism also influenced the development of fascist degenerationist ideas.[46] At the social and cultural level, eugenicist ideas acted as a stimulus to fascist fears pertaining to certain trends relating to modernity and 'mass society'. In some respects, such fears were a reflection of a more widespread contemporary concern about the continuing increase in urbanisation and its accompanying expansion of society's 'lumpen' and criminal element. Although pessimistic perceptions of the urban poor had long been a feature of the reactionary conservative imagination, such views would intensify as a consequence of the dramatic increase in industrialisation and urbanisation during the latter half of the nineteenth century.⁴⁷ Bourgeois *angst* concerning the urban 'mass' and the supposed debilitating effects of the modern urban milieu would be fuelled by the eugenicists' emphasis on biological heredity, with its stress on the genetic transmission of degenerate behaviour. Parallel explanations emanating from the fields of medical research, human psychology and criminal anthropology in Britain and the continent served to heighten anxiety still further. In the field of medical research, theories pertaining to the genetic transmission of sexual diseases, such as syphilis, aroused fears about the alleged link between urban centres and high levels of sexual deviancy. In a similar vein, degenerationist psychiatry attributed mental, sexual and social abnormalities, ranging from neurosis to deviancy, to a hereditary predisposition, while Lombrosian criminal anthropology sought to prove that urban criminality could be comprehended in terms of an individual's descent down the evolutionary scale. In this grim atavistic perspective on urban crime, the criminal was depicted as a biological throwback, a sort of reversion to a primitive state of savagery.⁴⁸ The pessimistic assessments of modern urban trends expounded by these positivistic explanatory models were also reinforced by naturalist novels of the period, particularly Zola's depressing literary realist observations of urban 'low life' during the French Second Empire.⁴⁹

Interwar fascism would inherit the view, with its pronounced eugenicist undertone, that a mass population of degenerate urban-dwellers with a tendency towards pathological behaviour was undermining social order and even culture itself. A variety of modern urban 'deformities' that included poverty, crime, improvidence, alcoholism and forms of sexual perversion were thought to be threatening civilisation from within. Fascism, on the other hand, emphasised the importance of hierarchy, discipline and order for the maintenance of social stability and cultural values. The question of 'racial' degeneration also preoccupied the thoughts of many fascists. Modern urbanisation was believed to be a cause of physical and mental deterioration, which, by multiplying the numbers of the 'unfit', expedited the process of racial decay. J. F. C. Fuller, writing in 1932, who was to become a senior official in the BUF, feared that a differential birth-rate, with 'degenerate stocks' demonstrating higher average fertility rates than other categories in the community, was leading to the deterioration of the race. Equally alarming for Fuller, for whom a 'differential birth-rate' contributed significantly to the destruction of Ancient Rome, was the modern tendency to do everything possible to foster the 'degenerate stocks' and 'reduce their death-rate'.[50]

The increase in the numbers of the 'insane and of the mentally deficient' and other such imagined manifestations and consequences of modern life, including those prone to 'unnatural vice' and suicide, also concerned the British fascist and Mussolini devotee James Strachey Barnes. For the Roman Catholic Barnes, such trends were symptomatic of an increasing decadence in modern society.[51] Fascist fears of decadence were invariably influenced by eugenicist Social-Darwinist ideas. Evolutionary frames of reference, and a perception of growing urban deprivation and an expanding population of the 'unfit', engendered alarm about the erosion of vitality and energy, or what Payne refers to as 'the reversal of development through entropy'.[52] As we shall see in a later chapter, for many fascists the city, or 'metropolis', was the principal agency of physical and moral degeneration and was thus the supreme symbol of cultural decadence in the modern age. Fascism, on the other hand, would identify the countryside and rural England as the true repository of an authentic national culture. The countryside was imagined to be a source of vitality and a spiritual antidote to the social dislocation and anomie that apparently disfigured life in the modern city.

Urbanisation was not the only feature of modernity that was responsible for the process of social and racial degeneration, according to the fascists. Modern democracy was equally to blame. For J. F. C. Fuller, democracy was a 'Satanic instrument' that was in conflict with Nature because it based its philosophy and practices on the Christian 'fallacy' that 'all men are equal'. As a consequence, the 'ignorant mass' is deified and sheltered through the implementation of 'humanitarian legislation' and 'social philanthropy' which protects the weak and 'ruins the strong'.[53] Fuller bemoaned a democratic morality which prevented the 'inefficient and worthless' from starving, was loathe to compel them to work, and yet allowed such types 'to marry and breed at the public expense'. Even worse, for Fuller, was the alarming increase in the numbers of the insane under humanitarian democracy. In a chilling diatribe punctuated by 'positive' eugenicist sentiments, he chastised democracy for lacking the will to 'insist on birth-control' and 'enforce segregation, sterilisation and the lethal chamber', amongst other remedies, to combat the ills he imagined were rife in modern Western civilisation.[54]

Eugenicist Social-Darwinism and perceptions of urban and

physical degeneration also contributed to the fascists' preoccupation with health and 'social hygiene', and their obsessive desire to cultivate the physically 'beautiful' body.[55] Racial and eugenicist Social-Darwinism acted as a stimulus, too, to more extreme forms of fascist elitism, with pessimistic observers of contemporary urbanisation and modern culture expounding the view that regeneration was dependent on the nation investing its hopes in its supposedly 'higher' types.

Karl Pearson's stance demonstrates that there was no necessary correlation between the ideas of eugenicist Social-Darwinism and a particular political belief system. Eugenicists could be located at all points of the political spectrum. Pearson was both a eugenicist and a socialist, suggesting a link between a number of left-wing thinkers and later British fascism. Others of a socialist persuasion, for example, also harboured eugenicist sentiments, including the Fabian socialists H. G. Wells and Sidney Webb.[56] Wells's views were particularly extreme. He advocated a variety of methods to ensure that the criminally insane, drug addicts, those with genetically transmissible diseases, as well as a range of other 'failures', were prevented from propagating, including sterilisation, being quarantined on special islands and the death penalty.[57] Wells's Fabian colleague George Bernard Shaw also flirted with eugenicist ideas, even serving as a lecturer to the Eugenics Education Society.[58]

Shaw's thinking provides other links with British fascism. His creative evolutionary vision and concept of the 'life-force' and his ideas concerning the emergence of a new 'superman' deeply impressed Oswald Mosley, for whom Shaw was a supremely 'creative thinker'.[59] Shaw believed, as did Mosley, that a life-force was at work in the evolutionary process which was struggling to create a more advanced type of existence. Shaw was keen for society to assist the life-force by cultivating and multiplying its 'highest types', an elite of heroic exceptional individuals, so as to expedite this transition to a higher state. Shaw's vitalism would enable humanity to transcend the limitations imposed on the historical process by the more gradual and random mechanisms of evolution.[60] This 'heroic vitalist' vision of progress, with the conscious intervention of the creative 'will-to-achievement' types serving to hasten evolution, would become an obsession for Mosley. As late as 1947 he wrote that 'to evolve a higher type has become a practical aim. Once again we postulate that the prime necessity of our age is to accelerate evolution. This generation must play the midwife to Destiny in hastening a new birth.'[61]

The concept of the conscious striving towards higher forms was not the only area of overlap between Shaw's thinking and British fascism. He identified closely with the contemporary vogue for efficiency in national affairs, a perception that partly motivated his desire to create a new elite of virile and heroic technical experts who would bring a greater degree of modernisation to *fin-de-siècle* Britain. Shaw's Fabian associates were also concerned about inefficiency in British society. Sidney and Beatrice Webb advocated the creation of a new supra-class party of 'national efficiency', whose aim would be to acquaint every sphere of British life with the principles of efficiency. This indeed was the professed aim of the Coefficients, a chosen elite of 'experts' of varying political complexions assembled by the Webbs in 1902, who would plan for the creation of such a party.[62] The Webbs and Bernard Shaw also favoured an imperialist orientation for Britain, a predisposition which underwrote their ambitious projects to fashion a new party of national efficiency. As Robert Skidelsky noted, in such Fabian schemes can be detected many of the political ideas embodied in Mosley's 'Centre Party idea of 1920', the New Party and the BUF.[63]

Robert Blatchford provides another link between fascism and the British socialist tradition. In the years prior to 1914, through the columns of his weekly socialist newspaper *The Clarion*, Blatchford frequently discoursed on a variety of themes that would later find their way into British fascist ideology.[64] Blatchford was opposed to the parliamentary party system, Cobdenite Liberal and Labour internationalism and class-war doctrines. In his writings, he also demonstrated a predilection for a strong leader, imperialism, martial values and the reorganisation of society along economic nationalist and protectionist lines, all distinct fascist themes.

The BUF attempted to appropriate the romantic utopian socialist William Morris for the fascist tradition, too, although in this case the connection is much more problematic.[65] It was Morris's aesthetic anti-modernism, most notably his antipathy to industrialisation and the increasing mechanisation of modern work, that received the most attention. The BUF imagined that there was a distinct line of continuity between Morris's anguished late Victorian critique of modernity and its own antipathy towards certain aspects of the modernisation process. Morris's celebration of the artisan, workshop production and the individual craftsmanship of the Middle Ages was thought to be consistent with the later spirit of national socialism.⁶⁶ The BUF also identified affinities between Morris's romantic view of unalienated labour and the Nazi work philosophy, *Kraft durch Freude*.⁶⁷ The attempt to claim Morris for fascism was not surprising. It was part of an ongoing effort by the BUF to identify itself with the Victorian reaction against the Industrial Revolution, an anti-materialist tradition that encompassed Thomas Carlyle, Samuel Coleridge, John Ruskin and Matthew Arnold.⁶⁸ The BUF cited another feature of Morris's romantic socialism as a forerunner of a fascist culture. Morris was critical of encroaching urbanisation and the modern city, while revelling in a nostalgia for the apparently timeless beauty of the English countryside. The Mosleyites would harbour similar views during the 1930s.⁶⁹ Other links between Morris and fascism were thought to exist. The BUF attempted to identify a spurious 'racial' component in Morris's thinking. It saw in Morris's mystical reverence for Iceland an intuitive awareness of a North European racial community and a common 'Nordic' racial heritage, to which the English apparently belonged.⁷⁰

At a more general level, we can identify other links with the socialist tradition. We should note the socialist, anti-capitalist strain in the economic programme of the BUF, for example. Mosley frequently discoursed on the disruptive effects of unregulated capitalist economics. 'Financial capital' was especially savaged. It was accused of being unaccountable, anonymous and predatory. The BUF, instead, proceeded to celebrate the 'virtuous' organic 'producers state' and the notion of direct producers' labour, a more authentic form of personal and communal property in its eyes. Thurlow has also traced aspects of Mosley's economic thought to the Independent Labour Party (ILP).⁷¹ Mosley took up the ILP's underconsumptionist argument concerning the need to reconcile consumption with production. He was convinced that there was a serious under-utilisation of existing productive capacity in Britain, a condition which he believed partly had its roots in the prevailing fetish amongst economists of the neo-classical *laissez-faire* type for the gold standard, deflationary policies and an export-orientated economy. The chronic inability to harness the combined potential of modern production techniques and scientific innovation, and a reluctance to exploit the home market, led to the paradox of underconsumption and poverty in the modern age of plenty, according to Mosley.

British fascism's ideological roots, however, were not restricted to the domestic context. It absorbed ideas from a number of continental intellectual sources, too. Oswald Spengler, for example, would have a crucial influence on Mosleyite fascist thought.[72] In addition, domestic fascism drew on ideas that developed out of the anti-rationalist and anti-positivist revolt of the *fin de siècle*.[73] The origins of much of this critique can be traced to a number of key intellectual figures of this period, principally Friedrich Nietzsche, Henri Bergson, Georges Sorel and Gustave Le Bon. Each of these thinkers, in their own way, challenged the assumptions of rationalism and positivism by highlighting the significance of non-rational motivation in individual and group behaviour. According to Nietzsche, Bergson, Sorel and Le Bon, individuals are swayed by appeals to the non-rational rather than the rational or logical elements within their make-up, which led each of them to conclude that the irrational was the primary motive force of cultural activity.

Nietzsche, for example, the arch-opponent of liberal rationalism and its related doctrine of individual self-improvement through progress, called on people to forsake reason and return to a more intuitive and passionate existence. This new, unfettered culture of virility, a new morality of the 'will', in Nietzsche's view, was the only means of ensuring survival in a world where traditional certainties, including Christianity and its system of ethics, had apparently been destroyed by the forces of liberal progress and modernity. Mosley and the BUF would acknowledge their intellectual debt to Nietzsche on numerous occasions.[74] To the Mosleyites, the irrational, or Dionysian, life sketched out by Nietzsche held out the promise of a new and exciting mode of existence, one pregnant with depth and new meaning. The French philosopher Henri Bergson also favoured the non-rational in people. Bergson repudiated the positivist notion that the creative thrust of existence could be explained by materialism, determinism or Darwinian mechanism. Rather it was the *élan vital*, or vital instinct, which supplied the creative evolutionary impulse or 'life-force' which thrust people and nature forward to new and ever higher forms of development. Taking its cue from the concepts developed by Bergson, fascism believed that in vitalistic intuition and the *élan vital* it had discovered an alternative source of creative energy to that of Cartesian rationalism and positivism.

The French ex-engineer Georges Sorel, too, endorsed the creative force of the irrational. As a revolutionary syndicalist, he was committed to the goal of worker emancipation. Sorel determined to discover the source of proletarian motivation, concluding that it was non-rational 'myths' which moved the masses to decisive action. As propagandistic statements or devices operating 'above' logical thought, myths would appeal to the emotions and cultivate an 'epic state of mind' in the people, instilling in them the urge to rise up and challenge the status quo.[75] Sorel's myths were thus an energising force that served the overt political purpose of igniting the spark of revolt in disenfranchised humanity. Like Sorel, fascism would recognise the value of irrational, emotion-generating myths as tools of mass mobilisation and propaganda weapons in the struggle for power. The fascist myth would prove to be an essential instrument for mobilising popular energies, irrespective of its rational content or truth-value.

The French social psychologist Gustave Le Bon was also interested in the role of non-rational elements in individual and group behaviour. He, too, challenged the Cartesian assumption that reason was the definitive element in people's mental and emotional make-up.[76] According to Le Bon, the quintessential feature of the modern era was the 'crowd'. He claimed that individuals, on entering the crowd, or mass society, invariably succumb to the irrational in their nature and act according to instinct, impulse and emotion. Just as significantly, Le Bon claimed that the crowd was highly susceptible to the power of suggestion and thus could be manipulated. The crowd performs another function, too. On entering the mass, individuals dissolve into the collective whole, as it were. As George Mosse has noted, Le Bon's contribution to fascist thought concerned his observation that people were basically irrational in their mentality and emotions and were therefore more likely to be swayed by charismatic leaders utilising mass suggestion and emotive propaganda rather than by appeals to reason.[77] Oswald Mosley, the most perceptive of Britain's fascist leaders, understood the significance of charismatic leadership, the power of mass suggestion and the need to appeal to the emotional side of the mass audience. Like all interwar fascist leaders, he was mindful of the need to make the lonely individuals of mass society feel as if they, when dissolving their individuality into the collective whole, were participating in something unique. Thus when isolated individuals were invited to enter the massed ranks of fascism, they were invited to enter into a mystical union with their fellow 'Britons', to join them in a unique historical drama to rekindle the national spirit and usher in a phase of national regeneration.

Notes

1. *FQ*, 1, 3 (July 1935), pp. 360–4.
2. *Blackshirt*, 21 September 1934, p. 9.
3. *FQ*, 1, 3 (July 1935), pp. 360–4.
4. W. E. D. Allen, *Fascism in Relation to British History and Character* (London, BUF Publications, 1933), pp. 5–6. Allen would later write for the BUF under the pseudonym 'James Drennan'.
5. *Blackshirt*, 21 September 1934, p. 9.
6. *Action*, 23 April 1938, p. 13.
7. Allen, *Fascism*, p. 5.
8. W. Joyce, *Twilight Over England* (Metairie, Sons, n.d.), pp. 13–14.
9. *FQ*, 11, 2 (April 1936), pp. 277–88.
10. *FQ*, 11, 3 (July 1936), pp. 427–35.
11. Ibid. See also *Blackshirt*, 6 July 1934, p. 4; 16 November 1934, p. 6; and 4 January 1935, p. 2.
12. See, for example, D. Brooks, *The Age of Upheaval. Edwardian Politics 1899–1914* (Manchester, Manchester University Press, 1995).
13. B. Semmel, *Imperialism and Social Reform. English Social-Imperial Thought* (London, Allen and Unwin, 1960), p. 248. See also D. Watts, *Joseph Chamberlain and the Challenge of Radicalism* (London, Hodder and Stoughton, 1998).
14. B. S. Farr, *The Development and Impact of Right-Wing Politics in Britain, 1903–1932* (New York, Garland Publishing, 1987), pp. 3–4.
15. Ibid., p. 89.
16. F. Coetzee, *For Party or Country. Nationalism and the Dilemmas of Popular Conservatism in Edwardian England* (Oxford, Oxford University Press, 1990), p. 20.
17. See P. Kennedy, *The Rise of Anglo-German Antagonism 1860–1914* (London, Allen and Unwin, 1980).
18. Coetzee, *For Party or Country*, p. 20.
19. Ibid., p. 39.
20. L. Witherell, *Rebel on the Right. Henry Page Croft and the Crisis of British Conservatism, 1903–1914* (Delaware, University of Delaware Press, 1998), on Croft. Semmel, *Imperialism and Social Reform*, pp. 177–87, on Milner.
21. Semmel, *Imperialism and Social Reform*, p. 170.
22. L. Susser, 'Fascist and Anti-Fascist Attitudes in Britain Between the Wars.' (Ph.D. thesis, University of Oxford, 1988), p. 216.
23. G. Searle, 'The Revolt from the Right in Edwardian Britain', in P. Kennedy and A. Nicholls (eds), *Nationalist and Racialist Movements in Britain and Germany Before 1914* (London, Macmillan, 1981), pp. 25–6.
24. Semmel, *Imperialism and Social Reform*, pp. 175 and 238.
25. Ibid., p. 185.

26 K. Lunn, 'Political Anti-Semitism Before 1914: Fascism's Heritage?', in K. Lunn and R. Thurlow (eds), *British Fascism* (London, Croom Helm, 1980), pp. 20–40.
27 Farr, *The Development and Impact*, pp. 25–6.
28 Coetzee, *For Party or Country*, p. 25.
29 Farr, *The Development and Impact*, pp. 25–6.
30 Coetzee, *For Party or Country*, p. 25.
31 Farr, *The Development and Impact*, pp. 25–6.
32 B. Kidd, *Social Evolution* (London, Macmillan, 1894).
33 Semmel, *Imperialism and Social Reform*, p. 37.
34 Ibid., p. 37.
35 *Hackney Gazette*, 15 January 1934, p. 7.
36 Susser, 'Fascist and Anti-Fascist Attitudes', p. 171.
37 *Blackshirt*, 16 November 1934, p. 6.
38 *Blackshirt*, 4 January 1935, p. 2.
39 P. Hayes, 'The Contribution of British Intellectuals to Fascism', in Lunn and Thurlow (eds), *British Fascism*, p. 177.
40 Ibid., pp. 173–5. See also R. Thurlow, *Fascism in Britain. A History, 1918–1985* (Oxford, Blackwell, 1987), pp. 17 and 87.
41 Semmel, *Imperialism and Social Reform*, pp. 46–8.
42 Ibid., p. 49.
43 E. Barkan, *The Retreat of Scientific Racism. Changing Concepts of Race in Britain and America Between the Wars* (Cambridge, Cambridge University Press, 1992), pp. 156–7.
44 Thurlow, *Fascism in Britain. A History*, pp. 88–9.
45 Ibid., pp. 17 and 158.
46 On degenerationist ideas, see J. E. Chamberlain and S. L. Gilman (eds), *Degeneration. The Dark Side of Progress* (New York, Columbia University Press, 1985).
47 S. Payne, *A History of Fascism 1914–1945* (London, UCL Press, 1995), pp. 29–30.
48 P. Weindling, *Health, Race and German Politics Between National Unification and Nazism 1870–1945* (Cambridge, Cambridge University Press, 1993 edition), pp. 81–4. Criminal anthropology was pioneered by the Italian psychologist Cesare Lombroso.
49 Ibid., p. 87.
50 J. F. C. Fuller, *The Dragon's Teeth. A Study of War and Peace* (London, Constable, 1932), p. 13.
51 J. S. Barnes, *Half a Life Left* (London, Eyre and Spottiswoode, 1937), p. 293.
52 Payne, *A History of Fascism*, p. 30.
53 Fuller, *The Dragon's Teeth*, pp. 14–17.
54 Ibid., p. 15.
55 On 'social hygiene', see Weindling, *Health, Race and German Politics*.

56 Semmel, *Imperialism and Social Reform*, p. 51.
57 J. Carey, *The Intellectuals and the Masses. Pride and Prejudice Among the Literary Intelligentsia, 1880–1939* (London, Faber and Faber, 1992), pp. 123–7.
58 Semmel, *Imperialism and Social Reform*, p. 51.
59 O. Mosley, *My Life* (London, Thomas Nelson, 1968), p. 224. See also Susser, 'Fascist and Anti-Fascist Attitudes', pp. 33–4.
60 Thurlow, *Fascism in Britain. A History*, p. 19.
61 O. Mosley, *The Alternative* (London, Abbey Supplies, 1947), p. 287.
62 Semmel, *Imperialism and Social Reform*, pp. 72–7.
63 R. Skidelsky, *Oswald Mosley* (London, Macmillan, 1981), p. 58.
64 Semmel, *Imperialism and Social Reform*, pp. 222–33, on Blatchford.
65 See 'William Morris, National Socialist', *BUQ*, II, 3 (July–September 1938), pp. 61–8. See also *BUQ*, II, 4 (October–December 1938), pp. 52–62.
66 On the BUF's support for craft-based production, see *Action*, 16 April 1938, p. 14.
67 Strength through Joy.
68 We will return to this theme in a later chapter. See below, Chapter Ten. On the Victorian anti-materialist tradition, see R. Williams, *Culture and Society, Coleridge to Orwell* (London, Hogarth, 1990) and P. Keating, *The Victorian Prophets* (London, Fontana, 1981).
69 This theme is explored in a later chapter. See below, Chapter Ten.
70 *BUQ*, II, 4 (October–December 1938), pp. 52–62.
71 R. Thurlow, 'The Return of Jeremiah: The Rejected Knowledge of Sir Oswald Mosley in the 1930s', in Lunn and Thurlow (eds), *British Fascism*, p. 105.
72 Spengler's influence is discussed in later chapters. See below, Chapters Four and Ten.
73 On the significance of the *fin de siècle* for fascist ideas see Zeev Sternhell's seminal book, *The Birth of Fascist Ideology* (Princeton, Princeton University Press, 1994). See also W. Laqueur, 'Fin-de-siecle: Once More with Feeling', *Journal of Contemporary History*, 31 (1996), pp. 5–47.
74 See, for example, O. Mosley, 'The Philosophy of Fascism', *FQ*, 1, 1 (January 1935), pp. 35–46. For a fuller discussion of the Nietzsche–BUF intellectual link see below, Chapter Four.
75 M. Biddiss, *The Age of the Masses. Ideas and Society in Europe Since 1870* (Harmondsworth, Penguin, 1977), pp. 128–30.
76 G. Le Bon, *The Crowd: A Study of the Popular Mind* (London, Fisher Unwin, 1896).
77 G. Mosse, *Nazi Culture. Intellectual, Cultural and Social Life in the Third Reich* (London, W. H. Allen, 1966), pp. xxiii–xxiv.

CHAPTER TWO

THE EARLY POSTWAR CONTEXT AND THE PRE-FASCIST GROUPS: INCIPIENT FASCISM?

The origins of British fascism can be traced to a range of intellectual currents and developments that germinated in the period prior to 1914, as we have seen. Domestic fascism also grew out of the traumatic experience of the Great War. The early postwar years, however, would prove to be just as crucial for the emergence of a native fascism. The period 1918–22, in particular, was a time of deep anxiety as Britain confronted the problems of postwar readjustment and reconstruction, and it is in this conjuncture of circumstances that many of domestic fascism's more immediate precursors lay. This period spawned an atmosphere of instability and uncertainty that was to prove conducive to the emergence of a number of radical right and proto-fascist groups, which would provide crucial organisational, ideological and personal links with the overtly fascist parties of later years.

In early postwar Britain, many on the right and centre of the political spectrum believed that the established order was disintegrating under the impact of developments on the international and domestic fronts. The signs of disintegration began to be observed from 1917, with the instability not subsiding until 1922. Events overseas threatened to undermine hopes of a prompt return to peace and stability following the bloodletting of the Great War. The nation's psychological structure had already been disturbed by the horrific experience of the war. The 745,000 fatalities sustained by Britain, with a further 1.6 million permanently debilitated by wounds and the effects of gas, shocked and traumatised the nation. Lenin's Bolshevik Revolution in 1917, however, appeared to be a harbinger of a terrifying new epoch of violence and revolutionary upheaval which threatened to derail attempts to hasten a return to peace and normality. The Spartacist rising in Berlin, and the estab-

The early postwar context and the pre-fascist groups

lishment of 'Soviet Republics' in Bavaria and Hungary during 1919, seemed to vindicate these pessimistic assessments. The formation of the Communist Party of Great Britain in 1920 merely heightened the prevailing sense of anxiety.

Imperial stability was also being endangered by postwar developments. Despite significant territorial acquisitions, the extension of British control over stretches of the prostrate Ottoman Empire (courtesy of the secret Sykes–Picot agreement) and the procurement of mandates over Germany's former imperial possessions in Africa and the Pacific, victory in the Great War did not guarantee unequivocal imperial security. The Empire became imperilled from other directions. Encouraged by both Bolshevism's and Wilsonian liberal internationalism's rhetoric of national self-determination, nationalist movements within the Empire proliferated. Imperialists in Britain were particularly anxious concerning the drift of events in India. Many believed that the introduction of limited self-government at the provincial level, provided by the 1919 Government of India Act, would have the effect of loosening the imperial grip in that country.[1] The forces of disintegration within the Empire were also thought to be at work in Ireland. Events there since 1916 had seen the eclipse of Irish constitutionalism and the resurgence of 'physical force' republicanism and an inclusive, self-consciously Gaelic, Irish nationalist movement embodied in Sinn Fein.[2] Sinn Fein's electoral advances during the 1918 General Election would spread panic amongst those committed to the maintenance of the Union. The 1921 Anglo-Irish Treaty was also greeted with dismay. Conservative-Unionists feared a 'domino effect'. The Treaty and partition were not only a forewarning of an end to the Union but set a dangerous precedent for like-minded independence movements within the Empire. General concerns about imperial security were not eased by initiatives in postwar diplomacy. The ban on capital naval vessel construction and establishment of fixed naval ratios for the major sea-powers, pushed through at the 1921–22 Washington Conference at the Americans' behest, saw a major contraction of the imperial battlefleet and seemed to herald the decline of British maritime power.[3]

Developments on the domestic front also gave cause for concern. The Great War affected Britain's postwar economic performance. The international economy had been severely damaged by the 1914–18 war.[4] The destruction of the Hohenzollern, Hapsburg and Romanov empires threw the economies of central and eastern

Europe into confusion. To add to this, Europe's transport and communications network was virtually destroyed in the conflict. The war also damaged the international monetary and exchange rate system, reduced the real value of the currencies of the belligerent nations in Europe and precipitated a postwar inflationary spiral from which Britain did not remain immune. In 1920 prices in the United Kingdom stood at three times the prewar level.[5] The rate of growth of world trade also slowed after 1918, relative to the prewar position, affecting Britain's comparative share. Britain's export market was also injured by the economic performance of its former wartime allies. A resurgent United States and Japan, both emerging from the war in a healthy economic condition, began to assail Britain's traditional markets in continental Europe, South America and Asia after 1918.[6] Between 1913 and 1923 British exports to Latin America declined by over one-third, the vast majority of these markets falling to the United States.[7] The First World War depleted Britain's financial reserves, too. Britain emerged from the conflict a debtor nation, having borrowed vast sums to sustain the war effort, including £1,027 million from the United States. The United States loomed large in other areas also. Wall Street was growing in financial influence after 1918, to the detriment of the City of London.

Britain's economy was also beset by structural problems. Long-term recovery could not be sustained by a reliance on the traditional staple industries of iron and steel, shipbuilding, coal and textiles. Despite some early signs of vigour, these sectors began to experience extreme difficulties. This was due to an over-expansion of productive capacity during the brief postwar boom, technically deficient plant, high production costs, exchange rate fluctuations, overseas competition, the development of indigenous primary goods industries, and the changing nature of demand in the world economy. In 1921 British shipyards languished, for example, as three hundred contracts for new ships were cancelled.[8] In 1912 the British cotton industry exported 6,900 million yards of cloth. In 1924 this figure had dropped to 4,500 million.[9] The Indian market, in particular, had contracted significantly. Between 1913 and 1923 the export of cotton piece goods to India had dropped by 53 per cent.[10] This bleak postwar picture helped contribute to the dramatic escalation in domestic unemployment, over two million by June 1921, as the economy slid into depression following the brief postwar boom.

A resurgence of trade union militancy after 1918 also generated anxiety.[11] In 1921 alone, 85 million working days were lost due to

The early postwar context and the pre-fascist groups

strikes.¹² The First World War once again provided an important backdrop to these developments. Trade union power and influence had increased during the war, a situation greatly stimulated by organised labour's crucial importance to the war effort. The widespread formal sanctioning of collective bargaining procedures by the state and employers' organisations was emblematic of this trend, further encouraging vigorous trade union growth. The number of workers in trade unions had spiraled to over eight million by the beginning of 1919, around double the August 1914 figure. There were many that feared this growth in the ranks of organised labour. After 1918, some feared, too, that the British worker was becoming dangerously infected by radical foreign ideologies which stressed class conflict. Syndicalist ideas had penetrated the Triple Alliance, a coalition of miners, railwaymen and transport workers that was formed in 1914, and the Shop Stewards' Movement, a militant unofficial craft-based organisation that first emerged in the engineering industry in 1915 as a reaction against the government's 'dilution' of labour schemes.¹³ The trade union movement also demonstrated pro-Bolshevik inclinations. The raising of the Red Flag in George Square, Glasgow, during the mass strike of 27 January 1919, and the formation in 1920 of 'Councils of Action' against possible British intervention in the Russian-Polish War, indicated sympathy for the ideals of the Russian Revolution within the labour movement.

The electoral advance of the Labour Party between 1918 and 1922 also aroused foreboding. The Great War boosted Labour's electoral profile, with the party gaining Cabinet experience in the wartime Coalition government. With the 1918 Constitution, drafted by Sidney Webb, providing the party with a sturdier organisational base and a more clearly defined political programme and purpose, Labour made an immediate electoral impact when hostilities ended. In the Coupon Election of 14 December 1918, a refined Labour Party with redefined aims amassed over two million votes or 22.7 per cent of the total poll, winning fifty-seven seats in the process, compared to the 371,772 votes that it accumulated during the previous General Election in December 1910.¹⁴

The postwar years were not only pregnant with the threat to political stability, property and future economic prosperity. Culture, too, appeared to be under attack. Many were of the view that Britain was being assailed by deadly forces which threatened to destroy authentic culture. The arts were felt to be adversely affected by a new climate of change. The advance of modernism in literature and, to a lesser extent, the visual arts, for example, with its commitment to original, innovative forms of cultural expression, was an indicator of a new and dissident mood in the arts.[15] There was a growing fear of 'mass culture' also, a mood partly precipitated by the growing trend towards a 'mass democracy'. The Great War, with its impersonal 'mass' armies and 'mass' slaughter, seemed to confirm this drift towards a dehumanising mass society. Indeed, the Great War represented a watershed in many areas of British culture. The 'machine war' of 1914–18, for example, appeared to confirm man's increasing subordination to the machine. Similarly, the Great War's industrialisation of war and killing fuelled disquiet about industrial society and materialism. As the BUF's J. F. C. Fuller was to put it later, the 1914–18 conflict was 'a materialist orgy of destruction, a perfect counterpart of the materialist orgy of construction which preceded it'.[16] Many also worried about the evident erosion of respect for established ideals and values such as authority, patriotism, seniority and even abstract notions of glory and honour, which seemed to be further casualties of the war.[17]

The anxiety felt within sections of the propertied classes as a consequence of the international and domestic dislocations of 1918–22, then, was to give rise to a profusion of anti-labour, anti-socialist, nationalist and expressly middle-class defence groups and publications. Some of these organisations and publications were simply obscure entities which provided a convenient forum for a variety of insignificant fringe cults, reactionary eccentrics, rabid period anti-semites and sentimental die-hard conservatives seeking a nostalgic return to the imagined security of the Edwardian past. Nevertheless, in broad outline it is possible to detect traces of an incipient fascism of the type of genus that characterised the fully matured variety of the later 1920s. Certainly, the traffic of ideas and personnel flowing from the early postwar anti-labour groups into the fascist parties of subsequent years would seem to suggest a significant degree of overlap between the two. We shall return to the question of the relative importance of these early postwar organisational and publicistic forms to the emergence of 1920s fascism at a later stage of this chapter.

Prominent amongst the postwar organisations was Brigadier-General Henry Page Croft's National Party (NP), which was formed in 1917 against the backdrop of the final critical phase of the Great War. It advocated protection for British companies, industrial harmony, propriety in government and a paternalistic approach towards the working classes. Under the impact of the labour agitation of the early postwar years, the NP would also adopt an uncompromising anti-Bolshevik and anti-syndicalist stance.[18] In this period of unrest the NP took on an almost exclusively middle-class profile. National Party members who became associated with 1920s fascism were Basil Peto and Reverend Gough, both stated to be members of the British Fascisti.[19] Beyond these personal connections, according to Barbara Farr, the lasting importance of the National Party for later British fascism concerned its attempt to transcend party and class politics, to mobilise a threatened middle class and to promote a corporatist doctrine of industrial relations.[20] With Croft being a committed tariff reform activist and an inspiration behind a number of pre-1918 imperialist pressure groups, most notably the Reveille movement and the Imperial Mission, the NP also provided a bridge between the prewar social-imperialist movement and 1920s fascism. For Farr, the National Party 'represented a redirection of the "Imperial Mission" into national, British unity'.[21]

The British Commonwealth Union (BCU) was another organisation that was fiercely hostile to the organised labour movement. Conceived in October 1917, it functioned as a political adjunct of anti-socialist business interests, engaging in covert anti-labour operations under the direction of the Irish-Catholic Patrick Hannon, who would serve as Conservative MP for Birmingham between 1921 and 1950.[22] Hannon provides another linkage between prewar social-imperialism and 1920s fascism. Vice-President of the Tariff Reform League between 1910 and 1914 and influential in a battery of other pre-1918 imperialist organisations, Hannon would later become a member of the British Fascisti, sitting on its Grand Council.[23] He also provides a connection, of course, between the postwar anti-labour groups and 1920s fascism, as does another BCU activist, Major-General T. D. Pilcher, who became a London official of the British Fascisti.[24]

Patrick Hannon was active in another of the postwar anti-Bolshevik organisations, the Comrades of the Great War (1917–21), serving as its first General Secretary.[25] The 'Comrades' was an ex-servicemen's group, lavishly supported by financial donations from British industrialists and businessmen, which sought to appeal to 'patriotic' elements in the armed forces.[26] Hannon's presence in this organisation highlights the ideological importance of pariotism and the Great War experience for the formulation of fascist beliefs.

Another avowedly 'patriotic' contemporary organisation, which endeavoured to mobilise patriotic labour and counter the growing appeal of the Labour Party to the working classes, was the British Workers' League (BWL). Super-patriots and imperialists, with a strong productivist orientation, and stressing the intrinsic unity of interests between employer and employee, BWL activists sought to keep alive the social-imperialist tradition in British politics. This aim would win the BWL the enthusiastic backing of the prewar stalwart of the tradition, Lord Milner. The BWL's political wing, the National Democratic Party, had a flurry of success at the 1918 General Election, winning ten seats.[27] The BWL also had ties to Patrick Hannon's British Commonwealth Union, receiving covert financial donations from that organisation.[28]

The British Empire Union (BEU) was another anti-Bolshevik patriotic organisation that stressed the intrinsic unity of interests between employer and employee. Formed in 1916, as an offshoot of the Germanophobic Anti-German Union, it sought the eradication of the roots of worker discontent against the employer by advocating measures such as profit-sharing and a high wage economy based on the United States capitalist model.[29] Stridently imperialist and protectionist, the BEU also sought to increase Empire ties through a preferential trade arrangement.[30] According to one historian, the BEU's anti-Bolshevik predilections led it to conspire clandestinely to assist in the development of the British Fascisti.[31] The BEU's programme certainly anticipated some later propagandist planks of the British Fascisti. Besides their shared ideological anti-Bolshevism and sentimental attachment to Empire, the BEU and the British Fascisti both campaigned to ban the 'seditious' and 'blasphemous' teaching of the 'Red' Sunday schools.[32] There was also an association at the personal level.[33] One member of the BEU, Maxwell Knight, is particularly deserving of mention in this regard. According to John Hope, Knight was a prominent Fascisti official, serving as its Deputy Chief of Staff and Director of Intelligence.[34] Knight's political work was not confined to these two organisations. He was also a leading MI5 agent during the interwar years.[35] The BEU survived into the 1930s and beyond, occasionally fraternising with Mosley's BUF.[36]

The Economic League (EL), an employers' association founded in 1919, also endeavoured to check the advance of socialism by stressing the apparent benefits of capitalist free enterprise to a sceptical working class. The EL was one of the most efficiently organised and durable of the postwar anti-labour organisations. It had a 'dirty tricks' department that carried out covert anti-labour operations, including the systematic surveillance and blacklisting of political 'subversives' for business interests.[37] 'Some degree of collaboration' also existed between the Economic League and the British Fascisti, according to John Hope. He stated that senior Economic League officials fraternised with the Fascisti, and that the League's Assistant Director and then Director (1926–39), John Baker White, sat on the British Fascisti Grand Council.[38]

Other anti-socialist groups responded in kind to the growth in class consciousness amongst the working classes. The Middle Class Union, which later metamorphosed into the National Citizens' Union (NCU), was formed in 1919 and sought the mobilisation of an exclusive middle-class constituency. The propaganda activities of the NCU and the British Fascisti also overlapped, with the former, as with the British Empire Union, opposing the 'Red' Sunday schools. The NCU was committed to maintaining essential public services in the event of serious labour unrest, another key British Fascisti goal.[39] There were other areas of convergence. Prominent members of the NCU professed an allegiance to fascism, such as its Vice-President, Sir J. R. Pretyman Newman, an Irish landowner and Conservative MP for Finchley, and Colonel Sir Charles Burn, a former Conservative MP for Torquay, who would become a member of the British Fascisti's Executive Committee.[40] Another BF official, the Tory MP Sir Burton Chadwick, Parliamentary Secretary to the Board of Trade (1924–28), was also stated to be a NCU member.[41] The NCU proved to be a resilient body, surviving into the late 1930s. As the years passed, it found itself drifting increasingly towards the fascist and anti-semitic fringe. In 1927, the notorious anti-semite Colonel A. H. Lane of the Britons became the NCU Chairman, while another Britons notable, the Reverend Prebendary Gough, also became a member. By 1938 the NCU was collaborating with the extreme anti-semitic and quasi-fascist body, the Militant Christian Patriots.[42]

The Anti-Socialist Union (ASU), which launched its anti-labour crusade in 1908, was active after 1918, too, for a short time operating under a new title, the Reconstruction Society, before reverting back to its original name. The ASU claimed that it organised almost ten thousand meetings between 1918 and 1922.[43] The postwar ASU shared many of the ideas associated with the other anti-labour groups, including anti-Bolshevism and the promotion of schemes to wean workers away from socialism, such as prudent social reform and profit-sharing. There is a connection between the ASU and 1920s fascism, with the prominent BF member Nesta Webster apparently drafting the ASU instruction manual.[44] Some leading ASU activists also provide some links between this organisation and 1930s British fascism. Ralph D. Blumenfeld, the Editor of the *Daily Express*, a prewar tariff reform enthusiast and a member of the ASU's Executive Committee, became associated with the BUF, while the ASU Chairman, the Conservative MP William Ashley, would become Chairman of the militant pro-Nazi group, the Anglo-German Fellowship.[45]

Other less durable postwar organisations which rallied to the defence of property and order included the Liberty League, which enjoyed a brief reign in 1920 before the Treasurer absconded with the funds, the National Security Union, which surfaced momentarily in 1919, and the Duty and Discipline Movement, which was launched around the same time.[46] The Liberty League has some significance apropos 1920s fascism. A leading figure in the League was Lord Sydenham of Combe, a former Governor of Victoria, Australia, and Madras, and a prominent period anti-semite who later became a member of the Centre International d'Études sur la Fascisme (CINEF), a body which sought to stimulate inquiries into Fascism.[47] There was also a body calling itself the Order of the Red Rose, which appeared in 1917.[48] The Order was anti-semitic and opposed to 'finance capitalism', and included amongst its members William Sanderson, later of the Imperial Fascist League, and George Mudge, later to join the Britons. In addition, the National Political League (NPL), the National Propaganda Movement Central and the Council of Economic Leagues would make an appearance during the sensitive early postwar years.[49] The latter body sought to ward off the socialist threat to private property, while the NPL aimed to construct a cross-class alliance to combat the 'Red' menace. The fact that the NPL believed the Labour Party to be a communist body furnishes us with an insight into its mentality. A patriotic women's organisation, the Victory Corps, was formed in January 1923. Patriotic, Christian and operating 'above party', the Corps developed the notion of the female pressure group, an idea that was incorporated into the British Fascisti.[50] There was also the Vigilantes Society, which was active during 1918, and the Silver Badge Party of Ex-Servicemen, a disgruntled veterans' group which apparently harboured a grievance about the government's handling of the national war effort.⁵¹ These latter two postwar patriotic organisations have particular significance in that Henry Hamilton Beamish, later to become President of the extreme anti-semitic Britons Society, had links with both. We shall become more acquainted with H. H. Beamish below.

Not surprisingly, the anti-Bolshevik paranoia of the immediate postwar period led to a spurt of publications. Some were marginal and quirky super-patriot journals with a short life-span, such as the *Englishman* and Lord Alfred Douglas's *Plain English* and *Plain Speech*.⁵² Others limited their appeal to particular constituencies, such as *The Veteran*, which sought to politicise ex-servicemen and inoculate them against the Bolshevik 'virus'.⁵³ Still others were survivals from the prewar phase of radical right tariff reform imperialism, such as Leopold Maxse's *National Review* and Cecil Chesterton's *The New Witness*. Leo Maxse's postwar writings testified to the lingering Germanophobia among some British imperialists. His antipathy towards Germany did not dissipate as a result of that country's defeat in 1918. He continued to inveigh against the German menace, castigating Lloyd George for missing the opportunity to destroy German power comprehensively at the Paris Peace Conference and Conservative Coalitionists for limply following in tow.⁵⁴ These latest anti-German outbursts were part of a wider current of right-wing anti-Germanism, different in kind from the Edwardian variant, which drew much of its impetus from a new strain of political anti-semitism that flourished against the backdrop of the political anxiety of the years after 1918. This new species of anti-semitism had its basis in a conspiracy theory of Jewish behaviour, which in turn was rooted in the notorious anti-semitic forgery the *Protocols of the Elders of Zion*. With the advent of the 1917 October Revolution, traditional radical right anti-Germanism and this new strain of political anti-semitism would become interwoven with anti-Bolshevism, to produce a heady ideological cocktail on the postwar extreme right from which many 1920s fascists would later draw sustenance.

This conspiratorial frame of mind can be detected during the Great War, when a clutch of disaffected die-hard conservatives which included Leo Maxse and Cecil Chesterton, aggrieved at the gridlock in the trenches, alleged that there was a 'hidden hand' at the centre of government. According to their detractors, this clandestine group, comprised partly of naturalised English Jews of German origin with divided loyalties, was subverting the war effort and conspiring to bring about a German victory.[55] The conjuncture of 1914–18 provided fertile soil for the reception of such ideas. The xenophobia and internal strains engendered by the exceptional circumstances of the war led to the assumption in some sections of society that Imperial Germany had entered into an unholy alliance with 'international Jewry'. This arrangement had been cemented by the supposedly mutual German and Jewish goal of world domination, an agenda that would be, it was thought, significantly advanced by the destruction of the British Empire.[56] The advent of the Bolshevik Revolution lent an even more implausible edge to this conspiracy theory. It was thought that the 'Ashkenazi-German alliance' was the 'hidden hand' behind the Bolshevik agitation in Russia.[57] This new and sinister German-Jewish-Bolshevik axis had apparently been constructed as Imperial Germany and 'international Jewry' sought to gain from the disintegration of the Tsarist Empire. These views were not confined to the lunatic fringe of the far right. Even the British Foreign Office and the normally staid London *Times* subscribed to the view that the October Revolution was engineered by Berlin, acting in concert with Jews, with both apparently profiting from the Bolshevik-incited internal chaos in Russia.[58] The publicity given to the *Protocols* at this time merely encouraged the growth of these conspiracy theory fantasies. The *Protocols* was a document purported to reveal the inner workings of a secret council of Jewish 'Elders', instructing their co-religionists to destabilise Christian civilisation prior to a Jewish and Masonic bid for world power.

The anti-Bolshevik publications of the early postwar period provided a useful outlet for the myth of the 'hidden hand'. Leo Maxse's *National Review* devoted much column space to uncovering the supposed Judaeo-German-Bolshevik bloc. Lord Alfred Douglas's *Plain English* believed in the *Protocols'* authenticity and the covert Judaeo-German alliance, going as far as to allege that Churchill, on orders from Jewish financiers, conspired to allow the German imperial fleet to escape in the wake of the Battle of Jutland.[59] The Boswell Printing and Publishing Company, founded in late 1921 by the 8th Duke of Northumberland, similarly aimed to alert the unsuspecting British public to the apparent German-Jewish-Bolshevik plot against the Empire. The Duke of Northumberland was a wealthy landowner and coal owner who, during his flirtation with the far-right fringe, collaborated with 1920s fascist notables such as Nesta Webster, the Lintorn-Ormans and Lord Sydenham of Combe.

The early postwar context and the pre-fascist groups

The Boswell Press was probably the most influential publishing outlet on the postwar anti-Bolshevik radical right, its numerous books, pamphlets and journals, including the obsessive conspiracy theory books of Nesta Webster, frequently focusing on the theme of the 'hidden hand'.[60] The Duke of Northumberland thought he had identified a world-wide web of intrigue against the Empire, a network of conspiracy sponsored by Russian and Jewish 'adventurers' which threatened imperial interests in Ireland, India and Egypt.[61] Pan-Germanism, the original 'hidden hand' financing and directing Bolshevik agitation, was also implicated in this global anti-British conspiracy, according to Northumberland.[62] The subversion was not confined to Britain's overseas possessions. Its tentacles also reached into the domestic sphere. The conspirators had apparently penetrated the trade unions and the Labour Party, with aspects of the Labour Party's programme thought to be 'indistinguishable' from Bolshevik communism.[63]

The *Patriot*, a proto-fascist journal founded by Northumberland in early 1922, would become one of the main vehicles for disseminating the myth of the 'hidden hand' in the years following the crisis period of 1918–22. In 1925 it urged the British public to remain ever vigilant, declaring that 'uninterruptedly, since the end of 1918, British home and Imperial interests have been the object of secret attack by Socialists disguised as "Labour" and by Jewish Bolshevists, rebel Irish and Irish Americans, all assisted by Germans'.[64] The *Patriot* was possessed of a vivid and fantastic imagination with respect to its adherence to the Jewish conspiracy myth in particular. In the minds of many of its contributors, the conspiratorial Jewish presence loomed large in the modern historical drama. Jews were alleged to have been the controlling force behind William of Orange, Frederick the Great, Sun-Yat-Sen, Herbert Hoover, Pierre Laval, Nero, Kaiser Wilhelm II and Ramsay MacDonald.[65] Similarly, the baneful influence of Jews could be discerned in the French Revolution, the Illuminati, Japanese militarism, the Versailles Peace, the Weimar Republic, the Dawes Plan and the Ku-Klux-Klan, amongst other historic phenomena.[66] The myth of the 'hidden hand' and a Jewish conspiracy would find its way into the discourse of 1920s British fascism via such bodies as the *Patriot*, which had ideological and personal links with the British Fascisti, most notably Nesta Webster, a frequent contributor to its columns. A leading BF official, Webster has been by described by Richard Thurlow as 'the grand dame of British conspiracy theory'.[67]

Of the groups and publications that emerged in the context of the early postwar unrest, the *Patriot* would remain one of the most durable, surviving until January 1950. Its relationship to fascism was also more clearly defined than most of its contemporaries, whereby, almost from its inception, it began to acquire a distinctly pro-fascist profile. It enthusiastically welcomed the advent of Mussolini's Fascist experiment in Italy, for example, forged close links with the British Fascisti, and acted as an information outlet for fascist parties that included the BF and the National Fascisti.[68] In addition, the *Patriot* regularly opened its columns to fascist writers, including Lord Sydenham, J. F. C. Fuller and Oswald Mosley.[69] The *Patriot's* political outlook was guided to a large extent, too, by the ideas of Nesta Webster of the BF, a leading writer for the journal.

The *Patriot* was the 'pet project', conceived during late 1921, of the Duke of Northumberland, which aimed to expose the activities of the 'enemies' of Britain and the Empire.[70] A non-commercial venture with no paid staff, the *Patriot* prided itself on the quality of the 'special information, of a nature not appearing in the general newspapers', it provided for its readership.[71] Hilary Blume estimated that the *Patriot* had a weekly circulation of around 3,000 copies.[72] Besides subscribing to the fantasy of the 'hidden hand' and a Jewish conspiracy, and endorsing Mussolini's Fascism, as we know, the *Patriot* professed an admiration for strong government, aristocracy, monarchy and martial values. It also expressed an aversion to Bolshevism, socialism, militant trade unionism, Irish Republicanism, mass democracy, women's suffrage, freemasons and pacifism, and was disparaging of so-called modern 'fads' like psychoanalysis and modern art.

We now arrive at the point where we should consider one of the most extreme of the post-1918 formations on the radical and far right, the Britons Society. The Society was founded in July 1919 for the purpose of protecting 'the birthright of Britons' and eliminating 'alien' influences in British economic and political life. Its members were obsessive anti-semites who believed that Jews were conspiring to Judaise the world and, to this end, were engaged in covert attempts to manipulate the affairs of British governments and dominate the nation's economic life. The Britons proceeded to put together a package of extreme measures to solve the so-called 'Jewish question'. These included drastically tightening up the 'inadequate' immigration and naturalisation laws and barring all citizens of non-British parents from sitting in Parliament, holding other public offices, both civil and military, and voting.⁷³ Compiling a register of 'foreigners' and requiring them to carry an identity card represented another 'solution'. At various periods, the Society also advocated the forced return of Jews to Palestine on a permanent basis, expulsion to Madagascar and, in its more extreme moments, extermination.⁷⁴

From its inception, the Britons peddled the simplistic notion that a heightened public awareness of the 'hidden hand', the curtailment of the rights of aliens and the eventual expulsion of the Jews would solve all the nation's ills. The organisation failed to develop a political programme and was silent on most of the relevant political and social issues of the day. It had a far narrower range of concerns than the other postwar patriotic organisations, although in many respects it was part of the same ultra-conservative, nationalist, elitist and imperialist tradition which spawned these groups. It was the 'Jewish question' that preoccupied the Britons, to the virtual exclusion of all other considerations. According to Gisela Lebzelter, antisemitism 'functioned as an all-embracing framework for the articulation of diffuse criticism and discontent'.⁷⁵ The Society spread its anti-semitic message principally through publishing activities, which took the form of pamphlets, brochures, leaflets, and monthly periodicals such as *The Hidden Hand*. This anti-Jewish 'hate literature' was swelled occasionally by the publication of anti-semitic books, published under the imprint of the Judaic Publishing Company and the Britons Publishing Company. From 1922, the group also published the *Protocols*. Public meetings, and even electioneering, provided other outlets for the Britons' views.⁷⁶ However, these types of activities remained extremely limited, with the Society devoting itself almost exclusively to publishing during its life-span.

The Irish-born Henry Hamilton Beamish was the original inspiration behind the Britons, serving as its President between July 1919 and 1948, the year of his death. Beamish, born in 1874, was a restless and widely travelled individual who fought in the Boer War before eventually settling in South Africa. He would serve with a South African infantry regiment during the Great War. Mid-1918 found Beamish in England where he attempted to enter Parliament on an Independent, super-patriotic ticket. Not surprisingly, Beamish lived overseas for the greater part of his presidency of the Britons. This decision was prompted as much by his reluctance in 1919 to pay a sum of £5,000 libel damages to the then First Commissioner of Works, Sir Alfred Mond, as by his restless disposition. In an act which paid homage to the 'hidden hand' myth, Beamish had alleged that Mond, a leading Jewish industrialist, was a traitor who had assisted the Germans during the First World War. Following his hasty departure from Britain in December 1919, Beamish became a roving ambassador for anti-semitism, 'enlightening' all who were prepared to listen on the 'Jewish world conspiracy', even claiming at one point to have 'taught Hitler'.[77] Although it is extremely unlikely that Beamish exerted any influence over Hitler, the Britons' President did establish links with the National Socialist German Workers' Party (Nationalsozialistische Deutsche Arbeiterpartei, NSDAP). Beamish gave occasional lectures in Nazi Germany and spoke at NSDAP gatherings.[78] The Nazis also ran advertisements for the Britons in their newspapers.[79] Beamish determined to retain firm links with the English anti-semites, however. Apart from his nominal presidency of the Britons, he also served as Vice-President of the racial-fascist Imperial Fascist League.[80] He was eventually domiciled in Southern Rhodesia, even serving as an Independent Member of the Rhodesian Parliament.[81] Beamish was interned in Rhodesia during the Second World War.

Another executive member of the Britons was Dr John Henry Clarke, chief consulting physician to the London Homeopathic Hospital, who was its Chairman between 1919 and 1931. Clarke was a Britons author who wrote, amongst other works, *England Under the Heel of the Jew* in 1921. Its rigidly uncompromising anti-semitic tone becomes apparent from Clarke's opening salvoes in the Preface where he asserted that 'a Jew cannot become an Englishman. He cannot do the work of an Englishman in the spirit of England. His "religion" forbids it; his blood makes it impossible.'[82] Another leading figure in the group was Victor Marsden, foreign correspondent with the *Morning Post* and translator of the *Protocols*. Arthur Kitson, the inventor and monetary reform campaigner, whose opposition to the gold standard was reputedly based on the *Protocols*, was another member, as was Bessie Pullen-Burry, an explorer with links to a number of geographical societies. Lieutenant-Colonel A. H. Lane, author of *The Alien Menace* (1928), was also attached to the Britons, as was another notorious period anti-semite, Joseph Banister.[83] Lane's book *The Alien Menace* was an alarmist and, at times, crude and vicious attack on London's Jewish immigrant community. Some well-known fascists were to become members of the Britons Society, including Lord Sydenham of Combe, whom we have met, Brigadier-General Robert B. D.

The early postwar context and the pre-fascist groups

Blakeney, the BF's President between 1924 and 1926, Anthony Gittens of the Imperial Fascist League, and the IFL's Leader Arnold Leese.

Historians of British fascism have primarily been dismissive of the Britons' impact on contemporary society. Richard Thurlow stated that it 'remained a small lecturing and debating society, with a miniscule middle-class membership', which gained little public support between the wars.[84] David Baker was broadly of the same opinion, claiming that the Britons were a highly marginal presence in British society, 'both by the eccentricity of their views and by the secrecy under which they operated'.[85] An earlier historian of the Britons, Gisela Lebzelter, took a similar line. For Lebzelter, the Britons Society was more of an elite club than a political party with ambitions to build a mass base.[86] She suggested that its failure to make a greater impact was due to ongoing financial difficulties and the absence of an able leadership.[87]

These dismissive appraisals do not mean, however, that the Britons Society had little significance for far-right politics during the interwar years. Lebzelter believed that it provided a 'niche' for other obsessive period anti-semites, while its literature was instrumental in sustaining the fantasy of the Jewish world conspiracy.[88] Its important role in developing and disseminating a stock of anti-semitic ideas which were then taken up by other anti-Jewish movements is also stressed by Blume, who contends that the Society was content to 'supply the polemics' whilst leaving considerations of manpower to others.[89] The Britons' significance at the level of ideas was taken up even more forcefully by Richard Thurlow. Thurlow believed that the Britons Publishing Society was to have a 'lasting effect on British racist thought', influencing the racial nationalist ideologies of groups such as the IFL and the postwar National Front.[90] In this sense, argued Thurlow, interwar anti-semitic organisations such as the Britons helped contribute to the revival of British fascism after the Second World War.[91] The Britons group do not only provide links to a tradition of thought on the far right that lay in the post-1945 era. Its polemics and personnel, the latter particularly in the persons of those such as Beamish, Lane and Banister, also connect it to the pre-1914 tradition of intolerance and activism on the radical right.[92] In this sense the Britons have links to the East End anti-alien campaign of 1900–5, and thus are a product of the same anti-alien culture which spawned the likes of the British Brothers' League (BBL).[93]

There is also a connection between Beamish's group and contemporary eugenic ideas. One of the Britons' leading members was George P. Mudge. A lecturer at the London Medical School, Mudge was a eugenicist who helped found the Eugenics Society. In addition, Colin Holmes has informed us that Karl Pearson's eugenic views were warmly received by the Britons.[94] Finally, the Britons have significance for the interwar far right in that they had some direct connections to contemporary fascist groups through certain of their personnel, such as Lord Sydenham of Combe, Brigadier-General Robert B. D. Blakeney and Arnold Leese.

It remains, finally, to formulate an overall view of the early postwar anti-labour and anti-semitic organisations and rightist publications, and assess their importance for the emergence of 1920s fascism. As suggested earlier, it is tempting to view the anti-labour groups as the more immediate precursors of the avowedly fascist parties of the later 1920s. There are some evident links. We have noted and identified the existence of a continuity of personnel. Also, as Richard Thurlow has demonstrated, particularly with regard to the Boswell Publishing Company, 1920s fascism had its roots firmly embedded in the right-wing publishing activity that came out of this earlier period of radical right activity.[95] There is also a discernible continuity of ideas connecting the two phases of right-wing activity, the mutual ideological anti-Bolshevism, the super-patriotism and the sentimental idealisation of Empire not least among them. The political anti-semitism of this period also survived, resurfacing in the xenophobic, conspiratorial fantasies of 1920s fascist anti-semites.[96] Also, as Farr observed, a tradition of right-wing activism germinated in the immediate postwar years which was inherited by the 1920s fascist parties.[97]

Despite these undeniable areas of overlap, we should guard against indulging in what Eley called a 'pre-fascist teleology' with regard to the postwar anti-labour groups, in particular. In other words, we should avoid ransacking the immediate past in search of assemblages of particular political and ideological dispositions that in some way anticipated or mirrored the policies and activities of fascism.[98] In its more extreme manifestations, such an approach has evident determinist leanings. We also run the risk, if we fix our analytical gaze too closely on the pre-fascist groups, of failing to appreciate adequately the unique specificity of the fascist phenomenon and the fascist historical 'moment'. If we fail to distinguish between individual political forms or patently different manifestations of the political right, moreover, it will have the effect of depreciating the value of 'fascism' as an analytical concept. In short, the term 'fascism' becomes a blunt and imprecise analytical instrument. We have here, in this desire to establish meaningful linkages and causal connections, a further example of a process that Roger Griffin has referred to as the erosion of 'fascism's lexical value'.[99] Thus we have the British Empire Union, for example, described by one historian as displaying 'decidedly fascist characteristics'.[100]

It is clear on closer examination that the political and ideological profile of the postwar anti-labour groups did not contain an appropriate number of generic fascist characteristics.[101] There was no constructive attempt by these groups, for example, to imagine or formulate an alternative notion of the state. There is simply no evidence of a desire to overthrow the existing order and replace it with a new type of state based on the myth of a revitalised national community. There was also a noticeable absence of a leadership cult within these anti-labour formations. The quintessentially fascist predilection for authoritarian solutions and elite leadership was simply not in evidence. The majority remained essentially narrowly based pressure groups representing specific sectional interests, such as the Economic League and the British Commonwealth Union. The notion of constructing a mass-based political movement would have been foreign to such groups. So, too, would the practice of indulging in the mass theatre and secular rituals of fascism, with the choreographed mass assemblies and solemn evocation of ancient national myths. There is also no indication that such groups were prepared to embrace a culture of political violence. One historian has suggested that 'paramilitarism' was a feature of the early postwar anti-socialist activity, that the period had thrown up a sort of *squadristi* in waiting, to be deployed in the event of a post-revolutionary collapse of civil order, and that the fascists later took this 'on board'.[102] Certainly, the creation of groups such as Henry Page Croft's People's Defence League, a blackleg and strike-breaking organisation that surfaced following the January 1919 mass strike on the Clyde, was a move in the direction of militant right-wing activism. Nonetheless, this development, and others like it in this period, hardly amounted to an endorsement of political violence and paramilitarism at the level of ideology.

Neither was there a repository of 'palingenetic political myth', the regenerative urge at the heart of authentic fascist doctrine, within this early postwar anti-labour discourse.[103] And there is no evidence of a desire to create a new 'fascist man', develop a cult of the physically beautiful body, or instigate a revival of traditional rural values based on a *Blut und Boden* outlook.[104] There was no overt attempt to appeal to youth, either, or build specifically mass-based youth organisations. Nor was there a concerted attempt on the part of the various groups to co-ordinate their goals, harmonise their tactics or achieve ideological symmetry. We could continue *ad nauseam*. Although it is vital not to underestimate the significance of the pre-fascist groups for the fascist parties that came after them, therefore, we should not forget that each, in the main, belonged to a different organisational and ideological realm.

Notes

1 See B. N. Pandey, *The Break-Up of British India* (London, Macmillan, 1969).
2 D. George Boyce, *Nationalism in Ireland* (London, Routledge, 1991).
3 See E. Goldstein and J. Maurer (eds), *The Washington Conference, 1921–22. Naval Rivalry, East Asian Stability and the Road to Pearl Harbor* (London, Frank Cass, 1994).
4 D. S. Landes, *The Unbound Prometheus. Technological Change and Industrial Development in Western Europe from 1750 to the Present* (Cambridge, Cambridge University Press, 1969).
5 Ibid., pp. 360–1.
6 On Anglo-US rivalry see B. J. C. McKerchner (ed.), *Anglo-American Relations in the 1920s. The Struggle for Supremacy* (London, Macmillan, 1991).
7 A. S. Milward, *The Economic Effects of the Two World Wars on Britain* (London, Macmillan/Economic History Society, 1972), pp. 50–1.
8 C. L. Mowat, *Britain Between the Wars 1918–1940* (London, Methuen, 1955), p. 280. Other historians, however, have been more guarded in their evaluation of Britain's economic performance after 1918, suggesting, more controversially, that its economic difficulties began after the Second World War rather than in the years following the Great War. See, for example, S. Pollard, *The Wasting of the British Economy. British Economic Policy 1947 to the Present* (New York, St Martin's Press, 1982).
9 Mowat, *Britain Between the Wars*, p. 281.
10 Milward, *The Economic Effects*, p. 50.
11 P. Renshaw, 'Anti-Labour Politics in Britain, 1918–1927', *Journal of Contemporary History*, 12 (1977), pp. 693–705.

12 A. J. P. Taylor, *English History 1914–1945* (Oxford, Oxford University Press, 1965), p. 163.
13 J. Lovell, *British Trade Unions 1875–1933* (London, Macmillan/Economic History Society, 1977), pp. 52–3.
14 M. Pugh, *The Making of Modern British Politics 1867–1939* (Oxford, Blackwell, 1982), p. 200.
15 For more on this, see below, Chapters Nine and Eleven.
16 J. F. C. Fuller, *The Dragon's Teeth. A Study of War and Peace* (London, Constable, 1932), p. 23.
17 S. Hynes, *A War Imagined. The First World War and English Culture* (London, Bodley Head, 1990).
18 On the NP's wider programme, see M. Cowling, *The Impact of Labour 1920–1924* (Cambridge, Cambridge University Press, 1971), p. 77.
19 J. Hope, 'British Fascism and the State 1917–1927: A Re-Examination of the Documentary Evidence', *Labour History Review*, 57, 3 (Winter 1992), p. 75.
20 B. S. Farr, *The Development and Impact of Right-Wing Politics in Britain, 1903–1932* (New York, Garland, 1987), pp. 34–41.
21 Ibid., p. 40.
22 Ibid., pp. 43–50 and 56.
23 Ibid., pp. 49–50.
24 Hope, 'British Fascism', p. 75.
25 Farr, *The Development and Impact*, p. 50.
26 C. Wrigley, *Lloyd George and the Challenge of Labour. The Post-War Coalition 1918–1922* (Hemel Hempstead, Harvester Wheatsheaf, 1990) p. 39.
27 Ibid., p. 7.
28 Farr, *The Development and Impact*, p. 47.
29 R. Benewick, *Political Violence and Public Order* (London, Allen Lane, 1969), p. 39. See also P. Panayi, 'The British Empire Union in the First World War', in T. Kushner and K. Lunn (eds), *The Politics of Marginality. Race, the Radical Right and Minorities in Twentieth-Century Britain* (London, Frank Cass, 1990), pp. 113–28.
30 K. D. Brown, 'The Anti-Socialist Union, 1908–49', *Essays in Anti-Labour History. Responses to the Rise of Labour in Britain* (London, Macmillan, 1974), pp. 255–6.
31 Hope, 'British Fascism', pp. 75–6.
32 Ibid., p. 255.
33 J. Hope, 'Fascism and the State in Britain: The Case of the British Fascist', *Australian Journal of Politics and History*, 39, 3 (1993), p. 371.
34 Ibid., p. 368. Knight's Fascisti links are also mentioned in, R. Thurlow, 'State Management of the British Union of Fascists in the 1930s', in M. Cronin (ed.), *The Failure of British Fascism. The*

Far Right and the Fight for Political Recognition (London, Macmillan, 1996), p. 30.
35 Ibid.
36 Benewick, Political Violence, p. 40.
37 A. McIvor, '"A Crusade for Capitalism": The Economic League, 1919–39', Journal of Contemporary History, 23 (1988), pp. 631–5.
38 Hope, 'British Fascism', pp. 76–7. White is also mentioned in PRO HO45/24967, Members of the Council of the British Fascisti.
39 Benewick, Political Violence, pp. 40–1.
40 Ibid., p. 41. H. S. B. Blume, 'A Study of Anti-Semitic Groups in Britain, 1918–40' (M.Phil. thesis, University of Sussex, 1971), p. 110 for additional information on Burn.
41 Hope, 'British Fascism', p. 75. On Chadwick's BF associations, see also Blume, 'A Study of Anti-Semitic Groups'.
42 Blume, 'A Study of Anti-Semitic Groups', pp. 232–3.
43 Brown, 'The Anti-Socialist Union', p. 251.
44 Hope, 'British Fascism', p. 76.
45 Brown, 'The Anti-Socialist Union', p. 254. On Blumenfeld and the BUF, see also Who Backs Mosley? Fascist Promise and Fascist Performance (London, Labour Research Department, 1934), p. 12.
46 G. C. Webber, 'Intolerance and Discretion: Conservatives and British Fascism, 1918–1926', in T. Kushner and K. Lunn (eds), Traditions of Intolerance. Historical Perspectives on Fascism and Race Discourse in Britain (Manchester, Manchester University Press, 1989), pp. 162 and 157, on the Liberty League and the National Security Union. Wrigley, Lloyd George, p. 16, on the Duty and Discipline Movement.
47 G. C. Webber, The Ideology of the British Right, 1918–1939 (London, Croom Helm, 1986), p. 29.
48 Ibid., p. 159.
49 Blume, 'A Study of Anti-Semitic Groups', p. 100.
50 Farr, The Development and Impact, p. 55.
51 The Vigilantes Society is referred to in G. Lebzelter, Political Anti-Semitism in England, 1918–1939 (London, Macmillan, 1978), p. 53; R. Thurlow, Fascism in Britain. A History, 1918–1985 (Oxford, Blackwell, 1987), p. 66, mentions the Silver Badge Party.
52 G. C. Webber, 'Intolerance and Discretion', p. 157.
53 Ibid.
54 Cowling, The Impact of Labour, pp. 78–80.
55 Thurlow, Fascism in Britain. A History, pp. 47–8.
56 Lebzelter, Political Anti-Semitism, pp. 14–16.
57 N. Cohn, Warrant for Genocide. The Myth of the Jewish World Conspiracy and the Protocols of the Elders of Zion (Chico, CA, Scholars Press, 1981), pp. 149–56.
58 Ibid., pp. 150–1.

The early postwar context and the pre-fascist groups

59 Ibid., p. 155.
60 Webster's *World Revolution, Secret Societies and Subversive Movements* and *The Socialist Network* were all published by the Boswell Press. See C. Holmes, *Anti-Semitism in British Society, 1876–1939* (London, Arnold, 1979), p. 303.
61 Cowling, *The Impact of Labour*, p. 81.
62 Blume, 'A Study of Anti-Semitic Groups', p. 91.
63 Cowling, *The Impact of Labour*, p. 82.
64 *The Patriot*, 15 October 1925, p. 505.
65 D. M. Geiger, 'British Fascism as Revealed in the British Union of Fascists Press' (Ph.D. thesis, New York University, 1963), pp. 43–4.
66 Ibid.
67 Thurlow, *Fascism in Britain. A History*, p. 58.
68 *The Patriot*, 2 November 1922, p. 198, on Italian Fascism; 12 August 1926, p. 159, on the NF.
69 Geiger, 'British Fascism', p. 41.
70 Holmes, *Anti-Semitism*, p. 207.
71 *The Patriot*, 15 January 1925, p. 196.
72 Blume, 'A Study of Anti-Semitic Groups', p. 97.
73 See G. Lebzelter, 'Henry Hamilton Beamish and the Britons: Champions of Anti-Semitism', in K. Lunn and R. Thurlow (eds), *British Fascism* (London, Croom Helm, 1980), pp. 41–56; and Blume, 'A Study of Anti-Semitic Groups', pp. 54–87.
74 R. Eatwell, *Fascism. A History* (London, Vintage, 1996), p. 178, mentions extermination.
75 Lebzelter, *Political Anti-Semitism*, p. 54.
76 Blume, 'A Study of Anti-Semitic Groups', pp. 75–6.
77 C. C. Aronsfeld, 'The Britons Publishing Society', *The Wiener Library Bulletin*, 20, 3 (Summer 1966), p. 33.
78 Lebzelter, *Political Anti-Semitism*, pp. 52 and 64.
79 Aronsfeld, 'The Britons Publishing Society', p. 33.
80 Thurlow, *Fascism in Britain. A History*, p. 68.
81 Cohn, *Warrant for Genocide*, p. 282.
82 Dr J. H. Clarke, *England Under the Heel of the Jew. A Tale of Two Books* (London, Judaic Publishing Company, 1921), p. iv.
83 On Banister, see Holmes, *Anti-Semitism in British Society*, pp. 39–42.
84 Thurlow, *Fascism in Britain. A History*, pp. 67 and 69.
85 D. Baker, 'The Extreme Right in the 1920s: Fascism in a Cold Climate, or "Conservatism With Knobs On"?', in Cronin (ed.), *The Failure of British Fascism*, p. 18.
86 Lebzelter, *Political Anti-Semitism*, p. 65.
87 Ibid., pp. 66–7.
88 Ibid., p. 67.
89 Blume, 'A Study of Anti-Semitic Groups', p. 87.

90 Thurlow, *Fascism in Britain. A History*, p. 67.
91 Ibid., p. 64.
92 Ibid., pp. 66 and 70.
93 The BBL conducted a campaign of mass opposition in the East End against Jewish immigration between 1901 and 1905. See Holmes, *Anti-Semitism in British Society*, pp. 89–97.
94 C. Holmes, *John Bull's Island. Immigration and British Society 1871–1971* (London, Macmillan, 1988), p. 141. On Pearson, see above, Chapter One.
95 Thurlow, *Fascism in Britain. A History*, p. 46.
96 Ibid., pp. 24–5.
97 Farr, *The Development and Impact*, p. 33.
98 G. Eley, *From Unification to Nazism. Reinterpreting the German Past* (London, Allen and Unwin, 1986), p. 254. The same degree of caution should inform our investigations of the pre-1914 period, too.
99 R. Griffin, *The Nature of Fascism* (London, Routledge, 1991), p. 2.
100 Hope, 'Fascism and the State', p. 371.
101 The attempt to arrive at an acceptable scholarly definition of fascism has proved to be a long and arduous intellectual journey. See R. Griffin (ed.), *International Fascism. Theories, Causes and the New Consensus* (London, Arnold, 1998).
102 Hope, 'British Fascism', pp. 74–5.
103 See Griffin, *The Nature of Fascism*, pp. 32–6.
104 Blood and Soil.

CHAPTER THREE

THE ARRIVAL OF FASCISM: THE BRITISH FASCISTI AND THE IMPERIAL FASCIST LEAGUE

The first political organisation in Britain openly to proclaim itself to be a fascist party was founded on 6 May 1923 by the then 28-year-old Rotha Lintorn-Orman. The idea for such a venture apparently came to her whilst she was weeding the garden of her dairy farm in Somerset![1] The fledgling fascist party would refer to itself as the British Fascisti during its first year of life, an indication of its founder's admiration for Mussolini's new fascist experiment in Italy. On 27 May 1924 it was incorporated as a limited company, thereafter to be formally known as the British Fascists Ltd. The BF's Leader was the granddaughter of Sir John Lintorn Arabin Simmons, a celebrated Field Marshall and a former Governor of Malta (1884–88). Like her grandfather, Rotha Lintorn-Orman would serve in the military with distinction, though in a less elevated capacity. During the Great War she served in an ambulance unit in Serbia, twice receiving the Croix de Charité for displays of courage in action.[2] Barbara Farr suggests that Lintorn-Orman's experiences of the horrors of war helped shape her particular brand of fascist anti-socialism. Lintorn-Orman believed that the radical left, aided by the weapon of the General Strike, was attempting to turn England into a battleground similar to Serbia in 1916.[3] The Fascisti's heroic mission, therefore, was to save England, and ultimately the Empire, from the socialist 'menace'. Socialism, and similar supposed scourges which were apparently disfiguring England's political landscape, needed to be uprooted by a firm and resolute hand, indeed in the same manner as the weeds that plagued her garden in Somerset.

Another pivotal figure during the BF's formative period was a retired Brigadier-General, Robert B. D. Blakeney, who replaced Lord Garvagh as the BF's President in September 1924 following the latter's resignation the previous January. Blakeney was both a political pragmatist and an efficient organiser and administrator who at one time was a general manager of the Egyptian state railway (1919–23). Besides anglicising the party's name, he was responsible for placing the BF on a firm organisational footing and developing its disciplined paramilitary profile. Following his departure from the BF in 1926, Blakeney would continue to hover on the fascist fringe, at different times joining both the IFL and the BUF. The party's Vice-President during these early years was Rear-Admiral A. E. Armstrong. Many of the BF's senior personnel hailed from military, naval and aristocratic backgrounds. Besides Blakeney and Armstrong, there was Brigadier-General Sir Ormonde Winter, former Deputy Chief of Police and Director of Intelligence in Ireland (1920–22), the 8th Earl of Glasgow, who commanded the BF's Scottish units, and Colonel Sir Charles Burn, the Conservative MP for Torquay between 1910 and 1923.[4] Lord Ernest Hamilton, the son of the Duke of Abercorn, and Sir Arthur Hardinge, the first cousin of Viscount Hardinge of Penshurst, were other leading figures. Arthur Hardinge was a Fellow of All Souls and a former Ambassador to Spain who became the party Treasurer in May 1926.[5] Some of the most prominent fascists of the interwar period were members of the BF at one time or another, including Nesta Webster, Arnold Leese, William Joyce, E. G. Mandeville Roe and Neil Francis-Hawkins.

Structurally, the BF was hierarchical. It also adopted a paramilitary organisation and style. At the apex was the decision-making body, the Fascist Grand Council, on which sat nine individuals, both men and women. Below that was an Executive Council.[6] The BF was then divided into various sections, which included sections for intelligence, transport, and propaganda and publicity.[7] There was an infantry section, too, composed of units of seven members or less. These were the Fascisti shock troops who would eventually grapple with the Red revolutionaries on the streets. In a time of civil emergency the BF's military machine, such as it was, would crank up a gear, with the units merging to form troops, companies and divisions. The BF's battle order was further subdivided into men's, women's and cadets' units, the latter embracing those members below sixteen years of age. Divisional or district commanders, operating within a county-based geographical framework, supervised the activities of the units. It was the role of BF General Headquarters in the capital, however, to oversee the entire operation. By the 1930s,

The arrival of fascism

separate area commands had sprung up in the Irish Free State and in Ulster.[8] All this paramilitary posturing looked impressive in theory, of course, but the reality was far different. It is doubtful whether the BF would have been able to muster enough members to influence events had they unfolded in the revolutionary direction that it feared.

The BF had different categories of member. There were mobile squads of young activists and older members who made up the reserves, while the monthly subscription, based on 6s. for active and 1s. for inactive, defined another membership category. A Fascist Order of Merit, introduced by Rotha Lintorn-Orman, helped to stimulate fascist enthusiasm amongst the members. In addition, a fascist corporate identity was engendered by a range of primarily members-only social and leisure functions and activities, which included dinners, garden fêtes, dances, balls, whist drives and playing in fascist soccer teams.[9] The BF had no prescribed official uniform in the early years, other than a Fascist badge and a black handkerchief which members carried. In time, however, the party leadership, ever keen to nurture the ceremonial side of the movement, had developed a 'distinctively British fascist regalia'.[10] By 1927 the BF had officially adopted a blue shirt, later adding dark trousers or skirts and a blue beret or fedora. Despite its evident affection for Mussolini, it is noteworthy that the BF did not wear the black shirt, a reflection of its desire not to be too closely associated in the public mind with the violent methods of his black-shirted *squadristi*.

We can identify a number of stages in the BF's development. Most historians of the BF agree that, from its formation until 1926, there was very little evidence of fascism in its ideology or programme.[11] As one historian has noted, 'set beside the history of European fascism, the BF seems a particularly insubstantial and confused expression of fascist ideology and tactics'.[12] This was partly due to the BF's founder, who had only a limited understanding of Italian fascist doctrine. Thurlow believed that the BF mirrored Lintorn-Orman's 'own experience of the Girl Guides, public service and a military background rather than any emulation of continental examples or ideologies'.[13] The BF's President, Brigadier-General Blakeney, had only a vague understanding of fascism in this early period, too, regarding it, famously, as an adult offshoot of the Boy Scout movement.[14] Native rather than continental influences shaped the BF's outlook at this stage. In many respects, the BF was simply a more radical version of the patriotic anti-labour organisations that sprang up after the Great War. Like the individuals who gravitated towards these pre-fascist bodies, the British Fascists were super-patriots who harboured an intense aversion to Bolshevism, radical socialism and militant direct action trade unionism, which were thought to pose a serious threat to property, civil order and ordered government. The BF advocated a non-partisan approach to industrial relations and politics, promoted the ideal of class-friendship and presented itself as the defender of the established order and the status quo. In programmatic terms, this commitment to the status quo meant upholding the established Constitution and the authority of Parliament and the Crown. Historians have interpreted this pledge to uphold traditional institutions such as Parliament and the Constitution as evidence of the innate conservatism at the core of the BF's ideology.

The BF also had a sentimental attachment to Empire. Barbara Farr suggests that the British Fascists were 'successors to the missionaries of Empire' on the prewar radical right.[15] Indeed, the promotion of inter-Empire trade and a cult of loyalty to Empire would remain cornerstones of BF policy throughout its period of existence.[16] There was also a reverence for traditional British values and belief systems and the British way of life. This took a number of forms. Besides its attempts to revive patriotic ideals and a healthy respect for monarchy, the BF sought to uphold Christian beliefs and practices. It deplored the ideological atheism of revolutionary Marxism and was generally alarmed by the increasing secularisation of contemporary Britain and the corresponding decline in religious observance. This concern took on an organisational form when, in June 1925, the movement embarked on a project to establish a national network of Fascist Children's Clubs to counter the 'Red Sunday Schools' and their allegedly poisonous effect on the innocent young mind, particularly that of 'slum children'.[17] The BF's ideology was also tinged with a heavy moralism. It promoted itself as the champion of traditional women's virtues, opposed the doctrine of free love and railed against the modern age's apparent lapse into sexual promiscuity and vice.[18]

There was very little, then, in its ideology at this stage that marked the BF out as distinctly fascist, save its extreme nationalism and anti-Bolshevism and some vague references to the importance of order, discipline, service and duty to political and social life. Even the BF's attempts to develop a cult of activism and political violence developed within the boundaries of constitutional legitimacy.

According to Barbara Farr, the Fascisti engaged in a form of 'constitutional right-wing activism' which sought to bolster the state rather than challenge its authority, while Robert Benewick argued that the BF was never interested in 'the systematic application of violence'.[19] It is difficult to escape the conclusion that, at this stage of its evolution, the BF was little more than a mobile counter-revolutionary defence force to be activated in a time of civil emergency. Thus, although it adopted the paraphernalia of fascism, it was not revolutionary either in outlook or intent. The BF argued that its 'British form of Fascism', essentially constitutional and law-abiding, was the model best suited to the native temperament.[20] A factional dispute in this early period of its life, which led to the first of a number of splits in the party, provided evidence of the BF's initial moderation. In late 1924 a faction of its more militant members peeled away from the parent body, apparently disaffected by the BF's brand of moderate conservative fascism. The defectors proceeded to form a rival body, the National Fascisti, which was committed to developing a more virile brand of fascism that more closely approximated to the model of Italian Fascism.[21]

The General Strike of 1926 marked the next decisive moment in the BF's development. Serious discontent in the coalfields and the prospect of widespread union support for the miners had been brewing since 1925. These developments, which culminated in the TUC General Council's official backing of the miners, prompted a number of voluntary right-wing organisations, including the BF, to offer to assist the government in the maintenance of essential services in the event of a General Strike. A few days prior to the strike deadline on 1 May 1926, the Baldwin government made its response known to the BF. Acceptance of the BF's offer was made conditional on the removing of the title 'Fascist' from its name, the winding up of its quasi-military organisation and the providing of an assurance to the government that it supported the principle of parliamentary democracy. This official rebuff of Fascisti support was to precipitate a major split in the BF's executive committee. While some elements in the leadership were for outright rejection of the government's edict, including Rotha Lintorn-Orman, others were prepared to come to terms. Following a vote on the Fascist Grand Council (40–32) which went in favour of the Lintorn-Orman faction, a number of senior figures resigned, including Robert Blakeney, A. E. Armstrong and the Earl of Glasgow. The defectors then proceeded to form the British Loyalists, a body whose organisational profile and policy met the basic requirements of the government's ultimatum.[22] In the wake of this haemorrhage of some of its leading personnel, Lintorn-Orman reassumed firm leadership of the BF.

The General Strike issue damaged the BF in other ways. It was not the prelude to the onset of a bloody Bolshevik revolution, as the fascist right had predicted. An exercise in moderation and restraint, the nine-day strike cruelly exposed the lack of factual substance at the heart of the BF's alarmist anti-labour rhetoric. With the failure of the General Strike and the waning of trade union militancy in its aftermath, there appeared little justification for a paramilitary civil defence force. These developments would effectively deprive the BF of a core element in its ideology, resulting in a loss of political direction. Farr suggests that the BF was left without 'co-ordination or ethos' in the post-strike period which manifested itself in a waning of dynamism, while, for Thurlow, Lintorn-Orman's party 'increasingly lacked purpose and credibility' after 1926.[23] The reduction in left-wing militancy and the easing of class conflict after 1926 were reflected in the BF's changing membership profile. Griffiths states that by 1930 many of the military types had departed, while in social-class terms the BF had 'moved down a notch or two'.[24]

The movement did not remain idle after May 1926, however, particularly in the realm of ideas and policy-making. In the post-strike years the BF began to acquire a more distinctly fascist ideology, as it struggled to recover the purpose and dynamism of the preceding period. The ideological anti-Bolshevism remained, as did the reactionary posture towards labour, an orientation that was mirrored in the glut of anti-trade union policies that appeared in its 1927 Manifesto. Sweeping trade union and industrial reforms were advocated. These extended to the outlawing of strikes, lock-outs and 'international trade union alliances', the abolition of the card vote and its replacement with a secret ballot, and the setting up of courts of compulsory arbitration.[25] The Manifesto also contained a number of political reforms of a punitive nature, which included the disenfranchisement of persons in receipt of poor law relief for a period of six consecutive months and those convicted of sedition.[26] We can detect a faint hint of incipient corporatism in the proposals for compulsory arbitration, as well as in the call in the Manifesto for an 'Organisation of employers and employees' to work collaboratively to obtain a 'high standard of efficiency and of living'.[27] According to Farr, a more clearly defined 'fascist feminism' also emerged during the post-strike phase, as women came increasingly to predominate on the BF executive following the departure of Blakeney and the other senior male members in May 1926.[28]

These developments in the direction of a more distinctly fascist outlook accelerated during the early 1930s. Due to the efforts of E. G. Mandeville Roe, a young schoolmaster and Mussolini enthusiast, a more clearly articulated concept of corporatism had emerged by 1931. In that year the BF advocated the setting up of fascist corporations and guilds. By 1933, in its 24-point political programme issued that summer, the BF was calling for the dismantling of the existing party system and its replacement by the Corporate State.[29] There was also a clear revolutionary tone to the BF's pronouncements at this point in its evolution. In the same 24-point programme the BF announced its intention to 'capture the political power of the state' for fascism.[30] We can detect a far greater reverence for the state, too, with it now being viewed as being above class and the expression of the national will. Other overtly fascist themes included the call for the destruction of the class system and the establishment of a meritocracy, and the purging of the 'International Financier' from the affairs of the state.[31] Although anti-alienism had been evident in the BF's ideology almost from the beginning, by 1933 this sentiment had hardened and developed into a full-blown anti-semitism. The BF's 24-point programme of mid-1933 called for Jews to be prevented from holding official offices in the state, exercising their voting rights and participating in the nation's financial, political and cultural life. There is also evidence of ideological pro-Nazism just prior to the BF's eventual demise in 1935, which may have contributed to the adoption of anti-semitism as official policy.[32]

These policy developments, however, emerged against the background of another internal crisis, more severe than its predecessors, which would eventually culminate in the BF's demise. The 1930s, then, was to mark another, more significant passage in the BF's history. The decisive moment here was the formation of Oswald Mosley's British Union of Fascists in October 1932. Faced with a rival fascist organisation of greater ideological and programmatic substance, superior resource potential and possessing a more capable and charismatic Leader, the BF found it increasingly difficult to compete. After October 1932, the Fascisti became progressively marginalised as the BUF proceeded to occupy the ideological high ground on the fascist right. This latter phase of the BF's life would be characterised by internal wrangling over the issue of merger with the Mosley group, and ever worsening balance sheets. A series of debilitating defections to Mosley would eventually destroy the BF as a viable political force. The party limped on through 1933 and 1934 before eventually expiring in September 1935. Reduced to a rump of Lintorn-Orman loyalists following the departure of the pro-Mosleyite dissidents, a group that included a number of senior figures and the majority of the active members, the BF was to suffer a further massive blow in March 1935. It faced the premature demise of its founder, who died from a combination of illness and alcohol abuse at the age of forty. When it was eventually wound up, the BF had incurred debts of £1,706.[33] Oscar Boulton's Unity Band would secure copyright of *British Lion* following the BF's dissolution.[34]

The predominant view in the historiography is that the BF was essentially a reactionary right-wing conservative movement which, in terms of outlook and policy, differed very little from Baldwin's Conservative Party. This interpretation has tended to dominate the literature of British fascism over the years. Webber, for example, believed that the BF never viewed itself 'as a serious political rival to the Tories', while its predominantly middle-class and upper-middle-class membership thought that in the BF they had found a party which satisfied their need for a 'stronger dose' of conservatism.[35] This was Thurlow's general impression, too. He tended to agree with Arnold Leese's judgement on the BF, that it was merely 'Conservatism with knobs on'.[36] Roger Eatwell argues in much the same vein, as does David Lewis. Eatwell suggests that the BF, despite its belated attempts to embrace radical fascist ideas such as corporatism, was unable to escape the shackles of its 'reactionary roots'.[37] For Lewis, the BF's ideology, as with other pre-Mosleyite fascist parties, was based on authoritarian reaction rather than fascism, with its members regarding fascism as the 'vigorous and independent right wing of conservatism'.[38]

The historians generally agree, too, quite correctly, that Lintorn-Orman's party bore the unmistakable mark of the early postwar anti-labour organisations, though John Hope argued that these links have been understated in the existing studies. Hope tends to *overstate* the connection, however, by claiming that there were *significant* organisational, ideological and personal links with the postwar radical right groups and that these bodies were 'deeply involved in facilitating the formation and development' of the BF.[39] In

The arrival of fascism

an important study of the female organisational structures within the Fascisti, Julie Gottlieb also stressed the linkages between certain pre-fascist organisational forms and the BF. She suggested that the Conservative Party-aligned Primrose League provided a model that the BF emulated to inspire its own particular mobilisation of women.[40] Gottlieb also saw a precedent for later female participation in fascism in the women's auxiliary services that sprouted up, both on the home and military fronts, during the Great War years.[41] 'Memories of the roles played by women during the war were central to the definition of the movement [the BF] and to constructing notions of self-worth', according to Gottlieb.[42] Moreover, 'right-wing women emerged from their war-time experiences with a renewed sense of patriotic endeavour', and some would later channel this enthusiasm into fascist female activism.[43]

There is virtual unanimity, too, in the historians' verdict on the BF's impact on the wider society and political life, which is generally described as negligible. Geiger, for example, stated that the BF attracted very little public interest during its lifetime.[44] Richard Thurlow arrived at a similar judgement, concluding that despite its paramilitary posturing, strike-breaking and other multifarious anti-labour activities, it 'made little impact'.[45] Benewick referred to the BF's 'innocuous' and often farcical activities, which included the sending of threatening letters to Labour leaders, the kidnapping of Harry Pollitt, and the offer, in 1932, to send 500 British Fascisti to assist the Bolivian government in its dispute with Paraguay.[46] These interpretations mirrored many of the contemporary assessments of the BF, such as that of the defector E. G. Mandeville Roe, who contemptuously dismissed his former party as 'Miss Lintorn-Orman's little tea-party at Earl's Court'.[47] A variation on this theme is the view that the BF had little consequence in terms of the development of a fascist ideological tradition in Britain.[48]

The BF was not adjudged to be completely irrelevant to the history of native fascism, however. Webber, for example, was correct to point out that it had some consequence if only for the fact that a number of interwar fascist notables, such as William Joyce, Arnold Leese and Neil Francis-Hawkins, had passed through its ranks.[49] Even Richard Thurlow conceded that the BF defectors to Mosley in the early 1930s, such as Francis-Hawkins, brought administration and discipline to the BUF.[50] The BF's stewarding methods, with their hint of political violence, were also important for the precedent they set for the BUF, according to Hilary Blume.[51]

The Fascisti was significant also in that it attempted to develop, through its founder Rotha Lintorn-Orman, a new concept of female right-wing political activism in Britain, a feature stressed by Barbara Farr. Farr referred to this novel departure as 'fascist feminism'. Lintorn-Orman was apparently 'forging a new role for women, combining voluntary service, militancy and right-wing politics into a fascist structure – a synthesis of female right-wing activism which can be termed "fascist feminism"'.[52] Julie Gottlieb, however, although conceding that the BF had a distinct feminine side and that there was a high degree of female participation in the organisation, sees something less radical than 'fascist feminism' in the BF's gender ideology. For Gottlieb, within the Fascisti movement 'traditional female roles were not radically transgressed'.[53] Lintorn-Orman, for example, 'cultivated an ultra-patriotic interpretation of female power, based on her myopic vision of women's duty and service to the nation; there was no room for women's rights in her political conceptions'.[54] Gottlieb pointed out that ideas on women's employment, the female franchise and sexual liberation were either understated in, or missing from, Lintorn-Orman's gender ideology, making it a 'fascism feminised' rather than a more meaningful expression of women's emancipation. Nonetheless, for Gottlieb, the fact that it 'gave temporary form to the fantasy of a fascism feminised and harnessed militant female activism in the name of a radical, if not revolutionary, nationalism', ensured that the BF merited an important place in the history of women's fascism.[55]

In general, though, the historiography tended to discount the BF. A distinct change of tone was observed in 1989, however, when Kenneth Lunn challenged most of the prevailing assumptions on the Fascisti. He suggested that the existing literature had 'undervalued' Lintorn-Orman's party and failed to appreciate its importance for later fascist organisations and ideology.[56] He claimed that there was significantly more fascist content in the BF's ideology and programme than had been appreciated in the earlier studies. For example, he pointed to the presence of a 'more "coded" version of fascist ideology' in the 1920s, including an ongoing opposition to parliamentary democracy and advocacy of dictatorship. He also took issue with those historians whom he believed underestimated the centrality of anti-semitism to BF ideology, as well as failing to note its virulent character. The level of BF branch activity and political activism was also much higher than had been hitherto appreciated,

The arrival of fascism

Lunn argued. Lunn remains a lone dissenting voice in the debate on the BF, however. When considering his claim that there was more fascist content in the BF's ideology, one might ask, for example, where is the evidence of an irrationalist anti-positivist culture, a rebirth mythology, the yearning for spiritual transcendence, and all the other ingredients that made up an authentic fascist ideology? It is difficult, too, to detect anything in the BF's ideology that resembled the Mosleyites' obsession with the new 'fascist man', their neoromantic fascination with the soil, or their desire to develop the philosophical side of fascism.

Another of the main fascist parties in interwar Britain was the Imperial Fascist League. The IFL's origins and history are inextricably bound up with Arnold Leese, one of the period's most fanatical, uncompromising and idiosyncratic of fascists. Leese was the nephew of a baronet, had a sheltered upbringing as a child, was a teetotaller and non-smoker in his adult life and extolled the virtues of a healthy diet.[57] For much of his professional working life, Leese was a veterinary surgeon who specialised in camel diseases. He would eventually write a definitive textbook on the illnesses of camels. The years before 1914 saw Leese practising his specialist profession in India and Kenya. After serving in the Royal Army Veterinary Corps in France and Somaliland during the Great War, Leese settled in England, opening a private practice in Stamford, Lincolnshire. In 1924 Leese entered the world of fascist politics when he joined the British Fascisti, forming a BF branch in Stamford. His conversion to fascism apparently owed its inspiration to Mussolini and Arthur Kitson of the Britons. Leese soon became disillusioned with the BF leadership's brand of moderate constitutional fascism, however, and decided to run the Stamford Fascists as an independent group. He then proceeded to dress the Stamford group in the black shirt, a symbolic action that confirmed his break with the BF. In 1926, in another move which ran counter to official BF policy, Leese contested the municipal elections in Stamford, along with another local fascist named Henry Simpson. Both were subsequently elected as 'Fascist' councillors for Stamford. Leese continued in his efforts to fashion an organisation that he regarded as a more truthful expression of the fascist ideal. In 1926, following a short period as a member of the militant BF splinter group the National Fascists, he established the Fascist League, a forerunner of the IFL, which eventually emerged in November 1928.[58] Captain Arnold Spencer Leese was aged forty-nine when the IFL was founded.

Leese was certainly present at the IFL's birth, although Thurlow stated that it was founded by Brigadier-General D. Erskine Tulloch and that Leese did not become its 'guiding spirit' until 1930.[59] Certainly, Thurlow's account, as well as the contemporary evidence from the security services, suggests that executive authority was not invested exclusively in Leese in this, the infant stage of the IFL's life. Indeed, the party was originally controlled by a three-man directorate consisting of Major J. Ballie, Leslie H. Sherrard and Leese himself.[60] In the wake of Ballie's and Sherrard's resignation in 1932, Leese became the party's supreme leader or 'Director-General', a position he would retain for the duration of the IFL's life-span.

The IFL adopted a paramilitary style and a hierarchical organisational structure. Its members were adorned in black shirts from the beginning. Full dress uniform would eventually comprise a black shirt, khaki breeches, khaki puttees, black boots, black cap and an armlet showing a Union Jack to be worn on the left arm. A swastika was superimposed on the Union Jack, the swastika having replaced the fasces as the party's emblem in 1933. In October 1933 the IFL membership was informed that only the party elite, and others who had enrolled prior to 15 September of that year, would be allowed to wear the black shirt.[61] The IFL was organised into three distinct divisions, the Lictors' Association, the Fascist Legions and the Activist Confederations. At the apex was the Lictors' Association, membership of which was preserved exclusively for the party elite, those of 'character' who were willing to serve and devote their energies to fascism. As this elite group was being trained for its future role as the governing aristocracy of a fascist Britain, entry into its ranks would be dependent on the approval of the Director-General. Even the internal structure of the Lictors' Association was hierarchical. It was composed of three orders, Lictors, Cadets and the Prefects, the latter comprising the IFL's Advisory Council. The rank-and-file membership, on the other hand, was grouped in the Fascist Legions, ostensibly a counter-revolutionary force of disciplined patriots primed to defend Britain and its Empire.[62] These Fascist Legionnaires were divided into Active and Reserve categories, which reflected members' varying shades of commitment to the movement. The Legions were further subdivided into separate formations, called Cohorts, Sections, Fasces and Maniples, which invariably had their basis in a military pattern of organisation. The Legions also contained a Women's Auxiliary Division. The IFL's third major divisional structure was the Activist Confederations, the party's economic and industrial wing, which aimed to educate the community about the apparent benefits of corporate beliefs and organisation. There were three Confederations in total, each of which was composed separately of employers, employees and professional workers. Supreme control of these Confederations was, as with most facets of the IFL's organisation, in the hands of Arnold Leese.

The IFL developed an elaborate organisational structure that was not in keeping with its size and political potential. Its membership base was pitifully small, as was the number of branch formations it was able to establish nationally. It probably attracted no more than a few hundred members in total during its lifetime. We know only of branches at Chalk Farm, Hackney, Shoreditch, Kentish Town, Maidenhead, Bristol, Newcastle upon Tyne and Glasgow.[63] There was also a small number of 'centres for enquiry' dotted at vast geographical intervals across England. There was a central Headquarters, but even this was a modest affair; George Catlin, a scholar writing in 1934, described it as 'two rooms without a telephone over a tailor's shop in London'.[64] Lack of funds always impeded the IFL's political progress. For the most part, it was sustained out of Arnold Leese's personal savings. Although the IFL was a pretentious organisation that failed to live up to the goals it set for itself, it was successful in attracting some prominent personalities from the fascist and anti-semitic fringe. These included the BF's former president Brigadier-General Robert Blakeney and the Britons notables Arthur Kitson, Lieutenant-Colonel A. H. Lane and Henry Hamilton Beamish. Indeed, there was a close affinity between the IFL and the Britons, both in terms of ideology and personnel. Other Britons members attached to the IFL were Anthony Gittens, Captain R. T. Cooper, Capel Pownall, Captain A. E. N. Howard and a Miss Beaumont.[65] Another individual associated with the IFL was John Hooper Harvey, whom Thurlow describes as a 'popular medieval historian and an expert on Gothic architecture'.[66] Others were H. H. Lockwood, an insurance agent who wrote for the IFL's newspaper, and William Sanderson, a freemason and writer. Sanderson had links with the English Mistery, a back-to-the-land group, of the reactionary 'muck and mysticism' variety, to which the Germanist and fascist fellow-traveller Rolf Gardiner also belonged.[67] In his book *Statecraft*, originally published in 1927, Sanderson subscribed to a mystical view of society. He believed that society was moving ever further away from the sources of ancestral power. Government, economics, property relations and race were based on lost 'Secrets', according to Sanderson, which had gradually been destroyed by modern 'industrial ideals'. Sanderson idealised the feudal Middle Ages. 'The underlying spirit of feudalism fostered the character and spirit of the race', he proclaimed.[68]

The IFL had a relatively coherent ideology and was more an overtly fascist party than most of its native contemporaries, including the British Fascisti. Its doctrine of Nordic supremacy and racial anti-semitism provided the IFL with much of its ideological coherence. Indeed, the IFL's ideology closely resembled that of Hitler's NSDAP, and, of all the fascist parties in interwar Britain, Arnold Leese's party was the one most closely linked to the German Nazis. This was not always the case, however. In its early days, the IFL gravitated towards Italian Fascism. Leese's ardour for Italian Fascism had even prompted him into a close association with the CINEF.[69] In particular, there was much enthusiasm for the Italian model of the Corporate State. Gisela Lebzelter has suggested that there was no evidence of racial anti-semitism in the IFL's ideology at the outset either, only traditional right-wing anti-alienism.[70] By 1931, Leese's paranoic nature had got the better of him and he turned away from Italian Fascism convinced that Mussolini was too favourably inclined towards the Jews.[71] By this stage the IFL had switched its allegiance to the German Nazis and we begin to see a greater attachment to the doctrine of Nordic racial supremacy, a descent into the realms of racial fantasy and fanaticism which was to gather pace during the 1930s. We will consider the character of the IFL's racial anti-semitism in a later chapter.[72]

Despite his growing suspicions of *Il Duce* and the Italian variant of fascism, Leese retained an affection for the Corporate State. It would remain a keystone of IFL policy. The British Corporate State would have an Upper House, composed of eminent persons who had served the state with distinction, and a Lower Industrial House, the 'Fascist equivalent of the House of Commons', made up of representatives from industry and other productive forces in the nation.[73] Members of the elite Upper House were to be appointed by the monarch following consultation with the Fascist government. The IFL argued that the key principles that underpinned the Fascist Corporate State were those of the old English craft guilds, with their aristocratic ideal of service and efficiency and tradition of 'fair play' between employer and hired craftsman.[74]

At one level the new form of Corporate State organisation

The arrival of fascism

reflected the IFL's disgruntlement with liberalism, notably the materialism and attachment to the principle of unfettered free competition, which were accused of destroying the standards of quality in workmanship. The Corporate State would also resolve the perceived problem of trade unionism, a practice that the IFL found equally repugnant. Trade unions were self-interested, unpatriotic and too aggressively class-conscious, according to the IFL, and forsook the principle of service for the good of the nation. At another level, the Corporate State reflected Leese's loathing of liberal democracy and its offshoots, the universal mass franchise, the party system and parliamentary government. He was convinced that democracy had failed the nation and that fascism could design a more efficient instrument of government. For Leese, the rule of elites was preferable to democratic 'mob rule' or the rule of the ignorant mass. Female suffrage, for example, was anathema to Leese because, according to him, it went against the grain of nature.[75] Although he favoured aristocratic rule, Leese was highly critical of existing elites in interwar Britain. He believed that England's traditional aristocracy had undergone a process of 'racial degeneration' by allowing Jews and other non-Aryans to enter its ranks. It thus no longer felt the instinct of the true aristocrat, a predisposition only open to those of 'pure' Aryan blood.[76] The *nouveaux riches* bourgeoisie, apparently infected with the modern sickness of materialism and individualism, were thought to be unfit to rule, too.[77] Rather, a new aristocracy of trusted men, a new 'governing caste of character and service', would emerge to replace the decadent elite of the old order. It was a new aristocracy of *race* that Leese hoped to create, for only those of pure Aryan stock could become members of the new governing caste. It was a racial fantasy, of course, which drew on myths and legends of selfless, highly moral, medieval knights, for the new aristocracy was imagined as a sort of knightly order of the truly pure of blood.

His views on race and aristocracy were not the only areas where Leese's fascist ideas veered towards the unconventional. His concept of leadership provided another case in point. Although an elitist, he did not favour rule by a single individual. In this way, he differed from many of his fascist contemporaries who adhered more strictly to the fascist Leadership principle and its ideal of rule by a single charismatic Leader, perceived as an almost God-like figure part human and part divine. Leese's occasionally idiosyncratic views were also reflected in his antipathy towards Christianity.

Unlike the BF, and even the Britons, he was hostile towards the Christian doctrine and the Church. For Leese, the Church was a 'judaized institution' which preached defeatism, internationalism and the insidious 'Jewish Masonic' doctrine of universal brotherhood with its message of liberty, equality and fraternity. Against this he set alternative, supposedly 'Aryan' values such as honesty, justice and love of truth.

In addition, of all the native fascist parties during the interwar years, the IFL was the one that most closely identified with eugenic ideas. Eugenic ideas featured in official IFL policy and informed many of its views on race. The proper role of the state, in the IFL's warped eugenic vision, was to 'care for the best blood' and prevent it from being 'contaminated by inbreeding with inferior racial stocks'.[78] Convinced that heredity, not environment, was the source of 'mental fitness', the IFL considered the low birth-rate amongst the middle classes, who comprised the 'more highly cultured elements of the population', a 'national menace', and promised that a future Fascist Corporate State would encourage them to produce larger families.[79] The IFL believed, too, that 'humanitarian' democracy was interfering with the 'laws of nature' by encouraging 'the propagation of the unfit at the expense of the fit'.[80] Chillingly, Leese's party also called for the 'sterilisation of conveyors of hereditary diseases'.[81]

In other areas, however, the IFL's ideology differed little from that of the other fascist parties. Apart from its hostility to liberalism, party politics, democracy and trade unionism, and support for a strong state and corporatism, which we have mentioned, the IFL was ultra-nationalist and opposed communism and socialism. Like the BF, Leese's party had a sentimental attachment to Empire and feared its break-up. It sought to preserve Empire unity by urging internal reorganisation and the strengthening of bonds between the imperial centre in London and the various imperial units scattered around the globe. Unlike the BF, however, and as always, racial ideas informed many of the IFL's views on Empire. Its attachment to Empire was underwritten by a belief in the inherent natural propensity of the European Aryan race to supervise and lead the non-white peoples.

In addition, like many fascist parties, we can detect a streak of irrational anti-modernism in the IFL's ideology. For example, much of what was of value in life and culture for Arnold Leese lay in a romantic pre-industrial medieval past. According to Lebzelter, his philosophy on life partly had its basis in ideals which he gleaned from medieval heroic legends.[82] The IFL also shared the view of many its fascist contemporaries that a thriving agricultural base was essential to the nation's economic and spiritual health. Warning the British people of the dangers of neglecting agriculture and the rural life, an IFL writer proclaimed that the 'preservation of the mental balance of our people is threatened by want of contact with nature'.[83] The IFL's economic ideas, for what they were, also overlapped at certain points with those of Oswald Mosley, though at a much lower level of analysis and sophistication. Like Mosley, the IFL attacked the 'tyranny' of international finance, advocated monetary reform in order to bring production and consumption more into line, and generally promoted the idea of a more demand-side economic policy to counteract the international trade crisis.[84] For Arnold Leese, as for Mosley, the creation of a more 'scientific' monetary system implied the abandonment of the gold standard. Crucial aspects of Leese's economic policy, particularly his prescriptions on monetary reform, bore the unmistakable mark of Arthur Kitson's influence.

Most historians of British fascism have discounted the significance of the IFL. Hilary Blume believed that the English public was blissfully unaware of its activities during the 1930s, while Eatwell referred to it as a 'talking shop for cranks' which was part of the 'one-man-and-his-dog fringe of British politics'.[85] Geiger also dismissed the IFL, referring to its 'lunatic fringe journalism' which made 'little pretence to logic or sense', as did Anderson, for whom the IFL was nothing more than a bodyguard for its eccentric Director-General.[86] Historians have correctly identified the BUF as a major factor in the IFL's political marginalisation during the 1930s. Once Mosley launched the BUF in October 1932, it was inevitable that rival fascist groups that sought to pursue an independent path would be squeezed, with some forced to go to the wall. Such was the fate of the British Fascists. Like Rotha Lintorn-Orman, Arnold Leese spurned Mosley and resisted his attempts at a takeover. Thereafter, he found himself in a war of attrition with the BUF, a conflict that he could not hope to win given Mosley's superior resources, adoption of a more coherent politico-economic programme, and firmer grasp on reality.

Leese tried gamely to carve out a separate niche for his party on the fascist right after 1932, by making the anti-semitic and racial components in the IFL's ideology more explicit so as to distance it from the BUF's 'Judaic Fascism'. In early 1933, in a move indicative of this descent into the dark underworld of racial fascism, the IFL began a collaboration with the 'Nordics'. The Nordics was a 'group of Britons conscious of the ideals of their Race', who were committed to spreading 'race-consciousness' among those in the nation of 'Nordic blood'.[87] According to the IFL, the BUF was far removed from the ideals of 'Nordic fascism'. Mosley's party apparently pursued a 'pro-Jewish policy', maintained Jewish contacts and was riddled with non-Aryans, occultists and masons.[88] Leese even peddled the line that the formation of the BUF represented a Jewish plot to destroy the IFL.[89] He also charged that Mosley's first wife, Cynthia Curzon, had Jewish ancestry. Leese's obstinacy and personal attacks on Mosley only succeeded in inviting the BUF's wrath, however. The IFL encountered fierce opposition from the Mosleyites during the 1930s, sometimes of an extreme 'physical force' nature, another factor which did not particularly assist its political development.

A further development, in 1936, also hampered the IFL's progress. On this occasion the state succeeded in putting Arnold Leese, the party's mainstay, out of action for six months. Unable to curtail his crude anti-semitic rhetoric, Leese accused Jews of engaging in the ritual murder of Christians and was subsequently charged, along with the printer of the IFL newspaper *The Fascist*, with seditious libel and causing a public mischief. Leese was acquitted on the more serious charge of seditious libel and found guilty on the charge of public mischief. He refused to pay the fine imposed by the court, however, and was sent to prison for six months. The cause of Nordic racial fascism received another heavy blow from the liberal state at the start of 1937, when the IFL was forced to shed its paramilitary image in order to evade prosecution under the Public Order Act. The Act, which became effective from 1 January 1937, contained provisions banning the wearing of political uniforms (Section 1) and prohibiting quasi-military organisations (Section 2). Despite these setbacks the IFL survived and continued to disseminate its highly individualistic brand of fascist propaganda right up to the war. According to John Morell, Leese's party even reaped some reward from its adoption of a vigorous anti-war policy and was thus probably at its strongest at the start of the war.[90] In September 1939 the IFL newspaper, *The Fascist*, was terminated. In November 1940 the state finally succeeded in muzzling Leese on a more permanent basis when he was interned under Defence Regulation 18b (1A).

The arrival of fascism

Although it failed to make an impact on the domestic political scene, or recruit a mass following, it would be a mistake to disregard the IFL's relevance for the British fascist right or indeed the interwar years as a whole, as some historians have recognised. Lebzelter, for example, thought that the IFL acted as a 'devoted mouthpiece' for German Nazi ideology in England.[91] Lebzelter and Blume are also of the view that, like the Britons, the IFL provided a 'political home' and a crucial source of anti-semitic propaganda for those in society who harboured an intense hatred of Jews.[92] Blume even went as far as to suggest that the IFL influenced many BUF members, and was thus instrumental in steering the BUF 'towards officially sanctioned anti-semitism'.[93] Blume's argument in this respect, however, lacks conviction and the advantage of supporting empirical evidence. We can state with more certainty that the IFL's inflammatory anti-Jewish rhetoric added to the climate of fear, insecurity and tension within Britain's Anglo-Jewish community, a point made by Richard Thurlow.[94] Apart from its unrelenting anti-Jewish written propaganda, IFL activists at the local level in London's East End engaged in acts of 'physical force' violence against Jews during the mid-1930s, which similarly contributed to the increase in tension within the Jewish community.[95] Thurlow also made what was perhaps the most interesting observation pertaining to the question of the IFL's significance. He connected Leese's fanatical group, in the form of an underground tradition of racial nationalism, direct action and premeditated racial violence, to certain post-1945 neo-fascist parties in Britain, including the National Front, the British Movement and the British National Party.[96] According to Thurlow, it was the Leese legacy, rather than the more intellectually coherent Mosleyite fascist tradition, which was to exert the most influence on the British fascist tradition as it evolved into the post-1945 period. Thurlow thus highlights the crucial role played by ideas and a tradition of thought, however extreme, bizarre and seemingly without logic, to the development of fascism.

Notes

1 C. Cross, *The Fascists in Britain* (London, Barrie and Rockliff, 1961), p. 57.
2 *British Fascism*, 1 March 1932, p. 1.
3 B. S. Farr, *The Development and Impact of Right-Wing Politics in Britain, 1903–1932* (New York, Garland, 1987), p. 55.

4   R. Benewick, *Political Violence and Public Order* (London, Allen Lane, 1969), p. 32.
5   Ibid.
6   In 1924 the Executive Council was renamed the Headquarters Committee.
7   Benewick, *Political Violence*, p. 30.
8   R. Griffiths, *Fellow Travellers of the Right. British Enthusiasts for Nazi Germany 1933–39* (Oxford, Oxford University Press, 1983), p. 89.
9   J. Gottlieb, 'Women and Fascism in Inter-war Britain' (Ph.D. thesis, University of Cambridge, 1998), p. 27; K. Lunn 'The Ideology and Impact of the British Fascists in the 1920s', in T. Kushner and K. Lunn (eds), *Traditions of Intolerance. Historical Perspectives on Fascism and Race Discourse in Britain* (Manchester, Manchester University Press, 1989), pp. 145–6.
10 Gottlieb, 'Women and Fascism', p. 27.
11 Cross, *The Fascists*, p. 58; Benewick, *Political Violence*, p. 28; Griffiths, *Fellow Travellers*, p. 86.
12 Gottlieb, 'Women and Fascism', p. 9.
13 R. Thurlow, *Fascism in Britain. From Oswald Mosley's Blackshirts to the National Front* (London, I. B. Tauris, 1998), p. 34.
14 R. B. D. Blakeney, 'British Fascism', *The Nineteenth Century* (January 1925), pp. 132–41.
15 Farr, *The Development and Impact*, p. 53.
16 PRO HO144/19069/31-3, British Fascists, Policy and Practice, 1 July 1926; HO144/19069/129-31, British Fascists, Manifesto, 1 October 1927; and *British Fascism*, Summer 1933, p. 8.
17 Farr, *The Development and Impact*, p. 74.
18 Cross, *The Fascists*, p. 58, on free love. See below, Chapter Nine, on sexual promiscuity.
19 Farr, *The Development and Impact*, p. 60; Benewick, *Political Violence*, p. 24.
20 *Fascist Bulletin*, 12 June 1926, p. 7.
21 See below, Chapter Five, on the NF.
22 Farr, *The Development and Impact*, p. 60.
23 Ibid.; Thurlow, *Fascism in Britain. From Oswald Mosley's Blackshirts*, p. 37.
24 Griffiths, *Fellow Travellers*, pp. 89–90.
25 PRO HO144/19069/129-31, British Fascists, Manifesto, 1 October 1927.
26 Ibid.
27 Ibid.
28 Farr, *The Development and Impact*, pp. 73–80.
29 *British Fascism*, Summer 1933, p. 8.
30 Ibid.

31 Ibid.
32 See *British Fascism*, March 1934, pp. 4–5.
33 Cross, *The Fascists*, p. 62.
34 Ibid.
35 G. C. Webber, 'Intolerance and Discretion: Conservatives and British Fascism, 1918–1926', in Kushner and Lunn (eds), *Traditions of Intolerance*, p. 63; G. C. Webber, *The Ideology of the British Right, 1918–1939* (London, Croom Helm, 1986), p. 28.
36 R. Thurlow, *Fascism in Britain. A History, 1918–1985* (Oxford, Blackwell, 1987), p. 24.
37 R. Eatwell, *Fascism. A History* (London, Vintage, 1996), p. 177.
38 D. S. Lewis, *Illusions of Grandeur. Mosley, Fascism and British Society, 1931–81* (Manchester, Manchester University Press, 1987), p. 29.
39 J. Hope, 'British Fascism and the State 1917–1927: A Re-Examination of the Documentary Evidence', *Labour History Review*, 57, 3 (Winter 1992), p. 75.
40 Gottlieb, 'Women and Fascism', p. 11.
41 Such as the Women's Army Auxiliary Corps and the Soldier's Parcel Fund.
42 Ibid., p. 12.
43 Ibid.
44 D. M. Geiger, 'British Fascism as Revealed in the British Union of Fascists Press' (Ph.D. thesis, New York University, 1963), p. 36.
45 Thurlow, *Fascism in Britain. From Oswald Mosley's Blackshirts*, p. 35.
46 Benewick, *Political Violence*, p. 34.
47 *Blackshirt*, 23–29 September 1933, p. 4.
48 Thurlow, *Fascism in Britain. From Oswald Mosley's Blackshirts*, p. 40.
49 Webber, 'Social Basis', p. 143.
50 Thurlow, *Fascism in Britain. A History*, p. 57.
51 H. S. B. Blume, 'A Study of Anti-Semitic Groups in Britain, 1918–40' (M.Phil. thesis, University of Sussex, 1971), p. 112.
52 Farr, *The Development and Impact*, p. 73.
53 Gottlieb, 'Women and Fascism', p. 20.
54 Ibid., p. 19.
55 Ibid., p. 37.
56 Lunn, 'The Ideology and Impact', pp. 140–54.
57 Cross, *The Fascists*, p. 63.
58 J. Morell, 'Arnold Leese and the Imperial Fascist League', in K. Lunn and R. Thurlow (eds), *British Fascism* (London, Croom Helm, 1980), p. 57; *The Fascist*, December 1934, p. 4, also refers to the Fascist League. *The Patriot*, 16 July 1925, p. 214, on Leese's NF association. See below, Chapter Five, on the NF.

British fascism 1918–39

59 Thurlow, *Fascism in Britain. A History*, p. 71.
60 PRO HO45/24967, Special Branch Report, 9 March 1936.
61 *The Fascist*, October 1933, p. 1.
62 G. Lebzelter, *Political Anti-Semitism in England, 1918–1939* (London, Macmillan, 1978), p. 72.
63 Ibid., p. 83; Thurlow, *Fascism in Britain. A History*, p. 72. *The Fascist*, March 1934, p. 4, on the Shoreditch Branch.
64 G. Catlin, 'Fascist Stirrings in Britain', *Current History*, 39 (February 1934), p. 542.
65 Lebzelter, *Political Anti-Semitism*, p. 76.
66 Thurlow, *Fascism in Britain. A History*, p. 73.
67 G. Boyes, *The Imagined Village. Culture, Ideology and the English Folk Revival* (Manchester, Manchester University Press, 1993), pp. 157–8.
68 W. Sanderson. *Statecraft. A Treatise on the Concerns of our Sovereign Lord the King* (London, Constable, 1932 edition), p. 87.
69 Griffiths, *Fellow Travellers*, pp. 97–8. On the CINEF, see below, Chapter Five.
70 Lebzelter, *Political Anti-Semitism*, pp. 73–4.
71 Blume, 'A Study of Anti-Semitic Groups', p. 192.
72 See below, Chapter Seven.
73 *The Fascist*, August 1933, p. 1.
74 *The Fascist*, March 1932, p. 1.
75 Lebzelter, *Political Anti-Semitism*, p. 71.
76 See IFL, *Race and Politics* (London, IFL pamphlet, n.d.). See also Eatwell, *Fascism*, p. 177.
77 Ibid.
78 *The Fascist*, February 1934, p. 3.
79 *The Fascist*, April 1929, p. 3.
80 *The Fascist*, November 1937, p. 3.
81 Ibid.
82 Lebzelter, *Political Anti-Semitism*, p. 69.
83 *The Fascist*, January 1936, p. 8.
84 See, for example, *The Fascist*, February 1931, p. 2.
85 Eatwell, *Fascism*, p. 179.
86 Geiger, 'British Fascism', p. 39; G. D. Anderson, *Fascists, Communists and the National Government. Civil Liberties in Great Britain, 1931–1937* (Columbia, University of Missouri Press, 1983), p. 49.
87 *The Fascist*, January 1933, p. 4.
88 *The Fascist*, October 1933, p. 1, and April 1937, p. 3.
89 Morell, 'Arnold Leese', p. 65.
90 Ibid., p. 59.
91 Lebzelter *Political Anti-Semitism*, p. 85.
92 Ibid.; Blume, 'A Study of Anti-Semitic Groups', p. 220.
93 Blume, 'A Study of Anti-Semitic Groups', p. 220.

94 Thurlow, *Fascism in Britain. A History*, pp. 74–5.
95 Ibid., p. 75. This was sometimes done in collaboration with East End Mosleyites.
96 Thurlow, *Fascism in Britain. From Oswald Mosley's Blackshirts*, pp. 227–44.

CHAPTER FOUR

THE BRITISH UNION OF FASCISTS

Like the majority of the interwar fascist parties, both in Britain and on the continent, the British Union of Fascists came to prominence on the back of a domestic internal crisis. The BUF was very much the child of the 1929–31 economic crisis, while its subsequent political life unfolded against the backdrop of the trade depression that came after it. Most of the BUF's principal economic and political ideas were framed in response to the 1929–31 crisis and its aftermath. What is more, these ideas, particularly in the economic arena, translated into detailed policy statements, a factor that set the BUF apart from its contemporaries on the interwar fascist fringe, the majority of whom failed to craft detailed or well-defined programmes. Indeed some historians have referred to the surprisingly 'programmatic fascism' of the BUF, when compared to its sister parties on the continent.[1] While it is important to stress this feature of its ideology, we should not let it obscure the fact that there existed a significant philosophical and even irrational element in the BUF's thinking, with many of these ideas hailing from a continental intellectual tradition.

When the Wall Street stock market crashed in October 1929, the ensuing economic slump in the United States seriously dislocated the global economy, precipitating a grave and unprecedented generalised depression. By mid-1930 some eleven million people in thirty-three countries were unemployed, twice the number prior to the Crash.[2] In Britain sharp and consistent monthly unemployment rises began to be recorded from late 1929. When Ramsay MacDonald's minority Labour government entered office in June 1929, unemployment stood at 1 million and was falling. By November 1929 it had climbed to 1.3 million, 1.7 million by April 1930, 2 million by July 1930 and 2.5 million before the year closed.

Britain's export market was seriously injured by the global slump, exports almost halving in value between 1930 and 1931. Britain's industrial infrastructure, particularly that based on its traditional staple industries of textiles, coal, iron and shipping, barely withstood the shock of the economic slump. It was in the context of the harsh economic setting of early 1930 that Oswald Mosley set his face against the prevailing economic wisdom of the day and promoted the ideas that would form the basis of his later fascist economic and political doctrine. At this point in his political career, Mosley was Chancellor of the Duchy of Lancaster, a Labour Cabinet Minister without Portfolio assisting the Lord Privy Seal, J. H. Thomas, with unemployment schemes.

Mosley's economic thinking developed in reaction to the fiscal orthodoxy of the 1929 Labour government, a *laissez-faire* 'Manchester School' approach that was heavily biased towards the international context and Britain's overseas export markets based on the traditional staple industries. According to 'orthodox' thinking, a domestic economic downturn was a phase of temporary disequilibrium that would soon right itself once the free market automatically adjusted itself and international trade revived. It was simply a matter of waiting patiently for the world economy to pick up again, so ran the 'orthodox' argument. In the interval, a number of harsh though necessary deflationary measures were required to steady matters until time and 'natural law' took effect, including public spending reductions and holding down wages. Inflation was to be averted at all costs, while every effort was to be made to balance the budget and resist the inclination to borrow, impose tariffs, which might trigger retaliation from overseas competitors, or intervene in the 'natural' working of the economy. A sound interim fiscal policy also implied an unswerving commitment to the retention of the gold standard, preferably at the prewar value of £1 to $4.68.

Mosley, on the other hand, situated himself in an alternative economic tradition that repudiated the 'orthodox' deflationary approach of the economic liberals of the Manchester School. Referred to variously as economic radicalism, economic nationalism, autarky and even radical capitalism, this tradition rejected the policy of imposing strict ceilings on public spending, wages and the level of borrowing, in favour of an expansive credit policy based on a strategy of deficit financing. This implied negotiating loans, making credit more readily available, and running up a deliberate budgetary deficit if deemed necessary, which would all serve the purpose of rekindling production and trade. There were a number of other related strands to economic radicalism. There was to be less reliance on conventional export outlets based around the traditional staple industries, and a stress on developing the domestic market and stimulating additional demand in the economy. The creation of new demand, which would evoke the economy's dormant productive capacity, would be achieved by such measures as forcing up wages to facilitate consumer spending, and ensuring that there was a relatively high level of both private and public expenditure. The latter was to be achieved, for example, by the creation of public works programmes. Treasury caution and inertia were to be replaced, therefore, by a more pro-active, dynamic and interventionist approach. Much of this new radical approach, of course, would mirror the demand-side economic thinking of John Maynard Keynes, and indeed Robert Skidelsky highlighted the intellectual contribution of infant Keynesianism to Mosleyite fascist economics.[3] Economic radicals like Mosley also thought that the home market would best develop behind a protective barrier of import controls or tariffs.

Most of these themes found their way into the 'Mosley Memorandum' which an impatient Mosley, furious at the lack of Treasury initiative and drive on unemployment, presented to Ramsay MacDonald on 23 January 1930. The Memorandum argued for the development of the home market, a reduced emphasis on the traditional export trade, and the setting up of import control boards and a flexible selective tariff policy that sought to avoid the potential pitfalls of outright protectionism.[4] It also called on the government to arrange loans amounting to £200 million to finance a number of projects designed to reduce unemployment, namely a constructive public works scheme, an emergency pension programme for sixty year olds, and the raising of the school leaving age ceiling. The adoption of an agricultural development policy would also help ease unemployment, it was argued. Easier credit was called for too, an aim that would be facilitated by the setting-up of a government-controlled development company in order to circumvent any financial difficulties caused by the banks. Mosley also proposed that a transport policy and a research and economic advisory department be set up, both centrally co-ordinated. More controversially, and here we move into the realm of incipient fascism, Mosley argued for a reform of the existing government machinery for dealing with the unemployment crisis. The theme of government reform would be developed and pursued with ever greater vigour in the months that followed the rejection of the Memorandum by a government sub-committee under the chairmanship of the ultra-orthodox Chancellor Philip Snowden in May 1930.

This did not amount to the first formal statement of Mosley's views on the economy, however. Many of the proposals contained in the Memorandum were prefigured in the ideas he developed during his early years in political life. Mosley had a varied political career during the 1920s. Following service in the 16th Lancers and the Royal Flying Corps during the Great War, the then 23-year-old Mosley entered Parliament as Conservative MP for Harrow in December 1918 as a member of Lloyd George's Coalition government. In November 1920 he left the Conservative Party in protest against the Coalition Unionist government's use of repression in Ireland during the bitter Anglo-Irish war.[5] He was returned as an Independent Conservative for Harrow in 1922, and again in 1923, before switching to the Labour Party in April 1924, under whose banner he unsuccessfully challenged Neville Chamberlain for the Ladywood seat in Birmingham later that year. Mosley was more successful in the Smethwick by-election of 1926, a seat he held for Labour with a healthy majority in the 1929 General Election. His first formal attempt to clarify his thinking on economic matters during his early political life took the form of the 'Birmingham Proposals' which culminated in a policy document he drafted in 1925, *Revolution by Reason*, co-written with his radical Labour colleague John Strachey.[6] In presenting the case for a more demand-side approach to the economy, the Birmingham Proposals questioned the remedies of classical economic liberalism and orthodox socialism, both of which argued that contemporary unemployment was a consequence of a maldistribution of rewards emanating from Britain's existing, though static, productive base.[7] Instead, Strachey and Mosley argued for an expansion in production, which would be brought about by the creation of supplementary demand to evoke the economy's dormant 'unused' capacity. An increase in demand could be achieved through a number of measures, including a state-induced rise in real wage levels, distributing consumer credits to the unemployed, and the issuing of producers' credits to manufacturers. The Birmingham Proposals also advocated state control of the supply of credit and currency to be achieved through the nationalising of the banking system.

By the time the New Party was formed on 1 March 1931, then,

Mosley having resigned from the Labour Cabinet on 20 May 1930, his economic thinking had reached a relatively high level of maturity and precision.[8] The New Party was a political hybrid that attracted to its ranks some Labour defectors including John Strachey and Robert Forgan, a number of dissident ILP members such as William Risdon and W. J. Leaper, and a lone Tory, namely W. E. D. Allen, the Conservative MP for West Belfast.[9] The New Party also attracted a few period intellectuals such as Harold Nicholson and C. E. M. Joad. The political programme of the New Party was set out in a pamphlet entitled *A National Policy*, which was published in March 1931, and amounted to a restatement of many of the concerns that had preoccupied Mosley since the mid-1920s. Once again, there was a focus on Britain's declining export and global trading position in relation to the traditional primary products, and the need to diversify through the development of the home market behind a barrier of selective protective tariffs. The latter would be attained by establishing Commodity Boards which would apply tariffs to failing industries hit by foreign competition.[10] The importance of planning was re-emphasised too, with a National Investment Board and National Planning Council providing financial assistance for industry. Emergency public works schemes to revitalise the economy were also mentioned. Where Mosley's thinking had moved on was in his prescriptions for political reform. Parliamentary debate was attacked for apparently being too leisurely and obstructive, while, in general, parliamentary procedure was accused of being inefficient. *A National Policy* also advocated that the business of government should be conducted by a Super-Cabinet of five or six ministers, rather than the current 'unwieldy' Cabinet of around twenty.

The New Party was a dismal failure. Most of its more moderate support leaked away once Mosley's nascent fascism became more apparent. John Strachey resigned on 23 July 1931 and C. E. M. Joad soon followed him. New Party meetings were marred by disorder and political violence, while it fared disastrously at the polls. In the October 1931 General Election, all twenty-four New Party candidates, including Mosley, failed in their efforts to capture a seat, attaining a paltry 0.2 per cent of the total poll. A decision to wind up the ailing party was eventually taken on 5 April 1932.[11] Mosley's rapid descent into fascism followed thereafter. As to whether the New Party was a fascist or proto-fascist party, Mandle observed that it did not have a fascist programme, though the tone was there.[12] It also had a youth wing, embraced a cult of physical fitness and activism, encouraged political violence, and advocated eugenics, all fascist characteristics.[13] Barbara Farr believed that national socialist ideas and policies 'existed in the New Party from the beginning'.[14] However, this latter viewpoint probably goes too far, for there was a great deal about the New Party that was not fascist. For example, there was no reference to the one-party state, corporatism or the need for elite rule, nor did its ideology have an underpinning in irrationalism, anti-positivism or organic ultra-nationalism, or indeed any of the other philosophical ingredients of a genuine fascist party. The final leap into open and genuine fascism would not take place until 1 October 1932, when Mosley formed the British Union of Fascists.

Mosley's first formal statement of the new fascist policy arrived in the shape of *The Greater Britain*, which was published in 1932.[15] There would be numerous subsequent reiterations and expansions of the new proposals for national regeneration in the months and years that followed, both in the BUF press and in the stream of propaganda pamphlets that left the Mosleyite printing presses.[16] Most of the by now familiar Mosleyite economic and political motifs were in evidence, though now even more detailed and supplemented by a number of additional explicitly fascist themes and policies. The BUF argued for demand-side economics to reflate the economy, a boosting of the home market to offset the negative impact of diminished overseas export outlets, an expansion of Britain's existing manufacturing product and a 'scientific' increase in purchasing power to co-ordinate consumption with the subsequent increase in production. A consumption boom would be facilitated in the short term by the issuing of consumer credits strategically directed towards society's more deprived members. If Mosley's belief that existing levels of consumption were inadequate to absorb production partly mirrored J. A. Hobson and the ILP's 'underconsumptionist' argument, the consumer credit measure had an antecedent in Major Douglas's 'social credit' idea of the national dividend to aid consumer spending.[17]

That the BUF pursued an aggressively modernist project, rather than an anti-modern agenda, was evident in Mosley's conviction that modern science was the panacea that would enable society to advance beyond the old economics of poverty to an age of material abundance. In a theme that expanded on his earlier Labour Party ideas on selective tariffs, Mosley advocated Empire autarky to insulate the domestic economy against the vicissitudes of the liberal international trading order. Mosley had first embraced the idea of a self-contained imperial trading zone in mid-1930, but he had to wait until the BUF was formed to give it free rein.[18] According to this autarkic model, the mother country and the dominions would observe reciprocal trade agreements, with the former focusing on manufacturing products and the latter on food output.[19]

If the notion of an Empire *Zollverein* represented a relatively new departure, the new policy of corporatism was indicative of the lurch to a more explicitly fascist doctrine. The BUF sought to apply corporate principles to virtually all the key sectors of industrial life. Alexander Raven-Thomson, the party's chief authority on the Corporate State, envisaged the restructuring of the economy into twenty virtually self-governing corporations on which would sit employers, workers and government-appointed consumer groups, all of whom would be equally represented.[20] In line with Mosleyite fascist theory, the corporations were consensus-orientated, aiming at the reconciliation of class interests. The corporations would work in harmony with a Fascist Parliament and a National Corporation of Industry, a more centralised body that would plan and regulate economic activity on a national scale. The National Corporation would function as a sort of parliament of industry, and as such would replace the House of Lords. The majority of the members of this new 'second chamber' of technical experts would be elected on an occupational franchise, the remainder subject to a wider electoral vote. The National Corporation would also work closely with a National Investment Board, an institution that would be set up to circumvent any potential problems arising from the supposedly pernicious activities of 'international finance capital'. Mosley's increasingly vitriolic attacks on 'international finance', which he accused of being preoccupied with shares speculation rather than long-term national reconstruction, reveal a further strand of his thinking that had succumbed to fascism. By the autumn of 1934 he had succumbed even further. By this stage he was convinced that 'international finance' was a Jewish preserve.

His views on the existing political system had become more extreme too. Parliament was denounced as an outdated nineteenth-century debating chamber, 'a non-technical assembly in a vastly technical age' according to Mosley, while the overall structure of parliamentary democratic government was deemed to be too cumbersome to undertake the pressing task of implementing a project of dynamic action.²¹ Mosley thus advocated its replacement by a strong executive based on the fascist Leadership principle. As in the New Party, government business would be in the hands of a Super-Cabinet of only four ministers without portfolio who would assist the 'Prime Minister' to co-ordinate national affairs.²² The New Party idea of legislation by Orders in Council was also retained.²³ Corporate principles would be applied here too, with elections to the Fascist Parliament, as with the National Corporation, being on an occupational, rather than a residential, basis.

For Mosley, the Corporate State held out the promise of 'rationalising' government, as well as industry. It also promised to bring about the rationalisation of the state, through the harmonious integration of all its various elements. It was conceived as a vibrant, finely tuned metabolism, an arrangement whereby each separate part remained in harmony with the organic whole. The BUF's fascination with biological analogies is evident here. The organic notion of the Corporate State was frequently expressed through the human body metaphor. The Corporate State, stated Mosley, envisaged 'a nation organised as the human body. Every part fulfills its function as a member of the whole, performing its separate task, and yet, by performing it, contributing to the welfare of the whole.'²⁴

If we turn to the historiography, most scholars now agree that a number of the BUF's key economic and political ideas germinated in the pre-First World War period, with Mosley taking up many of the intellectual arguments of the Edwardian radical right.²⁵ Certain of his proposals to restructure the British economy have their intellectual antecedents in the prewar anti-Cobdenite protectionist tradition of social-imperialism.²⁶ The notion of a self-contained imperial trading zone, for example, clearly bore the stamp of the tariff reform imperialism of Joseph Chamberlain. For one historian, Mosley was 'the intellectual heir of the most extreme wing of Chamberlainism, of protectionist social-imperialism'.²⁷ This focus in the historiography on the pre-1914 anti-Cobdenite radical right tradition has been crucial in revealing the domestic roots of the BUF's ideology. However, we also need to be aware of the vein of continental ideas running through Mosley's thinking. In much the same way, the existence of the rational and modernist strands within the BUF's doctrine, the 'programmatic fascism', the fascination with science and belief in the 'rational' Corporate State, should not disguise the fact that it contained a parallel philosophical and even irrational element. Economic and political rationalism was only one theme in the dialectic of Mosleyite fascism. A whole series of parallel emotions lay at the heart of the Mosleyite experience, though they were not always adequately acknowledged in the historiography of the BUF, particularly in the earlier work. Robert Benewick employed a somewhat simplistic structural-functionalist notion of ideology in his analysis of the BUF's outlook. He constructed a three-phase model by way of attempting to show how a particular ideological orientation, 'constructive economic analysis', 'political anti-semitism' and 'foreign policy', predisposed the BUF to act in accordance with a specific set of ideas or series of related policy goals.[28] While rightly emphasising the dynamic element of change in Mosleyite ideology, Benewick's 'definable policy positions', 'dominant at different stages in the development of the BUF', too readily assumed the functioning of a single homogenous set of cognitive mechanisms to explain the predisposition towards a particular policy goal. Benewick also drew too sharp a distinction between the different policy stages, or sets of core beliefs. More seriously, however, there was virtually no mention of the philosophical element within the Mosleyite creed. When contemplating the reasons for the BUF's ultimate political failure during the 1930s, Benewick suggested that it was due to its alienation from the British political culture. He argued that the BUF's political style, particularly its use of organised political violence, proved to be at variance with the essential moderation and tolerance of the national character and the peaceful evolutionary traditions of British institutions.[29] This argument had been put forward at an earlier date by D. M. Geiger in his unpublished thesis on the BUF.[30] However, as D. S. Lewis stated, it is naïve and smug to suggest that the BUF's failure was somehow 'preordained by the intrinsic nature of British society'. [31]

Like Benewick, Nugent's study of the BUF's ideas preoccupied itself almost exclusively with the 'programmatic' rational side of the Mosleyite doctrine and seriously underemphasised its philosophical aspects. According to Nugent, unlike most continental fascist parties the BUF 'was highly programmatic' and made little attempt to apply specific policies to a philosophical context.[32] Stuart Rawnsley pointed to the existence of a core set of beliefs within BUF ideology that pivoted on the desire for leadership, militarism, anti-semitism and the Corporate State.[33] Significantly, the ideological 'core' is limited to these features and there is no mention of philosophical concepts. Stephen Cullen, as with Benewick and Nugent, made great play of the BUF's 'programmatic fascism'.[34] His analysis also tended towards the functional in his construction of a six-part model – economic rationalism; hyper-patriotism; the ethos of the ex-servicemen of the Great War; the concept of the modern movement; anti-semitism; and peace – to explain the core pillars of its ideology. However, Cullen did not draw a sharp distinction between the different policy stages, or Mosleyite core beliefs, as did Benewick. Rather, Cullen suggested that the core elements of BUF thought operated as facilitative categories, which ensured a degree of continuity through the period of the movement's history between 1932 and 1940. Cullen also went further than both Benewick and Nugent in alluding to the presence of romantic and anti-modern themes in the Mosleyite discourse. Like Benewick, Cullen considered the question of BUF political violence, though the conclusions he arrived at are rather different, and far more controversial. Cullen claimed that the BUF was far more the victim than the instigator of offensive political violence and that 'BUF violence occurred almost exclusively in connection with the defence of their own events'.[35] In contrast, Cullen argued, communist-organised anti-fascist violence was far more prevalent.[36]

For D. S. Lewis, the BUF was neither a party of the traditional right nor a revolutionary party, but a movement of the 'authoritarian centre' that sought to absorb elements from both left and right.[37] In the final analysis, however, Mosley failed because he was unsuccessful in his attempt to bring about the reconciliation of apparently incompatible left and right elements. Other factors relevant to Mosley's failure, according to Lewis, concerned his personal weaknesses as a leader, his party's internal flaws, and his inability to overcome opposition from the anti-fascist forces and the liberal state.[38] Lewis suggested, too, that the absence of preconditioning factors in the form of a major economic crisis militated against the BUF's attempts to become a major political force. Whereas Lewis defined the BUF as a non-revolutionary party of the centre, Barbara Farr suggested that it was a dynamic revolutionary national socialist movement that stood in stark contrast to the moderate fascism of the 1920s as exemplified by the British Fascisti.[39]

Leslie Susser suggested that, like Italian Fascism and German Nazism, BUF fascism was 'Janus-faced', in that it displayed an uneasy ambivalence of attitude toward modernism and anti-modernism, a factor that ultimately contributed to its downfall.[40] The Mosleyites were never able to reconcile their goal of material progress with their desire for spiritual salvation from the consequences of modernisation. Endorsing Jeffrey Herf's reference to the 'reactionary modernism' of the Third Reich, Susser contrasted the British case with the experience of the Nazis, who, by aestheticising technology and viewing it as a projection of national spirit, resolved the tension between their 'reactionary irrationalism' and their rational forward-looking quest for industrial growth.[41] According to Susser, Mosley would never have dreamt of forging such a synthesis in a contemporary England that preferred to separate the spheres of matter and spirit. For Mosley, mastery of the machine would liberate the nation's spirit, not reflect it.[42] Susser further added that Mosley, as 'a would-be authoritarian moderniser' and romantic back-to-the-soil ruralist, was pre-empted at every turn during the 1930s by others on the non-fascist political spectrum quietly advocating similar arguments.

The focus on the modernist/anti-modernist dichotomy has generated important insights into the nature of Mosleyite fascism. So too has the work of other scholars who have illuminated the vein of philosophical thought running through the BUF's doctrine.[43] The BUF's observations on the condition of 1930s Britain, for example, were permeated with a pessimism that owed much to Oswald Spengler's gloomy meditations, which he left to posterity in the form of his ambitious tome *The Decline of the West*.[44] According to Spengler, each civilisation or 'culture' had a unique spirit, as in the 'Faustian' culture of Europe, and was governed by certain basic biological laws of formation, growth, decline and death, in the same manner as life forms in nature.[45] All civilisations or cultures in history had to obey these fundamental organic laws, which meant that every civilisation had to pass through its biological life-cycle and confront its grim destiny of inevitable decay and death. The BUF believed that Spengler's immense insight was to highlight Western civilisation's ailing health and alert the current generation to the threat of decay and the imminent decline of its 'Faustian' culture.[46] Mosley, however, repudiated Spengler's determinism and his fatalistic belief in the impending death of the Faustian culture of Europe. He believed that, crucially, Spengler's analysis had overlooked the productive power of science in the modern era. In fascism, a new and vital force had been discovered that, with the aid of science, would renew the youth of European civilisation and allow it to continue its evolutionary advance.[47] It was the heroic new 'Caesar-types', imbued with *élan vital* and the spirit of sacrifice exemplified by the youth of the Great War generation, that would set their face against the destiny of cultural decline, and in so doing, proclaim the rebirth of Faustian Europe. This was a new biological type that fascism promised to summon forth to save European culture, an individual in communion with his irrational nature, an intuitive and vibrant 'new fascist man' of action prepared to face adversity with a stoic disregard for his own personal safety.

In its original conception, of course, the idea of the *élan vital* can be traced back to the thinking of the French philosopher Henri Bergson, the supreme advocate of the creative power of the irrational. For the anti-rationalist Bergson, writing at the *fin de siècle*, the creative thrust of existence was provided by an enigmatic inner 'life-force', the *élan vital*, rather than any incontestable materialist 'laws' favoured by the positivists. There were domestic versions of the 'life-force' concept, too, one of which was formulated by George Bernard Shaw. Shaw's idea of the 'life-force' and meditations on the emergence of a new 'superman' made a profound impression on Mosley.[48] According to Shaw's creative evolutionary vision, a life-force was at work in the evolutionary process which was struggling to conceive a more advanced type of existence. Shaw believed that society should endeavour to assist the life-force by cultivating and multiplying its 'highest types'. This elite of heroic exceptional individuals would confront and transcend the contemporary age of inertia and accelerate this transition to a higher state. Shaw's vitalism would enable humanity to surmount the limitations imposed on the historical process by the more gradual and random mechanisms of evolution.[49] This 'heroic vitalist' vision, with the conscious intervention of the creative 'will-to-achievement' types serving to hasten evolution, would deeply influence Mosley. It would underpin his own vision of the new vital 'fascist man' striving to transport society to a higher plane of political and cultural existence which, he believed, was embodied in the new fascist order. Mosley, of course, the somewhat conceited aristocrat, imagined himself to be the supreme example of this 'higher type, the 'hero-king' of Greek mythology reborn, a figure part human and part divine.

We can discern the influence, too, of G. W. Hegel and Friedrich Nietzsche on aspects of Mosley's thought. Mosley was an ideological anti-Marxist who sought to refute Marxism on philosophical grounds. Classical or orthodox Marxism, clearly the only version of Marxism with which Mosley bothered to acquaint himself, promoted a model of economic determinism according to which the inevitable development of economic forces would necessarily and inevitably lead to the emergence of socialism.[50] In this 'evolutionist' model of Marxism, historical development was conceived as the development of an organic necessity. Significantly, because revolutionary change in the direction of socialism would be brought about by 'natural necessity', it was futile and unnecessary for individuals to voluntaristically force the pace of evolution. Mosley's reaction to this historical teleology, the notion that socio-economic change was an organic process whose outcome was predetermined in advance, was predictably critical.[51] Mosley believed in the Hegelian dialectical triad of thesis, antithesis and ultimate synthesis, whereby all history undergoes a process of change in which internal contradictions are resolved and transcended giving rise to new contradictions which then also require resolution.[52] The Hegelian dialectic clearly struck a chord with his belief in the evolution to higher forms of existence. However, Mosley rejected the central assumption of the Marxist dialectic that socialism would naturally emerge from the working out of the contradiction between labour and capital. He also attacked the Marxists' materialist model of history, on the grounds that it preoccupied itself with the world of form and matter and thus ignored Hegel's emphasis on Spirit as the motive force behind the dialectical process.

The BUF's attempts to refute philosophical Marxism also bore the mark of Nietzsche's insights on the 'will-to-power' and the 'superman'. Mosley repudiated the teleological assertion of orthodox Marxism that historical change was an organic process whose outcome was predetermined in advance; for him, this denied the role of individual self-assertion and the 'will' in the life process. Mosley, like Nietzsche, believed that individual striving and the force of 'will' would always overcome matter. In typical Nietzschian fashion, Mosley recoiled in horror, too, at the evolutionary Marxist assumption that the iron law of historical necessity rendered the role of voluntarism redundant. Following Nietzsche, Mosley claimed that fascism was a philosophy of passionate life that repudiated determinism, fatalism and all creeds that advocated surrender. Nietzsche, of course, championed the celebration of life, urging people to return to a more intuitive existence, a Dionysian life of passion as illustrated in the Greek myths.[53] According to Mosley, the BUF's fascism was strongly rooted in the Nietzschian doctrine. Vulgarising Hegel's dialectical method, he argued that

Nietzschian thought and Christianity were capable of synthesis, and that the two apparent opposites had been reconciled in fascism.[54] He declared, piously, that fascism had taken from Christianity the ethos of service, self-abnegation and self-sacrifice in the service of others. From Nietzsche, on the other hand, fascism had absorbed the idea of the virility of struggle and the 'superman' concept, the notion of the heroic 'natural aristocrat' resolutely opposed to the culture of surrender.

We should not forget, too, that the BUF was also intensely preoccupied with matters cultural during the 1930s.[55] We will consider the Mosleyite preoccupation with culture at some length in subsequent chapters, so there is no need to traverse the same ground here.[56]

The focus in the literature on the study of the BUF at the local level has also been helpful in throwing new light on the character of Mosleyite fascism, particularly with regard to its local membership profile and the local context of fascist recruitment.[57] There has also been a recent focus in the historiography on the role of women in the BUF, which has illuminated this hitherto under-researched aspect of the movement.[58] Martin Durham suggested that, contrary to received wisdom, the BUF revealed itself to be radical on women's issues.[59] Among the radical policies advocated by the BUF were women's right to work, equal pay and equality within the state. The BUF also promoted the concept of equal rights within the movement itself. The important activist role of the Blackshirt woman was stressed, too, by Julie Gottlieb. 'Complementing the principle of equality between the sexes was the ideal of co-operation between men and women in building a "Greater Britain"', she asserted.[60]

Having considered both the historiography and ideology of the BUF, including key aspects of Mosley's economic, political and philosophical thought, we will now turn to look at other features associated with the movement. Here we will particularly focus on the BUF's organisational and administrative profile, factionalism within the party, and its general political development. The rational or modernist currents within BUF ideology, the articulation of a detailed programme for economic and political change, always co-existed uneasily with the more irrational impulses within the Mosleyite discourse, as we have seen. Convinced that an economic crisis of major dimensions was imminent, BUF ideology, from the party's inception in October 1932, was invested with an 'apocalyptic' and messianic view of political struggle. This sense of urgency therefore dictated that Mosley reject the gradualist methods of the conventional political parties, in favour of a more dynamic political organisation and style that he judged more suitable to the crisis-ridden climate of British politics. The most noticeable effect of this apocalyptic outlook was the adoption of a paramilitary style that utilised an array of symbols that aimed to convey a sense of heroic struggle and dynamic action, or the notion of politics as drama 'expressed through secular liturgical rites and symbols' which drew inspiration from aesthetic concepts.[61] The negative political effects of this apocalyptic approach to contemporary politics could be seen at all levels of the BUF.

Firstly, militarisation created an excessively bureaucratised and expensive administrative structure at the centre which imposed inevitable financial strains on the BUF. Secondly, the party's paramilitary image led to the recruitment of some volatile individuals, while at the same time alienating potential support from more conventional constituencies.[62] A third factor concerned the overall shape and structure of the BUF in the early period, which was far too amorphous and technically ill-equipped to cope with the objective reality of Britain's political and electoral system. Activism and struggle might be ennobling in the BUF's view, but the 'old heroic fidelities' were qualities too vague to cope with the more technical machinations of electoral politics.[63]

By mid-1934, the National government had managed to bring about a relative upturn in the economy, which provided concrete evidence that the apocalyptic economic collapse predicted by Mosley was failing to materialise. During the same period, the adverse publicity occasioned by aggressive fascist stewarding at the Olympia meeting on 7 June began to exercise an important influence on the public perception of fascist methods.[64] In July 1934 the BUF suffered another major setback when the Rothermere press group severed its links with Mosley.[65] These events undermined Mosley's deterministic view of political crisis, and led to the realisation that the road to political power would demand a protracted political struggle of attrition with the democratic parties. Cumulative internal strains would not lead to a breakdown of the economic and political system. Nor would the BUF be swept spectacularly to power through a mass mobilisation of discontented social groups seeking spiritual and material liberation from a supposedly stagnating and outmoded liberal free-trade capitalism. In July 1934 Mosley had already announced that a more intensive electoral campaign was needed to aggrandise the BUF's support.[66] This trend in the direction of political legality and conventional forms of political behaviour was to accelerate within the coming months. Matters of organisation, however, would soon become entangled in sensitive and vexed questions concerning policy.

The most significant new development in policy that emerged in the aftermath of the summer reversals was the leadership's official endorsement of anti-semitism in September 1934.[67] However, not all elements in the BUF leadership favoured the new direction in policy. Very soon after the change of direction, the leadership divided into a number of mutually hostile ideological cliques, not all of whom were favourably inclined towards adopting an anti-semitic policy. The two most influential factions within the leadership were both disposed towards cultivating an electoral strategy with a view to eventually contesting parliamentary seats in a General Election. They remained seriously divided on other fundamental issues, though. The first group, the political-propaganda faction, which included William Joyce, John Beckett, A. K. Chesterton, William Risdon and Alexander Raven-Thomson, were doctrinal fascists who favoured pursuing a radical and uncompromising fascist propaganda campaign.[68] This faction believed that the way forward in propaganda terms was through platform oratory and the dissemination of literature, with the stress being on the radicalism of the message. Other, more indirect propaganda outlets, which appealed to the emotions rather than the intellect, and which utilised paramilitary marches, pomp and martial music, should be downplayed in the view of this faction. This group, however, favoured retaining the Blackshirt uniform as the enduring symbol of the supposedly virile and heroic struggle of fascism. An important theme in the radical fascist agenda, at least for ideological anti-semites such as Joyce, Beckett and Chesterton, was an unremitting hostility towards Jews.

The second faction, headed by Major-General J. F. C. Fuller and F. M. Box, a former Conservative Party political agent and the BUF's Director of Political Organisation, were equally well disposed towards a broad electoral strategy, although they favoured the development of a more orthodox political campaign based on the style and methods of the conventional parties.[69] This group hoped to broaden the appeal and political base of the BUF and was therefore antagonistic towards paramilitarism and populist demagoguey, which it thought was hindering the recruitment of a 'better type' of member and supporter. Box, in particular, was hostile to both 'physical force' methods and 'Jew-baiting', and believed that these methods, as well as the entire Blackshirt ethos, were antithetical to the future progress of the BUF.[70] This principled opposition, as well as Box's aggressive rationalisation drive to curtail the excess expenditures incurred by the political-propaganda section, ensured that he remained the *bête noire* of the Joyce–Beckett–Chesterton faction throughout the period of internal re-adjustment.[71]

A third faction, led by E. H. Piercy, a former Inspector of Police in control of the BUF's 'I' Squad or 'Storm Troop' section, favoured continuing with the overt paramilitary style and 'physical force' methods of the early days.[72] A relatively marginal but extreme group, inclined towards 'direct action' against both communists and Jews, made up the fourth element in the power configuration.[73]

The cumulative impact of the summer reversals, along with the combined electoral and organisational expertise demonstrated by Box and Fuller, strengthened the influence and hand of the moderates during the protracted period of ideological negotiation between the autumn of 1934 and the summer of 1935. This influence was most noticeable in matters pertaining to organisation. Following a recommendation by Box, centralisation was extended with the liquidation of Area Administration Headquarters, the regions and branches now becoming subject to supervision through a system of visiting National Headquarters inspectors.[74] At National Headquarters, the movement's excessive bureaucracy and expenditure also underwent stringent efficiency measures. The Box–Fuller axe fell most heavily on the extreme radical wing of the Blackshirt movement. The 'virile', paramilitary, barrack-room complexion of the BUF's early phase was de-emphasised, leading to the eventual abolition of National Headquarters and local defence forces in January 1935.[75] The increasingly inactive elite 'I' Squad 'Storm Troop' division simply atrophied, membership dwindling to fifteen by March 1935.[76] The network of fascist 'social clubs' was also eliminated by January 1935.

The desire to craft an efficient electoral machine was finally institutionalised by the major reform initiative of 21 January 1935. This reform would create a new Political Organisation embracing a new category of non-uniformed member.[77] The new Organisation was also equipped with executive powers to develop constituency organisations at the local level. These constituency organisations were eventually to cover the local wards under the direction of a political officer and agent operating from local constituency offices. The radical or revolutionary impulse within the movement did remain, however, albeit in an emasculated form. The uniformed elements were reconstituted within a revised organisational structure based on a unit system consisting of five-member action teams which were to engage in constituency work at ward level.[78]

Although this new 'Blackshirt Command' held joint executive powers with the political section, the thrust of the reforms, as Box and Fuller had intended, was in the direction of more conventional political styles and methods. An efficient electoral machine would aggrandise the BUF's vote and support within the constituencies, while the new non-uniform section would absorb a better category of member, thereby giving the movement a broader political base. In this task, although Blackshirt units provided the 'vital spirit of endeavour' with regard to doorstep canvassing and street propaganda, they were effectively subordinate to the political section on matters pertaining to the now more lucrative and highly valued work of political administration and instruction.[79] These fundamental organisational changes were given broad outline in the Policy Decision of 21 January 1935. With the successful implementation of the Box–Fuller initiatives, the BUF's new electoral strategy and more efficient administrative structure promised greater direction and purpose on the basis of a firmer organisational base.

The Box–Fuller model, however, was to prove a temporary experiment. In May 1935 a further central directive gave notice that the recently created Political Organisation would no longer have executive authority. All existing political organisations would henceforth be required to work under a reconstituted Blackshirt Organisation equipped with comprehensive and sole executive power.[80] The former Political Organisation would now function as a Department of Technical Instruction only, engaged in the operational specifics of electoral organisation.[81]

Although the May re-organisation developed and extended a number of the Box–Fuller initiatives (the creation of a three-tier membership system which retained a non-uniformed members' section, and the realignment of local branch organisations, with the boundaries of these new 'District' branches henceforth corresponding to the geographical profile of a parliamentary constituency or division), the new shift in focus served to reassert the authority of the radical element in the BUF.[82] By July 1935 Box had been transferred to the marginally influential Department of Technical Instruction, his revised political brief to embrace electoral concerns only.[83] With his influence on major issues of policy at an end, an important force for political moderation within the party apparatus had been effectively defeated. By mid-1935, both doctrinal fascists and ideological anti-semites within the BUF were firmly in the ascendancy.

The May re-organisation can be understood partly as yet another stage in the continual and chronic process of rationalisation and retrenchment that had afflicted the BUF since its formation. In addition, Mosley's lack of patience, and his messianic view of political struggle, did not always incline him towards the incrementalist and gradualist political strategies advocated by the moderates. The balance of forces within the party leadership had also shifted decisively against the Box faction by May 1935. The radicals' repeated assertions that recent internal reforms had eroded fundamental fascist principles would eventually influence Mosley's thinking. In addition, national and other factors also shaped developments.

The period between mid-1934 and mid-1935 was not an auspicious one for the BUF. It would be characterised by Mosley presiding over a sharply contracting membership base. Apart from minor successes, of which the Albert Hall rally in October 1934 was one, the party was unable to regain the momentum of earlier years.[84] Mosley's economic programme had lost its cutting edge following the improvement in the economy by mid-1934, and, as yet, there was no major national issue around which the membership and potential support could mobilise. The Italian-Abyssinian peace campaign would not gather momentum until the latter half of 1935. Regional campaigns which targeted local issues proved disappointing, too, with Mosley's Lancashire cotton campaign in January and February having little effect.[85]

This gloomy prognosis was mirrored in local and national membership patterns, which saw membership and support fall sharply in all regions during August and September 1934, register a marginal improvement in the following two months, only to plummet sharply again as March approached.[86] By early May 1935, many London branches were fragmenting, with resignations and disaffection widespread.[87] The condition of provincial branches followed a similar pattern, with only the Lancashire region reporting progress.[88] This far-from-optimistic picture had the effect of throwing the more ambitious projections of the Box–Fuller initiatives into sharp relief, with small memberships in particular making it extremely difficult to build efficient constituency and ward organisations in a locality.

It is important to consider the BUF's organisational development and the turn towards anti-semitism in the context of organised opposition from anti-fascist groups. The period between 1933 and 1935 was notable for the Communist Party's aggressive opposition to the BUF, inspired by the former's successful mass mobilisations against the fascists at Mosley's Olympia and Hyde Park meetings.[89] In the short term, leftist 'maximum force' tactics closed off many of the BUF's main propaganda outlets, thereby hindering its operational effectiveness. In other respects, such tactics precluded the possibility of the BUF conducting conventional political activity on the pattern of orthodox political parties as advocated by the moderates. Conversely, militant opposition had the effect of buttressing the arguments of radical fascists who wished to retain the pugnacious character of the early spirit of the movement. For many of these doctrinal fascists, 'maximum force' communism and Jewish anti-fascist militancy were part of the same continuous anti-patriotic tradition. These developments therefore assisted them in their efforts to push the BUF in the direction of aggressive populist street campaigning and militant, open anti-semitism.

These trends in the direction of open anti-semitism were given official sanction in a decision of October 1935, when radical elements within the leadership were given *carte blanche* to exploit, with whatever means available, the party's successes in the East End.[90] With the appointment of the abrasive ideological anti-semite 'Jock' Houston to the paid staff of BUF speakers the same month, and the resignation of the anti-'physical force' moderate F. M. Box announced in December 1935, the BUF's radical campaign was now fully under way.[91]

The eclipse of the 'moderate' Box–Fuller axis within the leadership apparatus by late 1935 represented an important tactical and ideological victory for the doctrinal fascists of the Political-Propaganda bloc. Despite this development, the fundamental issues of organisation and policy raised during the acrimonious factional disputes of the previous two years remained principally unresolved. The political and strategic imperatives which emerged as 1936 approached continued to demand the construction of an efficient and durable political machine. This continued preoccupation with organisational and administrative efficiency generated a renewed undercurrent of tension within the party apparatus. The following phase of readjustment, therefore, was again characterised by internal instability and personal rivalries between BUF elites. And, as with the earlier round of factional disputes, matters of organisation were inexorably linked to questions of policy and political strategy.

In early 1936 the BUF introduced a number of important innovations and structural changes. In January the arrival of *Action*, a new weekly newspaper, was announced.[92] A revised uniform system was also introduced in January. Issued to elite Division One members as a reward for commitment and service, the new paramilitary 'Action Press' uniform was designed to better represent the movement's evolving meritocratic structure.[93] The same month, the BUF's administrative structure again underwent reorganisation.[94] The Operations were henceforth divided into two administrative regions, Southern and Northern Zones, with the latter operating from a newly constituted Northern Area Headquarters in Manchester.[95]

A new administrative body, the Department of Organisation, was also created in January 1936. It would replace the former 'Blackshirt Organisation', and was invested with executive authority over the movement's entire administrative and political functions.[96] N. L. M. Francis-Hawkins, a meticulous bureaucrat formerly in charge of the now defunct 'Blackshirt Organisation', and former member of the British Fascisti, was appointed 'Director-General of Organisation' and was placed in overall control of the new department.[97] The promotion of Francis-Hawkins would eventually prove the most significant of the January changes. With B. D. E. Donovan and H. H. Hone, both close confidants of Hawkins, appointed Assistant Director-General Administration, 'Northern Zone' and 'Southern Zone' respectively, a rival source of political authority to the Propaganda group had emerged within the party apparatus.[98]

Relations between the two groups were already strained by late 1935, Francis-Hawkins incurring the hostility of the Propaganda section for his persistent attempts to aggrandise the power and influence of the 'Blackshirt Organisation' at the expense of rival departments within the party machine.[99] Fundamentally, the difference between the two groups pivoted on the issue of whether to give priority to matters of organisation or policy. Whereas the Francis-Hawkins faction advocated building an efficient political machine on the basis of a technically competent administrative base, the doctrinal fascists of the Propaganda bloc continued to argue for the promotion of a vigorous propaganda campaign with the stress on the intellectual content of the fascist message. To widen the division, the former group was convinced that the most effective way to win over potential supporters was to penetrate their psychological rather than intellectual constitution via the medium of paramilitary marches, bands and fascist symbolism.[100] This embittered debate between the 'Organisers' and the 'Policy' group remained a source of dissension within the leadership bloc during the following critical conjuncture of development.

In general, by mid-1936, apart from the increase in support in east London, both regional and national membership patterns were showing a marked downward trend. In March 1936 the BUF's national membership was estimated at 4,000 active members, this figure the culmination of a steady regression during the previous twelve months.[101] In many respects, east London and the anti-semitic campaign apart, a declining membership and the progressive geographical fragmentation of the national movement reflected the ineffectiveness of much of the BUF's political programme and strategy by 1936. National campaigns continued to play an important role for the BUF, providing the opportunity for temporary patriotic mobilisations around emotive contemporary issues. The death of King George V in January 1936 allowed for a recrudescence of the BUF's pro-monarchist sentiment, which was to reach its apotheosis in the abdication crisis of December 1936.[102] The outbreak of the Spanish Civil War, and Stalinist excesses in a fresh round of party purges and executions in the summer of 1936, would also give fresh impetus to the BUF's anti-communist propaganda.[103]

Elements of a new peace campaign were also being constructed in early 1936. Italian victory in Abyssinia in May 1936 had formally concluded the BUF's earlier 'Mind Britain's Business' peace campaign. Hitler's occupation of the Rhineland in March, however, generated further international tension and precipitated a new peace effort on the part of Mosley. This new peace campaign, moreover, was being put together at the same time as it became apparent that there was a closer approximation to the spirit of German National Socialism. This new departure resulted in a declining attachment to Italy and Italian Fascism, and was formally institutionalised by the acquisition of 'National Socialist' in the title of the movement in June 1936.[104]

The provisional and often unpredictable nature of these national campaigns, however, proved unsuitable as a basis for building a mass party, and BUF strategists continued to emphasise the long-term importance of developing industrial programmes and trade union propaganda.[105] To compound matters, the growing success of the east London campaign meant that this area was absorbing a disproportionate share of the BUF's political attention and resources.[106] More disconcerting for the BUF's progress was the deliberate undermining of its industrial propaganda programme by certain 'Organisation' officials within the leadership, who were less favourably inclined towards such a strategy.[107]

The evolution of Mosley's primarily ethnocentric and conspiratorial anti-semitism continued during 1936.[108] In his Albert Hall speech of 22 March 1936, his verbal attacks on the Jews and his characteristically xenophobic references to 'Jewish international power' were said to exceed by far his previous pronouncements on this matter.[109] An even closer attachment to the spirit of German National Socialism was in evidence also during this period.[110]

That year, 1936, also witnessed a proliferation of anti-fascist organisations and a mounting and varied campaign of opposition to the BUF. At least prior to October 1936, the majority of anti-fascist meetings in the capital continued to be organised by the Communist Party.[111] By the autumn of 1936 the anti-fascist bloc was beginning to alter its complexion, particularly in London, with parallel formations now engaging the BUF on a much wider front than hitherto.[112] At the Absa House Conference on 26 July 1936, the Jewish People's Council Against Fascism and Anti-Semitism was founded.[113] The Ex-Servicemen's Movement Against Fascism was formed in the summer of 1936, too, and by August 1936 was one of the largest anti-fascist movements in the capital outside the Communist Party of Great Britain (CPGB).[114] Similarly in mid-1936, in an attempt to counter the increasing defamation of the Anglo-Jewish community, a Co-ordinating Defence Committee was established by the Board of Deputies of British Jews, under the secretaryship of the Board's Press Officer, Sidney Salomon.[115]

A number of smaller, less prominent, *ad hoc* anti-fascist organisations functioned on the periphery of the main centres of fascist/anti-fascist confrontations. These groups, which included the British Democratic Association, the British Union of Democrats, and the Legion of Blue and White Shirts, managed to attract only marginal support and interest during their brief life-spans.[116] The Labour and trade union movements, and the National Council for

Civil Liberties, also engaged the BUF at this juncture.[117] A Council of Citizens of East London, which aimed to counter the BUF in the East End by restoring a 'spirit of harmony' to the area, was also formed in October 1936 under the secretaryship of Dr J. J. Mallon.[118]

By October 1936 it was becoming increasingly difficult to contain the dynamic of accelerating fascist/anti-fascist conflict in the area of the BUF's most visible presence in Britain, east London. On 4 October 1936 a large anti-fascist mobilisation physically checked the BUF's attempt to conduct a series of anniversary propaganda marches in the East End. The popular local mythology surrounding the 'Cable Street' events suggests that the anti-fascist mobilisation represented a practical and symbolic victory, the repercussions of which effectively checked Mosley's campaign in east London.[119] This interpretation requires some qualification. Contrary to the above view, the immediate portents for the Mosleyites following the Sunday disturbances were favourable.

In the following week, the BUF held its most successful series of propaganda meetings since its inception.[120] Audiences estimated in the several thousands attended BUF meetings in Stepney, Shoreditch, Bethnal Green and Stoke Newington.[121] More significant was the mood of these audiences, which was manifestly pro-fascist in orientation. The BUF's membership also increased significantly immediately subsequent to 4 October. From an original membership of 2,750 recorded earlier in the year, the 'London Command' recruited 2,000 additional members in the three weeks following the Sunday disturbances.[122]

In many respects, however, the events of October 1936 represented a parenthesis in the normal evolution of the BUF. For a brief period in October, the BUF had set in motion a significant mass-based, pro-fascist mobilisation in east London. But the potential for violence inherent in the evolving political situation eventually led the government to take firm legislative action to contain the conflict. On 9 November 1936 the Home Secretary introduced the first stages of the Public Order Bill into Parliament.

The Public Order Act finally became effective from 1 January 1937.[123] The wearing of political uniforms was to be prohibited in public places except on certain specified ceremonial occasions under Section 1 of the Act, while Section 2 forbade the formation of quasi-military organisations designed to usurp the normal functions of the police and army.[124] Section 2 prohibited the employment or display of physical force to promote political objectives.[125] A third section of the Act granted chief constables a discretionary power to regulate public processions for up to three months, and, subject to the consent of the Home Secretary and the Local Government Authority, prohibit all processions in a given area indefinitely. The Act's final sections banned the possession of offensive weapons at public meetings, and widened the legal scope and application of the offence of 'insulting words and behaviour' in public speeches which were likely to lead to breaches of the peace.

The Act's major provisions were targeted specifically at the BUF's political activities rather than fascism as a political or philosophical creed, and reasserted the role of the state as the principal social-control agency.[126] The Act, which both strengthened and extended the existing law, also reflected traditional police grievances against the BUF, particularly as enshrined in the determination to prohibit political uniforms and quasi-military organisations.[127] In addition, the Public Order Act clearly demonstrated the determination of the liberal-democratic state to preserve the political status quo.[128]

The BUF responded to the Public Order Act by instituting a series of comprehensive changes designed to de-emphasise its paramilitary structure. In December 1936 the Director-General of Organisation issued special instructions to de-militarise the party's administrative structure and operational procedures.[129] The new regulations and non-military titles were eventually encoded in a revised constitution which became operative in 1938.[130]

The effects of the Public Order Act on the subsequent progress of the BUF is difficult to gauge. Some historians have suggested that the negative psychological impact of the uniform ban, for example, was a causal factor in the BUF's long-term decline.[131] While it is important not to underestimate the effects of de-militarisation on the BUF's self-image, the perception it had of itself as a virile party of dynamic action, it is doubtful whether this seriously impeded its future political progress. Since its formation, there existed a particular ideological constituency within the BUF who believed that a paramilitary profile was damaging to the party's public image.[132] This particular grouping, therefore, welcomed the paramilitary downgrading and the shift towards a more conventional political approach.

In the months following the introduction of the Public Order Bill in Parliament, there was a noticeable decline in the incidents of public disorder arising from fascist and anti-fascist confrontations.[133]

The Public Order Act, though, did not completely stop the disorder or political violence.[134] Political violence was particularly in evidence at the BUF's fifth anniversary propaganda march in Bermondsey, on 3 October 1937, when 106 persons were arrested primarily for public order offences.[135]

The Public Order Act had an impact on the complexion of the east London anti-semitic campaign, too, which by late 1936 and early 1937 was characterised by a decline in the BUF's more abusive anti-semitic platform propaganda.[136] A decrease in the number of abusive anti-Jewish references by East End Mosleyite speakers was observed as early as August 1936, and was partly a result of the increase in police vigilance which followed the Home Secretary's July directives on fascist 'Jew-baiting'.[137] This more cautious and restrained approach on the BUF's part, however, also reflected inner tensions within its policy apparatus. Elements within the leadership were becoming increasingly concerned that the continuation of the existing aggressive policy of open anti-semitism was alienating public opinion and potential support.[138]

The Act's significance for anti-semitism concerned the way in which its deterrent measures continued to compromise the shape and form of anti-Jewish propaganda. Its effect was to accelerate divisions within the leadership with regard to the prominence to be given to a policy of open anti-semitism within the BUF's programme. It was significant that as early as November 1936, William Joyce, the foremost advocate of the policy of open anti-semitism, was already out of favour with Oswald Mosley.[139] Joyce's progressive marginalisation was to continue unabated during the months following the Public Order Act's introduction.

Despite the obstacles put in its way by the Public Order Act, the BUF continued to press its political campaign during early 1937. On 3 March 1937 it contested a number of east London seats, in Bethnal Green, Shoreditch and Limehouse, at the London County Council (LCC) elections.[140] The decision was consistent with Mosley's commitment to a long-term constitutional and electoral strategy conceived in the period of reappraisal following the mid-1934 reversals. The results of the March elections saw all six BUF candidates fail in their endeavours to gain representation on the London County Council.[141]

The March election unfolded at a critical conjuncture in the BUF's history, a period which witnessed the intensification of personal rivalry between the Francis-Hawkins and Joyce factions. The endemic rationalisation process within the BUF's administrative structure continued unabated throughout 1936. As at previous junctures, a phase of internal re-organisation became the occasion for manoeuvring by party functionaries seeking to strengthen their respective power bases within the party machine. The increasing pre-eminence of the 'Organisation' faction, gradually extending its influence under Francis-Hawkins's patronage, was further underlined by a series of tactical advances in late 1936 and early 1937.

On 19 October 1936 Francis-Hawkins assumed overall control of all Headquarters staffing arrangements and internal affairs of the movement, and by early November was stated to be the most powerful element in Mosley's advisory council.[142] The progressive transfer of powers to the Francis-Hawkins group was evidence of William Joyce's diminished influence on the major areas of decision-making. The Department of Organisation's overall control of the administration and direction of the March 1937 LCC election campaign provided further evidence of this internal transition.[143]

The subsequent failure to capture an east London seat at the LCC elections would lead to a further bout of recrimination. John Beckett, for example, accused the Department of Organisation of unfounded optimism regarding the party's election prospects, as well as technical incompetence in the administration of the overall campaign.[144] Only one week after the LCC elections result was announced, the BUF was hit by a major crisis.

On 11 March 1937 a widespread reduction in Headquarters personnel was announced, to be undertaken in conjunction with a fundamental restructuring of the movement's organisational machinery.[145] The rationale behind these drastic measures was to enable 'the Movement to husband its resources for the great fights that are to come'.[146] The re-organisation was precipitated by a 70 per cent reduction in expenditure, a clear indication that the BUF had experienced a drastic reduction in subventions hitherto received from foreign sources. In 1935, at the height of Mussolini's Abyssinian campaign, the BUF received a total of £86,000 from Italian sources.[147] In 1937 the total subsidy received from foreign sources had dropped to £7,630.[148] Among the administrative changes to be made was the termination of the North–South zonal system, the closing of the Northern regional offices in Manchester, and the subsequent concentration of all the BUF's administrative and political functions in the London Headquarters.[149] Staffing reductions also meant the dismissal of the BUF's paid regional organisers and a modification of the visiting National Inspectorate system.[150]

The significance of the March retrenchment on the composition and complexion of the party apparatus and the policy-making machinery was even more far-reaching. The dismissal of party personnel was comprehensive, extending to high-ranking officials at the apex of the movement, many of whom tendered their resignations in acrimonious circumstances.[151] At National Headquarters only a skeleton staff of fifty-seven paid and voluntary personnel remained from a previous total of 129.[152] Among the senior officials discharged were William Joyce and John Beckett and the majority of personnel from the Policy Propaganda Department.[153] All the paid national staff speakers, hitherto under the jurisdiction of the Policy Propaganda Department, were also dismissed. A decision of 15 March 1937 then placed Francis-Hawkins in overall control of the BUF's entire administrative and political machinery, finally and emphatically signalling that the destruction of the Joyce–Beckett power base in the movement was complete.[154]

The eclipse of the Policy Propaganda faction, and the eventual absorption of the BUF's political functions into a single, centrally administered command structure under Francis-Hawkins's stewardship, represented a comprehensive victory for those elements in the leadership who believed that bureaucratic efficiency should always prevail over doctrinal matters. It was also a victory for the quasi-military 'Blackshirt' elements within the leadership over rival fascists who preferred to emphasise the intellectual and ideological dimension of fascist politics. The most significant development in this regard was that the exodus of Joyce, Beckett and other doctrinal fascists represented the elimination of many of the more zealous ideological anti-semites from the major centres of decision-making. On 2 April 1937 Joyce and Beckett formed the violently anti-semitic, extreme pro-Nazi, National Socialist League.[155] The elimination of the Joyce–Beckett configuration appeared to signal, therefore, a re-orientation away from the more violent forms of anti-semitism.

Structural imperatives, principally a desire to stabilise a party machine that was rapidly imploding due to financial incompetence and mismanagement, was the principal factor behind the March retrenchment and the eventual demise of the Propaganda bloc. If the BUF was to continue to function as a viable political force, it was imperative, as Mosley correctly came to realise, to give priority to matters of administrative and financial efficiency over purely doctrinal concerns.

The cumulative effect of the LCC election defeat and the March retrenchment was a major downturn in the BUF's activities and political fortunes.[156] The provinces presented a particularly depressed picture. By mid-1937 there was no effective organisation in Birmingham, Lincolnshire, Manchester, Liverpool and Carlisle.[157] There was also no organisational machinery in place in South Wales, a situation exacerbated by the transfer of the area's solitary regional organiser, T. P. 'Tommy' Moran, to Northampton.[158] In the entire Lancashire area the combined active membership was estimated at a little in excess of 100, with a dearth of effective propaganda in most of the main urban conurbations in that region.[159] By October 1937, the total active membership in Lancashire had plummeted still further, and was half the mid-1937 figure.[160] With the Northern Headquarters now defunct, and the Regional Organiser and National Inspectorate systems moribund in the wake of the March crisis, Mosley's provincial organisational infrastructure appeared to be falling into irreversible decay as his party entered 1938.

This far-from-optimistic position was made worse by the wholly inadequate and inefficient voluntary National Inspectorate system, which, from the outset, suffered from a lack of quality personnel.[161] In the view of some contemporary observers, the BUF was entering into a state of terminal decline. In April 1937 the Home Secretary informed Neville Laski that it was the opinion of the Home Office that 'the Fascist movement was dying'.[162] A short time later, Laski himself expressed the view that 'I am satisfied that this man [Mosley] is at the bottom of the graph of his progress'.[163]

The November 1937 Metropolitan Borough Council elections would provide a temporary issue around which the membership could mobilise. The financial stringency and extension of decentralisation following the March crisis, however, meant that local BUF district formations were forced to subsidise their election efforts from local election funds.[164] Following rather low-key campaigns, the subsequent election results proved extremely discouraging for the Mosleyites, with no gains recorded, even in the BUF's East End strongholds.[165] During the same period concern was again expressed by Mosley regarding the BUF's current financial position.[166] At this same juncture, he embarked on another of his periodic administrative reorganisations with the various London districts being reorganised under a new London area system.[167]

By early 1938, the movement's prospects looked bleak, with an estimated active membership of just 5,800, and more than half of this figure concentrated in the London area.[168] Diminishing finances precipitated a further round of staffing reductions at National Headquarters in February 1938.[169] By Spring 1938, Mosley was deprived of one of his foremost propagandists, A. K. Chesterton, who resigned, reportedly disillusioned by the encroachment of the Francis-Hawkins faction into the area of policy-propaganda.[170]

The year 1938 also witnessed a further reorientation and change in the BUF's character, as the leadership continued to seek ways to circumvent the propaganda restrictions imposed on it by the Public Order Act. More vigorous attempts were made to attract private traders, small businessmen and professionals, with the leadership encouraging its membership cadres to penetrate private trading and professional bodies.[171]

Developments within the international arena, however, would initiate the most significant reorientation and change in profile. In March 1938 Hitler invaded Austria and, amid a growing international crisis that threatened to drag Britain into war, inadvertently helped re-launch the BUF's peace campaign. The gathering war clouds provided Mosley with substantial propaganda raw material, which he used to develop a new anti-war policy. This anti-war policy would be one of the main planks of the party's political programme from late 1938 through to September 1939. Moreover, this new policy shift was instrumental in reviving Mosley's waning political fortunes during this latter phase of the BUF's life.

The new policy received its biggest impetus as a result of the Czechoslovakian crisis of September and early October 1938. In the wake of this international event, the BUF proceeded to organise a series of high-profile demonstrations in the West End, Whitehall and Downing Street in September 1938.[172] The decrease in international tension that followed the signing of the Munich agreement of 29 September 1938 temporarily checked the momentum of the peace campaign by early to mid October 1938. By March 1939, the campaign had resumed in earnest. The German annexation of Bohemia which began on 15 March, and Chamberlain's guarantee to Poland later that month, generated a resurgence of intensive Mosleyite anti-war activity.[173] On 25 March Mosley declared that 'the jackals of Jewish finance are again in full cry for war'.[174] In April the BUF press attacked the system of security pacts and guarantees for creating a situation of 'collective insecurity' and increasing the likelihood of war.[175] The Polish state, apparently 'mortgaged to Jewry' and the City of London, was condemned, too.[176] The BUF's anti-war campaign would continue unabated until the outbreak of hostilities on 3 September 1939. It would reach its climax with the indoor public meeting at the Exhibition Hall, Earls Court, on 16 July, where Mosley addressed an audience of approximately 11,000.[177] The outbreak of war did not deter the BUF from pursuing its peace campaign. Thus the government, empowered by Defence Regulation 18b (1A), decided to wind up the BUF's campaign when it moved to arrest Mosley and leading party officials in May 1940. Finally, on 10 July 1940, the government, further empowered by Defence Regulation 18b (AA), pronounced the BUF an illegal organisation.

Notes

1 S. Cullen, 'Leaders and Martyrs: Codreanu, Mosley and Jose Antonio', *History*, 71, 4 (October 1986), pp. 408–30.
2 J. Stevenson and C. Cook, *The Slump. Society and Politics During the Depression* (London, Quartet, 1979), p. 2.
3 R. Skidelsky, *Oswald Mosley* (London, Macmillan, 1981), p. 302.
4 W. F. Mandle, 'Sir Oswald Mosley's Resignation from the Labour Government', *Historical Studies*, 10 (May 1963), pp. 493–510, remains the best discussion of the Memorandum and the events surrounding its release.
5 Particularly the deployment of the Black and Tans. See Skidelsky, *Oswald Mosley*, pp. 96–101.
6 O. Mosley and J. Strachey, *Revolution by Reason* (Birmingham, Birmingham Labour Party, 1925). See also J. M. Lipkis, 'The Odd Couple: Oswald Mosley and John Strachey', *Continuity*, 13 (1989), pp. 31–57.
7 R. Skidelsky, 'Great Britain', in S. J. Woolf (ed.), *Fascism in Europe* (London, Methuen, 1981), p. 260.
8 Mosley was expelled from the Labour Party on 10 March 1931.
9 W. F. Mandle, 'The New Party', *Historical Studies*, 12 (October 1966), pp. 343–55.
10 Ibid., p. 344.
11 Skidelsky, *Oswald Mosley*, p. 286.
12 Mandle, 'The New Party', p. 345.
13 R. Benewick, *Political Violence and Public Order* (London, Allen Lane, 1969), p. 78; B. S. Farr, *The Development and Impact of Right-Wing Politics in Britain, 1903-1932* (New York, Garland, 1987), p. 86, on eugenics.

14 Farr, *The Development and Impact*, p. 81.
15 O. Mosley, *The Greater Britain* (London, Greater Britain Publications, 1932).
16 See, for example, A. Raven-Thomson, *The Economics of British Fascism* (London, Bonner and Company, 1935). For a discussion of the BUF's ideas, see Benewick, *Political Violence*, pp. 132–68; N. Nugent, 'The Ideas of the British Union of Fascists', in N. Nugent and R. King, *The British Right. Conservative and Right Wing Politics in Britain* (Farnborough, Saxon, 1977); S. Cullen, 'The Development of the Ideas and Policy of the British Union of Fascists, 1932–40', *Journal of Contemporary History*, 22 (1987), pp. 115–36.
17 R. Thurlow, 'The Return of Jeremiah: The Rejected Knowledge of Sir Oswald Mosley in the 1930s', in K. Lunn and R. Thurlow (eds), *British Fascism* (London, Croom Helm, 1980), pp. 100–13.
18 Skidelsky, *Oswald Mosley*, p. 226.
19 Nugent, 'The Ideas of the British Union of Fascists', p. 141.
20 Ibid., p. 139.
21 Mosley, *The Greater Britain*, p. 21.
22 A. Raven-Thomson, *The Coming Corporate State* (London, Great Britain Publications, 1935), p. 34.
23 Mosley, *The Greater Britain*, p. 21. The 'Orders' would become law after a period of seven days if unchallenged by Parliament.
24 Ibid., pp. 26–7.
25 Skidelsky was an early forerunner here. Skidelsky, *Oswald Mosley*, pp. 234–45, on the link with Joseph Chamberlain, for example.
26 This link is discussed at some length in Chapter One above.
27 B. Semmel, *Imperialism and Social Reform. English Social-Imperial Thought* (London, Allen and Unwin, 1960), p. 248.
28 Benewick, *Political Violence*, pp. 132–68.
29 Ibid., pp. 12–14.
30 D. M. Geiger, 'British Fascism as Revealed in the British Union of Fascists' Press' (Ph.D. thesis, New York University, 1963), p. 310.
31 D. S. Lewis, *Illusions of Grandeur. Mosley, Fascism and British Society, 1931–81* (Manchester, Manchester University Press, 1987), p. 262.
32 Nugent, 'The Ideas of the British Union of Fascists', p. 145.
33 See comments in R. Thurlow, *Fascism in Britain. A History, 1918–1985* (Oxford, Blackwell, 1987), p. 146.
34 Cullen, 'The Development of the Ideas and Policy'.
35 S. Cullen, 'Political Violence: The Case of the British Union of Fascists', *Journal of Contemporary History*, 28 (1993), pp. 245–67.
36 I wonder about the relevance of such research as this. If Cullen's findings on this are accurate, it should come as no great surprise to scholars that anti-fascists organised a large amount of political violence against the BUF, given the Communist and Jewish memories of

the brutality of fascist and Nazi violence against their political opponents on the continent.
37 Lewis, *Illusions of Grandeur*, p. 56.
38 Ibid. pp. 262–8.
39 Farr, *The Development and Impact*, pp. 87 and 91.
40 L. Susser, 'Fascism, Literary Modernism and Modernization: The British Case', *Tel Aviver Jahrbuch für Deutsche Geschichte*, Part 18 (1989), pp. 463–86.
41 Ibid., p. 464. See also J. Herf, *Reactionary Modernism. Technology, Culture and Politics in Weimar and the Third Reich* (Cambridge, Cambridge University Press, 1984).
42 Ibid., p. 481.
43 The scholarship of Skidelsky and Thurlow has been crucial in this regard. Steven Woodbridge, too, has cogently analysed some of the pivotal philosophical ideas in 1920s and 1930s British fascist thought. Woodbridge concluded that British fascist ideology was a novel political movement, in that it aimed to unify, harmonise and invigorate the nation, society and 'race' in line with its 'anti-declinist' and synthesising philosophical vision. See S. Woodbridge, 'The Nature and Development of the Concept of National Synthesis in British Fascist Ideology, 1920–1940' (Ph.D. thesis, University of Kingston, 1997).
44 O. Spengler, *The Decline of the West. Perspectives of World-History. Vols One and Two* (London, Allen and Unwin, 1918, 1922).
45 J. Drennan, *BUF Oswald Mosley and British Fascism* (London, John Murray, 1934), pp. 194–201.
46 *Fascist Week*, 9–15 February 1934, p. 4.
47 Drennan, *BUF Oswald Mosley*.
48 O. Mosley, *My Life* (London, Thomas Nelson, 1968), p. 224. See also L. Susser, 'Fascist and Anti-Fascist Attitudes in Britain Between the Wars' (Ph.D. thesis, University of Oxford, 1988), pp. 33–4.
49 Thurlow, *Fascism in Britain. A History*, p. 19.
50 Economic determinism represents a vulgarised version of Marx's thought. The richness and complexity of Marxist thought can only be gauged by reading Marx's later economic writings in conjunction with his earlier humanist essays. For an example of this 'humanist' writing, see K. Marx, *The German Ideology*, in *Collected Works, Vol. 5* (London, Lawrence and Wishart, 1976).
51 Mosley, *My Life*, p. 329 contains a transcript of a speech he made to the English Speaking Union in March 1933 in which he attacks Marxist determinism.
52 Ibid., p. 321.
53 On Nietzsche, see F. Copleston, *Frederich Nietzsche. Philosopher of Culture* (London, Search Press, 1975); and R. Hollinrake, *Nietzsche, Wagner, and the Philosophy of Pessimism* (London, Allen and

Unwin, 1982). On Nietzsche and fascism, see W. Howard, 'Nietzsche and Fascism', *History of European Ideas*, 11 (1989), pp. 893–99.
54   O. Mosley, 'The Philosophy of Fascism', *FQ*, 1, 1 (January 1935), pp. 35–46.
55   In many respects this concern with culture flowed from the 'palingenetic' strain within its ideology. We are grateful to Roger Griffin for developing this concept. See R. Griffin, *The Nature of Fascism* (London, Routledge, 1993), pp. 32–6.
56   See below, Chapters Eight to Eleven.
57   See in particular, T. Linehan, *East London for Mosley. The British Union of Fascists in East London and South-West Essex, 1933–40* (London, Frank Cass, 1996); S. J. Rawnsley, 'Fascism and Fascists in the North of England in the 1930s' (Ph.D. thesis, University of Bradford, 1983); J. D. Brewer, *Mosley's Men. The BUF in the West Midlands* (Aldershot, Gower Publishing, 1984); A. Mitchell, 'Fascism in East Anglia: The British Union of Fascists in Norfolk, Suffolk and Essex, 1933–1940' (Ph.D. thesis, University of Sheffield, 1999); D. Turner, *Fascism and Anti-Fascism in the Medway Towns 1927–1940* (Rochester, Kent Anti-Fascist Action Committee, 1993); *The British Union of Fascists in Yorkshire 1933–40* (Trevelyan Scholarship Project, n.p., 1960: copy held at University of Bradford Library); L. Kibblewhite and A. Rigby, *Fascism in Aberdeen. Street Politics in the 1930s* (Aberdeen, Aberdeen People's Press, 1978); and C. J. F. Morley, 'Fascist Promise, and the Capitalist Alternative: An Analysis of Sussex Coast Fascism Between the Wars' (M.A. thesis, n.p., 1982: copy held at Wiener Library). There is also a useful unpublished local study of the BUF in Kingston, Surrey, by J. Wallder, which is currently deposited at the University of Kingston Library.
58   M. Durham, *Women and Fascism* (London, Routledge, 1998); J. Gottlieb, 'Women and Fascism in Inter-war Britain' (Ph.D. thesis, University of Cambridge, 1998); and T. Kushner, 'Politics and Race, Gender and Class: Refugees, Fascists and Domestic Service in Britain, 1933–1940', in T. Kushner and K. Lunn (eds), *The Politics of Marginality. Race, the Radical Right and Minorities in Twentieth-Century Britain* (London, Frank Cass, 1990).
59   Durham, *Women and Fascism*, p. 170.
60   Gottlieb, 'Women and Fascism', p. 77.
61   Z. Sternhell, 'Fascist Ideology', in W. Laqueur (ed.), *Fascism. A Reader's Guide* (London, Wildwood House, 1976), p. 363.
62   In April 1934 members were expelled from the BUF's Brixton Branch for their 'loose moral behaviour', while there was frequent trouble in the Paddington Branch associated with the ex-IRA man and Branch Organiser Patrick Mahon; see PRO HO144/20140/251-2, Special Branch Report, 11 April 1934; HO144/20140/288-9, Special

Branch Report, 15 March 1934.
63   The 'old heroic fidelities' of 'courage, service and self-sacrifice' according to A. K. Chesterton.
64   For the BUF's reaction to this adverse Olympia publicity, see *Blackshirt*, 15 June 1934, pp. 1–3, and 22 June 1934, p. 1.
65   See *Daily Mail*, 19 July 1934, pp. 12–13.
66   *Blackshirt*, 6 July 1934, p. 5.
67   Mosley's speeches at Belle Vue, Manchester, on 29 September 1934, and at the Albert Hall, London, on 28 October 1934, were pivotal in giving official endorsement to a policy of open anti-semitism within the BUF. See C. Holmes, *Antisemitism in British Society, 1876–1939* (London, Arnold, 1979), pp. 175–298.
68   PRO HO144/20144/233–6, Special Branch Report, 17 December 1934.
69   Ibid; see also HO144/20144/122–30, The Fascist Movement in the United Kingdom Excluding Northern Ireland, Report No. 5. Developments to the end of February 1935.
70   PRO HO144/20142/313–15, Special Branch Report, 18 October 1934.
71   For the smouldering resentment against Box, see PRO HO144/20145/221–5, Special Branch Report, 17 July 1935.
72   PRO HO144/20144/233–6, Special Branch Report, 17 December 1934.
73   Ibid.
74   PRO HO144/20144/276, Special Branch Report, 6 December 1934; HO144/20144/229–31, Special Branch Report, 20 December 1934.
75   On the January changes, see *Blackshirt*, 18 January 1935, pp. 1–2.
76   PRO HO144/20144/141–2, Special Branch Report, 6 March 1935.
77   *Blackshirt*, 18 January 1935, pp. 1–2; see also *Blackshirt*, 1 February 1935, p. 1; and PRO HO144/20145/203–6, Special Branch Report, 22 July 1935, Serial Orders 1/8.
78   The black shirt was to be accorded to those who rendered 'conspicuous service' to the 'cause'. See *Blackshirt*, 18 January 1935, pp. 1–2.
79   Ibid. See also PRO HO144/20144/122–30, The Fascist Movement in the United Kingdom Excluding Northern Ireland, Report No. 5, Developments to the end of February 1935.
80   See *Blackshirt*, 24 May 1935, p. 2; PRO HO144/20145/203–6, Special Branch Report, 22 July 1935, regarding the executive decision of 3 May 1935.
81   Ibid.
82   The three-tier membership system embraced a non-uniform Division Three category. Division One and Two members would have the 'privilege' of wearing the Blackshirt uniform. Divisional status One and Two was dependent on varying degrees of commitment to the fascist cause.

83 PRO HO144/20145/221–5, Special Branch Report, 17 July 1935.
84 PRO HO144/20144/261–9, The Fascist Movement in the United Kingdom Excluding Northern Ireland, Report No. 4, Developments October–November 1934.
85 PRO HO144/20144/122–30, The Fascist Movement in the United Kingdom Excluding Northern Ireland, Report No. 5, Developments to end of February 1935.
86 PRO HO144/20142/214–16, The Fascist Movement in the United Kingdom Excluding Northern Ireland, Report No. 3, Developments August–September 1934; HO144/20144/261–9, The Fascist Movement in the United Kingdom Excluding Northern Ireland, Report No. 4, Developments October–November 1934; HO144/20144/122–30, The Fascist Movement in the United Kingdom Excluding Northern Ireland, Report No. 5, Developments to end of February 1935.
87 PRO HO144/20144/45–48, Special Branch Report, 9 May 1935.
88 Ibid.
89 See J. Jacobs, *Out of the Ghetto* (London, Simon, 1978). For more general comment on the Communist Party of Great Britain, see Stevenson and Cook, *The Slump*, pp. 127–44.
90 PRO HO144/20145/11–17, Police Reports for the attention of the Prime Minister, 2 November 1935 and 24 October 1935.
91 On the Box resignation, see PRO HO144/20146/81–3, Special Branch Report, 18 December 1935. The resignation of Box went into effect in January 1936.
92 *Blackshirt*, 24 January 1936, p. 2.
93 The new uniform was issued to members who contributed two nights per week service to the movement and who sold thirteen copies of the new weekly newspaper, *Action*, or twenty-six copies of *Blackshirt* per week.
94 See *Blackshirt*, 10 January 1936, p. 5. See also PRO HO144/20146/90–91, Special Branch Report, 7 January 1936.
95 Ibid. The division between the two zones was the southern boundary of Lincoln, Rutland, Leicester, Worcester, Shropshire and Montgomery. Leicestershire and Rutland were to be only temporarily administered by the Southern Zone.
96 PRO HO144/20146/90–91, Special Branch Report, 7 January 1936. A 'Leaders Department' was retained under Ian Hope Dundas, which dealt with appointments, promotions and dismissals. This Department was formed in June 1935. See *Blackshirt*, 28 June 1935, p. 5.
97 Neil Francis-Hawkins had assumed control of the 'Blackshirt Organisation' on 22 June 1935.
98 B. D. E. Donovan had earlier succeeded Francis-Hawkins as Officer-in-Charge of the BUF's London Command, which administered all

branches in the London area, in January 1935. J. H. Hone had been a staff official under Francis-Hawkins in the 'Blackshirt Organisation' since August 1935.

99 PRO HO144/20145/11–17, Police Report for the attention of the Prime Minister, 2 November 1935 and 24 October 1935.
100 PRO HO144/20147/377–87, Special Branch Report, 24 March 1936.
101 Ibid.
102 On the BUF's tribute to King George V, see *Blackshirt*, 24 January 1936, p. 1. For the BUF's defence of King Edward VIII during the abdication crisis, see *Blackshirt*, 12 December 1936, p. 1.
103 The BUF did not involve itself overtly in Franco's Spanish campaign, although it undoubtedly sympathised with the rebels against the Republican government. See PRO HO144/21062/277–84, Special Branch Report, 2 November 1936, Policy of the British Union of Fascists and National Socialists.
104 On the announcement of the new title, see *Blackshirt*, 20 June 1936, p. 4. On the shift away from Italian Fascism, see PRO HO144/21060/52–5, The Fascist Movement in the United Kingdom Excluding Northern Ireland, Report No. 8, Developments from February 1936 to July 1936.
105 PRO HO144/21060/52–5, The Fascist Movement in the United Kingdom Excluding Northern Ireland, Report No. 8, Developments from February 1936 to July 1936.
106 PRO HO144/21062/402–7, The Fascist Movement in the United Kingdom Excluding Northern Ireland, Report No. 9, Developments from August 1936 to November 1936. See also *Blackshirt*, 17 October 1936, p. 4.
107 PRO HO144/20147/377–87, Special Branch Report, 24 March 1936.
108 On Mosley's anti-semitism, see Holmes, *Antisemitism*, pp. 175–298.
109 PRO HO144/20146/242, Letter from Special Branch to Sir R. Scott at the Home Office, 25 March 1936. For a verbatim account of Mosley's speech, see *Blackshirt*, 23 March 1936, p. 5.
110 PRO HO144/21060/52–5, The Fascist Movement in the United Kingdom Excluding Northern Ireland, Report No. 8, Developments February 1936 to July 1936.
111 PRO MEPOL2/3043/289–94, Metropolitan Police Report for August 1936, 9 September 1936.
112 PRO MEPOL 2/3043/253–61, Report for October 1936.
113 NCCL DCL 37/4, Jewish People's Council Against Fascism and Anti-Semitism (JPC), Statement of Policy, n.d. On the JPC, see also PRO MEPOL 2/3043/274–82, Report for September 1936.
114 PRO MEPOL 2/3043/289–94, Report for August 1936.
115 BD C6/2/1/1, The Jewish Defence Committee, Retrospect and Pros-

pects, n.d. See also BD C15/2/4, The Jewish Defence Committee, A Brief Survey of its Work, n.d.
116 See PRO MEPOL 2/3043/289–94, Report for August 1936; MEPOL 2/3043/274–82, Report for September 1936; and MEPOL 2/3043/253–61, Report for October 1936.
117 The NCCL was formed in 1934 and claimed that it was a non-political organisation.
118 PRO MEPOL 2/3043/253–61, Report for October 1936.
119 On the popular local 'legends' inspired by 'Cable Street', see N. Deakin, 'The Vitality of a Tradition', in C. Holmes (ed.), *Immigrants and Minorities in British Society* (London, Allen and Unwin, 1978), p. 167.
120 PRO MEPOL 2/3043/253–61, Report for October 1936.
121 Ibid.
122 PRO HO144/21062/257, Handwritten note from Special Branch to the Home Office, 21 December 1936.
123 For a detailed discussion of the Public Order Act, see D. G. Anderson, *Fascists, Communists and the National Government. Civil Liberties in Great Britain, 1931–1937* (Columbia, University of Missouri Press, 1983), pp. 159–202; and Benewick, *Political Violence*, pp. 235–62.
124 For a critical response to the Act from anti-fascist sources, see NCCL DCL 47/1, Public Order Bill, 13 November 1936. The left's view was that the new Public Order Bill represented a fundamental attack on civil liberties generally.
125 Ibid.
126 G. Lebzelter, *Political Anti-Semitism in England, 1918–1939* (London, Macmillan, 1978), pp. 127–32.
127 Thurlow, *Fascism in Britain. A History*, pp. 112–15. See also J. Stevenson, 'The BUF, the Metropolitan Police and Public Order', in Lunn and Thurlow (eds), *British Fascism*, pp. 135–49.
128 Thurlow, *Fascism in Britain. A History*, pp. 112–15.
129 MS BUF, Special Instruction, To: All Districts, From: Director-General of Organisation, 30 December 1936.
130 MS British Union Constitution and Rules (London, BUF, March 1938).
131 Benewick, *Political Violence*, p. 257; C. Cross, *The Fascists in Britain* (London, Barrie and Rockliff, 1961), p. 174.
132 This was the view taken by F. M. Box, the BUF's former Director of Political Organisation, in particular, before his fall from grace. It was also a major reason why the Division Three non-uniform membership scheme was instituted.
133 PRO MEPOL 2/3043/238–44, Report for November 1936. This report stated that the East End districts were quieter than they had been for a long time. See also PRO MEPOL 2/3043/234–7, Report

for December 1936.
134 The anti-fascist groups were concerned that the BUF's campaign in the East End during the summer of 1937 signalled a return to the unrest of October 1936. On this matter, see NCCL DCL 8/5, Letter from R. Kidd to Secretary of State at the Home Office, 7 June 1936.
135 The series of reports in PRO HO144/21087/1–149 discusses the Bermondsey disturbances.
136 PRO MEPOL 2/3043/234–7, Report for December 1936. See also MEPOL 2/3043/230–33, Report for January 1937.
137 PRO MEPOL 2/3043/289–94, Report for August 1936.
138 Ibid.
139 PRO HO144/21062/347–50, Special Branch Report, 6 November 1936.
140 On the March election, see PRO HO144/21063/241–6, Special Branch Report, 12 March 1937.
141 Ibid. On the March LCC elections and the BUF's wider east London campaign, see also Linehan, *East London for Mosley*.
142 PRO HO144/21062/258–62, Special Branch Report, 27 October 1936; HO144/21062/347–50, Special Branch Report, 6 November 1936.
143 PRO HO144/21063/241–6, Special Branch Report, 12 March 1937.
144 Ibid.
145 BD C6/9/1/3, 1937, MS British Union of Fascists and National Socialists, To: All Districts, From: Director-General of Organisation, 12 March 1937.
146 Ibid.
147 PRO HO45/25393/33–4, Special Branch Report, 6 July 1940. The Special Branch reported that it had located what it believed to be the BUF's secret bank account used to channel funds from foreign sources between 1933 and 1937.
148 Ibid.
149 PRO HO144/21063/252–6, Special Branch Report, 15 March 1937. Only four out of an original total of twenty-four National Organisers, and seven out of an original total of twelve National Inspectors, were retained on the BUF's paid staff.
150 Ibid.
151 BD C6/9/1/3, 1937, Letter from Secretary, Board of Deputies of British Jews, to Herbert Morrison, 19 March 1937, provides information on the 'state of affairs' at BUF National Headquarters.
152 Ibid.
153 Ibid. See also PRO HO144/21063/252–6, Special Branch Report, 15 March 1937.
154 Ibid.
155 PRO HO144/21063/9–12, Report from Special Branch to the Home Office on the subject of 'William Joyce', 29 June 1937. See below,

Chapter Five, on the National Socialist League.
156 On the downturn in London, see PRO MEPOL 2/3043/208–11, Report for March 1937; and MEPOL 2/3043/187–91, Report for May 1937.
157 PRO HO144/21063/21–2, Special Branch Report, 21 May 1937.
158 PRO HO144/21063/3–6, Special Branch Report, 17 June 1937.
159 Ibid.
160 PRO HO144/21064/66–70, Special Branch Report, 18 October 1937.
161 PRO HO144/21063/16–19, Special Branch Report, 1 June 1937.
162 BD E3/245, Memorandum of interview with Sir Russell Scott, Home Office, 4 p.m., 14 April 1937, Neville Laski.
163 *Neville Laski Papers*, Mocatta Library, University College, London, AJ/33/132, Letter from N. J. Laski to M. D. Waldman in New York, 6 July 1937.
164 PRO HO144/21064/178–82, Special Branch Report, 1 September 1937.
165 PRO HO144/21064/53–60, Special Branch Report, 3 November 1937. There were fifty-six fascist candidates in the Metropolitan Police district, none of whom were elected. See also BD C6/7/2/1, Memorandum of the Recent Municipal Elections, Constituencies with BUF candidates, London, n.d.
166 PRO HO144/21064/43–50, Special Branch Report, 11 November 1937.
167 Ibid.
168 PRO HO144/21281/7–11, Special Branch Report, 20 January 1938.
169 PRO HO144/21281/23–5, Special Branch Report, 10 February 1938.
170 PRO HO144/21281/33–6, Special Branch Report, 24 March 1938.
171 PRO HO144/21281/7–11, Special Branch Report, 20 January 1938. See also *Action*, 15 October 1938, p. 13.
172 *Action*, 1 October 1938, p. 7; PRO HO144/21381/88–90, Jew-baiting, Metropolitan Police Report for September 1938, 10 October 1938.
173 PRO HO144/21381/139–41, Jew-baiting, Metropolitan Police Report for March 1939, 14 April 1939; HO144/21381/177–9, Jew-baiting, Metropolitan Police Report for April 1939, 17 May 1939.
174 *Action*, 25 March 1939, p. 1.
175 *Action*, 8 April 1939, p. 4.
176 Ibid., p. 3.
177 PRO HO144/21281/150–53, Special Branch Report, 16 July 1939.

CHAPTER FIVE

THE MINOR PARTIES, 'ONE-MAN BANDS' AND SOME FELLOW-TRAVELLERS

Of the minor fascist parties during the 1920s the National Fascisti (NF) was the most significant. It was formed by a group of disaffected British Fascisti activists who split from the parent body in late 1924. According to a National Fascisti member, the dissidents were originally members of the BF's 'very active' branch at 184a Oxford Street, which seceded from the BF following a quarrel with the BF Grand Council.[1] Despite a number of attempts during the subsequent months by those, on both sides, who desired reconciliation to play down the quarrel, there existed fundamental differences between the breakaway group and the BF, in terms of both doctrine and method. The doctrinal differences centred on the dissidents' belief that the BF was insufficiently fascist and that its leadership had a poor understanding of the fundamentals of fascist ideology. According to one of the rebels, Arnold Leese, most of the members of the BF Grand Council 'simply do not understand fascism at all'.[2] The BF was 'merely blindly patriotic' rather than fascist, Leese claimed. What particularly irked defectors such as Leese was the BF's reluctance to confront the issue of democracy and the need to replace it with an alternative form of 'fascist' government. For Leese, true fascism implied a revolt against democracy, while 'sane' government meant abandoning the 'silly universal equal suffrage' of mass democracy and installing a new governing 'aristocracy' of character and 'brains'.[3] Further evidence of the BF's insufficient grasp of fascism, for rebels such as Leese, was provided by an official policy that allowed socialists and Jews to enrol as party members.[4] During the ensuing period the new breakaway party would attempt to craft a more virile form of fascism, one with a more positive revolutionary thrust, which more closely approximated to the model provided by Mussolini and the Italian Fascist Party.

The BF and the rebels disagreed over methods, too. The latter group favoured direct action and did not shirk from using violence against its political opponents. Here, as with doctrine, the NF would look to the recent experiences of Mussolini, and particularly the *squadristi*, for inspiration and guidance. According to the *Socialist Review*, then conducting an investigation into Britain's fascist parties, the NF 'were the real, authentic, black-shirt wearing, sword-carrying, fire-eating and would-be castor-oil administering emulators of the Italian model'.[5] This approach, the emphasis on 'deeds, not words', clearly embarrassed the BF's more moderate leadership, who feared that the violence would taint fascism in the eyes of the public and the government. Moreover, the NF's 'wanton and mischievous exploits' merely acted as a direct incitement to class hatred, thus injuring the cause of national regeneration.[6] Between 1925 and 1927 the BF was at great pains to distance itself from the NF's violent political methods.[7] The NF's penchant for 'physical force' fascism would prove a serious stumbling block during subsequent attempts at reconciliation. In a statement made in June 1926, a BF spokesman again urged the NF to 'rejoin the parent body'.[8] However, the BF made clear its belief that 'Italian methods' were ill-suited to the British character and circumstances. The 'British form of fascism must be adopted', it proclaimed, and this would be best achieved by following a 'constitutional' path, with violence used only as a weapon of last resort.

The NF's first President was L. A. Howard. At some point in 1925 the presidency passed to Lieutenant-Colonel Henry Rippon-Seymour, who retained it until he resigned that office in May 1927. The NF's Headquarters in July 1925 was stated to be 4a Chapel Street, Edgware Road, which comprised a suite of back rooms.[9] Fascist street-fighters needed to be trained, however, so the premises came complete with a drill hall and gymnasium. The NF continued to give physical fitness, athleticism and sport a high priority, for within a short time it was running a boxing and fencing club.[10] Political life in the capital for the NF, it seems, was both unstable and precarious. The *Socialist Review* reported that the NF moved its London Headquarters twelve times between late 1925 and early 1926.[11] Although the NF's operations and activities were centred in London, the *Socialist Review* reported that it had additional branches in Cambridge, Cardiff and Newcastle.[12]

There are a small number of impressionistic assessments of the NF's membership strength given in the contemporary and postwar accounts. According to Colin Cross, a group of around one hundred activists originally broke away from the BF to form the NF.[13] The *Socialist Review* 'investigator' put the total membership in London at 364, by late 1925.[14] Benewick believed that the party's total strength amounted to 'only a few hundred members'.[15] Although its members were very thin on the ground, the NF did boast a separate women's organisation.[16] William Joyce, like Arnold Leese, was another prominent period fascist who defected to the NF from the BF. Other known members included General Prescott Decie, Giles Edward Eyre, an interpreter and traveller by profession, F. G. Portsmouth and Raymond V. Fisher, the latter two both serving terms as the NF's Chief Political Officer. We also have the strange case of Colonel Victor Barker DSO, Secretary to the NF's President, Rippon-Seymour, who was, in fact, Valerie Arkell-Smith, a transvestite woman who had masqueraded as a man in order to escape the attentions of a violent husband.[17] Apparently Valerie Arkell-Smith was a master of disguises. During her time she had also posed as an actor, farmer, dog-breeder, scout-master and cricket captain.[18]

NF activists eagerly adorned themselves with the paraphernalia of Italian Fascism, including the black shirt and a badge displaying the lictor's axe and fasces, as if to emphasise their disapproval of the BF's moderate native version of fascism. Black peak-less caps were also worn.[19] Although funds were always scarce, the NF did manage to publish a newspaper, *The Fascist Gazette*, which superseded an earlier weekly news-sheet entitled the *Fascist*.[20] On 19 July 1926 the NF changed its name to the British National Fascisti, in order not to be confused with sister parties of the same name in continental Europe.[21]

The NF's political methods, not surprisingly, were aggressive. Its activists engaged in periodic street-fights with communists and socialists and broke up opponents' political meetings. On 16 January 1927 a Fascisti squad attempted to wreck a meeting in Trafalgar Square organised by the British Section of the International Class War Prisoners' Aid.[22] They also organised night-time raids on the premises of rival left-wing groups. On the evening of 16 April 1927, NF Blackshirts conducted a 'highly successful' series of raids on 'the 1917 Club and other centres of internationalism' in the capital.[23] They also staged dangerous publicity stunts. In October 1925 four Fascisti, armed with revolvers, seized a *Daily Herald* delivery van and crashed it into the railings of a London church. Fascisti

Blackshirts were also prone to displays of bravado and exhibitionism. In July 1925 a newspaper reporter observed three NF members parading outside their Headquarters armed with drawn swords.[24] Other activities included providing stewards for Conservative Party meetings, holding street-corner meetings and making threatening telephone calls to Labour Party leaders.

The NF's ideology, like its political methods, tended towards the extreme. It was militantly anti-socialist, whilst communism was described as the 'creed of wild beasts'.[25] To the NF, fascism was a rebellion against the democratic system, with its 'party feuds, chicanery, obstruction', party ambition and 'biased "Party" government'. The NF opposed the equal mass franchise and proposed to restrict the franchise 'to those really qualified to vote'. A 'National Fascist Parliament' would more truly represent the national 'will'. The Fascist Parliament would also 'deal drastically' with divisive left-wing 'subversives'. The 'right to strike' was considered to be a 'truly national menace' and would be abolished. In addition, the NF sought the re-incarnation of 'an Empire powerful and true', and the revival of the higher ideals of character, determination and the spirit of self-sacrifice exemplified by the dead of the 1914–18 war-generation. The NF was anti-'alien' and anti-semitic, too. It opposed 'alien immigration' and sought a revision of the Naturalisation Laws. One member, General Prescott Decie, complained about the numbers of 'Negroes' and 'Asiatics' living in London, many of whom were 'walking about with white girls'.[26] 'Negro' and 'Asiatic' immigration into Britain should be prohibited, he urged. Other NF members railed against Jews and the 'Bolshevik-Judaeic menace'.[27]

The NF was virtually moribund by May 1927, incapacitated by shrinking finances and an internal squabble which culminated in a violent confrontation at party Headquarters between Lieutenant-Colonel Rippon-Seymour, the NF President, and a rival group who had accused him of misappropriating party funds.[28] During the exchange, Rippon-Seymour brandished a sword and pointed an unlicensed colt revolver at one of his accusers. The party limped on, to no great political effect, until 13 May 1927, on which date it was finally disbanded.[29] The official reason given by the NF for disbanding the party was 'lack of support'.[30] The National Fascisti was a very minor factor in the affairs of interwar Brtiain. However, it had more significance apropos British fascism. It was the first native fascist party to officially don the black shirt and apply political violence in a systematic manner.[31] The brief NF experiment also represented the first attempt by native fascists to develop a more radical form of British fascism beyond that of the reactionary, negative, 'anti-' type that had been displayed up to that point by the British Fascisti.

The only other fascist body of note during the 1920s which had a bearing on the politics of the far right in Britain was the Centre International d'Études sur la Fascisme, which was formed in Lausanne in 1927. Like the National Fascisti, the CINEF professed an extreme devotion to fascism and took much of its inspiration from the Italian model of fascism. However, there the similarity ends, because the CINEF was very different in intellectual character and temperament from the NF. The CINEF was a sort of elite intellectual 'think-tank' on fascism. It professed to be an independent body whose object was to study fascism in an 'objective' and 'scientific' manner, and provide 'for the general public exact information' with regard to this new political creed.[32] Despite this claim to objectivity, however, the CINEF was little more than a propaganda vehicle for Mussolini and Italian Fascism.[33] The CINEF's relevance for British fascism lay in a number of areas. Firstly, through its publishing activities it provided an important source of propaganda for those on the far right in Britain who wanted fascism to be anchored in a more solid theoretical and intellectual base. Secondly, Arnold Leese became an active member, serving as the CINEF's British correspondent.[34] Thirdly, and more significantly, it enabled James Strachey Barnes to develop his fascist principles, ideas which would eventually be brought to the attention of a right-wing reading public in Britain.

Other British members of the CINEF, besides Leese and Barnes, were Lord Sydenham of Combe of the Britons, Professor Edmund Gardner, who taught Italian literature at the University of London, and Professor Walter Starkie, a Spanish scholar at Trinity College, Dublin. The latter two were founder members of the CINEF and served on its governing body. Both were sycophantic Mussolini-worshipers. Starkie, for example, referred to the Duce as a 'phenomenon of nature'.[35] Major J. S. Barnes, however, was probably the CINEF's leading figure. He was CINEF Secretary-General from 1927, and its principal representative in Britain. His literary output was also considerable. He wrote widely, contributing pieces on fascist theory to a variety of right-wing publications during this period. He also wrote two books on fascism, each of which went through two editions.[36]

Barnes was an Anglo-Indian who had been brought up in Italy by his grandparents, converting to Roman Catholicism in 1914. Although he was later educated in England, at St Aubyns, Rottingdean, Eton and Sandhurst, Barnes developed a keen dislike for the modern England that emerged out of the Industrial Revolution. 'Everything that I liked in England', he lamented, 'seemed to belong to a previous age – the pretty old world villages that once represented a thriving rural economy, the beautiful old Cathedrals and ancient foundations of learning which had been built by the Catholics before the Reformation, the dignified houses of an aristocracy which flourished before the advent of the newly rich, all the remnants of a refined handicraftsmanship in the exquisite furniture and household wares of the centuries before the industrial era.'[37] Barnes believed that the Great War had accelerated the decline of England which had set in with the Industrial Revolution. The 1914–18 war had led to the slaughter of the last of the 'Norman aristocracy', a class grouping whose effective assimilation of Latin culture had helped it to rule England with wisdom for generations.[38] Barnes's spiritual home evidently lay in Italy, where he went to live after the Great War. He would soon become infatuated with fascism, becoming a member of the Partito Nazionale Fascista (PNF) and a friend of Mussolini.

Barnes's fascism was partly motivated by religious convictions that drew inspiration from Catholicism and the Catholic Middle Ages. As a right-wing Catholic, his fascist ideology spoke of an affinity between fascism and Catholicism. Barnes believed that the modern era needed to return to the philosophical values of the Catholic Middle Ages, a 'spiritual, dualistic and transcendental outlook on life' that had been all but destroyed by the Renaissance and the modern secular age of liberalism.[39] Fascism, for Barnes, promised to bring about a conciliation between the modern era and the ideals of this earlier Christian age of faith. At the heart of Barnes's fascism was this emphasis on the spirit. Fascism resolved to bring about a profound spiritual reawakening in modern man. To its adherents, therefore, fascism was a spiritual and ethical revolution, a form of moral revolt grounded in religious principles, that promised to protect the postwar generations from the 'dissolving poisons of materialism'.[40] Barnes's fascist ideology was heavily saturated with palingenetic myth. His universal fascist 'spirit' would transcend the decadence of the modern age with its positivism, materialism and unbridled individualism. Fascism, he declared, 'is a definite revolt against materialism, that is, against all forms of interpreting the universe from a purely naturalistic or purely individualistic standpoint'.[41] Fascism would usher in 'a new age of faith', while 'God is to become once more the central principle of our conscious life'.[42] As well as a spiritual resurgence, fascism was a cultural and aesthetic revolt, according to Barnes. He believed the new generation of young Italians, imbued with fascist values, were developing 'a more genuine sense of Religion and artistic sensibility'.[43] Barnes's writings on fascism are of interest in that they sought to broaden British fascism's philosophical horizons and place it on a firmer theoretical footing than had existed hitherto. His doctrine highlighted the spiritual aspects of the fascist revolt and fascism's strong anti-materialist thrust, elements that, if not absent from, were certainly underdeveloped in the ideologies of the 1920s British fascist parties, particularly the British Fascists.[44]

The 1920s also spawned a small number of tiny fascist groups of a more ephemeral nature. Very little information exists on these groups, with many of them expiring shortly after their birth. Arnold Leese's short-lived Stamford Fascists and Fascist League we have already met.[45] There were also the British Empire Fascists and the Fascist Movement, tiny splinter groups which, like the National Fascisti, split away from the BF during the mid-1920s.[46] The British Empire Fascists advocated policies that hardly seemed likely to capture the imagination of the fascist right. According to the *Socialist Review* 'investigator', whom we have met above, they aimed to slash dramatically the salaries of high officials, including military salaries, and significantly reduce the rate of interest payable to British holders of War Loan.[47] There is also a reference in the literature to the Empire Fascist Movement, which may have been another miniature breakaway group from the BF.[48] So too, perhaps, was a body called the Yorkshire Fascists.[49] The Yorkshire Fascists proved to be more durable than the other splinter groups, for we know that they survived at least until 1930. In that year, the IFL press reported that IFL members were collaborating with their 'friends', the Yorkshire Fascists, in activities against communists.[50]

We also have the Loyalty League, which Barbara Farr stated was 'modelled on Italian Fascist lines'.[51] The League first saw the light of day in October 1922. It was a patriotic anti-communist organisation with an 'emotional' appeal, but despite its enthusiasm for Italian Fascismo it primarily viewed itself as a mouthpiece for the Conservative Party. The League sought co-existence with the BF during its time. Hilary Blume, too, has written of a group called the Loyalty League, which may or may not have been the same organisation as the one referred to by Farr. At any rate, Blume's Loyalty League was formed in 1923 and appears to have disbanded two years later.[52] The founding members were Professor Mudge, the Hon. Miss E. Akers Douglas and General Prescott Decie, the National Fascisti member whom we met above. According to Blume, General Decie was a senior figure in the Britons. Besides being antisocialist and imperialist, the Loyalty League referred to by Blume was rabidly anti-semitic, believing in the *Protocols* and the myth of the Jewish world conspiracy.

A body calling itself the Kensington Fascist Party had also made an appearance by the end of the 1920s. For a time, it was affiliated to the BF and the IFL.[53] By 1931, it was affiliated to Oscar Boulton's Unity Band, a group we shall meet below.[54] The Kensington group operated from its Headquarters at 13 Gunnerstone Road, London W14, under the leadership of Lieutenant-Colonel A. G. B. Lang.[55] All that we know of its ideology is that it feared the dissolution of the Empire, opposed the mass franchise or 'mob vote', and sought democracy's destruction.[56] Other than Lang, there is no information on its members, though it is likely that F. G. Portsmouth, who served as the National Fascisti's Chief Political Officer, joined the group. Interestingly, we can ascertain that Henry Hamilton Beamish of the Britons occasionally attended its meetings.[57]

By the time the 1930s got under way, three other fascist groups had turned up: the New Movement, the Legion of Loyalists and the British Union, the latter not to be confused with Mosley's BUF.[58] Like the Kensington Fascist Party, the latter two bodies collaborated with the BF and the Unity Band. They also shared with the Kensington group a deep hostility towards parliamentary government.[59] The New Movement was a fleeting phenomenon indeed. It almost certainly vanished soon after its initial appearance, though it did manage to obtain a mention in the IFL press.[60] The British United Fascists was another group with a short life story. It was formed in 1933 and had offices in Kensington.[61] That same year, the British United Fascists managed to upset Mosley's BUF because its premises were wrecked by a Mosleyite action squad, an act that certainly precipitated its speedy demise.[62]

Another minor group, the United Empire Fascist Party, was formed in December 1933 by C. G. Wodehouse-Temple, a director of an engineering company.[63] Serocold Skeels, a former IFL member and platform speaker, who had also acted as a representative for the IFL in Nazi Germany, was involved in its formation and became a prominent member.[64] Skeels would later become a Nazi agent, known to the authorities.[65] Not surprisingly, he was an extreme anti-semite, too, who used genocidal language during his all-too-frequent rabid denunciations of the so-called Jewish 'threat'.[66] Skeels would later be associated with the Nordic League, an extreme anti-semitic group that we shall meet below. The United Empire Fascist Party changed its name to the United British Party (UBP) shortly after its formation.[67] Skeels planned to stand as a UBP candidate in a parliamentary by-election at Cambridge but his candidature never materialised owing to his anti-Jewish views, which were found to be objectionable by the UBP Leader, C. G. Wodehouse-Temple.[68] The UBP put together a fourteen-point political programme which, on the face of it, appeared to be an exercise in fair-mindedness and moderation.[69] There was to be no animosity towards those of a different religious faith, a high wage policy, and a minimum standard wage and shorter working hours for all. There was barely a trace of an overt fascist outlook, apart from an obsession with the need to counter 'the menace of a socialist dictatorship', which would be achieved 'constitutionally', and a vague reference to the 'British Empire for the British peoples'. The UBP also railed against 'the dark powers of delay, apathy and obstruction'. A uniform was initially adopted, consisting of a grey tunic and Union Jack armlets, but the UBP later decided to become a 'non-shirt movement'.[70] Soon after its formation, the UBP placed advertisements in the press appealing for five hundred thousand members, which was a trifle over-ambitious to say the least. There is evidence that this party survived at least until late 1936, though it only had two branches, in London and Edinburgh.[71]

A group calling itself the British Empire Fascist Party (BEFP) appeared fleetingly in November 1933.[72] It was the inspiration of Lieutenant-Colonel Graham Seton Hutchison, a character we shall meet below, and had close ties with the British Fascisti. Seton Hutchison's enterprise soon fizzled out, though we do know that the BEFP crafted an ambitious 24-point programme of 'National Reconstruction'. Unlike the UBP's programme, this reconstruction plan was both overtly fascist and extreme in nature.[73] It called for the destruction of the party system and its replacement by the Corporate State, the outlawing of strikes, and the creation of a 'new aristocracy' based on merit not class. It also deified the state. The state was decreed to be supra-class, while all were to 'be within and none against the State'. An aggressive imperial policy was promoted. Britain should direct the imperial destinies and take a 'firm hand in India and Ireland'. The BEFP was fiercely anti-Marxist and rabidly anti-semitic, too. Jews were to be stripped of virtually all their political rights and prevented from participating as equals in the nation's economic and cultural affairs.

There is a brief mention in the secondary literature of a group called the Empire Fascist League, too, although no additional details are provided.[74] Mushroom groups even sprang up in Scotland during the interwar period, one of which was the Scottish Fascist Democratic Party, which was founded by William Weir Gilmour in the 1930s.[75] Gilmour had previously been associated with Oswald Mosley's New Party in Scotland. There was even a branch of blackshirted 'Italian Fascismo' in Edinburgh and Leith in 1924, formed by Scottish-Italians. The Edinburgh and Leith group evidently emerged in response to an attempt by the Mussolini regime in Italy to initiate fascist formations in Scotland.[76]

The 1930s threw up another fascist party, the Unity Band, which managed to outlive most of its contemporaries among the minor parties. It was founded *circa* 1930, by Lieutenant-Colonel Oscar Boulton, and was still active in late 1939. Boulton, educated at Harrow and Oxford and a director of a firm of timber merchants, virtually ran the Band single-handedly during the 1930s. It remained solvent courtesy of his financial input, while he was its mainstay in terms of journalistic and publishing output, which was considerable.[77] He was the author of two books which were published by the Boswell Press, and which dealt at length with his ideas and the Unity Band's policy.[78] He also penned 'Unity Band Monthly Notes' for the BF newspaper, the *British Lion*, for a time at the start of the 1930s. Then from 1932, when the Unity Band bought the copyright of *British Lion* from the BF following the latter's demise, the prolific Boulton became its main contributor.

In July 1930, soon after its formation, the Unity Band entered into an alliance with the BF.[79] Lines of co-operation were established which involved the Unity Band undertaking propaganda and educational work, leaving the 'militant work' to the BF. It was further agreed that, in the interests of co-operation, joint public meetings would be held and that representatives from each body would sit on the other's policy-making council.[80] The honeymoon did not last, however. Boulton broke with the BF in July 1932, a consequence, according to Farr, of ideological differences between him and the BF's leader, Rotha Lintorn-Orman.[81] After October 1932, when the BUF was formed, there ensued a conflict between the Unity Band and the BF for leadership of those fascist groups which resisted being swallowed up by Mosley's party.[82] Apart from Boulton, who was its Director, we know little of the Unity Band's membership, which consisted of those who subscribed to its newspaper. We do know, however, that a Captain Smith was its Secretary through to 1938 and that he was succeeded in that office by Frank Wheatley, an ideological anti-semite who had links with the Nordics, a body we shall encounter below.[83] The well-known period anti-semite Lieutenant-Colonel Arthur H. Lane of the Britons, author of the notorious *The Alien Menace*, was another Unity Band member.[84]

Like James Strachey Barnes, Oscar Boulton's fascism was underpinned by strong religious convictions. The Unity Band described itself as an 'association of Christian men and women', while its programme stressed the relevance of the Christian way of life and the need to recall 'the nation to God'.[85] Religion for Boulton, as for Barnes, Rotha Lintorn-Orman, the Duke of Northumberland and others on the Anglican and Catholic right, was an important mechanism of social cohesion and integration.[86] Boulton went even further, believing that the survival of civilisation itself was dependent on religion. He believed that the virtues of a community of civilised beings, 'duty, sacrifice, honour, generosity, and self-restraint', all had their basis in religion.[87] Barnes feared that civilisation was being threatened by revolutionaries, who espoused doctrines that ignored these fundamental virtues. The revolutionaries' claims to create 'progressive utopias' were based on appeals to the crude materialistic instincts and greed of the mob, according to Barnes, and thus threatened to return society to a primitive state of social savagery. Only a resumption of a Christian life could save civilisation, therefore.

Boulton's other ideas were, in the main, reactionary. He sought to restore Empire unity and reverse the trend towards separatism, initiated by the 1926 Imperial Conference and legalised by the 1931 Statute of Westminster.[88] He called for the restoration of absolute British authority in India, in the best interests of the Indian masses, for whom the British were 'trustees'. He also proposed to limit the power of trade unions by confining them solely to non-political functions. Barnes opposed 'alien' immigration, although, to his credit, he did repudiate ideological anti-semitism.[89] Modernist trends in art and culture ignited a fierce hostility in him, too.[90] His views on the role of women in society were even more reactionary. Indeed, Boulton was one of the most outspoken opponents on the fascist right of the post-1918 women's emancipation movement.

Boulton expressed a traditional view of women and their place in society. He repudiated the progressive notion that there should be equality between the sexes, which, for him, violated all the laws of nature and destroyed 'all the accepted codes of civilised humanity throughout the ages'.[91] The goal of sexual equality was absurd, according to Boulton, because the sexes were differentiated in terms of physical characteristics, mental attributes and the capacity to undertake life's various activities. He deplored the type of sexual equality dogma which encouraged women to 'make themselves as far as possible into the semblance of men', and to imitate 'all the male attributes and activities'.[92] He described as ludicrous, for example, the creation of women police, 'dressed up in a travestied imitation of the garb of the ordinary Constable, and suggesting irresistibly, some of the topsy-turvy parodies of a Gilbert and Sullivan opera'.[93] The modern 'Cock and Hen parliaments' also offended Boulton's traditional view of women's role in society. He therefore opposed the entry of women into Parliament as MPs.

For Boulton, it was man's sacred duty to preserve and protect the 'true womanly ideal'. Boulton had a clear notion of which virtues constituted the 'true womanly ideal'. 'Chastity, modesty, and gentleness of conduct and demeanour' were, for him, some of the traditional female virtues. The modern doctrine of sexual equality was a clear signal of encroaching degeneration and decadence for Boulton. This egalitarian trend threatened imperial security, too, and ultimately the survival of the race itself. Boulton's anti-feminist views ultimately led to conflict with Rotha Lintorn-Orman, whom Farr described as an advocate of 'fascist feminism', a schism that precipitated his departure from the BF in July 1932.[94]

In other areas of his fascist thinking, however, Boulton was more revolutionary than the BF. For example, unlike the BF, at least in its earlier moderate phase, he proposed to abolish parliamentary party government and replace it with a Directing Council and a House of Commons chosen on what he vaguely described as 'some approved standard of merit and capacity'.[95] Even this gesture towards fascist radicalism, however, stemmed from Boulton's reactionary outlook on life. He loathed mass democracy and the universal suffrage, a political arrangement whereby a Ramsay MacDonald or a Lloyd George could manipulate 'dexterously the passions of the mob'.[96] Indeed, for Boulton, the 'Flapper Franchise' represented 'the *ne plus ultra* of democratic absurdity'.[97] The decision, in 1928, to widen the franchise to include all women aged 21 and over, filled Boulton with despondency. No 'self-respecting nation of men', in his view, could tolerate being governed by women, while no nation would deserve to survive 'which handed over the choice of Government to its women'.[98] Although antagonistic towards democracy, Boulton stopped short of advocating a dictatorship. He believed that dictatorship, while suited to postwar Italian circumstances, for example, was not required in England.[99] He also rejected resorting to violence to overturn democracy.

Another one-man band during the 1930s was the National Workers' Party of Great Britain. It was originally founded as the National Workers' Movement in 1933 by Lieutenant-Colonel Graham Seton Hutchison, who was involved with the BEFP, as we know. The National Workers' Movement subsequently changed its title to the National Socialist Workers' Party, before it was eventually reconstituted as the National Workers' Party (NWP). Despite its title, the NWP was not very successful in recruiting workers. Indeed, apart from its self-appointed Leader, Seton Hutchison, there is evidence of only one other party member, Commander E. H. Cole, an ideological anti-semite who had links with the IFL and the Nordics.[100] One need not look beyond the person of Seton Hutchison, though, for an understanding of the NWP, for he was virtually its sole source of ideas. It would surely not have come to the attention of historians were it not for his extensive writings.

Like many leading British fascists between the wars, Seton Hutchison was a disillusioned First World War veteran who hailed from the officer class. His war service record set him apart from most, however. He had a distinguished record, which included being awarded the Distinguished Service Order and the Military Cross.[101] After the war he found some success as a writer of novels and spy stories. He also attempted to enter Parliament, standing as a Liberal candidate for Uxbridge in 1923. It was the war experience that shaped Seton Hutchison's main postwar interests and preoccupations, though. During the years after 1918 he became interested in the plight of ex-servicemen. He was the Old Contemptibles Association's first Chairman, and was a foundation member of the British Legion.

The minor parties

Prior to his attempts to establish himself as Britain's *Führer*, Seton Hutchison was a member of the BUF, but was expelled for 'improper conduct', an experience that left him very embittered towards Mosley.[102] A contemporary Special Branch officer described Seton Hutchison as a 'braggart and overweening', which may have had something to do with Mosley's decision to expel him. He was also a former member of the English Mistery. Seton Hutchison attempted to construct a genuine native national socialist party that looked exclusively to Germany for its inspiration. Fiercely pro-German, he was infatuated by Hitler and mesmerised by developments in the new Germany. He was thought to have been on good personal terms with leading figures in the Third Reich, including Hitler, whom he considered 'incorruptible, courageous' and 'devoted to his people as they are to him'.[103]

Not surprisingly, Seton Hutchison was also aggressively anti-semitic. He believed in the authenticity of that notorious forgery *The Protocols of the Elders of Zion*, as well as the mythical spectre of 'international Jewish finance'. There were links between Seton Hutchison's 'party' and the Britons. The NWP's Headquarters were at 40 Great Ormond Street, the Britons' offices.[104] Although the NWP's level of activism, for obvious reasons, was pitifully low, we do know that it managed to muster up an effort to intervene in the BUF's anti-semitic campaign in east London, for it is on record that it organised a provocative anti-semitic meeting in south Hackney in 1936.[105] Apart from its crude racial nationalism, the NWP's national socialism contained an appeal to workers and the unemployed. Again, drawing inspiration from the German Nazi model, Seton Hutchison dreamed of creating a truly classless community. An appeal was also made to ex-servicemen, based on the assumption that a spirit of kinship existed between British and German ex-fighting men. According to Griffiths, it was these three features of its ideology – the exclusive attachment to pro-Nazi policies, its attempts to woo ex-servicemen, and its claim to be a cross-class party that appealed to the working class – that lent the NWP some significance in relation to British fascism in the interwar period.[106]

Dismayed by the lack of support, Seton Hutchison finally wound the NWP up in 1938. His was not the only native fascist party of the 1930s that enthused about Hitler's Germany. After 1933, with the advent of the Third Reich, Germany displaced Fascist Italy as the principal focus of ideological interest for many on Britain's fascist fringe. Even the BUF began to look to Germany, rather than Italy, by 1936. A high percentage of the policies formulated by the minor fascist groups of the mid-to-late 1930s, with their distinctly pro-Nazi hue, would reflect this admiration for the new Germany. All these groups were uncompromisingly anti-semitic, for example, taking German Nazi anti-semitism both as a model and as a vindication of their own aggressive stance towards the so-called 'Jewish question'. Pro-Germanism and militant anti-semitism were not the sole defining features of these minor groups. All were promoting a vigorous anti-war line by the late 1930s, as they became gripped by terror at the prospect of a new Anglo-German war.

One of these pro-German groups was the National Socialist League (NSL), formed in March 1937. The NSL was a splinter group from the BUF. It was founded by British fascism's most avid Hitler worshipper, William Joyce, along with John Beckett and Angus MacNab, in the wake of their dismissal from Mosley's salaried staff at the time of the financial crisis that hit the BUF in March 1937.[107] Joyce and Beckett, we have met. Angus MacNab, educated at Rugby and Oxford, was editor of the *Fascist Quarterly* and the author of a viciously anti-semitic satirical column in the BUF press called 'Jolly Judah'. Another senior Mosleyite who went with Joyce into the NSL was Vincent Collier, a BUF national propaganda officer. All were to leave the BUF in acrimonious circumstances and, feeling slighted by Mosley, the disgruntled group set up the NSL in opposition to the Mosleyite brand of fascism. Mosley's 'insistence on personal autocracy and Continental "heel clicking"', declared William Joyce, was not the way forward for fascism in Britain.[108] Joyce's new party, on the other hand, would eschew a paramilitary organisation and insignia, and would be run by a 'council' rather than a single leader figure.

Apart from this, there was little that was original about the NSL. Its programme was similar to that of the BUF but with greater stress on Joyce's pet subjects, such as anti-semitism and the Empire, particularly, in the case of the latter, the need to maintain Imperial control over India. The NSL's attitude towards Jews was perhaps more uncompromisingly extreme than that of the BUF, which comes as no surprise given the personalities and outlooks of Joyce, Beckett and MacNab. The NSL advocated a heady 'blood and soil' anti-semitism that more closely mirrored the German Nazi example. Now ensconced in a party of his own, Joyce became even more shrill in his denunciation of the apparently Jewish-orchestrated financial-Bolshevik world conspiracy.[109] The NSL also proposed to

The minor parties

replace parliamentary government with a system of guild representation and a reformed House of Commons of 'experts', which probably drew inspiration from the BUF's ideas on fascist corporations. Despite securing the financial support of a stockbroker, A. C. Scrimgeour, an ardent Joyce admirer, the NSL failed to attract a mass following, or mount an effective challenge to the BUF. Its membership base was pitifully low. According to Mosley, around sixty BUF members left with Joyce and Beckett in March 1937 to form the NSL, but this number dwindled to twenty by the time of its demise.[110] Mosley's dismissive retrospective assessment is probably not too wide of the mark. It is unlikely that the NSL's membership exceeded fifty throughout its short life-span.[111] It did manage to add to the political tension in the East End by holding provocative antisemitic meetings in areas of Jewish concentration.[112] The NSL also set up a body called the Carlyle Club in 1939, in a vain effort to convince 'respectable' types to support national socialism.[113] Joyce probably modelled this body on the January Club, an organisation of the same type set up by the BUF in 1934. By 1938, however, the NSL was virtually moribund, though it only officially terminated its activities when war broke out in September 1939.

In October 1938 John Beckett left Joyce and the NSL. By mid-1939, following an involvement with the *New Pioneer* group, he became a prime mover in another of the 1930s pro-Nazi fascist groups, the British People's Party (BPP). The BPP was formed in May 1939 by the somewhat eccentric Marquis of Tavistock, the 12th Duke of Bedford as of 12 August 1940. Tavistock was a former socialist, Christian pacifist and Social Credit enthusiast. He also took a keen interest in the welfare of parrots and homing budgerigars, and wrote on such matters.[114] Tavistock became the BPP's President, while John Beckett was installed as its General Secretary. The BPP attracted a group of maverick fascists, fanatical antisemites, fascist fellow-travellers and naïve pacifists. Many of its personnel originally hailed from the political left, which invariably lent its programme a leftist tinge. We have already mentioned the previous socialist leanings of Tavistock, while Beckett was a one-time Labour MP for Gateshead (1924–29) and Peckham (1929–31) and held the whip for the ILP group in Parliament. The ex-ILP and BUF member John Scanlon would join Tavistock and Beckett on the BPP's Executive Council, while another ILP man, Ben Greene, would become its Treasurer. Ben Greene, a left-wing Quaker pacifist born in Brazil of a German mother, was cousin to the celebrated author Graham Greene.[115] The BPP also recruited Viscount Lymington (Gerard Wallop), the 9th Earl of Portsmouth from 1943, and Captain Anthony Ludovici, who was linked to the English Mistery, the English Array and the *New Pioneer* group.[116] Philip Mairet, a former editor of the *New English Weekly*, joined the BPP, too, as did Captain Robert Gordon-Canning, formerly of the BUF. H. St John Philby, an Arabian explorer and a 'Mohammedan', was another recruit.[117]

As mentioned, the BPP's political programme, to a large extent, mirrored the leftist origins of its Executive Council. In its twelve-point programme, it advocated the abolition of land speculation and class differences.[118] It also sought greater industrial security for labour, free of such menaces as international wage-cutting. In addition, it proposed to do away with a financial order based upon usury, 'which perpetuates social and economic injustice and which foments warfare between classes and nations', and replace it with a system of social credit. The BPP promoted a highly abstract notion of natural rights, too, arguing that all had the right to security and social justice. Freedom of education, and freedom of religion on the basis of 'absolute equality', were also campaigned for.[119] The only evidence of a more overt fascism and pro-Nazism in the BPP's programme lay in the allusion to the 'alien influence and infiltration' into British life, and the need for a re-orientation of the nation's foreign policy.

Like the National Workers' Party and the National Socialist League, the BPP failed to make an impact on the wider society. It did publish a newspaper, *The People's Post*, and attempt to build a mass following, but there is little evidence of it having an appeal beyond the small group which ran its affairs. During its time, Tavistock's party would principally be known for its aggressive anti-war posture.[120] Its main significance lay in the links it forged with other pro-Nazi, fascist and crypto-fascist 'peace' groups of the period. When war eventually came in September 1939, the BPP reconstituted itself as the British Council for Christian Settlement in Europe (BCCSE), with Tavistock, Beckett and Gordon-Canning remaining in executive positions.[121] During the war years the BCCSE was heavily involved in anti-war propaganda.

Most of the members of the British People's Party found their way into the group associated with the *New Pioneer*, a new monthly magazine of the far right that was launched in December 1938. Besides Viscount Lymington, who provided the primary inspiration for the magazine, John Beckett, Anthony Ludovici, John Scanlon, Ben Greene and Philip Mairet all gravitated towards it. Other contributors to the journal included A. K. Chesterton, J. F. C. Fuller, Henry Gibbs, Joan Morgan, all ex-BUF, and Rolf Gardiner. The *New Pioneer* promoted a curious medley of ideas. On the one hand, it wrote seemingly innocuous pieces on the virtues of home-baked bread and the cottager's pig, while on the other, it waxed lyrical about the Hitler revolution or indulged in sinister eugenic fantasies concerning urban degeneration and the supposed perils of racial intermarriage.[122] *New Pioneer* writers yearned for what seemed, to them, the bygone days of unpasteurised milk, and attacked the England of condensed milk and mass-produced tins from the 'centralised milk factory'.[123] It was the aim of thoughtful folk to spurn tinned foods and other 'devitalised foodstuffs', and return to an England 'symbolised by the pigs bred in the cottage garden', declared one writer.[124] But a more sinister note would soon be struck. London and Britain's seaports 'are already an international cocktail of dysgenics', complained Lymington in July 1939, as he attacked government plans to use Jewish refugee labour to work the land, a place 'where indigenous British stock has been kept pure'.[125]

This curious ideological mix of the absurd and the sinister reflected Viscount Lymington's own personal ideology. The *New Pioneer* project grew out of his earlier attempt to promote his vision of society which acquired form in the English Array, which he created in 1936. The English Array was the successor of the English Mistery, a reactionary ultra-royalist, anti-democratic body founded by William Sanderson. The Mistery was of the 'muck and mysticism' school of thought, too. Its leader, William Sanderson, wrote about grand and imposing lost 'Secrets', as applied to the 'mystery of race' and tradition.[126] Sanderson also hankered nostalgically after the feudal Middle Ages, viewing it as a lost golden age. He fantasised about 'regenerating' the English race, using his idealised image of the sturdy yeoman farmer as his ideal racial type. He also idealised the land and the agricultural system of production. 'The race must always depend principally on agriculture and wholly upon the development of land', wrote Sanderson.[127] When Lymington reconstituted the Mistery as the English Array, he took many of the former's ideas on land, agriculture, race and the pre-industrial past with him. The Gothic medievalist connotations went too. The English Array would extol the virtues of the English archers at Agincourt, 'properly manured vegetables', stoneground wholewheat flour, the cottage pig and 'unburnt stubble fields'.[128] It would also inveigh against the evil of tinned, imported and 'bureaucratically distributed food' and chemicals on the land. Such rural nostalgic and organicist ideas would invariably find their way into Lymington's *New Pioneer*, rubbing shoulders with the pro-Hitler outlook, the frantic outbursts against Jewish refugees and the impassioned anti-war statements.

In the same month that witnessed the birth of the British People's Party, May 1939, Captain Archibald Henry Maule Ramsay founded another of the pro-Nazi anti-war bodies, the Right Club. The Right Club was a clandestine group that endeavoured to create a more unified fascist anti-war movement. Like the BPP, its destiny was in the hands of a person who held convictions which were extreme and often idiosyncratic. Ramsay was an Eton- and Sandhurst-educated Scot with a commendable war record, who entered Parliament as Conservative MP for Peebles in 1931.[129] The turbulent international scene of the 1930s provided the backdrop to the development, in Ramsay, of an aggressive and paranoid anti-communist outlook. As a deeply religious individual, he was particularly appalled by left-wing atheism and Bolshevism's anti-Christian doctrine.[130] The anti-clerical atrocities committed by certain far-left elements within the Republican anti-Franco coalition during the Spanish Civil War merely confirmed Ramsay's loathing of 'Godless' communism. Given his conspiratorial and somewhat unbalanced frame of mind, it comes as no surprise to discover that Ramsay was an extreme anti-semite, too, who believed in the Jewish 'hidden hand' behind Bolshevism, the *Protocols*, and the myth of the Jewish world conspiracy. Needless to say, he was also aggressively pro-Nazi. Ramsay, like many on the fascist political fringe in the late 1930s, peddled the line that the dangerous deterioration in Anglo-German relations, and the concomitant drift to war, was the result of organised Jewish intrigue. In order to avert this, he connived to unite the disparate anti-war and pro-German factions on the far right, and eliminate Jewish influence from the Conservative Party.[131]

Although it recruited members, probably around 350, the Right Club was not a conventional political party with a cohesive, clearly defined political programme. Its relevance for interwar British fascism lay in its leading figure, Archibald H. Maule Ramsay, an individual whom Thurlow describes as 'the most significant figure on the fascist fringe of British politics', along with Oswald Mosley.[132]

The minor parties

The Right Club has importance also for its behind-the-scenes activity to weld the various fascist and quasi-fascist groups together into a more effective anti-war front, an effort that did not abate even during the sensitive months after September 1939, and the significance that this clandestine behaviour had in relation to the authorities' attitude towards the fascist groups at a time of acute national crisis.

Another of the pro-Nazi peace groups that needs to be mentioned is the Link. Like the Right Club, it was not a conventional political party, though it did form individual local branches. The Link was founded by Admiral Sir Barry Domvile in July 1937.[133] Domvile had a glittering naval career. He commanded a Royal Navy battle group during the First World War, and was a former Chief of Staff to the Commander of the Mediterranean Fleet (1922–25) before moving on to become Director of Naval Intelligence.[134] During the 1930s he became an ardent admirer of Hitler and the Third Reich. The Link was a self-styled Anglo-German friendship group that boasted an impressive membership of 4,300 by mid-1939, some of whom were fascists, ardent Hitler admirers and extreme anti-semites. It is likely, though, that the majority of the members, particularly of the rank-and-file, were naïve, well-meaning pacifists. The Link was officially wound up when war erupted between Britain and Germany.

The Nordic League (NL) was another of the shadowy pro-Nazi anti-war groups of the late 1930s. Archibald Maule Ramsay, of Right Club notoriety, was one of its leading personalities. The NL was founded in 1937, a secret organisation of 'race-conscious Britons' that had its origins in a fanatical racist and occultist order, the White Knights of Britain, Britain's nearest equivalent to the American Ku-Klux-Klan.[135] Although it established branches, organised public meetings, had a policy-making council, and attracted the support of many leading period fascists, including Henry Hamilton Beamish, Robert Blakeney, Arnold Leese, William Joyce and 'Jock' Houston, the Nordic League, like the Right Club, was not a conventional political party. The NL essentially provided a forum where the fascist faithful could gather and vent their spleen against the alleged Jewish menace, often in the most chillingly violent of language.[136] Its other purpose appeared to be an attempt to unite the fascist and anti-semitic right and bring direction to the fight against Jewry. The NL was officially disbanded at the outbreak of war, but reappeared in another guise, the Angles, during the war years.[137]

The Nordic League was probably the most fanatical and malevolent of the late 1930s pro-Nazi anti-war groups.

The Nordic League exerted an influence on another extremist anti-semitic body operating in this period of late fascism, the Militant Christian Patriots (MCP). The MCP more closely corresponded to a conventional fascist party. It formulated a programme of sorts, and generally operated more openly than many of its contemporaries on the fascist fringe. It sought to reach out to a wider audience through public meetings, street sales of MCP literature and its news organs, the *Free Press* from 1935 and a second newspaper *The Britisher* from 1937.[138] Historians disagree as to the exact origins of the MCP. Webber stated that Lieutenant-Colonel Arthur H. Lane, of the Britons, established the group in 1928, while Blume puts its foundation date at September 1935 and refers to Miss M. I. Nutt MacKenzie as the inspiration behind its formation.[139] We have more information on the MCP for the post-1935 period, mainly because its publishing activities were more copious from this date. A number of prominent fascists and anti-semites were attached to the MCP, including A. K. Chesterton, Cuthbert Reavely, both formerly of the BUF, Joseph Banister, a notorious period anti-semite and Britons member, and Captain Archibald Ramsay. William Joyce also fraternised with the MCP.[140]

As well as being one of the pro-Nazi appeasement groups, the MCP promoted many traditional fascist ideas. It was aggressively anti-communist, ultra-monarchist, and opposed liberalism and democracy. The MCP, not surprisingly given the rabid anti-semites associated with it, was fiercely anti-semitic.[141] It believed that Jewry sought world domination, and had secretly conspired to create an alliance between 'international finance' and Bolshevism to secure those ends. The MCP also railed against an assortment of other perceived enemies, including Fabianism, Zionism, the League of Nations, Occultism and Freudian psychology. Political and Economic Planning (PEP), a body founded in 1931, was also assailed because it promoted 'socialist' economic planning. The MCP attempted to give its views a spurious religious justification. It campaigned as an ultra-Christian body dedicated to re-introducing the spirit of militant Christianity into all areas of modern British life. To this end, it aimed to 'expose and militantly oppose all movements subversive of Christian faith and ideals'.[142] The MCP's journalistic efforts on behalf of militant, 'muscular' Christianity did not cease until April 1940.[143]

The minor parties

Notes

1. *The Patriot*, 9 July 1925, p. 188.
2. *The Patriot*, 16 July 1925, p. 214.
3. Ibid.
4. B. S. Farr, *The Development and Impact of Right-Wing Politics in Britain, 1903–1932* (New York, Garland, 1987), pp. 56–7.
5. 'Investigator', 'The Fascist Movement in Britain', *Socialist Review*, 1 February 1926, p. 23.
6. *Fascist Bulletin*, 21 November 1925, p. 1.
7. See PRO HO144/19069/29–30, Statement of the Policy and Aims and Objects of the British Fascists.
8. *Fascist Bulletin*, 12 June 1926, p. 7.
9. *The Patriot*, 9 July 1925, p. 188; *Daily Herald*, 31 July 1925, p. 1.
10. J. Wheelwright, '"Colonel" Barker: A Case Study in the Contradictions of Fascism', in T. Kushner and K. Lunn (eds), *The Politics of Marginality. Race, the Radical Right and Minorities in Twentieth-Century Britain* (London, Frank Cass, 1990), pp. 40–8.
11. 'Investigator', 'The Fascist Movement'. By late 1926 it had moved to more stable premises at 5a Hogarth Place, Earls Court, SW5. See PRO HO144/19069/90–94, *Fascist Gazette*, 8 November 1926, provides this address.
12. 'Investigator', 'The Fascist Movement'.
13. C. Cross, *The Fascists in Britain* (London, Barrie and Rockliff, 1961), p. 61.
14. 'Investigator', 'The Fascist Movement in Britain'.
15. R. Benewick, *Political Violence and Public Order* (London, Allen Lane, 1969), p. 36.
16. Wheelwright, '"Colonel" Barker', p. 43.
17. Ibid., pp. 40–8.
18. Ibid.
19. *John Bull*, 5 March 1927, p. 11.
20. *The Patriot*, 28 May 1925, p. 31, on the *Fascist*.
21. *The Patriot*, 12 August 1926, p. 159.
22. *Daily Herald*, 17 January 1927, p. 7.
23. *The Patriot*, 21 April 1927, p. 369.
24. *Evening News*, 30 July 1925, p. 4.
25. PRO HO144/19069/90–94, *Fascist Gazette*, 8 November 1926. The following discussion of the NF's policy has been based on this source unless a different reference is given.
26. *The Patriot*, 28 May 1925, p. 31.
27. *Daily Herald*, 31 July 1925, p. 1, on the Jews; *The Patriot*, 2 September 1926, p. 237, on the 'Bolshevik-Judaeic menace'.
28. PRO HO144/19069/104, *Daily Herald* extract, 10 March 1927.
29. *Daily Sketch*, 19 May 1927, p. 2.

30 Ibid.
31 Although Arnold Leese made the former claim for his Stamford Fascists, this group was attached to the BF and was not a party in its own right.
32 PRO HO144/19069/140–42, International Centre of Fascist Studies (CINEF); and *The Patriot*, 28 May 1925, p. 31.
33 R. Griffiths, *Fellow Travellers of the Right. British Enthusiasts for Nazi Germany 1933–39* (Oxford, Oxford University Press, 1983), p. 16.
34 Ibid., p. 97.
35 Ibid., pp. 19–20.
36 J. S. Barnes, *The Universal Aspects of Fascism* (London, Williams and Norgate, 1929); J. S. Barnes, *Fascism* (London, Thornton Butterworth, 1931).
37 J. S. Barnes, *Half a Life* (London, Eyre and Spottiswoode, 1933), p. 42.
38 J. S. Barnes, *Half a Life Left* (London, Eyre and Spottiswoode, 1937), pp. 297–8.
39 Barnes, *Fascism*, pp. 38 and 50.
40 Ibid., p. 43.
41 Ibid.
42 Ibid., pp. 50–1.
43 Barnes, *The Universal Aspects*, p. 166.
44 Barnes admonished a BF member, for example, for not appreciating that fascism sought an anti-materialist revolution, and was not based exclusively on reactionary anti-communism. See *The Patriot*, 7 February 1929, p. 141.
45 See above, Chapter Three.
46 Cross, *The Fascists*, pp. 60–1.
47 'Investigator', 'The Fascist Movement in Britain'.
48 Mentioned in A. K. Chesterton, *Oswald Mosley. Portrait of a Leader* (London, Action Press, 1937), p. 117.
49 Ibid.
50 *The Fascist*, May 1930, p. 2.
51 Farr, *The Development and Impact*, p. 55.
52 H. S. B. Blume, 'A Study of Anti-Semitic Groups in Britain, 1918–40' (M.Phil. thesis, University of Sussex, 1971), pp. 245–6.
53 Farr, *The Development and Impact*, p. 77.
54 *British Fascism*, June 1931, p. 8.
55 Ibid. and Griffiths, *Fellow Travellers*, p. 89, on Lang.
56 Ibid. See also *British Fascism*, May 1931, p. 7, on its anti-democratic mentality.
57 *British Fascism*, June 1931, p. 8.
58 Farr, *The Development and Impact*, pp. 77–8.
59 *British Fascism*, May 1931, p. 7.

60 *The Fascist*, June 1932, p. 3. The report also refers to a 'Mr. Moir', the New Movement's Propaganda Officer.
61 It is possible that this group may have formerly been the Kensington Fascist Party.
62 Cross, *The Fascists*, p. 82.
63 PRO HO45/25386/44–5, Special Branch, 22 January 1934.
64 *The Fascist*, February 1934, p. 4.
65 R. Thurlow, *Fascism in Britain. A History, 1918–1985* (Oxford, Blackwell, 1987), p. 80.
66 Ibid., p. 82.
67 *The Fascist*, February 1934, p. 4.
68 PRO HO45/25386/44–5, Special Branch, 22 January 1934.
69 Ibid.
70 Ibid.
71 See *Sunday Referee*, 11 October 1936, p. 11. It is possible that the UBP may have reverted back to its original title, because the *Sunday Referee* piece refers to the United Empire Fascist Party.
72 PRO HO45/ 25386/37–40, Special Branch, 22 January 1934, British Fascists Limited.
73 PRO HO144/19070/95, Metropolitan Police, 27 November 1933.
74 D. S. Lewis, *Illusions of Grandeur. Mosley, Fascism and British Society, 1931–1981* (Manchester, Manchester University Press, 1987), p. 29.
75 Cross, *The Fascists*, p. 108.
76 Farr, *The Development and Impact*, pp. 54–5.
77 See *British Lion*, January 1933, p. 11, on Boulton's financial input.
78 O. Boulton, *Fads and Phrases* (London, Boswell Publishing, 1930); O. Boulton, *The Way Out* (London, Boswell Publishing, 1934).
79 *British Fascism*, July 1930, p. 3.
80 Ibid.
81 Farr, *The Development and Impact*, p. 78.
82 Ibid. The Unity Band and the BF both opposed Mosley.
83 Blume, 'A Study of Anti-Semitic Groups', p. 265.
84 G. C. Webber, *The Ideology of the British Right 1918–1939* (London, Croom Helm, 1986), p. 154.
85 Boulton, *The Way Out*, p. 6.
86 Webber, *The Ideology of the British Right*, p. 63.
87 Boulton, *The Way Out*, pp. 97–8.
88 Ibid., p. 6.
89 See below, Chapter Seven.
90 See below, Chapters Eight and Eleven.
91 Ibid., p. 90.
92 Ibid., p. 95.
93 Ibid., p. 91.
94 Farr, *The Development and Impact*, p. 78.

95 Boulton, *The Way Out*, p. 6.
96 Ibid. p. 14.
97 Ibid., p. 12.
98 Boulton, *Fads and Phrases*, pp. 13 and 20.
99 Ibid., p. 14.
100 Blume, 'A Study of Anti-Semitic Groups', p. 257.
101 Griffiths, *Fellow Travellers*, p. 101.
102 PRO HO144/19070/94, Metropolitan Police, 27 November 1933.
103 Cited in Blume, 'A Study of Anti-Semitic Groups', pp. 258–9.
104 Ibid., p. 257.
105 *Hackney Gazette*, 10 August 1936, p. 5.
106 Griffiths, *Fellow Travellers*, p. 103.
107 On the retrenchment, see PRO HO144/21063/231–4, Special Branch Report, 24 March 1937.
108 *Liverpool Daily Post*, April 1937, p. 5.
109 R. Skidelsky, *Oswald Mosley* (London, Macmillan, 1981), p. 343.
110 O. Mosley, *My Life* (London, Thomas Nelson, 1968), p. 311.
111 Thurlow, *Fascism in Britain. A History*, p. 143.
112 See, for example, PRO HO144/21380/218–20, Metropolitan Police Report, 11 January 1938.
113 Webber, *The Ideology of the British Right*, p. 147.
114 A. W. Simpson, *In the Highest Degree Odious. Detention Without Trial in Wartime Britain* (Oxford, Oxford University Press, 1992), p. 97.
115 Ibid., p. 341.
116 Webber, *The Ideology of the British Right*, p. 146.
117 *The Patriot*, 6 July 1939, p. 10.
118 MS, British People's Party, Twelve Articles.
119 Ibid.
120 *The Patriot*, 6 July 1939, p. 10.
121 Simpson, *In the Highest*, p. 139.
122 See *New Pioneer*, December 1938, p. 16, on the former; January 1939, p. 50, on the Nazi revolution; and December 1938, p. 23, on eugenics.
123 *New Pioneer*, December 1938, p. 16.
124 Ibid.
125 *New Pioneer*, July 1939, p. 187.
126 See W. Sanderson, *Statecraft. A Treatise on the Concerns of our Sovereign Lord the King* (London, Constable, 1932 edition).
127 Ibid., p. 82.
128 P. Wright, *The Village That Died for England. The Strange Story of Tyneham* (London, Vintage, 1996), pp. 171–3.
129 On Ramsay, see R. Griffiths, *Patriotism Perverted. Captain Ramsay, the Right Club and British Anti-Semitism 1939–40* (London, Constable, 1998).

130 Ibid., p. 78.
131 Thurlow, *Fascism in Britain. A History*, p. 171.
132 Ibid., p. 79.
133 See Griffiths, *Patriotism Perverted*, pp. 39–42.
134 Simpson, *In the Highest,* p. 218.
135 Ibid. pp. 80–1.
136 Ibid., pp. 80–3.
137 Simpson, *In the Highest,* p. 72.
138 Blume, 'A Study of Anti-Semitic Groups', p. 230.
139 Ibid., p. 227; Webber, *The Ideology of the British Right*, p. 156.
140 PRO HO144/21381/230, Special Branch, 23 May 1939.
141 C. Holmes, *Anti-Semitism in British Society, 1876–1939* (London, Arnold, 1979), pp. 170–4.
142 *Free Press*, October 1935, p. 4.
143 See *Free Press*, April 1940.

CHAPTER SIX

THE MEMBERSHIP

The usual caveats need to be dispensed before we consider the membership strength of Britain's interwar fascist parties, and other areas of related interest such as the social-class and occupational profiles of fascist 'joiners'. The main problem concerns the paucity of documentary evidence and other forms of contemporary written material relating to these matters. To compound the issue of scarcity, there are often marked variations in the quality of the information emanating from the sources that do exist. Reliable material on the membership in the official fascist sources, in particular, is extremely scarce. This applies even to the largest of the period's fascist groups, the BUF. The national registers of the party's membership compiled at BUF National Headquarters, listing returns from the local branches, were probably seized by the security services in the raids on 23 May 1940 which followed the promulgation of Defence Regulation 18b (1A), and have yet to be released by the government.[1] Moreover, even if such registers have survived, it is likely that the information therein only relates to the BUF's active membership (Division 1), rather than the additional and more substantial body of recruits that resided in the non-active category. This is due to the practice, which BUF Headquarters initiated in 1937, of only registering active members in order to conceal the identities of non-active recruits.[2] The situation at local branch level is depressingly similar. Registers of membership compiled by the branch, which would have contained invaluable background data on Mosleyite recruits, did not survive the anxieties of the war years and Defence Regulation 18b (1A). The vast majority of these records were hurriedly destroyed by BUF branch officials, who were anxious to conceal the identities of local fascists from the authorities.[3] The whereabouts of branch records that may have escaped destruc-

The membership

tion remains a mystery. The picture is even bleaker for the other fascist parties of significance, the British Fascisti and the Imperial Fascist League. Both organisations were probably far less diligent than the BUF in compiling and maintaining accurate registers of members. If such records were kept and maintained, their current whereabouts remains unknown. No such records have appeared in the existing Special Branch and Home Office documents on the BF and the IFL currently deposited at the Public Record Office.

Historians have not drawn a complete blank, however. A few official documents and branch records from contemporary fascist sources, particularly the BUF, which yield fragments of extremely useful information on fascist 'joiners', have survived.[4] Newspapers published by the various fascist parties are also not without their usefulness. The fascist press frequently contained references to party members, including, on occasions, fairly detailed biographies of leading fascist officials and other categories of member. Fascist newspaper sources are less useful, however, if we are attempting to arrive at an estimation of a fascist party's membership strength. Membership figures put out by the fascist press are notoriously unreliable. The oral testimonies of ex-members of interwar fascist organisations have provided another very valuable source of information on the membership. In addition, there exists a small quantity of autobiographical and other material, both published and unpublished, from Mosleyite sources, which helps to add to our knowledge of the BUF's membership.[5]

There is also some invaluable material on the membership contained in the non-fascist sources. However, like the fascist sources, there are often marked variations in the quality of the information emanating from these quarters. The contemporary Special Branch and Home Office documents deposited at the Public Record Office probably constitute the most reliable of this material.[6] As always, there is significantly more data on the BUF. For example, the Special Branch monitored the BUF's progress between early 1934 and 1940, and compiled reports on a fairly regular basis. These reports mostly include information on the number of active BUF members at a national level. In a small number of reports, the national figures are supplemented by data on the size of membership in London. Occasional references to the distribution between active and non-active members are also provided.[7] Other Home Office and Special Branch files provide us with additional information on fascist recruits. For example, there is information on members of Mosley's organisation who were convicted of attacks against Jews, offences relating to public disorder at political gatherings, or, after January 1937, offences against the Public Order Act.[8] Details on the memberships of the other interwar fascist parties in these Special Branch and Home Office documents is much more sketchy.

Contemporary anti-fascist organisations also collected information on the interwar fascist parties and their memberships, although the status of this documentation varies widely in terms of quality and reliability.[9] The most detailed and informative data was gathered by the Board of Deputies of British Jews.[10] Finally, there are the contemporary newspapers, which provide the historian with some useful additional fragments of information on individual fascists.

If we turn firstly to the most significant of the 1920s fascist parties, the British Fascisti, we will see that there are conflicting views as to the size of its membership. For its part, the BF indulged in wildly inflated claims about its membership strength. The party boasted that it had 100,000 members by mid-1924.[11] This figure had leapt to 150,000 members by May 1926, according to the BF Leader Rotha Lintorn-Orman.[12] In October 1932, despite the impending formation of a serious rival in Mosley's BUF, the BF claimed that it had almost one million members.[13] Even as it approached its final death throes the BF was still claiming a huge membership. During 1933 and 1934, party propagandists put out figures of 400,000 and 416,000 members respectively.[14] The *Patriot*, the proto-fascist journal which supported the BF, concurred with this view, claiming that, at one point, its membership had stood at 400,000.[15]

In general, historians have taken a more sceptical view of the size of the BF's membership. Robert Benewick and Hilary Blume, for example, believed that even at its zenith, in the mid-1920s, it probably only attracted a few thousand adherents.[16] Webber sketched an even more damning picture. He thought that, apart from London, the BF was practically 'bereft of support', and that by 1934 the party had been reduced to a 'pitiful rump' of 300 members.[17] Other historians, though, have been more cautious about estimating membership levels. Richard Griffiths concluded that the evidence on this question was thin and inconclusive and thus declined to speculate on the BF's numerical strength.[18] An assessment greatly at variance with the more orthodox position taken by Benewick, Blume and Webber has been put forward by Barbara Farr. Her estimation is more in line with the claims made by the BF itself. Farr believed that

The membership

there were 'at least 1,000, perhaps 2,000' Fascisti units operating throughout the British Isles at the party's peak between 1925 and 1926.[19] Basing her calculations on an average of fifty members per unit, Farr therefore concluded that the BF may have had up to 100,000 recruits during that phase of its development. Kenneth Lunn has gone even further, hotly contesting the notion, promoted by historians such as Benewick, that the BF enjoyed only minuscule support. Basing his judgement on fascist press reports pre-eminently, which apparently revealed evidence of a high level of BF branch activity in England, Scotland, Wales, Northern Ireland and the Irish Republic, he suggested that recruitment levels may have been significantly higher than has generally been appreciated.[20] Surprisingly, however, given his vigorous dismissal of the orthodox view, Lunn did not put forward a figure of his own regarding the size of membership.

It is evident that in the absence of reliable documentary material, such as BF membership records or some additional statistics from government sources, historians have had to fall back on impressionistic assumptions and intelligent guess-work when they have come to assess the BF's membership strength. This has led to some skewed assessments. Farr's estimation that the party at one point had 100,000 members, for example, is well wide of the mark. Clearly, her judgement in this area needed to be informed by a more critical stance towards the figures on membership disseminated by the Fascisti propagandists. Lunn's considered argument for a revised upward estimation of the number of recruits occupies more solid ground, though his case is slightly marred by his apparent reluctance to put forward any new figures for consideration. Despite Lunn's worthwhile intervention, though, it is difficult to dismiss the Benewick–Blume–Webber model, namely the notion that the BF survived on a painfully thin membership base during its lifetime. Benewick was surely correct when he stated that, during its lifetime, the BF was 'plagued by frequent schisms and internal difficulties, which continually reduced the membership'.[21] Unfortunately, there are very few surviving pieces of documentary evidence that have a degree of genuine reliability on these matters. One to which the historian does have access, however, would seem to confirm this prognosis concerning the low level of recruitment. This is the Home Office report of 31 August 1933, which stated that, at that point in its life, the BF had between 300 and 400 members.[22] Another reasonably reliable piece of evidence, a Special Branch report of 22

January 1934, similarly puts the BF's membership at around 300.[23] Even taking into account the existence of a genuine rival in the recruitment stakes, Mosley's BUF, these are hardly impressive figures. The Benewick–Blume verdict of a 'few thousand' members during its peak recruitment period, 1925–26, is therefore probably correct, though one might suggest a modest upward revision of the numbers.

So from what sections of society did the BF recruit its members? We can identify a number of categories of member.[24] The first group was composed of aristocrats and members of the landed elite and others from the traditional governing classes. All other titled recruits will be included in this category, too. The BF was a reactionary rather than a radical fascist party. It sprang up in the aftermath of the political and labour disturbances of the postwar years with the professed intention of defending private property, civil order, the Constitution and the Empire against the apparent trade union, socialist and Bolshevik threat. The sociological composition of the membership, to a remarkable degree, reflected the reactionary character of the BF's political mission. It was very successful in attracting upper-class support, aristocrats and other elite types, namely those members of society who felt particularly imperilled by the threat to the status quo posed by the radical left. Such recruits included the 6th Marquis of Aylesbury, Earl and Countess Temple of Stowe, Baroness Zouche of Haryngworth, Lord de Clifford, Lady Ismay, Lord Langford, and the Dowager Countess of Westmoreland. Others in this category were the Countess of Eglington and Winter, Lord Ernest Hamilton, Lady Menzies of Menzies, Lady Mowbray, the 8th Earl of Glasgow, Lord and Lady Sydenham of Combe, and Viscount and Viscountess Downe. Dorothy Viscountess Downe, who would later join Mosley's BUF, was a friend of Queen Mary. Elite personalities held prominent positions within the party. The Earl of Glasgow directed the Scottish units, Viscountess Downe and the Countess of Eglington and Winter were Fascisti county commanders in North Riding and Ayrshire and Wigtonshire respectively, while Lady Sydenham of Combe was, for a time, in charge of Rotha Lintorn-Orman's pet project, the Fascist Children's Clubs.[25]

There was a bevy of other titled recruits, too, including the BF's Treasurer Sir Arthur Hardinge, a former Ambassador to Spain, Sir Gerald du Maurier, Sir Kenelm Coyley, Sir E. Lycett Green, Sir R. J. M. Walker and Sir C. Graham, Bt, DSO, JP, DL, a BF County

Commander in North Riding. There was also Sir Michael Bruce, a Fascisti Local Officer in Bournemouth, Sir Kenelm Coyley and Sir Burton Chadwick. Chadwick, who headed a company of Liverpool shipowners, was Parliamentary Secretary to the Board of Trade between 1924 and 1928.[26] Other titled recruits had links to the Conservative Party as well, such as Colonel Sir Charles Burn, a member of the BF's General Council, who was Conservative MP for Torquay between 1910 and 1923. Another was Sir Robert L. Bower, who was elected to Parliament as a Conservative MP for North Riding in 1931.[27]

The second category of member we can identify was composed of those from the military officer class. Again, as with aristocratic types and other titled recruits, the BF appeared to be remarkably successful in attracting this category of member. In identifying officers who had served in the Great War as being amongst the BF's leadership cadre, Farr suggested that such types 'mistakenly interpreted their experiences of front-line camaraderie as an *esprit de corps* which fortified class barriers', an experience which they hoped to carry over into the postwar world.[28] Other military officers holding senior positions within the BF, according to Farr, hailed from a paternalistic ex-colonial military background.

Military men proliferated throughout the Fascisti movement. They included such senior Fascisti officials as Brigadier-General Robert B. D. Blakeney, the BF's President from 1924 to 1926, and Brigadier-General Sir Ormonde Winter, who was in charge of BF units in the 'London Area'. Before he gravitated towards fascism, between 1920 and 1922, Winter was a Deputy Chief of Police and Director of Intelligence in Ireland. Military figures also occupied official positions at the local level, such as Brigadier-General E. P. Sevecold, a Fascisti official in Derby, and General J. Tyndale-Biscoe and General S. Geoghegan, who both officiated in Bournemouth. We also have a crop of military officers functioning as Fascisti county commanders, including Brigadier-General G. Soady in Kent, Captain D. Melville, MC, in Warwickshire, Colonel T. C. Gurney, DSO, in East Riding, and Captain W. Coates, JP, and Colonel M. J. Stapylton, OBE, in West Riding. Other county commanders included Captains C. Barrington and J. H. Rowlandson in the Western Command. To this group can be added Brigadier-General R. A. Carruthers and Major-General T. D. Pilcher, BF company officers in London and Camberley respectively. Pilcher had hitherto been involved with Patrick Hannon's pre-fascist anti-labour group, the

British Commonwealth Union, as we know.[29]

Others from the military officer class who joined the British Fascisti included General E. W. Appleby, General J. Spens, Major-General C. B. Knowles, Major-General Sir Francis Mulchay, Brigadier-General G. Soady and Major Sir Guy Graham. Still others included Major Sir Robert Bowen, Brigadier-General T. Erskine-Tulloch, Colonel H. W. Johnston, Colonel A. G. B. Lang and Colonel Dan Burges. Burges, who had won the Victoria Cross, was Governor of the Tower of London. Even the BF Leader, Rotha Lintorn-Orman, hailed from a military background. She was the granddaughter of a distinguished soldier, Field Marshall John Lintorn Simmons.[30]

Those who hailed from a naval officer background comprised a third category of recruit we can identify. Again, as with military figures, naval officers tended to rise to senior positions in the BF, both at the national and local level. For example, there was Rear-Admiral A. E. Armstrong, the party's Vice-President between 1924 and 1926, and Rear-Admiral W. E. R. Martin, the BF's paymaster. W. E. R. Martin was also a County Commander in Cornwall, as was Captain S. C. Warner in Sussex and Admiral Sir Reginald Tupper at Liss. Other Fascisti naval officers included Admiral Tuss and Admiral Richard Hyde. There was Lieutenant G. Edbrooke, too, a member of the BF's Portsmouth Branch.[31] Another Fascisti member was the Hon. Sir Admiral Edmund Fremantle, author of several books on the navy.[32]

A fourth category, alluded to by Farr, comprised those who gravitated towards the Fascisti as a result of their Christian beliefs, a group she described as 'fervent Church of England religious reactionaries'.[33] Many leading Fascisti professed firm Christian convictions, including Brigadier-General Blakeney and Nesta Webster. Indeed, for Farr, paternalistic ex-colonial military men such as Blakeney were instrumental in injecting 'the fervour of a Christian crusade into the Fascisti'.[34] There was also a handful of clergy who enrolled, such as the Reverend K. L. Kempthorne, a BF Local Officer in Falmouth.

A fifth category of member emanated from what may loosely be defined as the 'middle class'. These included those in professional occupations, such as the BF's Propaganda Officer, E. G. Mandeville Roe, who was a school-teacher, and independent commercial travellers like Neil Francis-Hawkins, a surgical-instrument salesman. As with all the categories of member, it is difficult to put an estimate on

The membership

the numbers of middle-class types that joined, owing to the dearth of detailed empirical studies of the BF membership within the existing literature. However, it is likely that individuals from this social-class group were there from the outset, though they probably increased in number by the end of the 1920s as the BF became less of a haven for reactionary anti-socialist aristocrats, jingoists, and retired generals, and more of an organisation with a clearly defined fascist identity aiming for a cross-class support base.

A type that Farr referred to as the 'newly enfranchised woman' made up a sixth category of recruit.[35] 'Genteel survivors of Victorianism attempting to redefine the responsibilities of women in post-war society', rather than ex-suffragettes or Conservative socialites, such women rose to senior positions within the BF. The importance of this category of 'joiner' is emphasised even more forcefully by Julie Gottlieb, who points to early native fascism's uniquely 'feminine side', and its 'high degree of female activism and propaganda directed towards women'.[36] Of such women, the Fascisti's founder and Leader, Rotha Lintorn-Orman, immediately springs to mind, of course, as does Nesta Webster. Farr mentions Mrs D. G. Harnett, Commander of the Ulster Units, as another such emancipated woman. Harnett was, in fact, the author Dorothy G. Waring. Described by Griffiths as a woman with a 'strong personality', in the late 1930s she would become a leading figure in Admiral Sir Barry Domvile's pro-Nazi group, the Link.[37] A Southampton Fascisti member, Mrs Foster Welsh, JP, the first woman Sheriff of the Borough of Southampton, was another.[38]

Kenneth Lunn has attempted to make a case for workers to be considered as a viable membership category within the Fascisti. He argued that 'the extent of working-class support has been neglected' in the historiography, and further, that it would be 'a mistake to see the members of the organisation as wholly middle or upper-middle class'.[39] He thus called for research to move 'beyond spotting famous names and ranks', and to engage in a 'systematic combing of sources' so as to ascertain the level of worker support for the Fascisti. Despite Lunn's important intervention in the debate, the case for significant worker support for the BF remains weak, however. The collective 'weight of examples' which he brought forward to support his position, which for him, 'suggests the need for a revision of the "middle-class" label often tagged to the BF', is clearly not numerous or substantial enough to warrant a readjustment of the prevailing membership profile. In addition, until the detailed empirical studies that he called for are undertaken, pronouncements on the degree of worker support for the BF will continue to remain in the realm of intelligent speculation. Undoubtedly, a sprinkling of workers did join the Fascisti during its period of life, though not in sufficient numbers to dislodge the prevailing image of a party whose recruits, in social-class terms, belonged to the upper class, upper middle class and middle class.

Some Fascisti members defy easy categorisation. One such individual was the eccentric veterinary surgeon and expert on camel diseases, Arnold Leese, who spent a short time in the BF between 1924 and 1926 prior to becoming the grandee of British racial fascism.[40] Another is Arthur E. R. Gilligan, a former captain of the England cricket team. Gilligan captained England during the Ashes tour of Australia in 1924–25.[41] Maxwell Knight, a leading MI5 agent in the interwar years, is another. Knight was the BF's Deputy Chief of Staff and Director of Intelligence.[42] John Baker White and Patrick Hannon are others. Both sat on the BF's Grand Council. For much of the interwar period, White was the leading figure in the anti-labour employers' association, the Economic League.[43] Hannon, who was active on behalf of the pre-1914 and postwar radical right, dovetailed his fascism with right-wing Conservatism during the 1920s.[44] Between 1921 and 1950, he was a Conservative MP for Birmingham. He was also stated to be on good personal terms with Neville Chamberlain and Winston Churchill.[45] Yet another who is difficult to categorise is Dr John Rudd Leeson, a BF member who was the first Charter Mayor of Twickenham, as is Mrs Foster Welsh, the Borough of Southampton's first woman Sheriff, whom we met above.[46] Even more difficult to categorise is E. E. Manuel, a Jewish anti-communist who enrolled in the BF's Hammersmith Branch.[47]

Apart from the BF and Mosley's BUF, the National Fascisti and the Imperial Fascist League were the only other noteworthy fascist parties between the wars. The significance of the NF and the IFL lay in areas other than the number of members they attracted, though. Both parties had pitifully small memberships. Originally formed from a nucleus of around one hundred BF dissidents in late 1924, the NF's total numbers never exceeded more than a few hundred.[48] Moreover, it is likely that the NF had very few adherents outside the capital. Blume and Cross put the IFL's membership at no more than 200, while Lebzelter put it at 150.[49] Indeed Blume dismissed the figures of 800 and 1,000 mentioned in some contemporary press

The membership

reports on the IFL's membership.[50] It is difficult to refute the paltry estimates given in the historiography, though a contemporary Home Office report suggests that the total national membership may have been slightly higher than the optimum figure of 200 proposed by Blume and Cross.[51] This report mentioned a figure of 140 for the party's London membership, while it also referred to additional IFL branches at Leeds, Liverpool and Manchester. A figure of between 300 and 500 may be more realistic in terms of the IFL's membership, therefore. Such low numbers make it virtually impossible, and indeed perilous, to estimate patterns of support for the NF and the IFL over time.

Of the NF and the IFL, Arnold Leese's party was the more significant, as we know. So why did it fail to attract a large following? We can identify a number of reasons for this. Firstly, from 1932, it had to compete for recruits with the BUF and invariably came off second best for most of the time.[52] Secondly, the IFL's uncompromisingly crude racial fascism, extremist policies, and a language and style of propaganda that often bordered on lunacy, were hardly likely to make it attractive to large numbers of people. Thirdly, Arnold Leese's elitist and racist approach to recruitment ultimately defined the limit of the IFL's numerical strength. Ironically, given his claim that the IFL was Britain's only authentic fascist party, Leese did not attempt to build it into a mass party. He believed that membership should be exclusively restricted to 'high calibre' types, those who conformed to his ideal of an 'aristocracy of character'. 'Ineffective' members were therefore ruthlessly weeded out. 'Every true Fascist movement', he declared, 'has to undergo a long period of trial, during which Adventurers, Melancholics, Intellectuals, Wasters and Careerists have to be gradually identified and eliminated.'[53] According to Leese, only one out of ten recruits demonstrated the necessary qualities, and remained in the party.[54] The other nine simply 'faded away' once they realised that they would be required to work. For Leese, the 'Mediterranean racial type of recruit' lacked the desired qualities, for although his work may be 'brilliant' while he was in the party, he was 'incapable of a prolonged strain or effort'.[55]

Unlike the British Fascisti, we simply do not know from what sections of society the NF and IFL gained its members. This is because, to date, there have been no attempts to investigate, in as detailed a fashion as the evidence permits, their social bases of support. The historiography awaits such an investigation. This is partly due, of course, to both the NF's and the IFL's derisory membership count which, just as with patterns of support over time, renders it difficult to build up an adequate sociological picture. As it is, we have to make do with a small number of impressionistic observations in the historiography. All of these pertain to the IFL. Hilary Blume, Roger Eatwell and Gerry Webber all thought that the vast bulk of Leese's recruits were drawn from the middle class.[56] Continuing in the same vein, Webber added that the IFL was 'noticeably lacking in young working-class "shocktroops"'.[57] Occasionally, a tiny detail on members' social background does crop up in the historiography. For example, we know that William Sanderson was a freemason and an author, H. H. Lockwood was an insurance agent, and John Hooper Harvey was a medieval historian. All of these IFL members we have met in a previous chapter.[58] The IFL's newspaper also claimed that the party recruited a Liverpool-based clergyman, the Reverend C. R. V. Cook, who was curate of St Stephen's Church, Byrom Street, Liverpool.[59]

If the historian is feeding off tiny morsels of information with the IFL, this is not the case with interwar Britain's pre-eminent fascist party, the British Union of Fascists. The BUF's membership strength was of a different order from the other native fascist parties, though as with the BF, historians have often disagreed as to the precise number of recruits. Robert Skidelsky, working on a ratio of three non-active members to one active member, estimated that the total national membership of Mosley's party hit a peak of 40,000 during the period of *Daily Mail* support between January and July 1934.[60] The numbers then dropped rapidly in the wake of the hostile publicity that followed the outbreak of fascist violence at the Olympia meeting on 7 June 1934, stabilised between 1935 and 1938, before returning to the 1934 peak of approximately 40,000 by 1939. In a later intervention in the debate, Skidelsky revised his estimate for 1939, suggesting a more modest membership base of 20,000–25,000.[61] Skidelsky's revisionist assessment was a departure from the earlier 'conventional' interpretation originally put forward by Colin Cross.

In his 1961 study of British fascism, Cross maintained that Mosley's party went into decline after the heady successes it experienced during 1933 and 1934. He stated that it was unable to stem the 'constant leakage of members' in the years following the 'breathtakingly rapid' advances achieved prior to July 1934.[62] The sharpest decline was thought to have occurred 'from 1938 onwards', culminating in the reduction of the BUF to a rump of about 1,000 active members by 1939–40. The Cross interpretation, of a sharply downward membership trend after the mid-1934 Rothermere peak, was broadly accepted by Robert Benewick in a later work.[63] This model was subsequently accepted by most historians and commentators on the BUF until Skidelsky's re-evaluation in 1975. According to Skidelsky, the discrepancy between the 'revisionist' and the 'classical' figures was due to the failure of both Cross and Benewick to take adequate account of two important developments after 1934. These were the upsurge in membership in east London between 1935 and 1938, and the recruitment of antiwar elements during Mosley's 1939 'peace campaign'.[64]

The first systematic attempt to estimate the BUF's membership strength that did not rely solely on impressionistic evidence and intelligent guess-work was undertaken in 1984 by Gerry Webber.[65] Basing his appraisal on figures contained in the government and Special Branch reports on the BUF held at the Public Record Office, Webber's findings were the most detailed yet compiled.[66] Significantly, he was broadly in agreement with Skidelsky's suggestion that the BUF did not enter into terminal decline after 1934, and was improving its position after 1935. Basing his appraisal on a ratio of one active to one-and-a-half non-active members, Webber therefore plotted a modest but progressive rise in the rate of recruitment between early 1936 and September 1939. He calculated that the BUF established an optimum total membership base of 40,000–50,000 by mid-1934, a figure that was spectacularly reduced to 5,000 by October 1935. The party's membership then rose progressively thereafter to 10,000 by March 1936, 15,500 by November 1936, and 16,500 by December 1938, before settling at 22,500 in September 1939. Webber's systematic tabulations of the Special Branch figures were later commended by Richard Thurlow, although he suggested 'a small downward revision of the total numbers' that Webber proposed.[67]

These larger numbers have helped place the study of the BUF membership on a very firm empirical and analytical foundation. It has enabled historians, for example, to sketch some extremely valuable portraits of the social types recruited by the BUF. It has allowed scholars, too, to explore the reasons which induced individuals to align themselves with Mosley during the 1930s.[68] As a result, it has been possible to put together a very useful social-class, occupational and motivational profile of a native fascist party of some numeric significance.

The first serious attempt in the postwar period to arrive at an understanding of the social types who gravitated towards Mosley was provided in 1946 by Frederick Mullally.[69] Mullally presented us with a picture of a 'typical' BUF member, a middle-class seventeen-year-old, 'Peter Fletcher'. Employed by the Britannia Electric Works, 'Peter Fletcher' was an 'old boy' of Clapham Academy and the son of a Roman Catholic civil servant from south London. In 1966 W. F. Mandle offered the world another portrait of a 'typical' Blackshirt, on this occasion, one of its characteristic leadership types. Mandle's was a study of the BUF's national leadership that drew on information contained in the various potted biographies of the fascist elite recorded in the Mosleyite press.[70] Mandle concluded his survey by suggesting that the composite fascist leader in 1935 was a widely travelled, extremely restless, public-school-educated, middle-class ex-army officer in his late thirties.[71]

There are a number of problems with these two early renderings of the phenomenon of fascist social type. Firstly, both accounts deploy a highly dubious methodology. Mullally's retrospective picture lacked the advantage of supporting empirical evidence and is thus wholly impressionistic, subjective and speculative. Mandle's findings, though set in more solid scholarly foundations, are also problematic in that they are based on a restricted sample of BUF officers who stood as prospective parliamentary candidates. Secondly, both accounts reinforce one of the postwar era's 'classic' theories of fascism, namely the notion of fascism as primarily the expression of the specific sectional interests of the middle class. The theory of fascism as essentially a middle-class revolt has been one of the dominant paradigms in postwar fascist historiography. It is an argument that has been promoted by both liberal and Marxist scholars of fascism. Liberal analysts of fascism, like Seymour Lipset, for example, believed that the middle class inclined towards fascism owing to their precarious economic position in a society experiencing crisis.[72] Modernisation was a catalyst here, creating profound economic and social upheavals that appeared to threaten the status of the middle class and disturb their inner mental universe. The advance of socialism was another catalyst. Apparently, a dread of the inherent levelling impulse within socialism impelled the threatened middle class into a reactionary, anti-socialist pact with the fascist devil out of a desire for self-preservation. The alleged symbiotic relationship between the middle class and fascism is assumed, too, in the classical Marxist theory that fascism was essentially a 'terroristic', antiproletarian instrument of bourgeois reaction.[73] Thirdly, and finally, the Mullally and Mandle assessments were reductionist, in that both analysts were unable to resist the temptation to define the membership in terms of a single stereotype.

Stuart Rawnsley's investigations into the BUF's activity and recruitment profile in the north of England marked a significant breakthrough in the treatment of the Mosleyite membership. It was the first study to make use of the personal memories and recollections of former Mosleyite joiners.[74] In his analysis, Rawnsley contested models of fascism that emphasised the homogeneity of class affiliation. He also found it difficult to locate anything resembling the traditional notion of the fascist stereotype, concluding that a range of different social groups and personality types made up the BUF's membership in the north of England. Just as significantly, Rawnsley's research showed that the working-class contingent within the northern membership was not inconsiderable. The northern BUF attracted to its ranks cotton workers in locations like Middleton, Nelson and Blackburn in Lancashire, railway workers and chemical plant operatives in Lancaster, and unemployed workers throughout the northern region. He did add, though, that Mosley made few gains in recruiting members from amongst the highly unionised sections of the working class, such as engineering workers and coalminers. In contrast, the unemployed, particularly those discarded by a declining textile industry, did join the BUF in significant numbers. Rawnsley noted, too, that the BUF's northern membership contained a high percentage of Catholics. He partly put this down to local Irish-Catholic appreciation of Mosley's stand, taken earlier in his political career, against the British government's decision to deploy the Black and Tans in Ireland during the 1919–21 Anglo-Irish War.

Like Rawnsley's study, John Brewer's monograph on the BUF in the West Midlands drew on the recollections of former Blackshirts.[75] Brewer analysed a sample of fifteen ex-Mosleyites, utilising the sampling and quantitative methods of sociology. Observing that, as a percentage of his total sample, 80 per cent would have been under thirty at the time of membership, he concluded that the Blackshirt 'movement was significantly one of youth'.[76] Amongst his other findings, he proclaimed that the traditional description of 'the movement as middle class is too simple'.[77] Analysing his age cohort, Brewer noted that there was a preponderance of 'lower class' types among the younger members and only 'as the age cohorts advance does the middle class bias emerge'.[78] Brewer's findings should be treated with caution, however. His membership sample was painfully small, making it hazardous to draw too many general conclusions on the BUF's sociological profile, even with regard to its West Midlands membership. Even the spatial distribution of Brewer's sample is problematic. His sample was too unevenly dispersed to allow for deliberation on the character of either the national or the regional West Midlands membership.[79]

My own study of the BUF's membership in east London and south-west Essex more openly challenged the classical view of fascism as essentially a middle-class revolt and the tendency to describe fascist joiners in terms of a single stereotype.[80] I also went much further than both Rawnsley and Brewer in pointing up the proletarian aspect of Mosley's membership. Of my sample of 311 local Mosleyites, 36 per cent were unskilled and semi-skilled workers and 15 per cent were skilled workers ('lower class'). The only other occupational sub-groups in my sample that recorded notable percentage rates were 'lower and intermediate white collar employees' at almost 14 per cent, 'self-employed merchants' also at 14 per cent, and 'independent master craftsmen' at nearly 8 per cent. All these three occupational sub-groups were from the 'lower middle and middle-middle class', in terms of social class. Interestingly, all three percentage rates fell well short of the figure of 36 per cent for unskilled and semi-skilled workers. With the 'lower class' element comprising the largest grouping in my sample with respect to social class, 51 per cent as against almost 39 per cent from the 'lower middle and middle-middle class', it was becoming apparent by this stage in the evolution of British fascist historiography that the 'middle-class fascism paradigm' was beginning to crack under the strain. The bulk of these 'lower-class' unskilled and semi-skilled workers were, of course, attached to BUF branches in the East End.[81] To me, this demonstrated that in the East End, the BUF 'acted as a rival focus of allegiance for large numbers of local workers who, for various reasons, rejected the traditional organisations of the Labour movement'.[82]

The workers in my sample of 311 local Mosleyites also engaged in a diversity of occupations. Amongst the 112 unskilled and semi-skilled workers there were some fifty-eight different occupations, embracing such types as dock worker, railway porter, ice cream vendor, coalman, hat blocker, news vendor, milk checker and soap boiler. A similar feature was evident with respect to the forty-eight skilled craft workers in the sample, who were involved in twenty-seven different occupations ranging from upholsterer to typewriter mechanic. Occupational heterogeneity appeared to be the norm with respect to Blackshirt proletarian recruits in this region, therefore. Like Rawnsley, I found that the majority of these proletarian recruits were from the non-unionised sections of the local labour market, though local Blackshirt branches did contain a sprinkling of workers with trade union affiliations, including some dockers and transport workers.

This high proletarian presence did not mean that non-workers did not figure prominently within the BUF's membership in the east London and south-west Essex region. In other respects, the local occupational profile mirrored that of other Mosleyite regional formations in Britain, and indeed fascist mobilisations throughout the continent, in that not insubstantial numbers of 'lower middle and middle-middle class' types could be found in local branches. As stated, 'lower and intermediate white collar employees', such as clerks, salesmen and commercial travellers, registered at almost 14 per cent, 'self-employed merchants' or shopkeepers at 14 per cent, and small independent master craftsmen and traders, which included costermongers and proprietors of small local businesses, at nearly 8 per cent. As Skidelsky put it, these were 'the intermediate groups which fell outside the labour–capital confrontation', the archetypal small men who craved protection and continued independence in a modern age where economic life was increasingly geared towards mass production and mass services.[83] Nonetheless, while it is correct to highlight this quintessential aspect of fascist mobilisations, the most recent research has demonstrated that it is no longer acceptable to focus exclusively on this social-class category and the occupational types that belonged to it, when considering domestic fascism's sociology. With the latest historiography revealing a substantial proletarian intake amongst fascist recruits, both in Britain and on the continent, the mythology of the 'middle-class thesis of fascism' has been virtually destroyed.[84]

Social-class and occupational analyses of fascist memberships undoubtedly help us to arrive at a greater awareness of the nature of fascism, not least because they impel us to focus on the structural or objective determinants of recruitment. Having said that, it is imperative that we do not confine our consideration of the membership to this area alone. We also need to heed those sociological categories that have a broader focus than social-class or occupational stratification. The BUF's apparent ability to appeal to youth is one such case in point. This is a generic fascist trait, with numerous scholars highlighting the youthfulness of the fascist and Nazi membership cadres between the wars.[85] In part, fascism was a 'generational revolt', a rebellion of youth against age and the perceived old and decadent bourgeois world of tradition, compromise and delay. Rawnsley's research has highlighted, too, the attraction of Mosley for Catholics, as we have noted above. Set against the wider landscape of the Spanish Civil War, the BUF also won the support of many Irish Catholics in Stepney between 1936 and 1938, as my work has shown.[86]

According to W. F. Mandle, the BUF also lured into its ranks society's rootless types, those who found it difficult to adjust to the changed circumstances of the postwar years.[87] He further pointed out that the BUF attracted its fair share of 'misfits and failures', as well as public-school-educated 'gallant gentlemen', and that occasionally such types 'were one and the same'. Mandle's work revealed, too, that like its predecessor the British Fascisti, the BUF attracted a sizeable crop of ex-military types, many of whom would form its leadership cadres. As a variation on this theme, it is worth noting that the BUF recruited war veterans of all ranks, many of whom were seduced by Mosley's anti-war message. Richard Thurlow cast his analytical net even wider, suggesting that the BUF appealed to a 'broad spectrum' in society which included displaced idealists, war socialists, authoritarian personality types, violent males, anti-Jewish elements, and the politically uncommitted.[88] Thurlow thought that its basic appeal was to those 'with initiative who had experienced bottlenecks in mobility patterns in society', a group that included 'cranks, criminals, alcoholics and worse'.[89] Thurlow did acknowledge, however, that among the BUF's membership could also be found individuals of character, resourcefulness and intellectual ability, who were attracted to Mosley because they, like him, felt themselves to be outsiders who were 'alienated from conventional establishment values'.

Women constituted another clearly definable category of member. It has been estimated that women made up 25 per cent of the BUF's membership.[90] Women joined the BUF, it seems, for the usual variety of motives that differed little from those of the male Blackshirts. These included ultra-patriotism and a desire for an improvement in economic performance and social welfare.[91] Women were also attracted by the BUF's radicalism on women's issues, for, as Martin Durham has pointed out, contrary to received wisdom, the BUF made a conscious attempt to avoid setting itself up as a 'bulwark against feminism, but, remarkably, as perfectly compatible with it'.[92] Among its radical policies, the BUF advocated equality within the movement and the state, women's right to work, and equal pay. Although there was no typical Blackshirt woman, many of the women fascists' political roots were to be found in Toryism, according to Julie Gottlieb.

We should also be mindful of changes in the BUF's sociological profile brought about by shifting patterns of support during the period of its lifetime. The historiography posits that, initially, between 1932 and mid-1934, its main appeal was to disaffected ex-Conservatives, the patriotic anti-socialist 'Rothermere fascists', many of whom believed (mistakenly, as it turned out) that in the BUF they had found a more virile and activist form of Conservatism.[93] After 1935, and continuing through to 1938, the party's sociological profile began to alter. Mosley's East End campaign, in particular, brought in a surge of fresh recruits of a proletarian and petty bourgeois nature, attracted as much by social, cultural and political issues of a specifically local character, as anti-semitism.[94] To this sociological picture of the party between 1935 and 1938 should be added the isolated outposts of support in areas like Manchester and Yorkshire. By late 1938, Webber has argued, the BUF's social profile had changed once more, with the party gathering to its peace banner significant numbers of pro-appeasement and anti-war protestors mainly of a middle-class character.[95]

The issue of motivation represents another fruitful line of enquiry into the problematic of membership. What were the factors which motivated individuals to join Mosley in his dangerous fascist adventure during the 1930s? Some historians have used oral history techniques to help answer this question. Fresh insights into joiners' motivation, as well as the workings of the inner fascist consciousness, have been spawned as a consequence.[96] Motivation to join the BUF flowed from a variety of sources. The least surprising motives were patriotism, invariably of the extreme and belligerent variety, an unstinting belief in the sanctity of Empire coupled with a desire to prevent its disintegration, and militant anti-communism. Anti-semitic beliefs, too, of course, would propel some into Mosleyite fascism.[97] The decision to enrol also sprang from more conventional economic and social welfare motives. Mosley's fascist movement emerged against the backdrop of the international slump in trade and the domestic economic depression of the 1930s and he invariably won over some individuals who were anxious about Britain's economic plight. An abstract fear of impending national economic decline would drive many towards fascism, as would a more personal dread or experience of unemployment. Mosley's programme of national economic renewal, as initially outlined in the Mosleyites' bible, *The Greater Britain*, excited many potential fascist joiners who saw in its surprisingly detailed policy proposals the best means of counteracting the economic slump.[98] Others joined Mosley because he promised to relieve poverty and social distress, and they believed him. Disillusionment with the existing liberal order, the established political parties, and the political culture, practices and rituals of liberal democracy were other motivating factors.

For many palingenetic fascists, of course, domestic economic malaise, social distress and the apparent inertia of liberal democracy and the party system were symptoms of decadence and encroaching national decay.[99] A perception of decadence and decline pervaded the Mosleyite consciousness and informed numerous fascists' observations of contemporary cultural life, too, as we will see in subsequent chapters.[100] This deep sense of foreboding, moreover, cut across the social class divide. It is at this deeper level of thought and consciousness that we can grasp the essence of the BUF's ideology and discern a fundamental fountain-head of fascist motivation. Mosley's Spenglerian analysis of contemporary economic, social, political and cultural conditions, with its bleak apocalyptic vision of the impending death of Europe's 'Faustian culture', spoke to such individuals. But more than this, Mosleyite fascism seemed to offer salvation, for contained within it was a dialectic of despair and hope. Contemporaneous with its pessimistic belief in crisis and decline, the BUF nurtured a 'heroic vitalist' vision of rebirth and regeneration, an ideology that drew on the Nietzschean and Shavian notion of the emergence of a new 'superman', Goethe's revolutionary 'Faustian' man, and Nietzsche's 'will to power'. Mosley's promise to revive the spirit, both in the inner personal realm and at the level of state and nation, would underpin such thinking. It was a seductive creed and message that appealed to those of a particular psychological frame of mind who feared the dissolution of self and nation and yearned for transcendence.

The BUF seduced potential recruits in other ways, too. Fascism consciously practised the art of seduction. Fascism aestheticised politics through its carefully choreographed marches and mass gatherings, secular rituals and display of paramilitary paraphernalia. Fascist political theatre generated a highly charged atmosphere that appealed to the emotions, mesmerising and then ensnaring the unwary.[101] Along the same lines, others signed up because they found the prospect of wearing fascist uniforms and insignia pleasing, because it appealed to their vanity. Again, on the same continuum, Julie Gottlieb has pointed out that the highly charged atmosphere created through fascist theatre was as much sexual as political. It spawned romantic encounters between youthful uniformed male Blackshirts and young female admirers, which, on occasions, led some women to join up so as to be near the object of their desire.[102] Stuart Rawnsley discovered that potential joiners could be lured in to the party by the prospect of courtship, too. Amongst his sample of northern Blackshirts was one Mrs B, who enrolled in the BUF's Moss Side Branch in 1934 'because she lived next door to the local headquarters and took a fancy to one of the fascists in his smart uniform'. The two would eventually marry.[103] The BUF's Leader was an integral part of fascist theatre, too. Many individuals were enticed into the party by Mosley's presence alone. In many ways, Mosley was the quintessential charismatic fascist leader-figure, the type whom masses of individuals were drawn towards throughout continental Europe between the wars.

There were many other motives for joining, of course. There was what Brewer referred to as 'the appeal of the cosh and castor oil'.[104] That fascism attracted men of violence throughout Europe during the 1920s and 1930s is beyond question. However, we cannot ignore the fact that domestic Mosleyite fascism also attracted individuals who were repelled by violence as expressed through wars between nations. The memory of the Great War, with its nightmarish images of the mass 'slaughter of the innocents' in the trenches of western Europe, haunted war veterans like Mosley, A. K. Chesterton and Henry Williamson and shaped much of the BUF's ideology. The BUF promised to remember forever the sacrifice of the war generation, keep alive the spirit of the dead heroes of the Great War and fight to prevent the outbreak of another European war. It was a message that struck a chord in some war veterans and anti-war pacifists who were thus motivated to join the BUF. Still others became fascists because they found the fascist and national socialist movements of continental Europe appealing and were excited at the prospect of being part of a domestic equivalent. Some enrolled simply because of a family affiliation. Wives joined husbands in the ranks, and vice versa, as did father and son and brother and sister. At another level, some romantic ruralists were attracted by the BUF's heady 'blood and soil' rural ideology, which stressed the supposed moral and spiritual advantages of country life, among other things. Individuals even joined for reasons that did not have the remotest connection to fascist ideology. One such person was a working-class trade union shop steward named Tom Pickles, one of Rawnsley's sample of northern Blackshirts, who enrolled with the BUF's Manchester Branch in 1933 because of the influence of some friends and the attraction of the sports facilities in the fascists' gym.[105] We should not ignore, either, the purely local context of Mosleyite recruitment, which in certain places like east London was very significant.[106] Clearly, there were numerous motives for joining Mosley's fascist party. Attempts to define motivation, or indeed any other feature pertaining to fascist joiners, such as social class, in terms of a single stereotype is reductionist and poor scholarship. Such characteristics can only be discerned through careful and often painstaking empirical research and cannot be inferred in advance on the basis of what are often suspect theoretical premises.

Notes

1 Historians continue to speculate as to how much Home Office material on the BUF remains held back by the government, despite the release of the Mosley papers in 1986. See C. Holmes, 'Internment, Fascism and the Public Records', *Bulletin of the Society for the Study of Labour History*, 52, 1 (April 1987), pp. 17–23. Through the instrument of DR18b (1A), the government achieved its aim of crippling the BUF. Between May and July 1940 some 784 Mosleyites were detained, including Oswald Mosley.
2 See R. Skidelsky, *Oswald Mosley* (London, Macmillan, 1981), p. 332.
3 My own research into local fascism in east London and Essex reveals that this was the fate of most branch records in that region.
4 During the course of my own research on fascism in east London and south-west Essex, I was able to consult a number of membership registrations, albeit an incomplete set, for the BUF's Epping Branch, and some official internal BUF bulletins announcing local appointments, promotions and resignations within the movement. I also gained access to a set of records detailing the names and place of residence of BUF district officials in the London area. See T. Linehan,

The membership

East London for Mosley. The British Union of Fascists in East London and South-West Essex, 1933–40 (London, Frank Cass, 1996).

5   See in particular *Mosley's Blackshirts. The Inside Story of the British Union of Fascists 1932–40* (London, Sanctuary Press, 1986); J. Charnley, *Blackshirts and Roses* (London, Brockingday, 1990); and *Comrade. Newsletter of Friends of O.M.*

6   The bulk of these documents are in the class of Home Office Supplementary Registered Papers in the HO144 series and the HO45 series.

7   See PRO HO144/21062/402–7, The Fascist Movement in the United Kingdom Excluding Northern Ireland, Ninth Report, Developments From August 1936 to November 1936, for a breakdown between active and non-active categories.

8   Again, these documents can mostly be found in HO144 and HO45.

9   The quality of information on the BUF produced by organisations such as the Communist Party of Great Britain (CPGB) and the National Council for Civil Liberties (NCCL) is, unfortunately, extremely poor. Dealing mostly in generalisations and stereotypes, these bodies rarely focused on such detailed matters as the social basis of fascism.

10 Unlike the NCCL and the CPGB, the Board of Deputies of British Jews approached the question of fascist membership in a spirit of dispassionate enquiry.

11 H. S. B. Blume, 'A Study of Anti-Semitic Groups in Britain, 1918–40' (M. Phil. thesis, University of Sussex, 1971), p. 107; C. Cross, *The Fascists in Britain* (London, Barrie and Rockliff, 1961), p. 59.

12 *Fascist Bulletin*, 1 May 1926, p. 2.

13 *British Fascism*, October 1932, p. 7.

14 Blume, 'A Study of Anti-Semitic Groups', p. 107. The BF expired in September 1935.

15 *Patriot*, 5 September 1935, p. 178. On the *Patriot's* political outlook, see above, Chapter Two.

16 R. Benewick, *Political Violence and Public Order* (London, Allen Lane, 1969), p. 31; Blume, 'A Study of Anti-Semitic Groups', p. 107.

17 G. Webber, 'The British Isles', in D. Muhlberger (ed.), *The Social Basis of European Fascist Movements* (London, Croom Helm, 1987), p. 143.

18 R. Griffiths, *Fellow Travellers of the Right. British Enthusiasts for Nazi Germany 1933–39* (Oxford, Oxford University Press, 1983), pp. 95–6.

19 B. S. Farr, *The Development and Impact of Right-Wing Politics in Britain, 1903–1932* (New York, Garland, 1987), p. 56.

20 K. Lunn, 'The Ideology and Impact of the British Fascists in the 1920s', in T. Kushner and K. Lunn (eds), *Traditions of Intolerance. Historical Perspectives on Fascism and Race Discourse in Britain*

(Manchester, Manchester University Press, 1989), pp. 145–8.
21 Benewick, *Political Violence*, p. 31.
22 PRO HO144/19069/210–12, British Fascists Ltd and Rival Fascist Bodies, 31 August 1933.
23 PRO HO45/25386/37–40, Special Branch, British Fascists Limited, 22 January 1934.
24 As with the appraisal of recruitment figures above, we are governed by the existing information at our disposal, which is patchy. Therefore, any conclusions we arrive at can only be tentative. The following analysis of the membership is primarily based on the findings of Blume, 'A Study of Anti-Semitic Groups'; Griffiths, *Fellow Travellers*; Benewick, *Political Violence*; and J. Hope, 'British Fascism and the State 1917–1927: A Re-Examination of the documentary Evidence', *Labour History Review*, 57, 3 (Winter 1992), pp. 72–83, unless stated otherwise.
25 Farr, *The Development and Impact*, p. 74.
26 Benewick, *Political Violence*, p. 33.
27 Farr, *The Development and Impact*, p. 75.
28 Ibid., p. 56.
29 See above, Chapter Two, on the BCU. See also Hope, 'British Fascism', p. 75.
30 Farr, *The Development and Impact*, p. 53.
31 Lunn, 'The Ideology and Impact', p. 146.
32 Benewick, *Political Violence*, p. 33.
33 Farr, *The Development and Impact*, p. 56.
34 Ibid.
35 Farr, *The Development and Impact*, p. 56.
36 J. Gottlieb, 'Women and Fascism in Inter-war Britain' (Ph.D. thesis, University of Cambridge, 1998), p. 8.
37 Griffiths, *Fellow Travellers*, pp. 92 and 313.
38 Lunn, 'The Ideology and Impact', p. 145.
39 Ibid., pp. 146–7.
40 See above, Chapter Three, on Leese.
41 On Gilligan, see *British Lion*, June 1927, p. 10, and 28 August 1926, p. 8.
42 See above, Chapter Three, on Knight.
43 See above, Chapter Two, on the EL.
44 See above, Chapter Two, on Hannon.
45 Farr, *The Development and Impact*, p. 56.
46 *British Lion*, October–November 1927, p. 8, on Leeson.
47 Farr, *The Development and Impact*, p. 75.
48 Benewick, *Political Violence*, p. 36.
49 Blume, 'A Study of Anti-Semitic Groups', p. 209; Cross, *The Fascists*, p. 63; G. Lebzelter, *Political Anti-Semitism in England 1918–1939* (London, Macmillan, 1978), p. 83.

50 Blume, 'A Study of Anti-Semitic Groups', p. 209. *Sunday Referee*, 11 October 1936, p. 11, refers to '800 paying members'.
51 PRO HO144/19069/210–212, British Fascists Ltd and Rival Fascist Bodies, 31 August 1933.
52 This pattern was reversed occasionally, such as in late 1934 when an indeterminate number of Mosleyite dissidents from the BUF's Wolverhampton and Belfast branches joined the IFL. See PRO HO144/20144/229–31, Special Branch Report, 20 December 1934.
53 *The Fascist*, December 1934, p. 4.
54 Ibid.
55 Ibid.
56 Blume, 'A Study of Anti-Semitic Groups', p. 21; R. Eatwell, *Fascism. A History* (London, Vintage, 1996), p. 179; Webber, 'The British Isles', p. 143.
57 Webber, 'The British Isles', p. 143.
58 See above, Chapter Three.
59 *The Fascist*, November 1930, p. 3.
60 Skidelsky, *Oswald Mosley*, pp. 331–2.
61 R. Skidelsky, 'Great Britain', in S. J. Woolf (ed.), *Fascism in Europe* (London, Methuen, 1981), p. 275.
62 Cross, *The Fascists*, pp. 130–2.
63 Benewick, *Political Violence*, pp. 108–10.
64 Skidelsky suggested that Cross and Benewick interpreted the figure of 9,000 BUF members quoted by the then Home Secretary, Sir John Anderson, in a statement he gave to the House of Commons in 1940, as referring to the total active and non-active membership. Skidelsky, on the other hand, believed that the Anderson figure only included the active membership.
65 G. C. Webber, 'Patterns of Membership and Support for the British Union of Fascists', *Journal of Contemporary History*, 19, 4 (October 1984), pp. 575–606.
66 This material was unavailable to earlier researchers.
67 R. Thurlow, *Fascism in Britain. A History, 1918–1985* (Oxford, Blackwell, 1987), pp. 122–5.
68 The utilisation of oral history methods by some historians has assisted in this task. It has enabled the historian, through interviews with ex-members of Mosley's party, to probe into the motivational structures of fascist joiners.
69 F. Mullally, *Fascism Inside England* (London, Claude Morris, 1946).
70 W. F. Mandle, 'The Leadership of the British Union of Fascists', *Australian Journal of Politics and History*, 12 (December, 1966), pp. 360–83.
71 Ibid., p. 369.
72 R. Griffin (ed.), *International Fascism. Theories, Causes and the New Consensus* (London, Arnold, 1998), pp. 45–8.

73 See above, Introduction, on the Marxist theory of fascism.
74 S. J. Rawnsley, 'Fascism and Fascists in the North of England in the 1930s' (Ph.D. thesis, University of Bradford, 1983), and S. J. Rawnsley, 'The Membership of the British Union of Fascists', in K. Lunn and R. Thurlow (eds), *British Fascism* (London, Croom Helm, 1980), pp. 150–65.
75 J. D. Brewer, *Mosley's Men. The BUF in the West Midlands* (Aldershot, Gower Publishing, 1984). See also J. D. Brewer, 'The British Union of Fascists: Some Tentative Conclusions on its Membership', in S. U. Larsen, B. Hagtvet and J. P. Myklebust (eds), *Who Were the Fascists? Social Roots of European Fascism* (Oslo, Universitetsforlaget, 1980), pp. 542–56.
76 Brewer, *Mosley's Men*, p. 7.
77 Brewer, 'The British Union', p. 545.
78 Ibid., p. 544.
79 Two of Brewer's fifteen respondents, for example, hailed from places as far apart as East Anglia and Birmingham.
80 Linehan, *East London for Mosley*.
81 Of the 232 East End fascists, 43 per cent were unskilled and semi-skilled workers, while almost 15 per cent were skilled workers.
82 Ibid., p. 216.
83 Skidelsky, *Oswald Mosley*, p. 327.
84 For a continental example, see D. Muhlberger, *Hitler's Followers* (London, Routledge, 1991).
85 See J. Linz, 'Some Notes Towards a Comparative Study of Fascism in Sociological Historical Perspective', in W. Laqueur (ed.), *Fascism: A Reader's Guide* (London, Wildwood, 1976), p. 81.
86 Linehan, *East London for Mosley*, pp. 81–4. Stepney Mosleyites astutely played up the issue of the leftist anti-clerical, anti-Catholic outrages in Spain for all it was worth, a factor of the Civil War that, to the consternation of Stepney's Catholics, was virtually ignored by left-wing organisations in the Borough.
87 Mandle, 'The Leadership', p. 369.
88 Thurlow, *Fascism in Britain. A History*, p. 125.
89 Ibid., p. 130.
90 Gottlieb, 'Women and Fascism', p. 44.
91 Ibid., p. 77.
92 M. Durham, *Women and Fascism* (London, Routledge, 1998), p. 170.
93 Thurlow, *Fascism in Britain. A History*, p. 125.
94 Linehan, *East London for Mosley*.
95 Webber, 'Patterns of Membership', pp. 593–4.
96 The work of Rawnsley, Cullen, Brewer, Gottlieb, Andrew Mitchell and my own work on east London spring to mind in this regard.
97 On BUF anti-semitism, see below, Chapter Seven.

The membership

98   O. Mosley, *The Greater Britain* (London, Greater Britain Publications, 1932).
99   On 'palingenetic' myth, see R. Griffin, *The Nature of Fascism* (London, Routledge, 1981), pp. 32–6.
100 See below, Chapters Eight to Eleven.
101 A number of Cullen's ex-Blackshirt respondents joined the BUF because they were intrigued by its theatre and 'dynamism'. See S. Cullen, 'The BUF, 1932–1940: Ideology, Membership and Meetings' (M.Litt. thesis, University of Oxford, 1987).
102 Gottlieb, 'Women and Fascism', p. 79.
103 Rawnsley, 'The Membership', p. 155.
104 Brewer, 'The British Union', p. 548.
105 Rawnsley, 'The Membership', p. 155.
106 See Linehan, *East London for Mosley*.

CHAPTER SEVEN

BRITISH FASCISM AND ANTI-SEMITISM

A number of points are in need of clarification before we proceed any farther. Firstly, there is no necessary or natural correlation between fascism and anti-semitism. As Zeev Sternhell has noted, racism was not a 'necessary condition for the existence of fascism', but was, on the contrary, a factor in fascist 'eclecticism'.[1] Although the majority of interwar Britain's fascist parties and groups professed anti-semitic beliefs, there were some that did not. Of the major parties, both the BUF and the IFL adopted an official anti-Jewish policy. For almost the entire period of its life, however, anti-semitism did not feature in the official ideology of the only other fascist party of note, the British Fascisti. The BF did not incorporate anti-semitism into its official programme until 1933, ten years after the party was launched.[2] There were other groups that would have no truck with an anti-semitic policy at all, such as Oscar Boulton's Unity Band, as we shall see below.

Secondly, the analyst and student of fascist anti-semitism needs to be alive to the fact that there are numerous strains of the anti-semitic virus, ranging from the common-or-garden anti-semitism, which was not systematically defined, to the more virulent racial-biological kind with its potentially genocidal implications. All the various strains of anti-semitism were present to some degree in domestic fascism. The character of a particular variant of fascist anti-semitism depended, of course, on conditioning and contingent factors. One such factor would be the presence or otherwise of xenophobic racist anti-semites within the decision-making hierarchy of an individual fascist party who may have been pushing for a more aggressively anti-Jewish policy. Another would concern the degree to which a prior tradition of nativist anti-semitism or racism existed within a national polity or community experiencing the onset of fascist anti-Jewish propaganda. The prevailing images, or stereotypes, of the Jew in society are another such contingent factor. Such stereotypes may have been sustained through institutionalised discrimination or popular mass culture. Context is also crucial to an understanding of the character of a specific strain of anti-semitism. Some historians, as we shall see below, believed that it is imperative to contextualise a particular variant, manifestation or outbreak of anti-semitism in terms of the interplay of wider political, socio-economic, cultural, and even international considerations.

Thirdly, and more obviously, a tradition of anti-semitism existed in Britain long before the advent of domestic fascism, much of it potent and highly articulate, as Colin Holmes's admirable *Anti-Semitism in British Society, 1876-1939* demonstrated.[3] By the same token, this scholarship reveals that anti-semitism in Britain was as much a home-grown product as a continental import, if not more so. This anti-semitic tradition had even embedded itself in the forms of English culture. Bryan Cheyette, for example, has shown how negative cultural stereotypes of the 'bad' Jew were much in evidence in the English literature of late Victorian and Edwardian England.[4] These Jewish literary stereotypes derived their meaning from a specifically English liberal tradition that defined Jews and their behaviour according to the degree to which they had assimilated into liberal society and its political and cultural traditions.[5] We have looked, too, in a previous chapter, at another pre-fascist manifestation of anti-semitism, the strain of 'conspiratorial' political anti-semitism that surfaced during the Great War and which fed off fears aroused by the Bolshevik Revolution and the domestic instability of the years after 1918.[6] Pre-eminently, this species of anti-semitism had its basis in that notorious forgery *The Protocols of the Elders of Zion*, and found expression in the fantasy of the 'hidden hand' and the 'German-Jewish-Bolshevik' conspiracy to destabilise the British Empire. Outlets for the myth were provided by publications such as Leo Maxse's *National Review*, Lord Alfred Douglas's *Plain English*, the Duke of Northumberland's Boswell Press, the *Patriot*, and organisations like the Britons.[7]

If we begin with the anti-semitism of the British Fascisti, we will observe that it was small beer in comparison with some of the variants we shall encounter below. According to Colin Cross, it was of the 'mild, doctrinaire type which excludes Jews from golf clubs'.[8] As already mentioned, the BF did not adopt anti-semitism as official policy until 1933, ten years after the party was formed. Prior to that date, only a vague form of 'anti-alienism' featured in BF pronouncements, though it is possible that this may have functioned as a coded language to conceal some resentment against Jews on the part of some elements within the party. Nonetheless, while it is important to accept the possibility that anti-semitism may have circulated amongst some Fascisti members, it is important not to overstate its virulence or the extent of its penetration into the party as a whole. A shift in orientation did occur by the early 1930s, however, with anti-alienism developing into a full-blown anti-semitism. In its 24-point programme of mid-1933, the BF announced that Jews should be prevented from voting, holding official offices in the state, and playing a part in the nation's financial and cultural life. The BF was becoming more ideologically inclined towards the German Nazis by the latter phase of its life, a reorientation which may have nudged it in the direction of anti-semitism at the level of official policy.[9] Nesta Webster stands as an anomaly in the story of the BF and anti-semitism. If the BF, for much of its life, was lukewarm in its attitude towards anti-semitism, this was not the case with Webster. She already harboured extreme anti-semitic views when she joined the BF in 1926 and retained them throughout her time in the party. She was an anti-semite of the arch conspiratorialist variety, who swallowed much of the message contained in *The Protocols*, believed in the myth of the German-Jewish 'hidden hand' behind the 1917 Bolshevik Revolution, and thought that Jews were plotting against the British Empire.[10] Webster also levelled a classic chimeric accusation at Jews, carried over from medieval anti-semitism, that they were aiding Satan in his grand design to undermine Christianity.[11] Personality mechanisms might have been at the root of Webster's anti-Jewish beliefs. An insight into her general psychology can be gauged from the fact that she believed in the occult, mysticism, reincarnation, telepathy and the existence of ghosts.[12]

The anti-semitism of the Imperial Fascist League was of a very different order from that of the BF. The IFL advocated a doctrine of racial anti-semitism and Nordic supremacy that would set it apart from the great majority of its contemporaries on the interwar fascist fringe. Initially, when the IFL was formed in November 1928, the 'Jewish question' did not occupy the centre ground of party policy. A vague form of traditional right-wing anti-alienism rather than a systematically defined anti-semitism prevailed.[13] By the spring of 1930 a change in thinking was becoming apparent, with Jews now being specifically targeted by IFL propagandists and blamed for a range of ills apparently affecting contemporary Britain and its Empire. Before long the 'Jewish question' would become the IFL's ruling passion, an obsessional anti-semitism that derived much of its impetus from the idiosyncratic personality of Arnold Leese, the party's leader. This descent into the dark regions of racial fanaticism accelerated in 1933 when the IFL merged with 'The Nordics'. The Nordics was a small but extreme racist group, committed to spreading race consciousness amongst Britons of 'Nordic blood' and improving the nation's 'racial fitness'.

According to Leese and the IFL, Jewry sought world supremacy and with it the domination of the Gentile race. Pursuing their goals through stealth and cunning rather than through open confrontation, the hand of the Jew was to be found behind all the various manifestations of subversion, disruption and disintegration in every country, including Britain. It was a ludicrous fantasy, of course, that linked this aspect of Leese's thought to the elaborate anti-Jewish conspiracy theories of Leo Maxse's *National Review*, the Boswell Press, the *Patriot*, Nesta Webster and others of this ilk. Leese, too, believed in the authenticity of *The Protocols*. In his hands, however, the myth of the Jewish world conspiracy would reach new heights of absurdity. The tentacles of Jewish subversion and disintegration apparently reached into virtually every sphere of domestic life, aesthetic, religious, ethical, social, industrial, financial and political. For example, Jews' pernicious presence could be found lurking behind postwar decadence in art, culture, mysticism, modern psychology, democracy, international communist subversion, class war doctrines, international finance, freemasonry, and all opinion-forming media outlets including the press and broadcasting.[14] They also sought to corrupt conventional morals, marriage and family life. If this was not enough, 'Jew power' was also behind crime, the 'white slave traffic', First World War casualties, anti-patriotism, the League of Nations, disarmament, unemployment, and attempts to undermine the Empire and eradicate the aristocracy. We could also throw in a variety of supposed Jewish malpractices, including corruption in public life and financial and banking irregularities.

The IFL's hatred of Jews knew no bounds. Leese even revived the Jewish ritual murder myth. The first known incident of this kind was recorded in Norwich, England, in 1144. The charge would recur in later years, such as the infamous incident in Lincolnshire in 1255, which revolved around the unsolved murder of a nine-year-old boy, Hugh of Lincoln. According to the Lincolnshire myth, some local Jews had abducted and then murdered the boy for religious ritual purposes because they required the blood of a Gentile child for the Passover ceremony.[15] The ritual murder charge led to the demonisation of Jews in medieval England and fuelled later Christian anti-semitism, while chimeric accusations of this kind provided a sanction for acts of persecution and collective violence against Jews down the centuries. Incredibly, Leese resurrected the myth in the modern context of 1930s England. In mid-1936, in an article in the IFL's newspaper, he stated that Jews regularly engaged in the ritual murder of Christians so they could procure fresh blood to mix in their ceremonial Passover bread.[16] This typically bizarre outburst led to Leese's prosecution on charges of seditious libel and creating a public mischief. He was eventually found guilty on the latter charge and, after refusing to pay the fine imposed by the court, received a six-month prison sentence.

Not surprisingly, given the eccentric nature of his views, Leese advocated bizarre measures to solve the 'Jewish problem'. He proposed that Jews be compulsorily confined to Madagascar and segregated on the southern half of that island where they could be stewarded by representatives from a soon-to-be-established 'League of Nordic Nations'.[17] It is likely that Leese picked up the seed of the Madagascar solution idea from his mentor, Henry H. Beamish of the Britons, although this may not have been the sole origin. The idea had a wide circulation amongst Europe's anti-semites, including the German Nazis, who considered the possibility of dispatching Jews to this location during the Second World War.

A crude but relatively systematic race theory underpinned Arnold Leese's and the IFL's fanatical hatred of Jews. It was a biological-racist view of Jews and Jewish behaviour that lent a dark and sinister edge to his anti-semitic rantings. For the IFL, the motive force of history and all cultural attainment was race, rather than an abstract guiding principle of progress as philosophical liberals liked to believe or class friction as advocated in the Marxist model of historical materialism. Within this racial interpretation of history, it was humankind's highest racial types who were responsible for propelling the historical and civilising process forward. Arnold Leese, the IFL, and its sister organisation 'The Nordics', believed that a hierarchy of different biological types existed in the human and social world, as in nature. Each of these different categories of human beings, moreover, was distinguishable according to specific physical, psychological and behavioural characteristics that were fixed and unalterable. The racial fascists of the IFL also introduced the principle of heredity into the equation, for these characteristics were apparently carried within the body and 'blood' of defined racial-biological groups and transmitted down the generations. This fixed biological endowment, a sort of physical and genetic blueprint, operated irrespective of external considerations such as environment or educational input. The racial fascist doctrine of biological differentiation and inherited characteristics sketched a depressingly static and inflexible model of the human world, where the worth or value of a particular race was not only biologically determined in advance, but precluded the possibility of the improvement of the so-called inferior races.

The ancestry of the IFL's distinctive brand of racial fascism can be traced to a nineteenth-century Anglo-Saxon tradition of racist thought that stressed the 'scientific' basis of race, rather than the continental tradition that tended to focus on the metaphysical and mystical dimensions of race. In a brilliant analysis, Richard Thurlow has convincingly demonstrated that the ideology of domestic racial nationalism upheld by the likes of Arnold Leese drew heavily on indigenous ideas, and should not be depicted as a simple derivative or imitation of German Volkish or Nazi racist thought.[18] In the continental tradition, which was strongly influenced by the thinking of Houston Stewart Chamberlain, the idea of race was based on subjective and irrational criteria rather than objective considerations. According to this mystical model of race, racial entities were established by intangible phenomena such as blood, landscape, spirit or an ethereal 'life-force'. Race was imagined to have emanated from mythical or mysterious sources that were not amenable to objective scientific scrutiny. Houston Stewart Chamberlain, drawing on Kant's notion of an 'essence' outside reason and pragmatism, claimed that all Germans possessed an inner 'race soul', a sort of mysterious inner substance that bound them together and conferred on them a unique and special status in the racial hierarchy.[19]

The 'scientific' racism that infused the race thinking of Arnold Leese received much of its impetus from nineteenth-century English Darwinian evolutionary doctrine and its later offspring Social-Darwinism. Darwinian evolutionary theory, in particular, would provide racist thought with a spurious 'scientific' credibility. It contributed, often inadvertently, a number of key ideas to the mode of racist thought that would characterise Leese's biological anti-semitism. To begin with, the theory of the 'survival of the fittest' and the best through evolutionary struggle appeared to reinforce the racist belief in Anglo-Saxon or Nordic supremacy. Anglo-Saxons apparently reigned supreme in the contemporary struggle for existence by virtue of their superior competitive instincts, innate moral and cultural qualities, and capacity for continued self-improvement. Darwinism's belief in the distinctiveness or uniqueness of species similarly supplied a spurious scientific rationale for the racist theory that people were divided into clearly differentiated races in the human world. Biological racism, with its rigid attachment to the theory of unalterable physical, psychological and behavioural traits, also owed a great deal to the Darwinian concept of the hereditary transmission of characteristics through evolution. Darwinism, too, advanced the notion that inequality reigned in nature, hierarchies based on force and the survival of the fittest of the species, an idea that seemed to rationalise the racist belief that you can have no equality between races or different racial types. The assumption that races are inherently unequal received further justification from the Darwinian conviction that nature reproduced species of unequal worth, or group inheritances of unequal value.[20] According to Arnold Leese, 'breeds of men have their characteristics just like breeds of dogs, and there is no equality either in men or in dogs'.[21] Finally, the omnipresent racial fascist dread of impending racial extinction owed something to the Darwinian proposition that only those species that proved capable of adapting to the harsh natural environment would survive.

Darwinian evolutionary doctrine's progeny, Social-Darwinism, made a significant contribution to racial fascist theory too. The idea of race betterment through the application of scientific methods, or eugenics, appealed to racial fascists who felt that the interventionist state could play a positive role in assisting the process of 'natural selection' by designing and implementing measures to improve the qualities of the race. The eugenic idea of the state as an instrument of racial improvement was sanctioned by the IFL, who looked forward to a time when the Fascist Corporate State would encourage the 'more highly cultured elements of the population' to produce larger families.[22]

The theory of genetics was another important forerunner of the IFL's biological-racist anti-semitism. Like Darwinism, Social-Darwinism and eugenics, genetics was another strand of thought that contributed to the so-called 'science' of racism. For racial fascists, genetics seemed to provide further 'scientific' evidence to support the proposition that biological factors explained differences between groups of human beings and that individual characteristics and conduct were predetermined. For example, August Weismann, a German biologist writing in the late nineteenth century, claimed that all life forms contained a distinctive hereditary substance, the autonomous 'germ plasm'. The 'germ plasm' constituted the essential element of germ cells, the hereditary material that is transmitted from generation to generation, and this unchangeable hereditary material was exempt from environmental change.[23] Weismann's explosive theory, which contradicted Lamarck's concept of acquired characteristics, served to sever heredity from the environment, thereby denying the possibility of change through individual self-exertion. We do know that Arnold Leese had some knowledge of genetic theory. In an article in the IFL press in June 1933, he cited the work of Gregor Mendel, like Weismann a leading figure in the field of genetics.[24]

Another strand of thought that fed into 'scientific racism' was anthropology. The science of anthropology undertook to inquire into humankind's evolutionary lineage, and its forms of language, religion and culture. Although anthropology first emerged in the late eighteenth century, it owed much to Charles Darwin's later insights on evolution.[25] Physical anthropology was a major branch of anthropology. Pre-eminently, it concerned itself with the naturalistic description of humankind's diverse groups, observing and then classifying their physical characteristics and differences. Within the context of late nineteenth- and early twentieth-century Europe, however, anthropology all too frequently became vulgarised, as imperialists and others sought a scientific and philosophical rationalisation for Anglo-Saxon imperialism and colonialism. Anthropology was often reduced to the crude classification and ranking of distinct 'racial types', where supposed race differentiation was based on outward physical criteria. For example, the relative worth or value of an individual was deduced from the physical make-up of the body or facial geography, such as the facial angle, the size of the skull, or shape of the jaw.[26] Anthropologists believed that it was possible to discover the inner moral and intellectual capacities of an individual from these outward physical characteristics. In a similar vein, the 'science' of anthropometry was prevalent during the late nineteenth century. Anthropometry was the practice of measuring skulls and the heads of living individuals in order to identify supposedly distinctive racial patterns among ethnic groups and establish their relative racial 'quality'.[27] The observations, classifications and comparisons made by physical anthropologists, though, were highly subjective and heavily value-laden, for they were guided in their judgements by aesthetic criteria derived from the ancient Greeks' classical ideal of beauty.[28]

Deductions about the worth of an individual or ethnic group from outward physical attributes became a staple element of 'scientific racism'. Along with Darwinian physiology, eugenics and genetics, this vulgarised version of physical anthropology would underpin the IFL's race doctrine. Arnold Leese, the IFL and the Nordics frequently inferred the 'quality' of ethnic groups by reference to physical traits which were based on aesthetic criteria. They were enthusiastic advocates, for example, of the myth of the innate beauty of the Aryan bodily form. Aryans, for Britain's racial fascists, exhibited physical purity. They had golden hair and fair skin, were tall in stature, strong-boned and well built, with a narrow face set upon a firm chin, and a medium to long skull.[29] This physical perfection was complemented by moral and mental purity. Aryans had certain innate moral and personal characteristics that distinguished them from the remainder of humankind. These characteristics included honesty, love of truth and justice, personal courage, and an attachment to the ideals of service and duty.[30] The IFL's views here amounted to a vulgarisation of the classical concept that the beautiful body posits a beautiful inner soul. The Aryan or Nordic was also perceived to be mentally alert, imaginative and intellectually inquisitive. In short, the Aryans were defined as a unique racial aristocracy, history's principal culture-bearers, who alone, of all the variety of racial types, possessed the appropriate personal and mental qualities to ensure the preservation of higher culture and the forward-thrust of civilisation.

Other true 'racial types' in Europe, according to the IFL, were the Mediterranean, Dinaric, East Baltic, and Alpine peoples. With the Aryans, they apparently constituted Europe's 'white races'. The Jews, for their part, would fall into a special category of IFL race analysis, as we shall see. Like the Aryans, all these groups were classified and evaluated according to distinct outward physical characteristics that seemed to coincide with their inner moral and mental state. Of the non-Aryan 'white races', only the 'Mediterranean' was thought to display positive physical and personal qualities, though of a lower order than the Aryan.[31] The East Baltic and Alpine peoples, on the other hand, were considered to be extremely low-grade racial material. The Alpine racial type, which could be found in large numbers in central France, south-east Germany, Switzerland, northern Italy, Galicia, Poland, Russia and the Balkans, did not meet the aesthetic criteria derived from the classical ideal of beauty. According to Arnold Leese, Alpines were 'clumsily-built' and square-headed.[32] They were also small and stocky, had short limbs and a short neck below a broad coarse-featured face.[33] These physical characteristics harmonised with their mental and personal traits. The Alpine racial type was purported to be intellectually slow, narrow-minded, unimaginative, humourless, ill-disciplined, lacked enterprise and was jealous by nature. Alpines had contributed very little to the advancement of civilisation, declared Leese, as had the East Baltic race, which predominated in eastern Germany, Poland, Russia and the Finnish interior. The East Baltic type bore a physical resemblance to the Alpine, though the former had 'Mongolian' features, a huge and heavy lower jaw and a weak chin, according to the racial fascists.[34] More imaginative than the Alpine, the East Baltic supposedly lacked resolution and was thus deemed to be uncreative by nature. The IFL declared that, being of poor racial fibre, both Alpine and East Baltic were impressionable and were thus easily lured towards that scourge of civilisation and culture, communism.

Such negative views on Europe's non-Aryan 'white races', however, paled in comparison to the IFL's assessment of the racial pedigree of the Jew. In Arnold Leese's distorted imagination, the Jew was neither a white person nor even a 'true racial type'. The Jew was of 'mixed blood, neither Eurasian nor Eurafrican, but a mixture of both', a 'mongrelised' being whose lineage could be traced to humankind's lowest stocks.[35] The Jewish 'Nation' was composed of three categories: Marrano, Sephardic, and Ashkenazim. The Marrano Jew apparently had a faint hint of Nordic blood within him, which was a consequence of intermarriage with the 'superior race'.[36] A blend of Oriental, Negro and Hither Asiatic blood, on the other hand, was thought to run through the veins of the Sephardic, or southern or Spanish Jew. The Negro racial component was very strong, for Leese, as could be observed in the Sephardic Jew's 'pouting lips and crinkly hair'.[37] The third type of Jew, the Ashkenazim, or German or eastern Jew, had a small amount of white Alpine blood in him, though this was 'swamped' by Mongoloid yellow and Hither Asiatic blood.[38] The Ashkenazim's ancestors were apparently the converted Jews of the Khazar Empire, who thrived in southern Russia *c.* 800 AD.[39] Leese reserved his worst invective for the Ashkenazim. He singled out the Hither Asiatic blood as the source of the Ashkenazim's supposedly evil nature.[40] The typical Hither Asiatic, according to Leese, had distinct physical characteristics, among which were a short head, weak chin, excessive bodily hair, swarthy skin and a narrow cunning face.[41] In nature and temperament, the Hither Asiatic race, which supposedly hailed from Asia Minor and which was composed of Armenians, Turks, Syrians, Kurds and Afghans as well as Jews, was declared to be mean, sensual, cruel, vengeful, treacherous and had a tendency towards homosexuality.[42] The hand of the Hither Asiatic was behind some of history's bloodiest episodes, for Leese, including the Spanish Inquisition and the Russian Bolshevik terror. In contrast to the Hither Asiatic's sadistic and bloody legacy, the Nordic had bequeathed to history Santa Klaus, the bringer (*sic*) of gifts.

The IFL's racial anti-semitism meant that of all interwar Britain's fascist parties, it was the one most closely linked to Hitler's NSDAP. In the historiography, Gisela Lebzelter, in particular, has stressed the close parallels between IFL and Nazi ideology.[43] However, though there were definite areas of overlap, Lebzelter's analysis overstated the connection. The IFL's racist doctrine should not be cast as a pale imitation of Nazi anti-semitism. Anglo-Saxon 'scientific' racism was the principal ancestor of the IFL's racial fascism, rather than the continental tradition of metaphysical or mystical racist thought which formed a significant, though not exclusive, slice of Hitlerite anti-Jewish thought. We should add, too, that with the IFL's anti-semitism we embark on a journey into the realms of racial fantasy. Arnold Leese's chimeric accusations against Jews, with their rigid train of thought and Manichean bent, had little basis in reality or reason and can only be comprehended in terms of the personality-disturbance or psycho-pathological model of anti-semitic belief systems. In other words, if we are to discern the motivating factors behind Leese's anti-semitism we need to delve into his personality. As Colin Holmes quite correctly recognised, with the fanatical and uncompromising 'high priests' of Jew-hatred such as Leese, there was an 'inner drive' towards anti-semitism that had its roots in a highly prejudiced or even psychologically impaired personality.[44]

If we now turn to the BUF's anti-semitism, we will observe that it was a different animal from that of the IFL's anti-Jewish hatred. As to its true nature, however, historians have yet to arrive at a consensus. One school of historiographical thought has defined Mosleyite anti-semitism as a blend of political anti-semitism, political scapegoating and cynical political opportunism. In this model, anti-semitism served its purpose as an ideological instrument of Mosleyite fascist political mobilisation. According to this 'orthodox' or classical interpretation of BUF anti-semitism, Mosley and the BUF leadership cynically exploited the dynamic of anti-semitism in order to resuscitate the party's political prospects, which were waning by 1934.[45] The year 1934 was certainly a difficult one for Mosley. A torrent of adverse press publicity, sparked by aggressive fascist stewarding at the BUF's Olympia meeting of 7 June, and the decision by the Rothermere press group to sever its links with Mosley the following month, for example, precipitated a haemorrhage of respectable support. The dip in the BUF's fortunes forced Mosley, according to Benewick, to 'construct a rationale to account for the failure of his movement, and at the same time to justify its continued existence and hold the allegiance of his followers'.[46] Similarly, in Mandle's judgement, by mid-1934 'the BUF was in need of an issue to revive its flagging fortunes'.[47] The outcome was the identification of a convenient Jewish scapegoat that was cynically exploited for reasons of political expediency. By September 1934 the BUF leadership had officially endorsed an extreme anti-semitic policy, with Mosley's speeches at Belle Vue, Manchester, on 29 September 1934, and at the Albert Hall, London, on 28 October 1934, being pivotal in this regard. Significantly, this policy development led Mosley to east London, with its large Jewish population, where from 1934 the bulk of the BUF's main propaganda effort in Britain was centred.

According to this perspective on BUF anti-semitism, therefore, anti-semitism was both an ideological tool of political mobilisation and a functional device to raise inter-ethnic tension within a community in order to garner support. In addition, there is the assumption that Mosley's anti-Jewish rhetoric was wholly insincere in that it did not have its basis in a set of beliefs that were genuinely held. Thus for Robert Benewick, 'political anti-semitism was more a weapon than a belief'.[48] A variation on this latter view was put forward by Colin Cross, who suggested that Mosley was a reluctant anti-semite who adopted the anti-semitic line under pressure from radical anti-Jewish elements in his party.[49] According to Cross, anti-semitism was the one area of fascist policy that found Mosley 'leading from behind'.[50]

Other attempts to comprehend the character of the BUF's anti-semitism were grounded in psychological and personality theory. W. F. Mandle's study in 1968, for example, drew on concepts from this paradigm, as did Benewick's, though neither did so exclusively. In this model, there was a stress on personality disturbance, prejudice and the authoritarian personality. Influenced by Freudian concepts, fascist anti-semitism is, here, viewed in terms of aggression projection, a form of displaced aggression arising from a refusal to probe 'inside oneself' and a personal failure in interpersonal relations, particularly pertaining to a child–parent relationship.[51] Prejudice, in this case against Jews, was therefore thought to serve a vital function in that it resolved an inner emotional conflict and re-established 'mental equilibrium' within the psychologically disturbed individual. Thus we had Mandle informing us that 'Mosley himself had a poor relationship with his father', the assumption being that this had some bearing on his later adoption of an anti-Jewish policy.[52] Similarly, during the BUF's anti-semitic campaign, according to Benewick, the highly visible Jew became 'a tangible object for projection and an outlet for frustration' for the prejudiced individual.[53]

The later historiography expressed some dissatisfaction with both the classical model of political anti-semitism and the person-orientated psychological approach. The question was asked whether one could arrive at a truly close understanding of BUF anti-semitism using these models of analysis. Some historians wondered whether the latter approach, for example, can ever be a viable tool of historical analysis given the speculative nature of its concepts and its falling back on hypotheses that are too often unsupported by empirical evidence. As Colin Holmes stated with regard to the BUF, 'we simply do not have sufficient proof to say that, in general, members possessed personalities which required the support of prejudice'.[54] This is not to discount completely the personality-disturbance model of course, for as we have seen with some extreme anti-semites like Arnold Leese, it is very apposite. It is only to recognise that, by itself, it cannot tell the whole story, nor even, perhaps, a significant part of it.

The political opportunistic model has been criticised in the later historiography, too. It has been attacked for being mono-causal, reductionist and too narrowly focused. It has been accused, for example, of failing to contextualise the conflict between the BUF and the Jewish community in terms of wider 'objective' considerations of a political, economic, social and cultural nature.[55] Some historians have adopted an interactionist or convergence perspective in an effort to comprehend BUF anti-semitism. In a seminal essay written in 1980, Colin Holmes argued that major outbreaks of anti-semitism tended to arise out of specific social milieux, were a product of a complex interaction of circumstances involving both agents in the conflict equation, and were part of a broader historical narrative of memory where perceptions in the present were impregnated with memories from the past.[56]

Thus for Holmes, BUF anti-semitism developed against a particular historical backdrop, which he identified as the 1929–31 world economic crisis and its domestic offshoot, the depression of the 1930s. Mosleyite fascism represented an ultra-nationalist response to the economic crisis which, according to Holmes, began to target Jews, who were accused of being a sectional interest within the nation with separate goals and external loyalties. In this sense, Holmes demonstrated that the BUF's anti-semitism should not be viewed in isolation from the remainder of its fascist ideology. The interactionist context then came into play. When sections of the Anglo-Jewish community, alarmed by these attacks and the growth of domestic fascism, and cognisant of the treatment of their co-religionists in Nazi Germany, understandably and legitimately organised opposition to Mosley, this, in turn, had the effect of further accelerating anti-semitic feeling within the BUF. Other interactionist pressures, for Holmes, included the 'historic role of Jews as members of a middle-man minority group'.[57] For the historian of anti-semitism, it is often less challenging and less problematic dissecting the mentality and utterances of the fascist anti-semite, but, as David Feldman observed, 'the political opposition and social competition presented by Jews' must be considered when investigating BUF anti-semitism.[58] Finally, for Holmes, there existed in 1930s Britain an 'anti-semitic folk memory' that drew on such recollections as the Marconi scandal, the propaganda of the British Brothers' League in the East End and the myth of the Jewish 'hidden hand' behind Bolshevism, which nourished the anti-Jewish antipathy and helped exaggerate the conflict in the present.

Robert Skidelsky took a more extreme and controversial interactionist line in his 1981 biography of Oswald Mosley. Skidelsky argued that it was the physical disruption of Mosleyite meetings by Jewish anti-fascists, a sort of pre-emptive strike that sought to strangle the BUF at birth before it grew into maturity on the scale of the German NSDAP, that helped to bring forward the anti-semitic sentiment in the BUF.[59]

Within the context of this discussion of the historiography, it needs mentioning, too, that some scholars have criticised the interactionist paradigm. Bryan Cheyette, for example, chastised convergence theory for 'over-determining' the sociological, and understating the role of ideology. Cheyette advocated a 'discourse' theory of anti-semitism, a methodological approach that has received widespread usage in literary analysis and postmodernist critical theory in recent years.[60] It also owes much to Michel Foucault's idiosyncratic approach to historical analysis and Edward Said's appraisal of Orientalism.[61] The emphasis here is on the notion of anti-semitism as a series of discourses or 'representations', rather than a 'natural' depiction of Jews. These anti-semitic 'narratives', or 'texts', were already prevalent in wider British society and culture, and could be drawn upon by the anti-semite. Thus, according to Cheyette, it was the 'determining imprint of racial discourse' within the wider society that was responsible for the anti-semite's interpretation of social 'reality'. In this approach 'the problematic exists not at the level of specific instances of conflict, at the level of "interaction" between social groups, but in the realms of ideology'.[62] Advocates of this approach, however, run the risk of producing a sort of reductionist history of the type that they condemn in the work of those who stress the importance of the 'sociological' dimension. In other words, postmodernist history writing is in danger of 'over-determining' the ideological at the expense of the social context, whereby all history and social reality collapses into the 'text' and further, in the imposing words of Jacques Derrida, 'there is nothing outside of the text'.

So how, then, given the lack of a consensus within the historiography, should we attempt to define BUF anti-semitism? The researcher into BUF anti-semitism needs to be sensitive to the range of interpretations on offer and attempt, if possible, a multi-factoral or multi-causal analysis which appears to offer the most fruitful way forward. In other words, the historian should seek to take account of the ideological underpinning of BUF anti-semitism, the socio-economic backdrop to the conflict, the interactionist context, images or 'representations' of the Jew in domestic culture and society, and the Mosleyite manipulation of these cultural and historical anti-Jewish prejudices. We should also take due account of some of the more recent research, which provides us with a more accurate insight into the character of anti-semitism emanating from the BUF's leadership, particularly Oswald Mosley.

Here, once again, the political opportunistic version is problematic. By promoting the argument that Mosley's anti-semitism was a cynical tactical weapon of political mobilisation, it failed to recognise that his anti-Jewish rhetoric had its basis in anti-semitic beliefs that were genuinely held. Although little attempt was made at the level of official party ideology to develop a systematic anti-semitic theory, define anti-semitic terms, or fall back on racial biological categories, or indeed metaphysical and mystical frames of reference, Mosley's anti-semitism was real enough. It was rooted primarily in a conspiratorial and ethnocentric view of Jews. Mosley frequently used conspiratorial language to describe Jewish behaviour, such as his references, repeated *ad nauseam*, to that mythical entity 'international Jewish finance', an apparently self-interested body whose agenda ran parallel to the national interest. Ethnocentricism, or cultural antipathy, saturated Mosley's outlook, too. It is important to restate that the BUF's anti-Jewish beliefs cannot be viewed in isolation from the remainder of its fascist ideology. This is no more evident than with Mosley's ethnocentric anti-semitism, which to a large extent was the child of the mythic palingenetic ultra-nationalist core at the heart of BUF ideology. The BUF's gloomy preoccupation with decadence, its parallel belief that decadence was the harbinger of national decay and decline unless fascism could arrest the process and bring about a glorious national rebirth, underlay much of Mosley's ethnocentric anti-semitism. Thus the hand of the Jew was imagined to be behind a welter of apparently 'decadent' modern cultural forms and developments, including modern art, modernist literature, psychoanalysis, and 'cosmopolitan' culture in its more general sense.[63]

These conspiratorial and ethnocentric views can also, in part, be tracked back to the Enlightenment notion of Jews as an internationalist body who 'despite emancipation, would not assimilate to the cultural norms of the emergent nation states of Europe', an outlook held by many ideological anti-semites down the years.[64] Mosley's hostility to Jews was also informed by his reading of Oswald Spengler. The Mosleyite preoccupation with alleged Jewish cultural exclusiveness and divided loyalties owed something to Spengler's quasi-historical portrait of self-contained mutually exclusive cultural aggregations, with the apparently rootless Eastern Magian culture, represented by the Jew, contrasting and clashing with the organic Faustian culture of European man.[65]

It is worth restating that Mosley's anti-Jewish beliefs were not grounded in pseudo-scientific racial-biological theories of anti-semitism, or a hierarchy of race model, which clearly differentiated his 'Jew-hatred' from that of Arnold Leese and the IFL, nor are they in the tradition of metaphysical and mystical racial anti-semitism. Richard Thurlow has put this down to a 'Lamarckian' strand within Mosley's anti-semitism.[66] Whereas Leese believed that different groups of individuals had fixed characteristics that were biologically determined, leading him to infer their cultural potential from their supposed 'racial-biological' make-up, for the 'neo-Lamarckians' of the BUF it was culture not race that determined behaviour. In addition, Lamarck's belief that the development of species had been conditioned by material and environmental factors which were subject to changes over time, along with his conviction that environmentally acquired characteristics could be inherited, meant that no species, or 'race', could be imprisoned in its present characteristics in perpetuity.[67] Thus the potential for change underpinned Lamarck's theoretical model. As a Lamarkian, then, Mosley rejected the racist notion that biological inheritance prevented Jews from changing their behaviour, allowing him to make a distinction between different types of Jew and forms of Jewish conduct. From this, it followed that there were 'good' Jews that had adapted to the patriotic and cultural norms of the host nation, and 'bad' Jews that allegedly conspired to undermine the national interest, such as Jewish communists and 'international Jewish finance'. This important qualification, which was further rationalised by reference to Spengler's concepts, led to the construction of a typology of Jewish behaviour divided primarily along pseudo-ethical lines.

This is not to suggest, however, that Mosley's anti-semitism was any less repugnant than other manifestations of the genus. Though it was not anchored to a biological-genetic base, and there is no clear evidence that it would have led inexorably to a genocidal conclusion, his conspiratorial and ethnocentric 'Jew-hatred' should be roundly condemned. In addition, within the ranks of the BUF there were many who harboured more extreme anti-Jewish sentiments. The mentality of William Joyce, for example, concocted a dangerously potent ideological brew of conspiratorial, ethnocentric, categorical and racist anti-semitism, a frame of mind that would eventually impel him to throw in his lot with the biological-racist, and ultimately genocidal, anti-semites of Nazi Germany. Major-General J. F. C. Fuller, another senior BUF official, fused extreme conspiratorial anti-semitism with medieval or magical anti-semitism. 'For over 1,000 years', he contended, 'the Jews have been a world-wide power, a net of conspiracy and of race interests stretched over half the globe.'[68] According to Fuller, Jews had sought and attained the destabilisation of ancient Egypt, Babylon, Persia and Rome, fomented disorder after the Crusades, the French Revolution, the Napoleonic Wars and the Great War, and had almost entirely directed the Russian Revolution.[69] Fuller also revived the medieval notion of the Jew as the Devil's agent, assisting the latter in his grand design to destroy Christianity.[70] Christianity had been systematically undermined by the Jew down the ages through magic and mysticism, he claimed, the sources of which apparently sprang from the Qabalah and the *Zohar*, or *Book of Splendour*.[71] The Church had been assailed by Jewish-fostered magical cults, including witchcraft, sorcery and demonology, the latest expression of which was psychoanalysis, a new black magical cult that, by trifling with the mysteries of sex, struck at the heart of morality, the family and Christian civilisation.

The anti-Jewish rhetoric of another of Mosley's senior lieutenants, A. K. Chesterton, occasionally teetered over into crude racist language, though fundamentally, as David Baker has shown in a commendable biographical study, in the final analysis he remained in essence an ethnocentric or cultural anti-semite.[72] The BUF rank-and-file contained its fair share of extreme ideological anti-semites, too. In east London, such 'types' were much in evidence, not least the Bethnal Green Mosleyite E. G. 'Mick' Clarke, and 'Jock' Houston and James 'Bill' Bailey of the militantly anti-semitic Shoreditch Branch, all of whom were highly skilled in the crude 'art' of populist street-corner anti-semitism.[73] East London Mosleyites, such as the notorious Hoxton boxer Leonard James 'Dixie' Deans, were not averse to engaging in acts of 'physical force' violence against Jews either.[74]

As with the anti-semitism of the major parties, the picture pertaining to the minor fascist parties is not a uniform one. For example, while some of interwar Britain's smaller fascist parties and groups were fiercely anti-semitic, there were others that were indifferent to the so-called 'Jewish question'. Still others rejected anti-semitism outright. And even those that did promulgate an anti-Jewish policy, did so with varying degrees of clarity and coherence.

We should also observe that with many of the tinier and more ephemeral fascist groups it is difficult to offer any judgement at all on their stance towards anti-semitism. This is because, unlike the situation relating to the larger parties, the existing information on most of these groups is very patchy. Finally, it should be noted that we have met all the following fascist groups and period anti-semites in a previous chapter.[75]

Of the 1920s minor parties, the National Fascisti was anti-'alien' and anti-semitic, though there is little evidence that this developed beyond the plane of crude insults, directed against 'alien' immigration, the Naturalisation Laws and the 'Bolshevik-Judaeic menace'. The picture is somewhat different with the CINEF, the only other body of the 1920s minor fascist groups of some substance. James Strachey Barnes, the CINEF's principal representative in Britain, had little time for anti-semitism, particularly of the racist variety. He considered the anti-semite to be a 'fool' and professed an admiration for Jews, believing them to be a 'greatly endowed race'. Repudiating the claim by the anti-semites that there was a 'Jewish peril', he thought that every host nation should seek to assimilate its Jewish population, for a 'judicious admixture of Jewish blood' served to enrich other races, including the Nordic races.[76]

By the mid-1930s anti-semitism had moved more centre-stage, with most of the minor organisations then in existence taking the NSDAP as their model concerning the so-called 'Jewish question'. The National Workers' Party, that fiercely pro-Nazi one-man band run by Lieutenant-Colonel Graham Seton Hutchison, for example, embraced both conspiratorial and racist anti-semitism. Seton Hutchison believed in the authenticity of *The Protocols*, as well as the myth of 'international Jewish finance'. He also thought that Mosley's BUF lacked race-consciousness and was under Jewish influence.[77] The NWP may have fallen under the spell of the Britons' anti-Jewish fantasies as well as those spun by the German Nazis, for its headquarters were at 40 Great Ormond Street, the offices of the Britons.[78] Seton Hutchison's other failed experiment in fascism, the British Empire Fascist Party, which made a brief appearance in November 1933, similarly proclaimed an extreme anti-Jewish policy. In a BEFP Britain, Jews would have been stripped of all their political privileges and purged from the nation's economic and cultural life.

The National Socialist League adopted a line that was just as extreme, advocating a heady 'blood and soil' racist anti-semitism, which comes as no great surprise given the personalities and sycophantic attitude towards Nazism of its leading lights, William Joyce, John Beckett and Angus MacNab.[79] A similar pattern can be discerned in two late 1930s proto-fascist bodies, the Right Club and the Nordic League. Both were intensely pro-Hitlerite and anti-Jewish. Of the two, the Nordic League was the most violently anti-semitic. Formed in 1937, the NL was a clandestine body with a primarily upper-middle-class support base that had its origins in a fanatical racist and occultist order, the White Knights of Britain, Britain's nearest equivalent to the American Ku-Klux-Klan.[80] At its gatherings, genocidal language would frequently be used in relation to Jews. The arch period anti-semite, Captain Archibald H. Maule Ramsay, was a key figure in both organisations. Ramsay believed in the Jewish 'hidden hand' behind Bolshevism, *The Protocols*, the 'Jewish world conspiracy' fantasy, and was a fervent anti-Zionist.[81]

Ramsay was also associated with the Militant Christian Patriots, another body that had formulated an anti-Jewish policy. A number of anti-semitic personalities, besides Ramsay, were attached to the MCP, including A. K. Chesterton, Joseph Banister, and J. F. Rushbrook, formerly of the IFL. The MCP were classical conspiratorialists. They believed that Jewry aimed at world domination, and was working to secure this goal through 'international finance' and Bolshevism. In the fiction of the MCP, Zionism represented another instrument through which Jewry sought world supremacy.[82] The MCP were hostile to Jewish immigration into Britain, too, believing that Jews were a racially exclusionist 'middleman minority' group whose ways were inimical to traditional British patriotism.[83] In this, the MCP drew on a historical stereotype of the Jews as a sojourning minority group, whose relationship to the host nation would always remain transient and temporary. As its title implies, the MCP viewed itself as a defender of the Christian faith and Christian civilisation against those that allegedly sought to undermine it, including Judaism, 'Jewish Bolshevism' and Zionism. It is partly within the context of this fanatically Christian outlook, according to Colin Holmes, 'that its anti-semitism should be considered'.[84]

However, even in the more heavily charged atmosphere of 1930s far-right politics, with the air thick with pro-Nazism and ideologically driven anti-semitism, it was not a uniform picture. The United Empire Fascist Party, one of the more ephemeral of the 1930s groups, which shortly after its formation in December 1933 became the United British Party, repudiated anti-semitism. In the UBP's programme, for example, it declared its intention to support the rights of those belonging to all religious faiths. This principle was soon to be upheld by the UPB when its Leader, C. G. Wodehouse-Temple, forced its candidate Serocold Skeels, a notorious period anti-semite, to stand down prior to contesting a by-election in Cambridge on account of his anti-Jewish views. Even in the case of the Marquis of Tavistock's BPP, another of the pro-Nazi groups operating in the period of late 1930s fascism, the situation is not clear-cut. The BPP refrained from adopting a policy of open anti-semitism for reasons of political expediency, despite the efforts of some militant anti-semites within the party leadership to prevent this.[85] Old habits did die hard, however, and some residual anti-semitism survived, albeit in a heavily diluted form. This can be observed in the BPP's allusions to the 'alien' infiltration of British life, and its attacks on the system of 'usury' which apparently perpetuated social and economic injustice. Lieutenant-Colonel Oscar Boulton's Unity Band, whose life spanned the entire 1930s, did indeed eschew anti-semitism, at least at the level of official party ideology. Indeed Boulton, who admired the qualities of the 'gifted' Jewish 'race', and was dismissive of the 'Nordic nonsense' espoused by the German professors of 'race culture', preferred tolerance to persecution.[86] 'We had certainly no reason to complain of our native Jews', he declared, 'whose fidelity to the country which they now claimed to be their own, and latterly the devoted patriotism of many of them in its defence, left nothing to be desired.'[87] The case of Oscar Boulton and his Unity Band during the 1930s, and indeed James Strachey Barnes in the preceding decade, reveals that there was no necessary correlation between fascism and anti-semitism. The analyst of fascist anti-semitism needs to be alive to this fact, just as he or she should be aware of the existence of a number of different strains of the anti-semitic virus, most of which were present to some degree in domestic fascism during the interwar period.

Notes

1   Z. Sternhell, *The Birth of Fascist Ideology* (Princeton, Princeton University Press, 1994), p. 5.
2   See above, Chapter Three.
3   C. Holmes, *Anti-Semitism in British Society, 1876–1939* (London, Arnold, 1979).

4 B. Cheyette, 'Jewish Stereotyping and English Literature 1875–1920: Towards a Political Analysis', in T. Kushner and K. Lunn (eds), *Traditions of Intolerance. Historical Perspectives on Fascism and Race Discourse in Britain* (Manchester, Manchester University Press, 1989), pp. 12–32.
5 On the same theme, see also D. Feldman, *Englishmen and Jews. Social Relations and Political Culture 1840–1914* (New Haven, Yale University Press, 1994). For a general history of modern Anglo-Jewry, see G. Alderman, *Modern British Jewry* (Oxford, Oxford University Press, 1992).
6 See above, Chapter Two. See also D. Cesarani, 'Joynson-Hicks and the Radical Right in England After the First World War', in Kushner and Lunn (eds), *Traditions of Intolerance*, pp. 118–39.
7 See above, Chapter Two.
8 C. Cross, *The Fascists in Britain* (London, Barrie and Rockliff, 1961), p. 122.
9 See *British Fascism*, March 1934, pp. 4–5.
10 Holmes, *Anti-Semitism*, pp. 155–6; R. Thurlow, *Fascism in Britain. A History, 1918–1985* (Oxford, Blackwell, 1987), pp. 57–61.
11 R. Thurlow, 'Satan and Sambo: The Image of the Immigrant in English Racial Populist Thought Since the First World War', in K. Lunn (ed.), *Hosts, Immigrants and Minorities* (Folkestone, Dawson, 1980), p. 43.
12 N. Webster, *Spacious Days. An Autobiography* (London, Hutchinson, 1950), pp. 173–4.
13 G. Lebzelter, *Political Anti-Semitism in England 1918–1939* (London, Macmillan, 1978), pp. 73–4.
14 *The Fascist*, July 1931, p. 2.
15 Nineteen Jews were falsely accused of the murder and subsequently executed.
16 *The Fascist*, July 1936, p. 5.
17 J. Morell, 'Arnold Leese and the Imperial Fascist League', in K. Lunn and R. Thurlow (eds), *British Fascism* (London, Croom Helm, 1980), p. 69.
18 Thurlow, *Fascism in Britain. A History*, pp. 86–90.
19 G. Mosse, *Towards the Final Solution. A History of European Racism* (Wisconsin, University of Wisconsin Press, 1978), pp. 105–6.
20 H. Fein (ed.) *The Persisting Question. Sociological Perspectives and Social Contexts of Modern Anti-semitism* (Berlin, Walter de Gruyter, 1987), p. 18.
21 *The Fascist*, October 1931, p. 3.
22 *The Fascist*, April 1929, p. 3.
23 A. Weismann, *The Germ-Plasm. A Theory of Heredity* (1892).
24 *The Fascist*, June 1933, p. 2.
25 Mosse, *Towards the Final Solution*, pp. 2 and 17.

26 G. Mosse, *The Crisis of German Ideology. Intellectual Origins of the Third Reich* (London, Weidenfeld and Nicolson, 1964), p. 100.
27 P. Rich, 'The Quest for Englishness', in G. Marsden (ed.), *Victorian Values. Personalities and Perspectives in Nineteenth-Century Society* (London, Longman, 1990), p. 217.
28 Mosse, *Towards the Final Solution*, p. 2.
29 *The Fascist*, March 1933, p. 1.
30 IFL, *Race and Politics. A Counter-blast to the Masonic Teaching of Universal Brotherhood* (IFL pamphlet, n.d.); *The Fascist*, March 1933, p. 1.
31 IFL, *Race and Politics*.
32 *The Fascist*, October 1931, p. 3.
33 IFL, *Race and Politics*.
34 *The Fascist*, October 1931, p. 3.
35 *The Fascist*, October 1934, p. 2.
36 *The Fascist*, July 1936, p. 5.
37 *The Fascist*, June 1932, p. 3.
38 *The Fascist*, October 1938, p. 2.
39 *The Fascist*, June 1932, p. 3.
40 *The Fascist*, October 1938, p. 2. However, in this racial fantasy, the Sephardic Jew also had a high quantity of Hither Asiatic blood.
41 *The Fascist*, July 1936, p. 5.
42 Ibid.
43 Lebzelter, *Political Anti-Semitism*, pp. 76–9.
44 C. Holmes, 'Anti-semitism and the BUF', in Lunn and Thurlow (eds), *British Fascism*, pp. 117–8; see also Holmes, *Anti-Semitism*, pp. 172–3.
45 Historians who have promoted a version of this line include R. Benewick, *Political Violence and Public Order* (London, Allen Lane, 1969) and W. F. Mandle, *Anti-semitism and the British Union of Fascists* (London, Longman, 1968).
46 Benewick, *Political Violence*, p. 151.
47 Mandle, *Anti-semitism*, p. 23.
48 Ibid., p. 134.
49 Cross, *The Fascists*, pp. 122–8.
50 Ibid. p. 119.
51 Fein, *The Persisting Question*, p. 21.
52 Mandle, *Anti-semitism*, p. 22.
53 Benewick, *Political Violence*, p. 151.
54 Holmes, 'Anti-semitism and the BUF', p. 118.
55 See, for example, T. Linehan, *East London for Mosley. The British Union of Fascists in East London and South-West Essex, 1933–40* (London, Frank Cass, 1996), pp. 4–5.
56 Holmes, 'Anti-semitism and the BUF', pp. 114–34.
57 Ibid., p. 128.

58 D. Feldman, 'There was an Englishman, an Irishman and a Jew: Immigrants and Minorities in Britain', *Historical Journal*, 26, 1 (1983), pp. 185–99.
59 R. Skidelsky, *Oswald Mosley* (London, Macmillan, 1981), pp. 385–410.
60 A good introduction here is T. Eagleton, *Literary Theory* (Oxford, Blackwell, 1983).
61 See, for example, M. Foucault, *The History of Sexuality* (New York, Random House, 1985) and E. Said, *Culture and Imperialism* (London, Chatto and Windus, 1993).
62 B. Cheyette, 'Hilaire Belloc and the Marconi Scandal: A Reassessment of the Interactionist Model of Racial Hatred', in T. Kushner and K. Lunn (eds), *The Politics of Marginality. Race, the Radical Right and Minorities in Twentieth-Century Britain* (London, Frank Cass, 1990), pp. 131–42.
63 For a more detailed focus on these cultural themes, see below, Chapters Eight, Nine and Eleven.
64 Thurlow, 'Satan and Sambo', pp. 39–63.
65 Ibid., p. 47.
66 Thurlow, *Fascism in Britain. A History*, p. 17.
67 Mosse, *Towards the Final Solution*, p. 18.
68 *FQ*, 1, 1 (January 1935), pp. 66–81.
69 Ibid.
70 Thurlow, 'Satan and Sambo'.
71 *FQ*, 1, 1 (January 1935), p. 78. The *Zohar* was a thirteenth-century book devoted to esoteric Jewish mysticism. It speculated on such themes as the mystery of creation and the question of evil.
72 D. Baker, *Ideology of Obsession. A. K. Chesterton and British Fascism* (London, I. B. Tauris, 1996), pp. 144–6.
73 See Linehan, *East London for Mosley*.
74 Ibid., p. 44.
75 The reader should refer to Chapter Five above, for more information on these groups and individuals.
76 J. S. Barnes, *Half a Life* (London, Eyre and Spottiswoode, 1933), p. 301. It might be argued, of course, that assimilation was simply another form of intolerance, given that Jews were being urged by the advocates of assimilation to accept the values and cultural norms of the host community. However, in Barnes's case, we should be careful not to assume that his use of the term 'assimilate' had the meaning ascribed to it by later scholars of anti-semitism.
77 R. Griffiths, *Fellow Travellers of the Right. British Enthusiasts for Nazi Germany 1933–39* (Oxford, Oxford University Press, 1983), p. 103.
78 H. S. B. Blume, 'A Study of Anti-Semitic Groups in Britain, 1918–40' (M. Phil. thesis, University of Sussex, 1971), p. 257.

79 On Joyce's post-BUF racist thought, see W. Joyce, *Twilight Over England* (Metairie, Sons, n.d.)
80 R. Griffiths, *Patriotism Perverted. Captain Ramsay, the Right Club and British Anti-Semitism 1939–40* (London, Constable, 1998), pp. 45–7.
81 Ibid., *passim*.
82 Holmes, *Anti-Semitism*, p. 171.
83 Ibid.
84 Ibid.
85 Griffiths, *Patriotism Perverted*, pp. 55–6.
86 O. Boulton, *The Way Out* (London, Boswell Publishing, 1934), p. 73.
87 O. Boulton, *Fads and Phrases* (London, Boswell Publishing, 1930), p. 50.

CHAPTER EIGHT

DEFINING CULTURE

Culture was at the centre of the fascist political project in interwar Britain. British fascism was a cultural phenomenon as much as it was a movement for political or economic change. According to Alexander Raven-Thomson of the BUF, fascism was 'a new and revolutionary creed of national and cultural regeneration'.[1] Cultural concerns permeated most aspects of British fascism, giving shape and coherence to many of its ideological preoccupations and perceptions. Like other areas of thought associated with British fascism, this cultural disposition did not have a distinct and readily perceivable historical and intellectual genealogy. At the intellectual level, the cultural ideas of British fascism drew on and absorbed concepts from a variety of both European *and* native sources. With regard to the former, British fascist culture developed within the broad European-wide cultural critique of liberal rationalism and positivism that originated in the 1890s, and was thus an organic element of it. *Fin-de-siècle* anti-rationalist thinkers like Nietzsche, Bergson, Sorel and Le Bon all developed concepts that found their way into the fascist cultural outlook, as we have seen in a previous chapter.[2] In other respects, though, fascist culture had its roots in cultural traditions and concerns, as well as specific material developments and forces, which were distinctly British. So how did Britain's fascists between the wars see culture? What did they understand by it, and how did they seek to define it? This chapter will address these matters.

For many native fascists, authentic culture emerged from the collective soul of the people. According to this *Volkish* notion of culture, there was an organic link between the people and culture. Fascist and Nazi *Volkish*, or populist, notions of culture between the wars drew inspiration from the romantic tradition, according to

George Mosse. This outlook can partly be traced to a neo-romantic perception that the people shared fundamental characteristics with Nature. The people were imagined to be a primitive, yet authentic force – simple, direct, full of innate goodness and possessed of a passionate honesty of basic emotions, indeed like Nature itself.[3] The people were also thought to represent something *eternal* and *enduring*, quintessential features of true culture for fascists. British fascists believed that by endorsing a popular culture of folk songs, medieval dances and ancient festivals, the 'eternal' or fundamental beneath the artificial veneer of modern bourgeois society would be rediscovered. At the same time, the maintenance of the traditions of folk culture would provide an antidote to the alienation of modern life. In this sense, then, folk culture was deemed to have its roots in a more edifying pre-industrial past.

Such an orientation towards popular culture would also help to maintain the nation's 'biological health'. For a Mosleyite, the embrace of popular cultural tradition, 'folk-lore, dialect and language and the observance of ancient festivals and customs', was crucial 'to the biological well-being of the race'.[4] Participation in such activities would also awaken the people from the modern stupor of 'individual self-absorption into which they had sunk', arousing them to a new communal consciousness.[5] Although references to race did feature in the BUF's lexicon, it did not develop a coherent or explicit theory of race. Racial terms were not defined with any precision, while some of its propagandists promoted a non-hierarchical, inclusive, rather than exclusive, notion of race. Thus popular traditions other than those found in 'Anglo-Saxon' England were considered to be authentic sources of cultural vitality. A Mosleyite celebrated the Gaelic folk genius of the Irish, for example. He waxed lyrical about the rich cultural heritage produced by such rural idylls as Connemara, an environment graced by 'the laughing lustrous eyes of the girls, the strong rugged men' and 'the sweet sound of the Gaelic and the peat reek filling the air'.[6] From such sources emanated music and poetry of such wild beauty, he proclaimed.

This populist view of culture also served to invest the people's everyday activities with cultural significance. Culture and life merge in this perspective, forming a natural, seamless unity. The everyday activities of the people became 'aestheticised' in the eyes of some British fascists, no more so than in the realm of work and labour. Fascists discovered true art and beauty in the individual craftsmanship associated with the artisan and the small workshop. James

Defining culture

Strachey Barnes mourned the disappearance of a refined tradition of 'handicraftsmanship' embodied in the 'exquisite furniture and household wares of the centuries before the industrial era'.[7] In this idealised view of work, the beauty and joy apparently inherent in physical labour was stressed, too. Work was defined as a truly creative activity. We can identify a strain of aesthetic anti-modernism within this particular cultural perspective, with many native fascists bemoaning the encroaching mechanisation of work, which they associated with the relentless march of industrialisation and factory mass production.[8] Fascists decried the legacy of the Industrial Revolution, and in so doing sought to place themselves in a long-standing cultural tradition that was distinctly British.[9] This tradition ran through the nineteenth-century writings of Samuel Taylor Coleridge, Thomas Carlyle, John Ruskin and the romantic socialism of William Morris, amongst others.[10]

The people were not the only repository of culture according to the British fascists. Authentic culture was also associated with the countryside and the soil. Rural England was depicted as a site of unequalled beauty and, as such, was considered to be a vital part of the nation's cultural heritage.[11] The land also shared certain characteristics with the people. It was considered to express something eternal and enduring, an apparently timeless place which transcended the present and within whose bosom the spiritual essence of the 'race' or nation was believed to reside. The fascist propensity to aestheticise work also came into play here. The beauty and joy to be discovered in physical labour was no more evident than in the working life of the countryside. Rural labour, though arduous, was idealised. To love the 'hard handle of the plough' and the 'sweat of harvest gathering' was to live a sublime existence which maintained the ancestral bond with the sturdy yeoman types who graced the England of old. Fascism's firm commitment to the land would ensure that 'once again the Yeomen of Britain will return', proclaimed Oswald Mosley.[12] To partake of the more genuine existence of rural life would replenish the spirit, too, the vital well-spring of creativity and culture for many fascists. The land even became synonymous with fascism itself, in the minds of some fascists. 'The soil is National Love and National Love is Fascism', a BUF member declared somewhat cryptically.[13]

The fascists did not only define culture through the medium of popular traditions, the people's working practices and the apparently timeless beauty of the English countryside. True culture was also created by society's higher types, its geniuses, and was embodied in the nation's high art. In this sense culture was defined in terms of the celebration of individual genius and specific works of exceptional artistic creation. Thus, parallel with their celebration of folk culture, British fascists exalted the creative genius and artistic masterpieces of Michelangelo, Titian, da Vinci, Schubert and Wagner, as well as Milton, Shakespeare, Elgar, Turner, Wordsworth and Keats within a specifically English cultural context.[14] It is 'high culture' that is being endorsed here, the idea that culture dwells in a select body of canonical works which transcend the values of a particular historical period. High culture supposedly affirmed the universal, eternal and immortal. Sculpture for a Mosleyite should express 'life itself with the undying elements of our earth', while music was 'appealing in its aspiration of immortality'. In a similar vein, literature should convey 'the never dying record of man's nobility'. These were the 'eternal realities of man', realities on which fascism 'founds its greatest appeal'.[15] For fascists, this was a state of perfection and majesty to which only a few 'exquisite' individuals could aspire. A member of the Unity Band wrote of Shakespeare's 'supreme genius' and praised 'his immortal works'.[16] High culture offered an opportunity to gain sublime insight into the human condition, embracing both its beautiful and tragic dimensions.[17] Supposedly possessed of an inner radiance, the canon of high culture held out the promise of a profound and sublime experience for those who desired to partake of it. 'We persist in proclaiming our preference for the "sweetness and light" emanating still from the great Masters', declared Oscar Boulton of the Unity Band.[18]

The elevated, elitist view of culture implicit in the fascists' endorsement of high culture or 'immortal art' owed something to the Nietzschean idea of an innate aristocracy of artists soaring majestically above the mass or 'herd', who were incapable of producing culture. This notion of the artist-aristocrat or 'artist-hero', a truly cultured being who had unique powers of insight and creativity and a special claim on truth, was part of a long-standing domestic tradition of cultural thought, too. It was during the first half of the nineteenth century in England that the term 'artist' initially came to stand for a special kind of individual, as Raymond Williams has shown.[19] This elitist conception of the artist can be plotted through a resilient English cultural tradition whose spokesmen included Percy Bysshe Shelley, Thomas Carlyle and Matthew Arnold, and their twentieth-century equivalents, F. R. Leavis, Clive Bell, John

Defining culture

Cowper Powys and T. S. Eliot.[20]

Leavis, Bell, Powys and Eliot embraced the idea of the 'artist-aristocrat' partly in response to the onset of mass culture, as did Carlyle and Arnold in their own time. These cultural elitists believed contemporary trends in modern life, technological innovation, the mass-based popular press, the mass democratic suffrage, and increased leisure time and disposable income were creating a 'mass society' and a philistine mass population. This philistine mass was the eager consumer of mass culture. But mass culture lacked a heroic base, claimed its detractors. All noble thought, inspiration and individuality were being stifled by popular mass culture. Cultural elitists claimed that mediocrity, the anonymous individual and a standardised life were the main features of mass society, while the effect of a mass-based culture was a crude levelling down of taste. Mass culture's goal of catering for the emerging mass consumer market invariably led to the production of standardised thoughts and objects that pandered to the cheap uncritical emotional response and banal tastes. Cultural elitists feared that high culture and authentic selfhood were being contaminated by this all-consuming mass culture, which worked towards and depended on the 'homogenisation of difference'.[21] These self-appointed guardians of high culture endeavoured to erect barriers to keep the horde of 'barbarians at the gate' at bay. One should shield oneself from the 'bustling ineptitude of the unenlightened' mass, the 'enemies of light and imagination', by cultivating detachment and 'interiority', urged John Cowper Powys.[22]

Many of Britain's fascists shared these concerns about mass culture and the arrival of 'uniform mass man'. James Strachey Barnes attacked 'mass ideas, culture in tabloid form, which is no culture at all', a product of a super-capitalist machine civilisation that 'turns out men like sausages'.[23] A BUF member referred to the 'massed hordes of the big cities' that 'come to heel as one man' at the behest of the publicity experts of the 'gutter-press', cinemas and the 'chain stores'.[24] 'Skilled in mass-psychology', the publicity man can evoke 'any response he needs' from the mass who do not have the mental equipment to resist. A. K. Chesterton, too, complained of the 'cultural agencies', the theatre, cinema and newspapers, which 'were feeling their way towards the wholesale exploitation of credulity and cheap emotionalism'.[25] William Joyce applauded the true man of culture like G. K. Cherstertson, who resisted 'pandering to a debased public' and thus kept 'aloft the torch of English literature'.[26]

Some fascists were convinced that it was the liberal utilitarian 'greatest happiness of the greatest number' principle that initially threatened culture with 'contamination' by bringing the masses to the centre of the political stage. The culprit here was modern mass democracy, election 'by brute numbers' and the counterpart of the materialism of mass wealth, according to Joyce's BUF colleague J. F. C. Fuller.[27] The new spirit of the age, proclaimed Fuller, 'is in fact a revolt against the ignorance of massed multitudes'.[28] Fuller feared that the modern age was being 'fused into an amorphous mass by a venal, sensation-loving press which stood for the spirit of democracy'.[29] Fuller did not have much time for the masses. 'It is totally useless attempting to convert the masses of mankind by logic', he asserted, 'for the masses remain stably [sic] unintelligent, cowardly and brutal.'[30]

A conception of beauty was an important feature of the fascist identification with high culture. 'True culture', through its various forms such as art and literature, was meant to articulate a universal ideal of beauty. Nesta Webster, a leading figure in the British Fascists, decried those who sought to undermine the traditional 'conception of Beauty' in art, proclaiming that 'we are for real beauty as conceived by sane and normal minds trained to true aesthetic standards'.[31] Attempts to subvert traditional conceptions of beauty in art merely served to prepare the way for moral perversion according to Webster.[32] Another BF member applauded the genius of Michelangelo, Rembrandt, Beethoven and Bach, 'who have given beauty to the world, and before whom we ordinary mortals bow our heads'.[33] Oscar Boulton of the Unity Band also believed that art, music and literature should adhere to traditional and accepted norms of beauty. For Boulton, 'Beauty' in art, as in life, was one of the 'supreme and celestial attributes'.[34]

The devotees of racial fascism also equated true culture with the universal law of beauty. In this instance, the perception of beauty was informed by race doctrine and had its basis in a racial stereotype. The Nordics, a racial nationalist group aligned to the Imperial Fascist League, proclaimed that 'the uniform standard of physical beauty' amongst Greeks, Romans, Celts, Goths, a standard which later permeated medieval and modern Europe, derived from a 'Nordic racial aristocracy', or those males 'fair of skin and hair' and with blue eyes.[35] For the Nordics, the physical attributes of the Nordic racial aristocracy were the 'nearest to human perfection', a 'truth' apparently not lost on the 'great cultures' of the ancient world, including the Greco-Roman civilisations, who proceeded to invest their deities with these characteristics. The fascist obsession with the 'beautiful body' is apparent here, a stereotypical ideal form which drew much of its inspiration from the classical Greco-Roman model of the perfect body. This image of the perfect physical form was enshrined in the athletic, muscular postures displayed in the figurative sculpture of classical Antiquity. This stereotypical, 'perfectly proportioned' muscular form would be adopted and taken to extremes in fascist and Nazi monumental sculpture, as exhibited in the work of the likes of Arno Brecker and Josef Thorak. The deliberately imposing muscular figures of Josef Thorak, which recalled the 'classic motif of armour in the form of a torso', inflated this 'perfect' muscular man into a warrior, 'the emblem of personal and individual invulnerability'.[36]

The ideal of beauty was not exclusively equated with physical characteristics. British fascists occasionally equated beauty with ethical values, such as 'Truth' and 'Honesty', which lent a spurious moral basis to many of their pronouncements on culture. For a Mosleyite, the task of revitalising British culture was dependent on the discovery of a new 'integrity' of 'Truth', which he associated with aesthetics. 'Honesty alone can bring man to Beauty, for where lies Truth, however bitter, there lies Beauty.'[37] 'It is only from the finer instincts that true cultural progress comes', declared another Mosleyite.[38] Britain's fascists made little attempt to clarify or define these aesthetic or ethical terms with any precision. It was usually a nebulous and pious notion of the beautiful, or vague allusions to the relevance of aesthetics to politics, that underwrote much of their stated mission to regenerate society. The development of an 'aesthetic sensibility' in those identifying with fascist goals would assist in the practical task of solving social and economic problems, for James Strachey Barnes.[39] The BUF's A. K. Chesterton, too, as David Baker has shown, believed that art was the source of truth and virtue and that aesthetics had relevance for political practice. Chesterton believed that knowledge could be gained from aesthetics by metaphysicians such as himself, and that this knowledge could be utilised to inform one's understanding of the political world.[40] Chesterton's error, according to Baker, and the mistake of other metaphysicians of a similar 'culture despair' frame of mind, was that he refused to recognise the need for an epistemological separation between politics and art.

Identifying with a universal ideal of beauty was not the only feature of high culture that appealed to British fascists. Clarity of form was thought to characterise the work of the immortal Masters. Form and clarity in art, along with beauty and harmony, were supreme and 'heavenly' attributes for the Unity Band's Oscar Boulton.[41] A. K. Chesterton was scathing of those modern artists who, he claimed, contemptuously discarded the discipline of the art form. He slammed the modern poet, for example, whose verse, he insisted, contained neither harmonious relationships nor beauty, but consisted of nothing other than the 'maniac association of fantastic dissimilarities' without sense or order.[42] This yearning for clarity of form was not confined exclusively to art or governed solely by aesthetic considerations. Oscar Boulton, like other interwar fascists, applied the same criteria to everyday life. Form and clarity, he believed, should characterise social and other types of relationships in society. This craving for form and clarity can be traced to psychological and political factors. As George Mosse has noted, the fascists' yearning for discipline of form in art in many ways reflected a deeper, more fundamental craving for order and certainty amid the trials of the modern world.[43] The desire for strictness of form also reflected the fascists' dread of flux, anarchy, chaotic change and personal dissolution, dangers they associated with the turbulence of modern political and social life.[44] The haughty disdain of order that was deemed to be characteristic of much modern art was, for A. K. Chesterton, making chaos and anarchy into an intellectual cult which merely served the goals of the Bolshevik revolutionaries.[45] It is not surprising, then, that Britain's fascists primarily preferred the traditional in art. Classical and representational art would become the favoured modes of expression for most fascist cultural commentators in interwar Britain.[46]

High culture also satisfied the fascist hankering for permanence. The canon of high art expressed permanence for cultural elitists like the British fascists, because it was thought to emphasise the highest good and fundamental truths. These higher values and fundamental truths, moreover, were considered to be universal, timeless and immutable. No art form or artistic tradition expressed permanence more effectively than that bequeathed by classical Greece and Rome. The German Nazi and Italian Fascist predilection for the classical, or Greco-Roman tradition, in architecture is well documented.[47] British fascists sought to enlist this tradition for their political project, too. A Mosleyite wrote of 'the unrivalled glories of Greek and Roman classical art'.[48] A regard for the classical tradition was considered to be the bedrock of a great and virtuous society and a mark of a truly civilised nation.

While native fascists acknowledged the contribution of individual creative genius to the nation's overall cultural advancement, not all subscribed to the view that genius was an exclusively individualist product. The BUF's Alexander Raven-Thomson, for example, preferred to place individual genius within a wider communal setting. According to Raven-Thomson, there was an organic relationship between individual inspiration and the traditional repository of 'communal' or national culture handed down to the present by past generations.[49] Artists could not attain creative fulfilment, nor adequately apply their creative energy to the cause of developing the culture of the age, unless they drew inspiration from the rich vein of the nation's cultural heritage. In this mystical, organic notion of culture, individuals of culture, in order to realise their genius, must take part in a 'cultural communion' with the great artists of the past. This organic definition of culture, with its stress on *contemporaneity*, or the blending of the past with the present, reasserted the view that authentic culture was universal, timeless and immutable.

Raven-Thomson was a vigorous exponent of the organic model of culture. For him, culture was the ultimate expression of the nation's achievement, the culmination of its conscious exertions towards higher forms of existence and creative excellence. Culture was imagined both as the expression of a nation's grandeur, a sublime testimony to its greatness and evolutionary development, and as the culmination of a great collective endeavour. Underlying Raven-Thomson's cultural perspective was the belief that the nation was a biological organism similar to other living organisms in nature. He believed that the entire edifice of nature was characterised by a series of what he called 'biological integrations'.[50] With each new biological integration, life forms pass to a higher stage of organic complexity, where old laws of combination have disappeared and new natural laws hold sway. Through these repeated 'biological integrations', a single primitive substance would progress to ever higher levels of development. This ascent to more advanced forms of biological existence was consistent with the most fundamental truths in nature and scientific knowledge for Raven-Thomson. This 'sublime series of evolutionary progressions from plane to plane of higher development' had culminated in the advent of 'civilisation', a superorganism which represented the highest and most complex biological stage of the evolutionary process to date. However, civilisation as it was then organised under modern democracy, with its claim that the individual was both the pinnacle of perfection and of more consequence than the collective whole, and where personal self-seeking was elevated to a moral law, threatened to arrest the process of evolutionary development.[51] The democratic organisation of society by reducing civilisation to a mere instrument of materialist gratification tended towards *dis*-integration, therefore, with its consequent death of culture, rather than integration to a higher level of social organisation and cultural attainment.

Fascism, on the other hand, had set itself the historic mission of continuing the evolutionary advance. Raven-Thomson was convinced that fascism was a profound and revolutionary new force in 'Nature-history', representing a more complex and superior stage of biological intergration, and as such would overcome the organic forces of decay that were supposedly destroying 1930s Britain. The trend towards disintegration would be reversed by restoring to civilisation its deeper organic purpose through the inauguration of the corporate organisation of economic, social and cultural life. In its recognition of the primarily organic character of social interaction and organisation, the Corporate State was a 'superorganic integration' which served to expedite the evolutionary process.

Raven-Thomson believed that an awareness of *purpose* was a fundamental biological mechanism that guaranteed vigorous life. An organism would die unless it demonstrated this urge to sustain vigorous life, a 'will-to-life' that was supposedly inherent in the entire scheme of existence. 'No active organism can adopt a self-limiting purpose. There is always striving towards an external goal or development would cease', he declared.[52] This awareness of life had positive implications for culture. A restoration of national or communal purpose would check the process of cultural decline supposedly inherent in the modern democratic scheme of things. It would thus guarantee the survival of culture and prepare the way for a new cultural advance. Mosleyite fascists like Raven-Thomson sought inspiration for this organic vision of life in a past age of achievement. It was the purposeful Elizabethan age which represented the 'high point of national life' for Raven-Thomson, ushering in a truly creative phase of culture embodied in the philosophy and science of Bacon and the drama and poetry of Shakespeare.[53]

Like many of his fascist contemporaries in interwar Britain, Raven-Thomson believed that any restoration of national and cultural purpose had to have its foundation in a *spiritual* reawakening. For many British fascists the spirit was the force which animated culture. This was as true in art as in other aspects of cultural activity. The authentic artist for one BUF member, whether in literature, painting, music, sculpture or architecture, worked 'from the soul outwards', his artistic creation representing a 'reflection of his spirit's unity with the divine ultimate reality'.[54] An obsession with the spiritual, the desire to ignite a revolution of the spirit, pervaded the fascist enterprise. For many of its adherents, this was the essence of fascism. According to the Mussolini enthusiast James Strachey Barnes, the spiritual dimension was the key to a deeper understanding of the origins of the fascist revolt.[55] A Mosleyite, too, defined fascism as 'the spiritual interpretation of life translated into terms of practice'.[56] The 'spiritual' was defined in various ways. A BUF member suggested that an explanation of this 'mystic' element within fascist thought could be found in the teachings of Kant, who defined the spiritual urge as 'an aspiration to higher things, which comes from beyond time and material things'.[57] At other times, the spiritual was defined in terms of a turn inward towards the domain of the inner self. This was the realm of feeling, emotion, instinct and intuition, the subjective or irrational elements of human nature, believed by many fascists to be the well-spring of true insight and all that was of value in life. The novelist and BUF member Henry Williamson declared that 'intuition is the basis of all thought and faith and understanding among men'.[58] This focus on the subjective inner self linked fascist ideology to *fin-de-siècle* anti-positivist thinkers like Nietzsche, Bergson and Sorel, who similarly claimed that the irrational was the pre-eminent motive force of cultural activity.[59] The roots of fascist political activism could also be traced to this inner realm. According to another Mosleyite, fascism was 'a subconscious and intuitive form of insurgent and impatient antagonism against the downward trend' inherent in the 'conditions of life today'.[60] In a similar vein, the inner self, or 'soul', was thought to be a well-spring of true creativity. Culture in this sense was perceived in terms of the soul's longing for expression and gratification.

The spirit would be reawakened, according to Britain's fascists, if the nation cultivated a more austere, even ascetic, approach to modern life. Mosley's followers, for example, encouraged the new reconstructed man of fascism to live by a set of ideals that were deemed to have a universal and transcendent quality. These were the ideals of duty, service, courage, sacrifice, comradeship and respect for tradition, which invoked the spirit of the 'old heroic fidelities' in the view of A. K. Chesterton.[61] These high ideals would find their expression in fascist activism, an unswerving devotion to a cause for which there was no material reward, 'only an inward light of infinite radiance', in the words of Chesterton's fascist comrade Captain Robert Gordon-Canning.[62] Native fascists mainly preferred to deal in vague metaphysical abstractions when discoursing on the importance of the spirit to a cultural resurgence. Raven-Thomson's allusions to the spirit were influenced by the religious writings of the Russian dissident Nicholas Berdyaev. Berdyaev was a former Professor of Philosophy at Moscow University and a devoted member of the Russian Orthodox Church, who was expelled from Russia by the Bolsheviks in 1922 because of his outspoken religious views.[63] Berdyaev believed that only by returning to a new age of spiritual and religious faith, comparable to the Christian Middle Ages when Europeans were aware of a 'great divine purpose' behind material life, could man recover a belief in his own cultural destiny. Echoing Berdyaev, Raven-Thomson called for a return to a new age of faith to stem the tide of cultural decline in 1930s Britain. Fascism 'recalls mankind to spiritual faith', he proclaimed.[64] It was fascism which was to be the new faith for the modern age for Raven-Thomson, a political philosophy which he believed found a natural harmony with the religious instinct in man. 'The moral code which has been laid down by religion is also the basis of fascist ethics', he pronounced.[65] Both fascism and religion were also, of course, questions of faith rather than reason, a point of convergence that would not have escaped Raven-Thomson's pious attention, though that, arguably, is where the similarity ends. James Strachey Barnes's deliberations on the importance of the spirit to a cultural resurgence were also motivated by religious convictions that drew inspiration from an earlier Christian age of faith. Fascism's spirit of heroic sacrifice recalled the warrior spirit of the crusading Christian knights for Barnes, while its desire to herald a new dawn of spiritual faith and belief in Divine Providence was motivated by genuine religious beliefs which had their roots in the Catholic Middle Ages.[66]

Fascism aimed to restore to civilisation its deeper organic purpose, and thus rekindle national and cultural life, via the medium of the Corporate State, as we have seen. The fascist Corporate State was not simply an instrument of sound government or efficient administration for Raven-Thomson. It was, more fundamentally, the

Defining culture

form through which the nation as an organic communal entity could find expression in the attainment of its national purpose or destiny.[67] In order to attain the 'divine' destiny, the Corporate State needed consciously to direct the nation's great cultural purpose. In essence, it would facilitate cultural advancement. In a practical sense, this meant that the fascist Corporate State would establish cultural standards, so as to elevate public taste and counter the apparently debilitating effects of contemporary commercial standards.[68] Additionally, it would endeavour to organise the nation's cultural life, including leisure activities. Raven-Thomson glanced approvingly at the corporate organisation of leisure in Mussolini's Fascist Italy and decreed that the Dopolavoro 'after-work' recreation scheme was a model worthy of emulation in a corporate Fascist Britain.[69] True artists of talent would also have an honoured role in national life. No longer would they be forced to bow to 'sordid' commercial taste and languish in anguished, self-indulgent, Bohemian isolation.[70]

The Corporate State would patronise the arts, too. A generous government subsidy to the arts was considered a vital national duty in a Philistine age of commercially driven mass culture. The future fascist state would bestow on a grateful nation one of the world's grandest opera houses, declared Raven-Thomson.[71] Another Mosley follower believed that national socialist patronage would provide the appropriate context for the flowering of artistic genius in the modern age.[72] The fascist organic state would also facilitate the entry of the 'people' into the nation's artistic life. Price reductions would enable the people to visit opera, concerts, theatres, and painting and sculptural exhibitions.[73] A truly organic relationship would therefore develop between professional artists, granted a wide and appreciative audience by state patronage, and the people, the grateful consumers of their creative work. Folk culture would also blossom under the aegis of the fascist Corporate State. A corporate recreational organisation would encourage the proliferation of recreational schemes devoted to reviving traditional handicrafts in the spirit of the medieval artisan. These after-work schemes would seek to rekindle the artistic impulse within the labour process, which was being stifled by factory production. Along the same lines, the after-work schemes would provide encouragement for 'amateur' handicraft talent. Raven-Thomson imagined a time when Britain would once again witness craftsmen creating the beautiful decorated hand-made furniture of Chippendale and Adam.[74]

This idea of the state as an organic form had a long ancestry that was rarely acknowledged by fascists such as Raven-Thomson. It was evident in the philosophical thought of Aristotle, Plato, Rousseau, Hegel and Burke and the sociological writings of Ferdinand Tonnies.[75] It was apparent, too, in Social-Darwinist thinking. Social-Darwinists perceived the nation-state to be a biological organism engaged in a fiercely competitive struggle for life similar to that experienced by other organic forms in nature. Britain's fascists were equally fond of using biological analogies, as well as metaphors associated with health, to describe the role and function of their own Corporate State. 'In the same manner as the human body is composed of many million cells, working for a common higher purpose, so the civilised community must be organised as a Corporate State, in which each human individual performs his functions in the higher interests of the whole', stated Raven-Thomson.[76] The body metaphor, whereby the Corporate State is conceived as a vibrant living organism with a finely co-ordinated metabolism, communicated the appropriate image in various ways. It helped to convey an image of the state as a healthy, combative athlete tirelessly combating the forces of cultural disintegration.[77]

Raven-Thomson's thinking on culture bore the unmistakable mark of Oswald Spengler. His morphological approach to matters cultural, for example, was not dissimilar to that of the German philosopher. Spengler's *The Decline of the West*, published in two volumes in 1918 and 1922, was an ambitious attempt to analyse the rise and fall of civilisations in history and predict the course of historical development.[78] According to Spengler, each civilisation, or 'culture', had a distinct spirit which was unique to it and which could not be consigned to another culture, as in the 'Faustian' culture of Europe and the 'Faustian-European culture-world' in other areas of the globe that had emulated the European model.[79] All cultures in history were governed by certain basic biological laws of formation, growth, decline and death, in the same manner as organic forms in nature, he claimed. These fundamental laws had to be adhered to, which meant that every culture had to pass through its biological life-cycle, with its dire implications of inevitable decay and death. Raven-Thomson believed that the modern generation in Britain and Europe owed Spengler an immense debt of gratitude for highlighting the ailing health of Western civilisation and alerting them to the threat of decay and the imminent decline of their 'Faustian' culture.[80] It is clear from Raven-Thomson's own thoughts on culture, however, that he spurned crucial aspects of Spengler's analysis. In particular, he rejected Spengler's determinism and his fatalistic belief in the impending death of the Faustian culture of Europe, believing that in fascism, European civilisation had discovered a political and cultural force that would renew its youth and cultural vitality.

Culture, then, was imagined in a number of ways by British fascists. Indeed, like fascism and its ideology, it did not project a single uniform identity. True culture, for the fascists, as we have seen, was meant to convey a sense of the eternal and enduring. In other words, it should express permanence, timelessness and immutability. Culture should also disseminate reassuring messages of stability and continuity. In this sense, culture should make meaningful connections with the national past – a past, moreover, that was heroic and glorious. Art and culture had to be sane and noble, too, in the opinion of a BUF writer.[81] Culture also needed to be clean and pure, purged of immoral and 'pornographic' associations. There would be little room for libertarian challenges to conventional morality in fascist art and culture. Similarly, like the human body, culture needed to be expunged of poisonous infections and 'genetic' defects which threatened health and mortality. Culture should also convey a reassuring message of truth and show mankind the way to morality.

In addition, through their endorsement of the organic Corporate State and its 'historic cultural mission', fascists like Raven-Thomson sought to depict culture as a reflection of the nation's aspiration to greatness, an expression of a conscious 'will-to-achievement' by an organically integrated collectivity. In the same vein, the function of culture should be to elevate and inspire. The nation's culture should also affirm communal rather than individual values and acclaim the virtue supposedly inherent in a society organised along functional, organic lines. Culture should thus emphasise, through its art and literature, that the shared community represented a higher form of civilisation and celebrate the reintegration of the hitherto alienated individual into the new organic society. In addition, the idea of culture as being *therapeutic* was promoted through this organic vision of society. Fascist propagandists boasted that fascist culture would restore the nation to spiritual health. The nation's soul, thought to be sick as a result of the excesses of a liberal-democratic society, would be healed through a revival of authentic cultural life. True culture, therefore, should also reflect the nation's spirit, but moreover a spirit rekindled and restored to health.

Underlying the organic definition of culture also was the idea of culture as an essentially unifying phenomenon. The organic state's historic mission was to forge a unified culture, a culture that transcended sectional interests within the nation. This was consistent with the more overtly political aim of constructing a unified nation and national identity. True culture, then, should depict social unity and a society characterised by mutual accord rather than conflict and anomie. The nation should be shown with its various individual units welded together by a common purpose based on supposedly shared aspirations and ideals and where the individual was content to bow to the state's higher purpose. Culture, then, should celebrate this new and glorious synthesis of the individual and the state. Fascist cultural forms, moreover, were meant to portray this act of individual submission as a joyful occurrence. Culture, therefore, should depict an optimistic and positive illustration of life as experienced in the integral national community. All this meant that culture acquired a definite *political* character within the fascist organic vision of life. Fascist culture was meant to convey and reinforce the idea of a harmoniously integrated society, united in its pursuit of prescribed political goals. As historians of continental fascist and Nazi art have demonstrated, interwar fascists and national socialists were convinced that culture and art should consciously serve definite social and political objectives.[82] Culture and art under fascism, therefore, tended towards the rhetorical, didactic, polemical and aspirational.[83]

The consequence of such an approach to culture, of course, was depressingly obvious. The fascist corporate notion of culture invariably discouraged cultural diversity and the individual autonomy of the artist or man of culture. What was being repudiated here was the humanist idea, developed in the writings of Kant and pivotal to the aesthetic thrust of intellectual modernism, of the sanctity of the individual artist's right to self-expression as a means of attaining personal freedom.[84] In the words of a BUF member, the fascist state's aim was 'to see each separate stream of individual artistic expression flow into the broad river of national culture'.[85] Such sentiments, of course, would translate into an intense hostility towards contemporary modernist art.[86] Fascist culture had other disturbingly obvious consequences. Rather than dispelling individual alienation, or curbing the supposed social blight of self-interested

Defining culture

individualism, the pious suggestion of community and a truly communal culture contained in the notion of the organic state meant, in reality, the subordination of the individual to an all-encompassing state aesthetic. In addition, as well as stifling individual self-expression and precipitating personal dissolution, the fascists' need for political expression through art would turn culture into a banal and unimaginative instrument of propaganda.

The racial fascists of the IFL, and their associates the Nordics, shared many of the views concerning the meaning and role of culture that we have touched on in this chapter. Where the IFL and the Nordics parted company with many of their fascist contemporaries was in their unwavering and dogmatic attachment to a racial notion of culture. In their view, race was the bedrock on which all authentic culture was built and the pre-eminent motive force of cultural attainment. Furthermore, according to the racial interpretation of history, it was humankind's *highest* racial types who were solely responsible for creating culture and propelling the civilising process forward. Culture was defined by reference to spurious biological criteria by racial fascists. They were wedded to the belief that a hierarchy of different biological types existed in the human and social world, as in nature, with the 'Aryan' or Nordic at the apex.[87] As the racial elite, the Nordics, alone of all the races, were imagined to represent the font of all culture. The 'higher culture of mankind responsible for the rise of civilisations has been due initially to one Race alone, the Nordic', claimed a spokesman for the Nordics.[88] Indeed, the highest pinnacles of cultural achievement from the earliest times and down through the ages were thought to be the creative product of this one racial group. 'The great cultures of the ancient world', declared the Nordics, 'had always the inspiration of leadership of Nordic men', while the progress of world culture 'has always depended on the exertions of the Nordic'.[89] 'Nordic Aryan men', in the view of an IFL writer, were 'the true chosen of God, who have created what is fine and noble in history' and were attached to the ideal of building a 'world of culture and beauty'.[90] Like the German Nazis, Britain's racial nationalists believed in a continuous and unbroken Aryan racial tradition, the idea that an Aryan or Nordic racial essence could be discerned in the highest forms of art and culture down the ages. Culture thus expressed the eternal and immutable creative essence of the race.[91] Racial fascists thought that culture should not only reflect the soul of the race, but demonstrate the Aryan genius, too. In other words, culture must emphasise and celebrate the greatness and majesty of the Aryan race, and proclaim its achievements. The Aryan had also, apparently, bequeathed to culture a uniform standard of physical beauty, a point that we previously touched on in this chapter.[92]

When applied to the practical world of politics and social policy, the racial fascist's fantasy version of culture had sinister implications. As society's racial aristocracy, the Aryan had a solemn responsibility to safeguard culture, to ensure its health and maintain its vigour. A ruling caste should 'wield power on behalf of our cultural ideals', stipulated the Nordics. In the same manner, the cultural progress of humanity itself was dependent on these guardians of culture. Because culture itself, the ballast of civilisation, was dependent on the Aryan racial aristocracy, it was judged to be imperative that this racial elect was preserved at a high level of racial health. There was a need, therefore, to prevent the racial guardians of culture from succumbing to the modern disease of 'degeneration' that resulted from 'interbreeding' with lower racial types. 'It is of the utmost importance for the future of civilisation that the world shall be ruled by the best blood', declared a Nordics writer, 'and that that blood shall be kept at a high level by selective breeding.'[93] History had taught the world, he went on, that 'the advancement of culture, mankind's highest mission, is only to be accomplished by the rule of the superior blood over the inferior, and where the blood of the Great Race is purest, there will the dominant power be also'.[94] The racial nationalists' notion of culture, and thus racist fascist aesthetics, was therefore inextricably linked with their dark, and potentially genocidal, eugenic fantasies.

Notes

1 *FQ*, 1, 2 (April 1935), p. 253.
2 See above, Chapter One.
3 G. Mosse, *Nazi Culture. Intellectual, Cultural and Social Life in the Third Reich* (London, W. H. Allen, 1966), p. 3.
4 *Blackshirt*, 23–29 March 1934, p. 1.
5 Ibid.
6 *BUQ*, 1, 2 (April–July 1937), pp. 78–83.
7 J. S. Barnes, *Half a Life* (London, Eyre and Spottiswoode, 1933), p. 42.
8 Chapter Ten below will explore these themes at greater length.
9 See, for example, 'William Morris, National Socialist', *BUQ*, II, 3 (July–September 1938), pp. 61–8.

Defining culture

10 See R. Williams, *Culture and Society. Coleridge to Orwell* (London, Hogarth, 1990).
11 For more on this theme, see below, Chapter Ten.
12 *Action*, 24 April 1937, p. 9.
13 *Action*, 28 January 1939, p. 5.
14 See *Blackshirt*, 11 January 1935, p. 11; 18 April 1935, p. 4; 27 December 1935, p. 2; 14 February 1936, p. 7; and *Action*, 8 April 1939, p. 13, on Wordsworth.
15 *Blackshirt*, 27 July 1934, p. 9.
16 *British Lion*, June 1932, p. 7.
17 J. Naremore and P. Brantlinger (eds), *Modernity and Mass Culture* (Indianapolis, Indiana University Press, 1991), p. 9.
18 *British Lion*, February–March 1934, p. 9.
19 Williams, *Culture and Society*, p.15.
20 Ibid., *passim*, on the nineteenth-century tradition. See also F. R. Leavis, *Mass Civilisation and Minority Culture* (Cambridge, Minority Press, 1930); C. Bell, *Civilisation* (London, Chatto and Windus, 1928); J. C. Powys, *The Meaning of Culture* (London, Cape, 1930); and T. S. Eliot, *The Idea of a Christian Society* (London, Faber and Faber, 1938).
21 A. Huyssen, *After the Great Divide. Modernism, Mass Culture and Postmodernism* (London, Macmillan, 1986), p. 9.
22 F. Gloversmith, 'Defining Culture: J. C. Powys, Clive Bell, R. H. Tawney and T. S. Eliot', in F. Gloversmith (ed.), *Class, Culture and Social Change. A New View of the 1930s* (Sussex, Harvester Press, 1980), pp. 16–18.
23 J. S. Barnes, *Fascism* (London, Thornton Butterworth, 1931), p. 147.
24 *Action*, 23 April 1938, p. 16.
25 *Action*, 6 August 1936, p. 9.
26 *Action*, 18 June 1936, p. 2.
27 J. F. C. Fuller, *The Dragon's Teeth. A Study of War and Peace* (London, Constable, 1932), p. 24.
28 Ibid., p. 25.
29 J. F. C. Fuller, *War and Western Civilisation 1832–1932. A Study of War as a Political Instrument and the Expression of Mass Democracy* (London, Duckworth, 1932), p. 181.
30 Fuller, *The Dragon's Teeth*, p. 210.
31 *Patriot*, 4 June 1925, pp. 49–51.
32 *Patriot*, 2 July 1925, p. 165.
33 *British Lion*, June 1929, p. 9.
34 *British Lion*, February–March 1934, p. 9.
35 *The Fascist*, February 1933, p. 4.
36 B. Nicolai, 'Tectonic Sculpture', in *Art and Power. Europe Under the Dictators 1930–45* (London, Hayward Gallery, 1995), p. 336.
37 *Action*, 10 June 1939, p. 16.

38 *Action*, 31 July 1937, p. 11.
39 Barnes, *Fascism*, p. 77.
40 D. Baker, *Ideology of Obsession. A.K. Chesterton and British Fascism* (London, I. B. Tauris, 1996), p. 92.
41 *British Lion*, February–March 1934, p. 9.
42 *Action*, 20 January 1938, p. 3.
43 G. Mosse, 'Fascism and the Intellectuals', in S. J. Woolf (ed.), *The Nature of Fascism* (London, Weidenfeld and Nicolson, 1968), p. 215.
44 On the theme of flux and personal dissolution, see K. Theweleit, *Male Fantasies. Vol. 1: Women, Floods, Bodies, History* (Cambridge, Polity Press, 1987).
45 *Action*, 20 January 1938, p. 3.
46 For more on this, see below, Chapter Eleven.
47 See, for example, T. Benton, 'Rome Reclaims its Empire', in *Art and Power*, pp. 120–9, and W. Nerdinger, 'A Hierarchy of Styles. Architecture Between Neoclassicism and Regionalism', in the same volume, pp. 322–5.
48 *Blackshirt*, 11 January 1935, p. 11.
49 *Fascist Week*, 6–12 April 1934, p. 7.
50 A. Raven, *Civilisation as Divine Superman. A Super-organic Philosophy of History* (London, Williams and Norgate, 1932); *Fascist Week*, 9–15 February 1934, p. 4.
51 Ibid.
52 A. Raven-Thomson, *The Coming Corporate State* (London, Great Britain Publications, 1935), p. 44.
53 Ibid., p. 45.
54 *BUQ*, 111, 3 (July–September 1939), p. 58.
55 Barnes, *Fascism*, pp. 36–54.
56 *Blackshirt*, 30 August 1935, p. 9.
57 *Blackshirt*, 12 October 1934, p. 8.
58 H. Williamson, *Goodbye West Country* (London, Putnam, 1937), p. 192.
59 See above, Chapter One.
60 *Fascist Week*, 26 January–1 February 1934, p. 4.
61 *Blackshirt*, 1 February 1935, p. 1.
62 R. Gordon-Canning, *The Inward Strength of a National Socialist* (London, Greater Britain Publications, c. 1938), p. 2.
63 *FQ*, 1, 2 (April 1935), p. 246; *Fascist Week*, 2–8 February 1934, p. 7.
64 *Fascist Week*, 9–15 February 1934, p. 4.
65 Ibid.
66 Barnes, *Fascism*, pp. 50–3.
67 Raven-Thomson, *The Coming Corporate State*, p. 44.
68 *Fascist Week*, 6–12 April 1934, p. 7.
69 *FQ*, 1, 2 (April 1935), p. 251.

Defining culture

70 Raven-Thomson, *The Coming Corporate State*, p. 42.
71 *Fascist Week*, 6–12 April 1934, p. 7.
72 See J. Morgan, 'Can Genius Survive National Socialism?', *BUQ*, 1, 3 (July–September 1937), pp. 65–6.
73 Raven-Thomson, *The Coming Corporate State*, pp. 42–3.
74 Ibid.
75 D. S. Lewis, *Illusions of Grandeur. Mosley, Fascism and British Society, 1931–1981* (Manchester, Manchester University Press, 1987), p. 43.
76 *Fascist Week*, 9–15 February 1934, p. 4.
77 W. van der Will, 'The Body and the Body Politic as Symptom and Metaphor in the Transition of German Culture to National Socialism', in B. Taylor and W. van der Will (eds),*The Nazification of Art* (Winchester, Winchester School of Art Press, 1990), p. 22.
78 O. Spengler, *The Decline of the West. Perspectives of World-History. Vols One and Two* (London, Allen and Unwin, 1918, 1922).
79 J. Drennan, *BUF Oswald Mosley and British Fascism* (London, John Murray, 1934), pp. 194–5.
80 *Fascist Week*, 9–15 February 1934, p. 4.
81 *BUQ*, 11, 2 (April–June 1938), p. 51.
82 See D. Elliott, 'The Battle for Art', in *Art and Power*, pp. 31–5; J. Petropoulos, *Art as Politics in the Third Reich* (Chapel Hill, University of North Carolina Press, 1996); and D. Thompson, *State Control in Fascist Italy. Culture and Conformity, 1925–43* (Manchester, Manchester University Press, 1991), p. 118.
83 Elliott, 'The Battle for Art'; Thompson, *State Control*.
84 Ibid. pp. 31–2; R. Griffin, 'Totalitarian Art and the Nemesis of Modernity', *Oxford Art Journal*, 19, 2 (1996), pp. 122–4.
85 *Blackshirt*, 27 July 1934, p. 9.
86 On the fascist attitude towards modern art, see below, Chapter Eleven.
87 On the character of racial fascism, see above, Chapter Seven.
88 *The Fascist*, March 1933, p. 4.
89 *The Fascist*, February 1933, p. 4.
90 *The Fascist*, January 1936, p. 1.
91 Mosse, *Nazi Culture*, p. xxiii.
92 On this see also, *The Fascist*, February 1933, p. 4.
93 *The Fascist*, April 1934, p. 4.
94 Ibid.

CHAPTER NINE

A HOST OF 'DECADENT' PHENOMENA

The British fascist imagination during the interwar period was racked by a morbid dread of impending national dissolution. There was a perception that Britain was being assailed by destructive forces which threatened the very survival of authentic culture. Like their continental fascist contemporaries, and taking their cue from Nietzsche's gloomy meditations on modern life, Britain's fascists believed that modern life carried within it the seeds of the destruction of culture. They became obsessed by a belief that culture needed to be inoculated against the deadly virus of modern life. A major source of this mortal threat to culture was modern liberalism and the various philosophical, political and socio-economic doctrines associated with it, namely materialism, individualism, rationalism, positivism, democracy and 'finance capitalism'. In postwar England, a Mosleyite lamented, the enthronement of the liberal 'bourgeois' system and its ideals, the 'slow sordid tragedy of the bourgeois triumph', had worked to 'crush and deaden the spiritual impulse which is the maintenance and vitality of a people'.[1] With this 'bleak death of the spirit' came an inevitable sapping of cultural vitality.[2] This was not the sole source of cultural decay, however. A number of parallel modern movements were thought to be injecting unhealthy substances into the body of the nation, too, including 'cultural Bolshevism', intellectual modernism and 'Americanism'. In addition, in their more wildly speculative moments, the fascists blamed 'Jewish cultural internationalism' for poisoning British culture. As we observed in the previous chapter, the essence of true culture for native fascists was located in such forms as the people, rural England and the nation's organic 'soul', and in supposedly eternal verities such as genius, beauty, clarity of form, duty, and faith in a divine purpose behind life. But in liberalism, 'cultural Bolshevism', intellectual modernism, 'Americanism' and 'Jewish cultural internationalism', they detected the very antithesis of culture, its negation or opposite.

These 'alien' forces, then, were accused of having spawned many of the evils supposedly afflicting post-1918 Britain. Philosophical liberalism was much maligned. Britain's fascists, for example, repudiated the self-confident and overly optimistic assumptions inherent in the liberal notion of progress. Liberalism apparently promoted a spurious notion of progress which had its basis in the narrow utilitarian 'greatest happiness of the greatest number' principle and was measured in terms of the individual's striving to attain material advantages and comforts. Rather, true progress, and thus a deeper sense of personal liberty, could only be realised by rejecting a life of ease and material comfort. Hedonistic individualism was to be spurned in favour of a new existence, which had its basis in sacrifice, self-denial and service to an ideal higher than the self. 'In self-abnegation the self is realised' and there is 'rapture in sacrifice', declared the Mosley loyalist E. D. Randall.[3] Liberal acquisitiveness, in contrast, was the fountain-head of decadence rather than culture. Ease and luxury were the 'father and mother of decadence', declared one fascist, and it is only when people and nations renounce liberal materialism and embark on the painful, solitary path of rebirth that they achieve greatness and undergo cultural advancement. Art, for example, owed its 'most sublime masterpieces' to periods of regeneration, to the 'fury of insurrection', the 'bright flame of revolution' and the 'ferocity of battle'.[4]

The British fascist mind between the wars was obsessed with the apparent modern phenomenon of decadence. Decadence was viewed as the harbinger of national degeneration and decline. It is not too difficult to detect the generic fascist roots of this gloomy prognosis. Roger Griffin has brilliantly made transparent and diagnosed the 'palingenetic' essence underlying the fascist preoccupation with decadence.[5] At the core of fascist palingenetic myth lay the conviction that decadence was a modern blight which reflected the sickness of Western culture and civilisation and heralded the onset of national decline. A dialectic of pessimism and optimism, however, characterised fascist ideology in its more mature palingenetic form. Thus fascists preoccupied with decadence and other symptoms of national decline believed that a movement of regeneration, alive to the need for revolutionary rebirth, could stem the tide of decadence and reverse the trend towards dissolution. Perceptions of decadence, therefore, would always travel hand in hand with visions of a glorious national rebirth.

Despite the belief in a future rebirth, pessimism weighed heavily on the fascist consciousness. Not surprisingly, given the perceived threat of decadence to Western civilisation and culture, fascist thinking on this subject was invariably melancholic and even apocalyptic. Biological metaphors and a variety of morbid images associated with life-threatening illnesses and death were deployed to comprehend and neutralise this imagined threat to culture. The BUF's A. K. Chesterton likened modern decadence to a range of deadly diseases assailing the body of the British nation. In one example, he equated the forces of decadence with invading armies of typhus germs, while in another, decadence was defined as a 'collective disease exactly as bubonic plague is a collective disease'.[6] The struggle against decadence for cultural pessimists like Chesterton was nothing less than a life and death affair. 'The battle between the forces of life and death is being continuously waged within us, not only in our blood but in the innermost recesses of us – in the country of the soul', he declared bleakly.[7]

Decadence was thought to manifest itself in a variety of modern cultural forms, ranging from sexual impropriety to psychology. Its origins were often traced to the recent past. A BUF activist believed that modern decadence was a fall-out from the Great War. It was a blight which displayed itself particularly in the 'neuroticism, eroticism, flabbiness and soullessness' of the 1920s, a trend which Noel Coward captured perceptively in his sentimental and rousingly patriotic 1931 spectacular, *Cavalcade*, according to this Mosleyite.[8] Britain's fascists were particularly alarmed by the changing manners and habits of the postwar generation of youth, the so-called 'bright young things', with their spirit of gay abandon, lust for entertainment and questioning of established moral and sexual conventions.

We can trace this libertarian trend amongst mainly middle-class and upper-middle-class youth to a number of influences. In one respect, it was a product of a general postwar restlessness. People wanted to forget and cast off wartime traumas. In particular, there was a cathartic desire to expunge the memory of the Great War on the part of the first postwar generation of youth. It also had its roots in the prewar feminist suffragette revolution, which helped pave the way for the emergence of the emancipated, independent and assertive young woman of the 1920s, the 'flapper', and a general relaxing of sexual conventions.[9] The proliferation of night-clubs and new dancing and musical styles after 1918, the latter mostly imported from the United States, encouraged this postwar mood, too. Jazz, rag-time dances, the fox-trot, the tango, one-steps and hesitation waltzes were quickening the pulse of youth and transforming the entertainment scene in Britain during the years after the Great War. It was a culture captured for posterity in Evelyn Waugh's *Vile Bodies*, amongst other literature of the period.[10] The BUF's James Drennan linked this libertarian youth culture to the historical conjuncture of the Great War also. For him, the 'cocktail-shaker' had become the symbol of a decadent generation of British youth who found themselves channelled down the path of self-indulgence and sexual promiscuity owing to postwar uncertainties.[11] Britain's lengthening dance-hall queues alarmed another of Mosley's followers, while another decried the 'orgy of dancing, bottle party madness and the 101 other things which our Bright Young Things offer us'.[12]

Another sign of modern British youth's decadence, in the view of the fascists, was their penchant for spectator sports. A Mosleyite thought that this 'obsession' constituted a 'grave, national danger'.[13] Another criticised the young males who gazed for endless hours at the 'hurtling shapes of racing-cars', while A. K. Chesterton satirised the young Briton who, 'tense with excitement, frantic with anxiety, now cheering, now groaning', turned up week-in week-out to cheer his favourite soccer team.[14] Chesterton questioned the sanity of the youth who was devoted to such pastimes which did not affect the destiny of the nation or individual 'one jot', wondering whether such a youth 'might well be regarded as a case fit for the pathologist'.[15]

Such criticism was not confined to young males. The 'flapper' generated particular unease. Capel Pownall, who was associated with the British Fascists and the IFL, deplored the encouragement of smoking and 'cocktailing' amongst young females.[16] The radical changes in women's fashion after 1918, with short skirts, low-cut blouses, short hair and a 'cylindrical' or tubular shape, announcing a more independent female mood, also caused offence. Capel wrote disapprovingly of the 'flagrant immodesty' in women's attire in modern Britain.[17] Young women were imagined to be avid consumers of the new movie culture, again American-driven, which swept Britain after 1918. Fascists spoke of impressionable 'goggle-eyed women' and their propensity to be manipulated by the Hollywood 'star machine'.[18] A female follower of Mosley wrote of the 'half-educated flapper' who enjoyed 'reading the vapid declarations of her favourite movie star', while for another BUF member, the 'sex-mad hero worship' of American movie stars by 'young silly impressionable girls' was a sure indication of the decadence of British youth.[19] Indeed, the thrust of mass culture – the Hollywood movie being a quintessential representative form – appeared to be tending towards the 'feminisation' of culture itself.[20] Because mass culture was perceived to lack a heroic base in that it apparently stifled all noble and imaginative thought, it was deemed by many cultural elitists to be more suited to women. Mass culture was accused of pandering to the emotions and banality rather than intellect, so it supposedly spoke more to women who were thought to be traditionally disinclined to favour elevated or abstract thought. The true artistic temperament, for those who saw culture as the exclusive preserve of the 'artist-aristocrat' like the Hitler enthusiast and fascist fellow-traveller Percy Wyndham Lewis, was primarily classical, rational, aristocratic and *male*.[21]

The Hollywood movie, of course, along with the likes of the 'sensational' popular newspaper and some of the new forms of American-driven popular music, was regarded as a key prop of the mass-culture industry. Fascists between the wars tended to adopt a 'mass manipulation' perspective on American cinema and the audience-consumer, fearing that it was having a wholly objectionable effect on not only the female mind but the public mind in general, which was regarded as impressionable, malleable and generally 'innocent'. This was not the only response to the Hollywood film, but it was a common one nonetheless. The view of BUF member John Rumbold was typical. He complained that the British Board of Film Censors had 'allowed hundreds of salacious bedroom comedies, putrescent leg-shows, horrifying gangster "melodramas" and suggestive farces to pass without comment for Universal consumption, regardless of the harm accruing from such "entertainment" in juvenile, adolescent and even adult minds'.[22] The people 'drug themselves with the third-hand drama of the cinema' and other forms of the mass-culture industry, groaned the Mosley loyalist Jorian Jenks. Writing in 1939, Jenks feared that 'the cinema is replacing the Church as a culture centre'.[23]

The disease of decadence supposedly infected young women of the aristocratic elite also. The Mayfair high society girl, according to the BUF activist Doreen Bell, 'who rises lunch time, and retires, worn out with the quest for pleasure and excitement, in the early

A host of 'decadent' phenomena

hours of the morning', was an affront to the nation.[24] The high society girl was thus a 'parasite' and one of 'the most despised members of the community'. The decadent ways of the 'idle rich' also offended Oswald Mosley. He attacked those who frequented city night-clubs to 'swill and guzzle' while their fellow 'Britons' languished in poverty. 'This dancing scum on the surface of national life stinks in the nostrils of the people', asserted Mosley.[25] Aristocratic decadence disturbed the fascists. They felt that Britain's aristocratic elite should be guided by high ideals, the ideals of duty, responsibility and service to the greater good. Too many of those at the 'top' of society were 'amusing themselves most of the time', to the obvious discomfort of the British Fascisti, who viewed this as a positive national danger.[26] Attacking the 'cocktail experts' and 'frequenters' of night-clubs and 'freak parties', the 'Society' members who had done much to defame national life since the Great War, an IFL member concluded that the post-1918 English elite had obviously forgotten the meaning of *'noblesse oblige'*.[27] As always, the IFL peered at this problem through the lens of race. Although it favoured aristocratic rule, the IFL was of the view that England's traditional aristocracy had succumbed to a process of 'racial contamination' by opening its ranks to Jews and other non-Aryans. Only those of 'pure' Aryan stock could feel the instinct of the true aristocrat, that of *'noblesse oblige'*, according to the IFL. For the Mosley loyalist Alexander Raven-Thomson, the misuse of leisure by the rich, with their wearisome succession of London Season 'events', was a 'crying scandal'.[28]

These displays of decadence by the youth of the interwar British elite and middle classes alarmed and offended the fascist mentality for a number of reasons. At one level, the self-indulgence and wild parties were viewed as a form of moral debasement which threatened to destroy the integrity of British youth, undermine traditional values, and damage the nation's overall social fabric. Mobilising that familiar aspect of fascist discourse, the morbid imagery of disease and death, one fascist declared disconsolately that the post-1918 generation of youth was 'decaying'.[29] Another fascist lamented that traditional British qualities as well as the 'finer feelings of the race' were being eroded by this postwar mood.[30] At another level, this lust for enjoyment was thought to betray a lack of pride in the country. The sturdy, virile and patriotic youth of the past had apparently been replaced by the 'slender-waisted youth' whose sole ambition is to 'concoct another cocktail and discover a new night club'.[31] In the same vein, such activities were deemed to represent a betrayal of the heritage of the past, particularly the imperial ideal and the Great War's spirit of heroic self-sacrifice. Some fascists feared also that the 'doctrine of work', on which the nation's industrial strength was based, was being undermined by the prevailing culture of pleasure and idleness. The BF, for example, believed that Britain could never teach the doctrine of work to the 'younger generation of workers', nor would it recover its industrial supremacy, 'while all this senseless, selfish luxury was being flaunted everywhere', particularly by those at the top of society.[32]

Still further anxiety centred on the perception that the decadent culture of the postwar years seriously injured national morale in an era of economic and political uncertainty. This was thought to have wider implications in terms of the nation's ability to navigate increasingly treacherous international waters. Indeed for some fascists, the pleasure-seeking habits and ostentation of the wealthier classes in depression-ravaged 1930s Britain, who unashamedly flaunted luxury in the eyes of the less fortunate in society, bore a striking parallel with an earlier historical phase of 'democratic decadence'. It was the 'rich debauchees' of the Roman republic and others of their ilk 'enfeebled by vice and idleness' who apparently sapped the vitality of Ancient Rome. The 'decadent republic' was accused of paving the way for the slave uprising of Spartacus and the revolt of Asia Minor against Roman power, which threatened to destroy Rome from within and without.[33] It was a 'man of destiny', Caesar, who eventually saved Rome by ruthlessly cleansing it of republican vice and corruption. The message for modern Britain was clear. Decadence, if left unchecked, threatened to unravel Britain's entire cultural and imperial fabric, with the result that it would follow the Roman example. Only Mosley, a twentieth-century 'Caesar', could challenge the destiny of decadence, renew the life of Britain and save the Empire.[34]

The fear that great nations passed away because of domestic decadence was commonplace amongst interwar fascists. It was the corrosive power of domestic 'immoralities', rather than the strength of external enemies, which toppled the might of Egypt, Carthage, Greece and Rome, according to a fascist writing in 1926.[35] The fear that Britain's internal enemies would thrive in such a climate, particularly communists, was another response, as was the perception that the youth generation, supposedly declining in intellect and political insight since 1918, would fall easy prey to the 'wire-pullers'

A host of 'decadent' phenomena

of liberal democracy, the smooth-talking politician and the press.[36]

The fascists, at least those who inhabited a mature palingenetic ideological world, were plagued by an even deeper anxiety, however. The postwar mood apparently undermined the pressing task of national regeneration. It did this in two ways. Firstly, the postwar culture of enjoyment inhibited political activism. It was thought to be indicative of an artificial, 'synthetic' civilisation, a bogus world of escapist 'make-believe' behind which youth shielded themselves from the 'savage gusts' of political truth.[37] Secondly, and more alarmingly, this hedonistic culture supposedly destroyed the spiritual impulse, the kernel of the regenerative urge. The logical and sole outcome of youth's feverish search for pleasure was spiritual entropy, 'death in life', in the words of A. K. Chesterton. It was the spirit of disillusionment, hopelessness and surrender, a materialist 'cancer' which pointed the way to degeneration and ultimate death.[38] Rather, youth required a 'mighty cause' and a fearless leader, who would rekindle the spiritual flame and steer them down the path of regeneration. Interwar fascists were fond of employing mountain imagery to convey a sense of their mission to regenerate society. Mountain metaphors seemed to neatly express what they believed was the essence of their regenerative quest, the idea of resolutely striving towards an almost insurmountable goal, and the thrilling rapture of scaling the heights of political achievement that comes with the moment of fascist victory. Thus Robert Gordon-Canning, Chesterton's colleague in the BUF, found it fitting to define fascism as 'the Spirit of Everest as opposed to that of the night club'.[39]

Another symptom of postwar decadence which began to reveal itself increasingly in the field of leisure and culture, to the fascist way of thinking, was the increasing prominence given to matters of a sexual nature. This was a 'lunatic obsession with sex', complained A. K. Chesterton.[40] The topic of sex certainly began to feature more conspicuously in public, intellectual and political discourses after 1918. The 1920s, in particular, witnessed a more open attitude towards the subject. This openness was assisted by the cumulative efforts of late Victorian, Edwardian and postwar sexual reformers, mostly women, to topple the bastions of Victorian sexual conservatism and repression and establish new sexual codes in both private and public life.[41] During these decades sex progressives questioned the culture of bourgeois domesticity, including the Victorian model of marriage and the family, and attempted to establish a more egalitarian relationship between the sexes.⁴² The sexual libertarianism of the 1920s was also fuelled by a greater public knowledge of sex, a development assisted by the writings and lectures of Dr Marie Stopes on contraception and the work of Sigmund Freud and Havelock Ellis on sexual psychology.⁴³

A veritable kaleidoscope of nightmarish new forms and practices appeared on the fascists' mental horizon as a result of the sexual revolution. Many fascists believed that this revolutionary wave had burst the dam of conventional decency and moral restraint, unleashing a tide of sexually promiscuous behaviour and decadent sexual perversity on modern Britain. In the fascist imagination the 'sex-obsessed individual', the 'sex pervert' and the effeminate 'half-a-man' were the products of the 'sexual revolution', rather than sexual enlightenment and sex equality. The mushrooming of societies for 'experimental sex week-ends' merely indicated the extent of the malaise for the BUF's A. K. Chesterton.⁴⁴ At the cultural level, these 'sinister' new trends found expression in a variety of contemporary forms. For example, fascists noted the increasing prominence given to sexual themes in the literature, cinema, theatre and variety shows of the postwar years.

Surveying the modern literature scene, fascists would freely give vent to their paranoia about the apparently unregulated sexual indulgence of the modern age. The *Patriot*, a proto-fascist journal with close links to the British Fascisti, frequently protested about the high levels of sexually explicit material contained in postwar novels. According to one contributor, writing in 1924, the great mass of modern novels was an 'open sewer spreading miasma on all sides'.⁴⁵ The *Patriot* proposed that legislation be introduced to safeguard the nation against the 'commercialised corruption' of 'sex literature'.⁴⁶ It held up for example the efforts of moral reformers in the United States, particularly the 'Clean Books League', to pressurise their government to introduce laws to curb the production of 'filthy books' in that country. The Unity Band picked up the 'sex literature' theme at a later date. One Unity Band writer condemned the tendency in modern literature to write about sex so that 'prurient hogs might wallow in that filth'.⁴⁷ The 'modern literary hack' was apparently more interested in sordid financial gain than moral principles. The 'modern sex lust scribbler' pandered to the most 'bestial qualities and tastes of sexomaniacs' so as to gain a 'little filthy lucre', in the opinion of this fascist. The BUF was equally shrill in its condemnation. One Mosleyite believed that the 'sex novel' placed the 'moral pervert on a heroic level', while another feared that the literature of 'sexual perversion and obsession' would undermine England's vitality and drain its moral resistance.[48] Pronouncements on these matters occasionally bordered on the hysterical. A BUF member charged that English literature was full of the 'ravings of the Onanists, Nymphomaniacs, Drug-fiends, Impotents, Pederasts, Homos, Masochists, and many other abortions'.[49] A similar note of moral outrage and alarm could be found in the commentary of the Imperial Fascist League. The arrival in England of the 'filthier brand of French novel' disturbed one IFL member.[50] Other categories of books with sexual themes were equally obnoxious to the fascist mind. Concern was expressed about the increasing volume of pornographic 'sex books', with their focus on 'homosexualism, sadism, masochism, [and] perversions of all kinds', which appealed only to 'the morbid or filthy minded'.[51]

Another trend associated with so-called 'sex literature' which the fascists found repugnant was the sprouting of 'sex book-shops' to cater for this 'vicious trade', notably in London's West End. They were particularly repelled by the tendency of these shops to display their wares openly in their shop windows, in the full view of passing children.[52] The inclination of some 'sex book-shops' to supplement their book stock with sex magazines, 'indecent prints' and 'purple postcards' similarly aroused indignation.[53] The popular newspaper was thought to be giving increasing prominence to the topic of sex, too. The British press, with its 'sex-laden and repellent news', a mere 'chronicle of vices' in the worst cases, was now suggestive of the worst type of American journalism according to a follower of Mosley.[54]

This objectionable preoccupation with sex was perceived to extend to the cinema, theatre and variety shows also. Once again, the *Patriot* sounded an early warning. In April 1925 it warned its readership about the pernicious effect on young impressionable minds of imported American 'movies', with their 'alluring titles', 'sex appeal' topics and the general promotion of immorality through the reiterated presentation of sexual 'irregularity'.[55] Concern about the effects of the 'sex film' on impressionable minds would become a recurring theme amongst interwar fascists. Oscar Boulton of the Unity Band complained that since the arrival of the 'film' and other modern media, sex 'positively shrieks' at the young from morning till night.[56] A BUF member attacked the 'vice' and 'sexual filth' of the American film, and then reflected on the 'elevating spectacle of pimply-faced adolescents' giggling through a celluloid exposure of the 'facts of sexual life'.[57] For another BUF cultural commentator, the 1930s movie was obsessed with 'titillation'.[58] Oscar Boulton found the modern theatre drama, with its lewd dialogue and obsession with this 'bedroom business', equally distasteful.[59] The same note was struck a decade earlier, when the British Fascisti press warned its readership of the prurient sex play, a 'putrid' and 'degrading thing' which contaminated the British stage with its 'nastiness'.[60] The IFL would later complain about the displays of nudity in theatre and cabaret, and the 'perverted type' who frequented the postwar stage, 'effeminate men' who pranced about making 'suggestive gestures and remarks'.[61] In a similar vein, the modern British music hall was denounced as nothing but 'an organ of filth'.[62] For a Mosleyite, too, the art of variety had rapidly descended into a succession of 'filthy jokes and sex-ridden songs'.[63]

No popular cultural medium excited more moral outrage in Britain's fascists and generated more paranoia about potentially threatening sexuality than jazz. With its celebration of sensuality, uninhibited dancing and the vitality of the human body, Jazz seemed to epitomise unrestrained sexuality. Indeed, a follower of the BUF pronounced that 'present day Jazz is to music what pornography is to the pictorial arts'.[64] A 'bastardisation of music', Jazz was 'the music of apes in rut', stated the senior BUF official J. F. C. Fuller.[65] 'Bottom-wagging jazz', declared Percy Wyndham Lewis, is the 'folk-dance of the Megalopolis'.[66] As representative of 'the savage type' of imported American music, 'music in its lowest form', Jazz was deemed to be only suitable for consumption by those lower down the evolutionary scale.[67] Jazz's relationship to black American culture, too, caused obvious discomfort and sparked crude racist remarks. A BUF writer referred to 'the hysterical thumping of nigger music', while another complained of 'Jew-boys wailing jazz and gold-toothed niggers disseminating the "culture" of the jungle and the swamp'.[68]

Other postwar leisure pursuits would provide further opportunities for fascists to reveal their homophobia and paranoia about the new age of apparently unregulated sexual licence. Vice flourished after dark in the clubs and street life of the city, according to the BUF. Shady sex-clubs and the 'strip-tease' dance, the latter apparently bearing the stamp of the burlesque theatres of New York, blighted the urban scene.[69] One irate BUF commentator complained that the 'fairest of our girls display their allurements' in 'strip-tease'

A host of 'decadent' phenomena

shows in 'foreign cabarets before the multicoloured scum of humanity'.[70] Such overt displays of female sexuality and the naked female body appalled many fascists. Prostitution was also considered to be rife. An IFL member complained that in certain London streets it was almost impossible for a man to avoid being accosted.[71]

These activities contained more than the seeds of cultural decay. Bodily disintegration beckoned to the unwary. According to Harold Sherwood Spencer of the Britons, writing in 1922, postwar Britain was 'filled' with female and male prostitutes with 'death-dealing diseases hidden behind their perfume and paint'.[72] Another sexual 'type' who was thought to be stalking the dark corridors of the city in increasing numbers was the homosexual, the 'sex-perverted man of the great cities' in the language of the BUF's James Drennan.[73] In the modern city, according to Drennan, a forbidding and unnatural place, the 'man-woman' flourished, while homosexuality had developed into a fashionable pastime bolstered by a flagrant exhibitionism and fuelled by the modern cult of psychological introspection.[74] Drennan's BUF colleague A. K. Chesterton was also gripped by homophobia. The founding of societies that campaigned for the revision of the homosexuality laws was a sure sign of advancing spiritual decay in postwar Britain, for Chesterton.[75]

In their efforts to imagine a domestic environment free of such 'unwholesome' traits and preoccupations, British fascists often looked to their more politically successful far-right counterparts on the continent, particularly Nazi Germany, for inspiration and guidance. In characteristically vulgar language, the Mosleyite James Drennan applauded Adolf Hitler for cleaning out the 'human sewers' of vice in the *Kurfurstendamm* quarter of west Berlin and hunting out 'with the sterilizer's needle the erotic scum of the rich apartment buildings' in that city.[76] Percy Wyndham Lewis was equally damning of the promiscuous culture of west Berlin during the Weimar years. For Lewis, west Berlin was the '*quartier-général* of dogmatic Perversity'. It was 'the Perverts' Paradise', where every variety of 'perversion' was liberally represented, from proletarian transvestites with 'harsh unshaven bristles as stiff as those of a toothbrush' trading in prostitution, to Hollywood-style cabarets, 'glitter and nigger-hubbub', selling 'super-sex and pink champagne'.[77] Henry Williamson, too, observed approvingly that the Nazis had 'cleaned-up' the Berlin night life of 'pornographic film shows' and beer halls where 'rouged youths dressed in girl's clothes awaited nightly custom'.[78] The IFL also welcomed Hitler's 'clean-up' of Weimar culture, including Berlin's night life, where 'vice and perversion flourished openly', and its theatre, which during the 1920s had become increasingly 'vicious in its tendency'.[79]

Many of the same fears expressed by the fascists concerning the boisterous leisure activities of the postwar youth generation surfaced in their imaginative reflections on this particular symptom of modern 'decadence'. A common concern was that changing sexual attitudes and norms were eroding the foundations of conventional morality. This posed a grave threat to public morals and family life. All this 'nasty sex nonsense', declared the BF's President, Brigadier-General Robert B. D. Blakeney, 'is upsetting the sanctity of home life'.[80] The new sexual trends had implications for national and imperial stability. As was often the case with such responses, the assessment was hardly reasoned or measured. For example, James Strachey Barnes opined that a nation of 'sexless, half-impotent and sex-obsessed individuals', with only a limited appreciation of the importance of the family, was not conducive to maintaining an Empire for long.[81] Racial fantasies, as ever, underlay the responses of the IFL. By undermining the permanence of the marriage tie, an institution apparently founded by the Ancient Aryans following their subjugation of the 'matriarchal Chaldeans', the culture of sexual promiscuity threatened the very basis of racial stability and thus civilisation itself.[82] Oscar Boulton also feared for civilisation. The overthrow of modesty, reticence and restraint in the domain of sex threatened to wreck civilisation and trigger a descent into barbarism, for these were virtues which distinguished the civilised being from the human animal.[83] At the forefront of fascists' concerns, however, was the belief that Britain's 'lunatic obsession with sex' reflected a disease of the 'soul' which was antithetical to the regenerative urge.

If the reactions of the fascists to the new sexual trends evoked a series of agitated responses which were often founded on fear and prejudice or downright fantasy as in the case of the IFL, the attempts to discern the causes of this phenomenon frequently bordered on the wildly speculative and absurd. As a supposedly quintessential symptom of decadence, postwar sex culture was most frequently linked with liberal individualism, particularly its hedonism, spirit of 'sordid' commercialism, tolerance and advocacy of freedom of expression, whether of the mind or body. American cultural influences were often cited disapprovingly also, as we have seen. Some fascists even pointed to the influence of Marxism, or 'cultural Bolshevism'. According to a BUF writer, it was the task of 'cultural Marxism' to plant the seeds of cultural disintegration because a climate of national and cultural decay aided the goal of revolutionary communism.[84] Thus when vice is pandered to and 'unhealthy tastes and tendencies are excited by suggestion', it was certain that the 'hidden hand' of Bolshevik cultural subversion was actively at work. In a similar fashion, claimed another BUF cultural commentator, communism promoted the culture of sexual promiscuity because it sought the destruction of the Christian institution of the family.[85] Nesta Webster of the British Fascisti, writing in 1925, also expressed concern about the 'free love doctrines of Moscow' and their effect on the institution of the Christian marriage.[86] Bolshevism, however, was only one of the links in a wider chain of global revolutionary subversion, which sought the destruction of the family, marriage and morality in favour of sexual promiscuity, for Webster. Christian Socialists and the 'red clergy' of the Church of England, amongst others, were part of the same conspiracy to undermine the Christian way of life as established 1,900 years earlier by Jesus Christ.[87] Webster's comrades in the *Patriot* also traced the postwar cult of sexuality to the 'hidden hand' of red subversion. One contributor believed that Bolshevism sought the inauguration of an era of unregulated sexual indulgence, in which people were urged to gratify the full range of their sexual appetites, as part of its calculated scheme to destroy the moral and religious basis of the British Empire.[88] The BF President Robert Blakeney, too, suspected that left-wing subversives were behind the cult of 'effeminacy', the 'nasty sex nonsense', 'immoral literature' and other forms of 'rotten decadence' afflicting modern Britain.[89]

More often than not, however, British fascists of a variety of ideological complexions were convinced that the 'hidden hand' of 'international Jewry' was behind these sexual trends. As ever, the responses were often confused and contradictory. For the *Patriot* writer cited above, the Bolshevik scheme to initiate an era of sexual licence in order to further its international revolutionary aim of destroying the British Empire was hatched with the connivance of Jews and Germans who nurtured a similar anti-British agenda.[90] The *Patriot* also traced the postwar 'sex literature' to the Jewish 'hidden hand', even citing the notorious forgery *The Protocols of the Elders of Zion* to support its position. Apparently it was *Protocol XIV* ('In countries so-called advanced we have circulated an insane and disgusting literature') which provided the proof of this diabolical conspiracy. Such ludicrous responses, of course, must be seen in context. In the years following the end of the Great War, the notion of the German-Jewish-Bolshevik conspiracy against the Empire, and the belief in the authenticity of the *Protocols*, still held sway amongst sections of the radical and far right.[91] Nonetheless, fascists' attempts to link sexual deviancy and promiscuity to Jewish influences continued unabated through the 1920s and 1930s. Many BUF cultural propagandists, for example, were convinced that Jewish commercial interests were behind the new sex culture and that Jews were prepared to debase culture for sordid financial gain. Occasionally these observations were based on crude racial stereotypes. J. F. C. Fuller believed that Jews had 'an instinct for sensuality and excitement' and were thus well disposed to promote sensuous films and indulge in lewd writing.[92] The IFL, less surprisingly, also resorted to crude racial stereotyping when discoursing on this subject. For one IFL writer the racial urge of the Jews, which could be traced to their Armenoid-Oriental ancestry, was always instinctively directed towards sexually promiscuous behaviour.[93]

Some fascists located the roots of the new sex culture in modern psychology and the methods of psychoanalysis. More often than not, the hand of the Jew was considered to be behind this new intellectual movement. Obtaining his imagery from the tradition of medieval or magical anti-semitism, J. F. C. Fuller thought that psychoanalysis was a new black magical cult obsessed with trifling with the mysteries of sex, a subversive anti-Christian doctrine which was Jewish in inspiration and design.[94] Its 'jargon' about repression and subconscious urges which were assumed to be primarily sexually motivated were insidious for Fuller, for it hit at the family and morality and undermined people's self-confidence by suggesting they were the mere play-things of irrational sexual urges. Needless to say, Sigmund Freud was frequently reviled in the fascist press. According to William Joyce, Freud was a 'Jewish pornologist' who merely 'presented pornography in the guise of scientific treaties'.[95] The attitude of the Imperial Fascist League towards psychoanalysis was characteristically extreme. The IFL leader Arnold Leese accused 'Freudism' of filling Britain's asylums.[96] He also thought it nonsensical on racial lines for 'Jewish psycho-analysts' to administer psychological treatment to Aryan patients. According to Leese, the subconscious sexual urges identified by Freud were simply the base instincts which governed Jews and as such could not feature in the psychological universe of the chaste Aryans.[97]

A host of 'decadent' phenomena

Intellectual modernism was also thought to be behind the cult of sexual decadence. It was the intellectual modernist literati of Bloomsbury who came in for the sharpest criticism. Bloomsbury writers and intellectuals were accused of being obsessed by Freudian 'sexual psychology'. In particular, they were charged with ceaselessly promoting sexual topics through their art. According to one BUF writer, Aldous Huxley was fascinated by degeneracy and the 'seamy side of psychology', a trait which was reflected in the literary characters to be found in his novels. In Huxley's *Eyeless in Gaza*, nasty 'degenerates' from sadists to licentious women abound for this Mosleyite, while every character in the book is the prisoner of psychologically introverted thoughts which revolve *ad nauseam* around the need for sexual gratification.[98] For William Joyce, English letters had been debased by the 'sickening miasma of Bloomsbury masochism'.[99] Such was the loathing felt by fascists for Bloomsbury intellectuals that on occasions the latter were re-imagined as a death-dealing disease. Reporting on a meeting of the 'British Sexological Society', in 1936, a Mosleyite described those in attendance as 'Bloomsbury bacilli'.[100]

The BUF's hostility to 'Bloomsbury' culture did not derive solely from the latter's alleged obsession with sex, however. 'Bloomsbury' developed into a general term of abuse in the Mosleyite lexicon for a wide spectrum of intellectual activity extending beyond the literary modernist elite. This hostility is all the more surprising given that the portents for a meaningful alliance between literary modernism and fascism appeared to be good during the interwar period. Both, for example, were antagonistic towards bourgeois materialism, aspects of liberal humanism and, with some of the more authoritarian modernists such as Ezra Pound, T. S. Eliot, D. H. Lawrence and Percy Wyndham Lewis, liberal democracy.[101] Both, too, deplored modern alienation and advocated a spiritual renaissance in society. Fascist and literary modernist thinking intersected at other points. Philosophical pessimism and 'cultural despair' was an attitude of mind common to both. Fascism and literary modernism were also contemptuous of 'mass culture' and the alleged 'Americanisation' of British culture. In addition, for both, the supremacy of elites in culture and other areas of society was deemed unavoidable. Fascists and literary modernists believed in the notion of a 'natural aristocracy' as the traditional trustees of culture.[102] Some modernists such as D. H. Lawrence also shared with fascism an affinity with the irrational or the primacy of intuition over reason. However, as Leslie Susser has pointed out, despite some obvious points of ideological convergence, British fascism held the modernist intellectuals in contempt during this period.[103]

So why the intense hostility? Susser correctly points out that one of the main reasons for this animosity was that fascism associated literary modernism with the decadence of the dying bourgeois culture it pledged itself to destroy.[104] Literary modernism's delicate sensibility, intellectual 'squeamishness' and inertia also aroused fascist indignation.[105] We should note other reasons for this antipathy, however. For many fascists, the intellectual modernists of Bloomsbury, by challenging the hegemony of traditional modes of written expression, were debasing English literature and subverting culture by advocating anarchy in the art form. A. K. Chesterton of the BUF deplored intellectual modernism's disdain for the conventions of form in literature, the obscurity of prose which, for him, reflected its spiritual turmoil and absence of a true inner vision. It was as true in poetry as it was in literature. The flagrant disregard of the principles of order represented in the lunatic 'association of fantastic dissimilarities' characteristic of much modernist verse offended Chesterton's sense of artistic propriety.[106] Oscar Boulton was mystified by the 'new poetry' of modernism, too, which, to him, had discarded 'rhyme and even rhythm of any kind'. What remained was 'a mere jumble of verbal affectations, serving only to conceal a poverty of thought and beauty by an obscurity of diction'.[107]

A. K. Chesterton despaired of the likes of James Joyce, T. S. Eliot and D. H. Lawrence. He believed their writings to be idiosyncratic and introspective, amounting to little more than a pretentious journey into the 'never-never lands of inanity'.[108] Another follower of Mosley accused James Joyce of playing with words and 'bastard sounds' in senseless and incomprehensible books, which had no relationship to great literature.[109] Such literary products, which, in the view of this BUF member, blithely eschewed clear thought and lucid expression, were considered a negation of art by these self-appointed guardians of the national culture. Language, for fascists like A. K. Chesterton, should not be an instrument to convey the inner torment of the individual, as was apparently the case with the literary modernists, but should be a means to establish contact between masculine minds seeking truth and the path that leads to human advancement. Similarly, good literature, according to another Mosleyite, should not concern itself with 'tricks with words' but should be composed 'of a beautiful combination of words resulting from the simple expression of human emotion'.[110]

There were other reasons for the revulsion. Culture of the Bloomsbury variety was thought to be indicative of an advanced state of *intellectual* decadence. Hostility towards intellectuals and exclusively intellectual activity featured prominently in British fascist ideology. For James Strachey Barnes, the 'over-specialised, logic-ridden intellectual' was an unbalanced, mentally stunted 'abnormality' who feared both spontaneity and reality.[111] In the BUF anti-intellectualism would become almost an obsession. Henry Williamson, for example, decried the 'slack-muscled professor', an unnatural being whom he associated with the culture of the town and the city.[112] As Williamson surveyed England's intelligentsia, the perception of decadence was never far from his thoughts. Himself a prolific and accomplished writer, Williamson feared and denounced the activity of living solely and intensely in the imagination.[113] For Williamson, the novelist, writing was an unnatural activity. 'Biologically speaking' writing was a 'decadence, an introversion, a rotting away of life'.[114] Another BUF member attacked the 'anaemic intellectualism' of the age, epitomised by those who opted for the 'sedentary life' and the modern-day propensity to dwell too long in 'musty libraries'. These activities were antithetical to a 'full, warm-blooded life', the 'things of death' which threatened the destruction of England's 'great culture'.[115]

Not surprisingly, the Bloomsbury literary intelligentsia were considered to be quintessential modern intellectual 'types'. 'Bloomsbury intellectualism', moreover, was imagined to be a particularly virulent strain of the virus of decadence because it had spread far beyond the circles of the literary intelligentsia. For the beleaguered fascists, the Bloomsbury 'type' seemed to dominate British intellectual and cultural life. The 'left-wing intellectual' of 1930s Britain, with his sports car, 'teddy-bear overcoat' and 'pale sallow complexion behind rimmed spectacles', was considered to be one such Bloomsbury 'decadent', as was the 'pansy', the 'long-haired apparition with the multi-coloured umbrella' and the 'tinted lips and eye-brows'.[116] The Bloomsbury 'specimens' of the left-wing variety who consumed the products of the 'Jew-Gollancz's' Left-Book Club were particularly loathed. Full of 'stale theories', their intellectualism apparently prevented them from experiencing a profound love of country or deep comradeship.[117] For the horrified Mosleyites, these 'products of perversion', the 'pansy and the

Marxist pink', had even polluted Oxford and her sister universities.[118] BUF undergraduates were urged to drive such 'filth and decay' from the campuses and restore Britain's ancient academic institutions to their former grandeur.

In many respects, this fascist assault on the supposedly decadent disease of 'intellectualism' can be traced to fascism's anti-rationalist perspective. Fascists accused rationalism of presiding over a fundamental divorce between intellect and emotion. By elevating mind and reason to a privileged position of authority within the human condition, rationalism was charged with denying man's subjective nature. The perceived cultural effects of this unnatural schism were perceived to be wholly negative. In stifling the emotional and intuitive side of man's nature, rationalism effectively blunted the motive forces of genuine creative endeavour. Fascism, on the other hand, proclaimed that it would restore the 'whole man', reconstruct fragmented modern man by eliminating this apparently artificial distinction between mind and inner feeling. This modern tendency towards intellectual abstraction could never compute the mysteries of the spirit for Britain's fascists, nor compete with the dynamic power of the will. Intellect was the mother of doubt and anxiety, an obstacle which blunted true creativity and inhibited vigorous action, a sterile and destructive province which deflected humanity from the path of freedom and truth.[119] The Mosley loyalist E. D. Randall declared boldly that he and his fascist comrades 'dare to deny the supremacy of mere intellect' which was 'powerless to appreciate in any length of time the truth which the senses grasped in a moment'.[120]

Notes

1 *Fascist Week*, 19–25 January 1934, p. 4.
2 Ibid.
3 *Action*, 12 February 1938, p. 7.
4 *Blackshirt*, 28 December 1934, p. 2.
5 R. Griffin, *The Nature of Fascism* (London, Routledge, 1993), pp. 32–6.
6 *FQ*, 11, 1 (January 1936), pp. 58–67.
7 Ibid.
8 *Fascist Week*, 25–31 May 1934, p. 6. On 1920s decadence in England, see M. Green, *Children of the Sun. A Narrative of Decadence in England After 1918* (London, Pimlico, 1992).
9 C. L. Mowat, *Britain Between the Wars* (London, Methuen, 1987

edition), pp. 211–15; R. Graves and A. Hodge, *The Long Weekend. A Social History of Great Britain 1918–1939* (London, Abacus, 1995 edition), pp. 41–4.
10 E. Waugh, *Vile Bodies* (London, Chapman and Hall, 1930).
11 J. Drennan, *BUF Oswald Mosley and British Fascism* (London, John Murray, 1934), pp. 85–6.
12 *Blackshirt*, 17 August 1934, p. 6; *Action*, 2 December 1937, p. 18.
13 *Blackshirt*, 23 February–1 March 1934, pp. 2–3.
14 *Blackshirt*, 4 January 1935, p. 6; *Blackshirt*, 7 December 1934, p. 6, on Chesterton.
15 Ibid.
16 Cited in H. S. B. Blume, 'A Study of Anti-Semitic Groups in Britain, 1918–40' (M.Phil. thesis, University of Sussex, 1971), p. 287.
17 Ibid.
18 *Action*, 6 August 1936, p. 13.
19 *Action*, 15 April 1939, p. 14, and 4 September 1937, p. 20.
20 On mass culture, see above, Chapter Eight.
21 J. Carey, *The Intellectuals and the Masses. Pride and Prejudice Among the Literary Intelligentsia, 1880–1939* (London, Faber and Faber, 1992), p. 185.
22 *BUQ*, 1, 3 (July–September 1937), p. 52.
23 J. Jenks, *Spring Comes Again. A Farmer's Philosophy* (London, The Bookshelf, 1939), p. 8.
24 *Action*, 28 May 1938, p. 14.
25 *Action*, 28 November 1936, p. 9.
26 *Fascist Bulletin*, 26 September 1925, p. 1.
27 *The Fascist*, February 1937, p. 3.
28 A. Raven-Thomson, *The Coming Corporate State* (London, Greater Britain Publications, 1935), p. 40.
29 *Action*, 2 December 1937, p. 18.
30 *Blackshirt*, 17 August 1934, p. 6.
31 *Action*, 2 December 1937, p. 18.
32 *Fascist Bulletin*, 26 September 1925, p. 1.
33 See *BUQ*, 11, 2 (April–June 1938), p. 15; *Action*, 12 February 1938, p. 10; *Blackshirt*, 21 December 1934, p. 4.
34 Ibid.
35 *Fascist Bulletin*, 20 February 1926, p. 3.
36 *The Fascist*, February 1937, p. 3; *Blackshirt*, 17 August 1934, p. 6; *Blackshirt*, 23 February–1 March 1934, pp. 2–3.
37 *Blackshirt*, 21 December 1934, p. 1.
38 Ibid.
39 R. Gordon-Canning, *The Inward Strength of a National Socialist* (London, Greater Britain Publications, c. 1938), p. 4.
40 *Fascist Week*, 5–11 January 1934, p. 8.
41 S. Pederson and P. Mandler (eds), *After the Victorians. Private*

Conscience and Public Duty in Modern Britain (London, Routledge, 1994), pp. 13–17.
42 Ibid.
43 Graves and Hodge, *The Long Weekend*, pp. 101–8.
44 *FQ*, 11, 1 (January 1936), p. 65.
45 *Patriot*, 4 December 1924, p. 70.
46 *Patriot*, 10 January 1924, p. 357.
47 *British Lion. The Official Organ of the Unity Band*, January 1933, p. 9.
48 *Blackshirt*, 18 April 1936, p. 5; *BUQ*, 11, 2 (April–June 1938), p. 51.
49 *Action*, 14 November 1936, p. 11.
50 *The Fascist*, January 1938, p. 5.
51 Ibid.; *The Fascist*, January 1938, p. 1.
52 Ibid.
53 *Blackshirt*, 21 August 1937, p. 2.
54 *Action*, 12 March 1938, p. 5.
55 *Patriot*, 23 April 1925, pp. 544–5.
56 *British Lion*, May 1932, p. 6.
57 *Action*, 26 February 1938, p. 15.
58 *BUQ*, 11, 3 (July–September 1938), p. 15.
59 *British Lion*, May 1932, p. 6.
60 *Fascist Bulletin*, 20 June 1925, p. 2.
61 *The Fascist*, January 1938, p. 1, and February 1937, p. 3.
62 Ibid.
63 *Blackshirt*, 27 March 1937, p. 5.
64 *Blackshirt*, 17 August 1934, p. 6.
65 *FQ*, 1, 1 (January 1935), pp. 76–7.
66 P. Wyndham Lewis, *Hitler* (London, Chatto and Windus, 1931), p. 181.
67 *Blackshirt*, 17 August 1934, p. 6.
68 *Blackshirt*, 11 January 1935, p. 11, and 22 November 1935, p. 6.
69 *Blackshirt*, 13 March 1937, p. 2, and 3 April 1937, p. 2.
70 *BUQ*, 11, 3 (July–September 1938), p. 18.
71 *The Fascist*, February 1937, p. 3.
72 H. S. Spencer, *Democracy or Shylocracy?* (London, The Britons, 1922), p. 30.
73 Drennan, *BUF Oswald Mosley*, p. 191.
74 Ibid.
75 *FQ*, 11, 1 (January 1936), p. 65.
76 Drennan, *BUF Oswald Mosley*, p. 194.
77 Wyndham Lewis, *Hitler*, pp. 21–8.
78 H. Williamson, *Goodbye West Country* (London, Putnam, 1937), p. 248.
79 *The Fascist*, June 1933, p. 3, and February 1937, p. 3.

80 *Fascist Bulletin*, 2 March 1926, p. 6.
81 J. S. Barnes, *Half a Life* (London, Eyre and Spottiswoode, 1933), p. 333.
82 *The Fascist*, January 1938, p. 7. The Chaldeans were an ancient people who lived in the coastal areas near the Persian Gulf in the sixth century.
83 *British Lion*, June 1933, pp. 6–7.
84 *BUQ*, 11, 3 (July–September 1938), p. 15.
85 *BUQ*, 11, 2 (April–June 1938), p. 52.
86 *Patriot*, 4 June 1925, pp. 49–51.
87 Ibid.
88 *Patriot*, 10 September 1925, pp. 394–5.
89 *Fascist Bulletin*, 2 March 1926, p. 6.
90 Ibid.
91 See above, Chapter Two.
92 *FQ*, 1, 1 (January 1935), p. 76.
93 *The Fascist*, March 1939, p. 2.
94 *FQ*, 1, 1 (January 1935), p. 79.
95 *Action*, 21 November 1936, p. 12, and 16 April 1936, p. 6.
96 *The Fascist*, October 1930, pp. 2–3.
97 *The Fascist*, January 1938, p. 7.
98 *Action*, 9 July 1936, p. 12.
99 *Action*, 18 June 1936, p. 2.
100 *Blackshirt*, 2 May 1936, p. 2.
101 L. Susser, 'Fascism, Literary Modernism and Modernization: The British Case', *Tel Aviver Jahrbuch für Deutsche Geschichte*, Part 18 (1989), pp. 463–86. See also J. Harrison, *The Reactionaries* (London, Victor Gollancz, 1966). On Wyndham Lewis, see A. Hewitt, 'Wyndham Lewis: Fascism, Modernism and the Politics of Homosexuality', *English Literary History*, 60, 2 (1993), pp. 527–44.
102 On the literary intelligentsia fascination with the idea of a 'natural aristocracy', see Carey, *The Intellectuals*, pp. 71–90.
103 Susser, 'Fascism, Literary Modernism', pp. 465–8.
104 Ibid., p. 468.
105 Ibid.
106 *Action*, 20 January 1938, p. 3.
107 *British Lion*, March 1933, p. 5.
108 *Fascist Week*, 9–15 March 1934, p. 4.
109 *Blackshirt*, 28 September 1934, p. 9.
110 Ibid.
111 J. S. Barnes, *Fascism* (London, Thornton Butterworth, 1931), p. 69.
112 Williamson, *Goodbye West Country*, p. 156.
113 On Williamson, see M. D. Higginbottom, *Intellectuals and British Fascism. A Study of Henry Williamson* (London, Janus, 1992).
114 Ibid., p. 388.

115 *Fascist Week*, 16–22 March 1934, p. 4.
116 *Action*, 26 March 1938, p. 7, and 17 July 1937, p. 11.
117 Ibid.
118 *Action*, 26 March 1938, p. 7.
119 *Action*, 21 August 1937, p. 12.
120 *Action*, 12 February 1938, p. 7.

CHAPTER TEN

THE CITY, THE COUNTRYSIDE AND THE MACHINE

In the fascist mind Bloomsbury 'intellectualism', together with changing trends in leisure and sexual behaviour, as we saw in the previous chapter, were decadent phenomena which heralded the dissolution of culture. However, in the view of many of Britain's fascists between the wars, the supreme paradigm of decadence and the ultimate symbol of the destruction of culture in the modern age was the city. Indeed, the modern city stood accused of having spawned many of the decadent habits and practices which were thought to be afflicting the postwar world. In the fascist imagination, the city metamorphosed into a dark, forbidding and threatening place where decadent practices flourished, including the leisure antics of the 'bright young things', sexual promiscuity and 'intellectualism'. The judgement of the BUF's James Drennan on the intellectuals' relationship to the city, for example, was a typical reaction. 'Like intelligent bluebottles on the muck-heap of all culture', the intellectuals 'sun themselves on its [the city's] foul odours and swell fat on its ordure', declared Drennan.[1] It was the city which nourished barren 'intellectualism', the cold, unfeeling rationality of the bourgeois man of logic. 'Shallow and rootless', the 'intelligent mind', in the opinion of Drennan's Mosleyite comrade Henry Williamson, was a product of 'sidewalks, steamheat' and 'cocktail nothingness', a culture of 'bricks and mortar decadence'.[2]

Disquiet about the modern city, of course, was not the exclusive preserve of the fascists. Contemporary writers on culture such as T. S. Eliot, who inveighed against London urban life in *The Waste Land* (1923), periodically poured scorn on the quality of existence in the modern urban environment. Those pioneers of enlightened town planning, too, Patrick Geddes and Lewis Mumford, expressed serious reservations about the evolving character of the modern urban milieu, suggesting that its sprawling and unplanned nature threatened the quality of life of its inhabitants, and even the global ecological balance.[3] It was the fascists, though, who engaged in the most sustained and impassioned polemic against the modern city. As with their reactions to the changing patterns of behaviour in postwar British culture, the fascist disquiet about cities was not an isolated reactionary 'anti-' phenomenon. Rather, it was an element of a coherent cultural *Weltanschauung*, which was underpinned by the omnipresent notion of decadence and perception of impending cultural decline. This was particularly the case with the 'Spenglerian' fascists of the Mosleyite variety, as we shall see.

During the 1920s, in its initial stages, fascist commentary on the city and the modern cityscape tended to be spasmodic and not clearly defined. Nonetheless, we can detect the outlines of a pessimistic vision of the city which, by the 1930s, with the arrival of the BUF on the political scene, had developed into a sustained critique. Writing in 1925 a British Fascisti member, for example, expressed concern about the physical condition of Britain's cities, pointing to their mean slums, poor housing, overcrowding and general scenes of squalor.[4] The poor quality of life of the slum-dwellers, however, was not the main concern of this BF writer. Rather, the appalling conditions of Britain's urban centres represented a grave danger to society because slum populations were easy prey for the 'Young Communists International' and other 'mob orators' assiduously planting the seeds of class bitterness and revolution in their ranks. The perception that modern cities were centres of revolutionary intrigue and subversion, and that the 'slum-dweller' was particularly receptive to seditious propaganda, would become a common fascist fear as the 1920s and 1930s unfolded.

Other threats emanated from the British city in the eyes of the BF. It was felt that the modern urban centre harboured a 'degraded' population, which dissipated national strength. According to one Norman Thompson, Britain's declining industrial and commercial position in global terms was mirrored in the deteriorating quality of its urban population. He feared that economic decline was creating a surplus population in the decaying industrial cities, the 'fittest' of whom were preparing to emigrate to more prosperous climes while those largely 'unfit' in both health and physique remained, to the detriment of the national good. Like 'all decadent and decaying matter', he declared, the 'unfit' would 'remain inert *in situ*, an incubus on the budget and the nation, until starvation and other disintegrating influences reduce their numbers to more appropriate dimensions'.[5] That such comments were underpinned by eugenicist ideas is indisputable, a frame of mind confirmed by Thompson's belief that around half of Britain's population fail to reach full 'normal' mental capacity owing to their poor heredity and that 'no amount of environment will put it right'.[6] Thompson's BF comrades also engaged in eugenicist fantasies. For the District Officer of the BF's Western Command, John Cheshire, the city 'mob' demonstrated in the Liverpool police strike of August 1919 that it respected neither property nor moral decency.[7] Cheshire longed for a time in the future when the eugenic elimination of the mentally and physically 'unfit', which he described as the 'militant Fascism of Science', would forever eliminate the blight of civil disorder from the civilised world.[8] Such dark meditations suggest that the fascists were the heirs of both the eugenicist and 'degenerationist' thinkers of the *fin de siècle*. The idea that increasing urbanisation in the modern world was breeding a physically and mentally deficient biological type with vicious habits was disseminated by such pessimistic tomes as Max Nordau's *Degeneration*.[9] Originally published in 1892, Nordau's book found an enthusiastic readership and went through a number of editions.

On occasions, the theme of biological decline acquired more sinister connotations. The city was also linked with 'race pollution' in the mind of the BF's Norman Thompson. Jews and other European immigrants, drawn 'largely from the lowest grades of their nations of origin', who had recently settled in England were not only largely responsible for the city slums and the 'multiplication of the unfit' but also 'the contamination of our British stocks'.[10] In a menacing twist to his depressing meditations on life in early postwar England, Thompson suggested that poison gases, so effective in time of war, were 'the only practical solution yet presented for slum cities and their dysgenic masses'.[11]

Many of these negative views of the city would be taken up at a later date by the Imperial Fascist League. Not surprisingly, the themes of biological retrogression and race deterioration surfaced in their writings. One IFL member believed that a by-product of increasing urbanisation and declining rural life was physical enfeeblement and that an exclusively urban civilisation was a civilisation in decay.[12] Another feared that London's ever-expanding population was leading to a 'loss of racial purity'. London was urged to heed the lesson of Rome and Athens which supposedly demonstrated that the city inevitably lends itself to race deterioration.[13] The IFL, too, saw a link between revolutionary 'subversives' and the city. 'Red' Clydesiders such as James Maxton were products of a foul atmosphere of 'forge smoke and Clyde filth'.[14] The IFL's aversion to an urban civilisation went further. It even advocated a policy of de-urbanisation as one solution for the nation's increasing ill-health.[15]

The Mussolini enthusiast and Italophile James Strachey Barnes's view of British cities was equally pessimistic. He, too, believed that a civilisation characterised by huge enveloping urban centres was tending towards 'biological decadence'.[16] He also warned against the modern city's increasing domination over its surrounding regions, a parasitic inclination that threatened to create an imbalance within the nation's economic life.[17] Barnes particularly 'loathed' the appearance and general ambience of the modern English city, a 'stinking and gloomy' place with depressing slums, an absence of light and air, and a 'hideously commercial' look, not least in its 'ghastly vulgarity' in advertisement.[18] Barnes's fascism, as we know, was saturated in nostalgia, so it comes as no surprise to discover that his ideal city was the city of the Middle Ages and the early Renaissance.[19] The same line of thought can be found in the writings of Rolf Gardiner, the admirer of the Nazi revolution and an ardent 'back-to-the-land' enthusiast. Gardiner bemoaned the modern world's fluidity, which was destroying the 'old England' of country mansions. For him, the cities of the 'new England' of the 1930s were 'un-English' and centres of 'sheer barbarism'.[20]

The majority of concerns about the modern city identified above were also present in the BUF's thinking on this subject. The followers of Mosley, too, believed that Britain's industrial cities were centres of squalor, deprivation and disease, poisoned environments which brutalised the inhabitants, destroyed their health and invariably imperilled the survival of the 'race'. The following response was typical. The consequence of forcing children to live in 'crowded cities, perpetually drinking the fumes of factory chimneys', one BUF member complained, was that they emerged into adulthood with stunted bodies and a low disease threshold.[21] For this same Mosleyite, the average Briton, a product of 'the ravages of our cramped, artificial and industrialised lives', was a 'weak specimen, undersized and under-developed', with bad teeth, poor eyesight and susceptible to consumption, rheumatism, cancer, mental illness and a variety of other debilitating conditions.[22] Race deterioration and cultural extinction beckoned unless Britain addressed such problems for this despondent fascist.

Henry Williamson's view of the city was equally bleak. Like Rolf Gardiner, Williamson was a national socialist of a neo-romantic bent whose meditations on postwar life in Britain reveal an intense fascination with nature and an antipathy towards modernity, which he associated with urban rather than rural values.[23] Williamson's writings were laced with numerous references to the city's debilitating effects on social and cultural life and expressed a nostalgia for a rural environment and way of life that, by the interwar period, was fast disappearing. His view of the modern city, like that of James Strachey Barnes, was also governed by aesthetic considerations. Prior to his conversion to fascism, Williamson recalled a visit to London and its suburbs soon after the Great War. He was appalled by London's green fields 'so foully ravaged', its 'dead houses' and bizarre concrete cliffs where once forests thrived, its 'roads dreary with sulphurous fog' and the overall 'strange and dreadful scene' that it presented to the visitor.[24] His mood was one of sorrow as he imagined a time when the corn grew on these same locations, the hares ran the stubble and field workers gaily sang harvest songs. It was a melancholy Williamson who 'looked with despair for any sign of beauty' amidst the capital's arid urban wastelands.[25]

The neo-romantic impulse behind Williamson's anti-urban agenda, the reverence for nature and the timeless heritage of the English landscape, was not confined to him alone. It ran like a thread through the BUF's cultural outlook. 'No country in the world has such a gentle fertile green landscape as England; some of our counties are almost parks', wrote one BUF member.[26] But this BUF member was pessimistic about the future well-being of rural England. He reflected on developments like the 'great arterial roads', observing that the Great West Road 'is now almost one unbroken stretch of mongrel houses from London to Oxford, spoiling the countryside in a most reckless way'.[27] Anxiety about the extent and pace of urban development and the corresponding disappearance of the countryside would be a recurring theme. Mosleyites deplored the encroachment of the city and its mechanised culture into rural England. 'The city spreads its tentacles of brick and stucco across the face of England and fumes of oil rise in lanes once only redolent with the scent of hedge-blossom', lamented one BUF member.[28]

In their unceasing celebration of the virtues of rural England, the

Mosleyites believed themselves to be the self-appointed guardians of the English pastoral ideal in the tradition of earlier romantic ruralists such as Richard Jefferies, the late nineteenth-century naturalist and novelist.[29] There were others in this tradition, too, such as Edward Carpenter, who in the 1880s set up a rural commune at Millthorpe outside Sheffield, modelled along the lines of the anarchist co-operative commune proposed by Peter Alekseyevich Kropotkin.[30] There was a thriving rural England literary genre in the late nineteenth and early twentieth centuries also. Rural nostalgia and quaint rustic images pervaded the novels of the period, such as Thomas Hardy's *Far From the Madding Crowd* (1874) and E. M. Forster's *Howard's End* (1910). Even that arch-trumpeter of England's imperial destiny overseas, Rudyard Kipling, succumbed to this mood for nostalgia. In *Puck of Pook's Hill* (1906) Kipling fixed his gaze inward and quietly meditated on the peaceful splendour of rural Sussex.[31] During these decades also, a host of modern-day, mostly urban, pilgrims embarked on solemn quests to discover the life and culture of villages and an England of quiet meadows, idyllic patchwork landscapes and village greens.[32]

All these devotees of rural England, including the BUF, held shared beliefs and concerns. There was an aesthetic concern about England's vanishing landscape and picturesque 'old world' villages. There was also a belief that the essence of the national character resided in rural society rather than in the city. Rural communities were perceived to be timeless and enduring places that preserved a form of social interaction that was both natural and harmonious.[33] At another level, it was imagined that rural England had the power to impede the process of time itself. In some magical way, it would act as a barrier to slow down the speeding juggernaut of modernity unleashed by the forces of 'Progress'.[34] For those who embraced its healing balms, the countryside promised deliverance from the rushing, frenetic, contemporary age. The concept of rural England as a refuge from modernity and its stresses was a related theme, a tranquil 'resting place' where the individual could achieve a more natural state of psychological and spiritual equilibrium. Such sentiments were deeply nostalgic. They flowed from a profound sense of loss and regret at the passing of an earlier way of life, which was genuinely felt. The BUF tapped into this rich vein of traditional rural nostalgia. Consistent with its fascist ideology, however, its views on the countryside were of an even more extreme kind.

In fascist ideology, particularly that of the 'mature' Mosleyite variety, 'true' culture was indelibly bound up with the countryside and the soil.[35] The land or countryside, as a timeless place expressing something eternal and enduring, was perceived to be a vital repository of the nation's spiritual values. In the same vein, rural England was imagined as a vital repository of the spiritual essence of the 'race' or the racial community which, with the BUF, was defined in metaphysical rather than biological terms. There was an almost mystical attachment to nature itself, too, in mature fascist ideologies. This reverence for nature was invariably underpinned by metaphysical assumptions. Nature was considered to be a vital place, the only source of life and truth. 'Only from nature could the truth arise', declared Henry Williamson.[36] It followed, therefore, for fascists like Williamson, that those closest to nature would be closest to the truth. Williamson harboured a neo-romantic fascination with the sun in particular. The sun was the source from which the life-force itself flowed. The sun generated 'the light that was life, the light that was truth', according to Williamson.[37] Fascist nature-worship invariably led to the related belief, too, that nature nourished the spirit, a vital well-spring of the individual's and the nation's cultural expression. In addition, the more balanced existence that rural life supposedly provided was productive of healthy minds and bodies. If a race and its civilisation is to survive, stipulated Oswald Mosley, it needed continual replenishment from the 'steady, virile stock which is bred in the health, sanity and natural but arduous labour of the countryside'.[38] Alongside its commitment to an autarkical revival of the agricultural economy, therefore, the BUF hoped that a restoration of a greater balance between town and country would check the process of race deterioration supposedly brought on by unrestrained urbanism.

The growth of the city, of course, threatened all this in the eyes of the Mosleyites. The city was looked upon as the antithesis of truth and life. Henry Williamson feared that the modern Englishman had lost the clarity of mind and mental fearlessness which would guarantee the creation of a better world because the 'town-mind had lost touch with the truths of sky, grass and sunshine'.[39] The lack of light, sun and air in the city and its destruction of the land, 'deadened to eternal impotence by down-thrusting weight of hewn-stone and brick and metal' in the colourful prose of one fascist, offended the Mosleyites. The city's effect on people was regarded as nothing short of dramatic. It had wrenched them from their natural environment and placed them in an artificial, 'nature-divorced' world of soaring concrete, iron, pavements and 'synthetic' pleasures. For the BUF cultural propagandist Francis McEvoy, the city masses had been 'deracinated' and had lost all spiritual anchorage.[40] In the BUF's judgement the modern city-dweller was a 'devitalised' individual who lacked vigour, courage and vision, and craved safety and comfort. E. D. Randall loathed the 'effeminate city-complex of individual security', while another Mosleyite, Theo Lang, decried modern man's 'mad search for comfort and convenience and ease', which drove him to erect his haven, the 'Metropolis'.[41]

However, rather than providing people with the comfort and security for which they yearned, the Metropolis was seen to be the agent of a whole gamut of neuroses. Deprived of the 'soothing balms of nature', the resident of the 'unnatural' city was cast as a new biological type, a desperate figure suffering from all manner of nervous strains, a neurotic racked by hyper-tension, fatigue and 'over-muchness'. Moreover, this devitalised and neurotic existence apparently bred a variety of 'perversions', some of which, the postwar era's so-called decadent leisure and sexual habits and 'intellectualism', we have looked at in detail. Other perceived urban-generated 'perversions' included anti-patriotism and Marxism. Henry Williamson, a First World War combatant who was haunted by the awful memory of the trenches, even linked the origins of wars to the city. He was convinced that modern wars were caused by neurotic city men, 'irritable' types who were unable to achieve inner harmony and looked for release through the excitement of war.[42] Wars were made by the 'pallid mob-spirit, by mass-escapists from indoor and pavement living', declared Williamson, the 'pale-faced men whose natural instincts are repressed'.[43]

The neurotic, 'unnatural' life of the city even threatened procreation. The city begat the 'Ibsenian intelligent woman' who was prepared to spurn even motherhood for inner freedom, the quintessential liberated modern woman portrayed to great effect by Nora Helmer, the fictional heroine of Henrik Ibsen's play *A Doll's House* (1879).[44] Fascism, on the other hand, promised a return to 'true womanliness'.[45] The 'intelligent woman', and indeed the homosexual, the 'man who is no longer man', flourished in the modern city because life in the city was *formless*, according to James Drennan. In this place of 'formless anarchy', where all life is unnatural, 'perversity' becomes the norm. We can once again discern fascism's dread of formlessness and flux and its desire to impose order on perceived chaos. Indeed, in many respects, fascism was a movement that sought consciously to bring order and discipline to the apparently 'formless' existence of the modern city.

It is clear from all this that the BUF's perception of the city was of a qualitatively different kind from that of rival fascists in interwar Britain. The main reason for this is the enduring influence of Oswald Spengler on Mosleyite fascist thought. Spengler's view of the modern city was characteristically pessimistic. For him, the giant world-city, the 'Megalopolis', was the final, awful destination of 'Culture' in the modern world.[46] Man's 'daemonic creation', the 'world-city', signified the final stage of the organic life-cycle of a culture, a dreadful climax which presaged the death of civilisation itself. The giant city was depicted as a nightmarish place by Spengler, a 'daemonic stone-desert', which would ultimately, like Mary Shelley's Frankenstein monster, devour its creators, the 'Culture-men' who had been spiritually formed by the land. According to Spengler, all civilisations and cultures were subject to fundamental biological laws of formation, growth and decline, so it comes as no surprise to discover that an evolutionary perspective underlay his view of the Megalopolis. The giant city was part of the same structural process of birth and death which governed the development of other historical and cultural phenomena. The emergence of the giant city was the culmination of a series of stages of evolutionary development, which began with primitive forms of human settlement and interaction. 'Growing from primitive barter-centre to Culture-city and at last to world-city', in the words of Spengler, the city 'sacrifices first the blood and soul of its creators to the needs of its majestic evolution, and then the last flower of that growth to the spirit of Civilisation; and so, doomed, moves on to final self-destruction.'[47] According to the remorseless logic of Spengler's grim prophecy, necropolis, the death of the city, was the next stage in the organic life-cycle, an outcome that was both inevitable and irreversible.

Spengler earmarked a key moment in this process of self-destruction, the city's propensity to uproot and disassociate itself from the environment that originally nourished its growth. In Spengler's eyes, the giant city was responsible for creating an ecological imbalance that was turning the countryside into a wasteland, a process which was tantamount to racial suicide. In Spengler's dramatic prose, 'the giant city sucks the country dry, insatiably and incessantly demanding and devouring fresh streams of men, till it wearies and dies in the midst of an almost uninhabited waste of country'.[48]

The 'artificial' existence, 'soullessness' and sterile 'intellectualism' of the Megolopolis, and its discouragement of fertility, were other harbingers of death. It is evident that the Mosleyites were greatly influenced by Spengler's writing on the Megalopolis, for the majority of these dark Spenglerian themes can be found in their analysis of the city, as we have seen. The BUF followed Spengler, too, in portraying the Metropolis as a place peopled by 'nationless nomads' who had no attachment to soil or nation. Life and culture in 1930s London for one follower of Mosley represented 'a vivid picture of internationalism in practice', a centre of cosmopolitanism which was coming more and more to resemble the international 'melting pot' of New York.[49] Offensive animal metaphors served to dehumanise sections of London's population. The capital apparently housed a 'huge mongrel population', while late at night in the West End, 'Greeks, negroes, and the ubiquitous Jews gather in great numbers, slinking from pavement to pavement, cafe to cafe like great slugs'.[50] A 'hybrid international and Jewish culture' permeated the capital's cultural life also, according to this fascist.

There is more than a strong hint of Spengler also in the BUF's characterisation of the urban space as geometric and 'mechanised', which engendered a machine-like, and thus soulless, existence for its inhabitants. Spengler compared the old city of Gothic cathedrals, town halls and high-gabled streets, and grand patricians' residences and palaces in the Baroque style, to the artificial abstractions of the modern Metropolis. In contrast to this older city aesthetic, the Metropolis, a mathematical and purely 'intellectual' concoction of the city-architect, aimed 'at the chess-board form', which, for Spengler, was the symbol of soullessness.[51] A BUF writer condemned the city, its 'geometric machine lines' and the homes of those who toiled in the city, which, in their 'uniformity, regimentation and mediocrity', served the purpose of moulding them for their 'planned, regimented, apportioned life in offices and factories'.[52] The suburbs were singled out for the most acute criticism. 'The machine-made regulation-pattern article' which was a feature of the 1930s suburban housing estate had 'whiped [sic] all character off the face of our towns', bemoaned one Mosleyite. As he surveyed the 'row upon row of modern, sanitary, neat little brick boxes', all of them 'exactly alike' and 'facing the same way' in streets of a uniform pattern, he yearned for a return of the old English village with its irregular streets and eccentric, contrasting houses built according to individual style and taste.[53]

Indeed, for many in the BUF the residential suburb was the supreme embodiment of the artificial, soulless and devitalised existence of modern urban life in 1930s Britain. The 1920s and 1930s witnessed a spectacular growth in suburban housing development in England.[54] The expansion of suburbia in the south-east was particularly marked. The growth of London's suburban 'outer ring' between 1921 and 1931, for example, saw population explosions in numerous districts hitherto partially rural, such as Carshalton by 105.2 per cent, Chingford by 132.6 per cent and Kingsbury by 796.3 per cent, the latter from 1,856 to 16,636.[55] This expansion partly reflected a desire on the part of the middle classes to flee the older parts of town and partly mirrored internal population movements from north to south. To the BUF the suburban phenomenon was wholly objectionable. Neither authentically urban nor rural but a miscegenation of both, England's dormitory suburbs were derided as satellite cities, 'pale, devitalised versions of the mother cities', and an 'anaemic ghost of the country' which they were ravaging at a ferocious pace.[56] The BUF's contempt for suburban man and suburban cultural life was total. The 'little men' of the suburbs, unwilling to confront and challenge the horror of the Megalopolis, sought escape by scurrying home every evening to 'drugged rest in the unsocial, unintellectual horror of suburban philistinism'.[57] According to E. D. Randall, the 'suburban bourgeoisie' had hidden themselves away in a 'dim little world of self-absorption'. They hankered after only two things in life, security and a small car, while the 'rows of artificial villas with narrow gardens growing synthetic shrubs' represented the limit of their ambition and concern.[58]

It is tempting to view the BUF's critique of the modern city and its progeny, the residential suburb, as a quintessential expression of reactionary fascist anti-modernism. Indeed, rarely does one encounter a positive view of the city or the suburbs in Mosleyite literature. The BUF's nostalgic reflections on the virtues of pre-urban rural life would seem to fit into the same pattern of anti-modernism. That the BUF identified with Spengler's bleak assessment of the city appears to offer further proof of the essentially reactionary thrust of its urban outlook. On closer examination, however, the nature of the BUF's urban project appears to be less unambiguously anti-modern. Rather than proposing a wholesale flight from the city, the BUF sought to 'rescue' it, to prise it free from the grasp in which it was apparently held by the powerful and destructive forces of liberal capitalist modernity. The city would not disappear in the new fascist order of things, but was to be recast anew in accordance with the BUF's overall mythic vision of a regenerated national community. If the BUF absorbed Spengler's gloomy prognosis on the modern city's character and mode of life, therefore, it did not accept his fatalistic assessment that the city was heading remorselessly towards inevitable self-destruction. As we noted above, fascism defined itself as a revolt against the apparently 'formless' existence of the modern city. The fascists believed that they had a mission to bring a sense of order and discipline to the city's formless anarchy. Thus fascism viewed itself as a force seeking to control the city and thereby sustain its cultural life, albeit along lines which conformed to its narrow definition of culture. The BUF's James Drennan, for example, believed that the experience of continental Fascism and Nazism demonstrated that these two movements represented consciously controlled attempts to master 'the City in cultural life', and therein lay their profound significance for modern Europe and its cultural life.[59] The Mosleyite strand of British fascism viewed its cultural mission in a similar vein. While following Spengler in many aspects of his thoughts on the city, the BUF refused to countenance his fatalism. Thus Mosleyite fascism represented a mutiny against the destiny of Megalopolitan destruction, or necropolis, as defined in Spengler's gloomy dystopian vision.

We can detect a definite modernising impulse at work in the BUF's urban project, therefore, albeit of a different ideological complexion from that of liberal capitalism's modernising agenda. Thus in a similar vein to Drennan, A. K. Chesterton wrote of the need to rebuild Britain's slum-infested major cities in order that they may 'capture the sun and air' and 'give life to lung and eye'.[60] This 'remaking [of] an entire environment' represented a mighty and heroic task of reconstruction that could only be undertaken by fascism, in Chesterton's mind, which alone of all its political contemporaries had the necessary courage, iron will and strength of purpose. It is important to qualify the above assessment, however. On many occasions the BUF's commentary on the place and role of the city in modern life came across as being vague and confused, which reflected an inability to resolve adequately the contradiction between the anti-modern and modern elements in its ideology. Too often in party discourse there was no clear unanimity of opinion, which reflected the fact that there was a strand of thought within the BUF that had not reconciled itself to the strong modernising impulse within the movement's political project. It is difficult to ignore the fact that in the writings of a number of the more romantic back-to-the-soil enthusiasts, such as Henry Williamson, E. D. Randall and Jorian Jenks for example, we can observe a yearning for a return to a more simple life in touch with nature that would unfold against the backdrop of a reconstructed economic system orientated towards agriculture rather than manufacturing. This romantic vision of a sturdy and contented yeomen farming population and an autarkical return to agricultural production was genuine and can only be interpreted as unambiguously anti-modern.

If fascists' attitudes towards the metropolis were characterised by unease, anxiety and even loathing, that other potent symbol of modernity, the *machine*, aroused similar emotions in them, emotions which, *prima facie*, strike one as a further example of a reactionary anti-modernist outlook. Apprehension about the machine and the machine age was prevalent in British fascist discourse. The BUF's James Drennan complained that the 'remorseless power of the Machine' was 'chawing into pulp the whole cultural life of the Europe' of history and tradition.[61] The senior BUF official Alexander Raven-Thomson remarked on 'the cruel, drab mediocrity of the machine age' and the need to curb it, while another Mosleyite, H. B. Raynor, warned that 'when man acclaimed the machine god, civilisations crumbled away in decadence'.[62] Rolf Gardiner, too, condemned the worship of mechanical power in the modern age, which he believed had its origins in 'the dead, flameless [sic] ideals of the nineteenth century'.[63] For the BUF, the machine age was the material expression of a number of parallel forces in the modern world that included free-trade capitalism, liberalism, communism, materialism and positivism, and it was initially spawned by the Industrial Revolution. In the words of the prominent Mosley loyalist J. F. C. Fuller, it was the Industrial Revolution that had propelled mankind 'into the dungeon of the steam age'.[64]

British fascism, particularly the BUF, viewed itself as a counter-revolution against the Industrial Revolution. Jorian Jenks, the BUF's agricultural spokesman, complained that, as well as creating England's 'dreary industrial slums', the Industrial Revolution had depopulated the countryside, a process which had detrimental long-term effects on the rural economy.[65] Another Mosleyite felt that when England entered the industrial age, it 'turned over an intensely romantic page' in its history, because industrialisation triggered a migration from country to town and destroyed the old England of independent yeomen farmers.[66] Similar accusations to the ones levelled at urbanisation and the city were directed at the new industrial age, such as the charge that industrialisation produced a physically enfeebled population which ultimately dissipated national strength. For the fascists, a population of physically deficient biological 'types' spelt race deterioration and even the decay of civilisation itself.

In berating the Industrial Revolution's legacy, the BUF attempted to position itself within a long-standing domestic tradition of anti-industrial thought that reached back to the pre-Victorian era. Unease about industrialisation, for example, could be discerned in the outlook of Augustus Pugin (1812–52) and his contemporaries in the neo-Gothic revival movement. In Pugin this anxiety translated into nostalgia for the Catholic Middle Ages, which he imagined to be a harmonious, ordered age that prized spiritual and aesthetic values above all else.[67] It was a comforting image which he set against the dominant one of environmental ugliness and social dissonance that characterised his own secular age of unfettered industrialisation. Pugin's answer to all this was to promote the idea of a return to a 'Christian' architecture, which eventually led to a flurry of Church and public building in the Gothic style. The tradition of nostalgic, romantic anti-industrialism can also be traced through the Oxford Movement of the 1830s, which, like Pugin, advocated that Church design should conform to a medieval style. This tradition can also be discerned in later 'Victorian Medievalism', with its desire to revive the cult of courtly romance and chivalric codes of conduct.[68] The 'Merrie England' myth which developed in the late Victorian era also contained within it a moral condemnation of industrialism and an appeal to an imagined golden English past. The myth was inspired by the writings of Richard Jefferies and sustained the medievalist socialist visions of the likes of Robert Blatchford and William Morris.[69] Anxiety about industrialisation featured in the thought of Thomas Carlyle, John Ruskin and Mathew Arnold, too. These eminent Victorians regularly inveighed against liberal utilitarian materialism and the ethos of 'Progress', fearing its effect on culture and the aesthetic sensibility, in particular.[70]

If British fascists believed that industrialisation had a detrimental effect on bodily health, was a chief agent of biological retrogression and threatened the survival of the 'race', they also thought that it struck at the deeper recesses of the soul by killing the artistic impulse within the work process. The principal target of their wrath

The city, the countryside and the machine

here was mass production. Mass production was accused of killing the artistic impulse because, firstly, it transformed work into a mechanical, soulless activity and, secondly, it was preoccupied with the production of standardised objects which ensured the alienation of the worker from the product of his or her labour. On the first count, British fascists claimed that since the Industrial Revolution, work had become an 'unnatural' mechanised activity, devoid of pleasure, creativity and beauty. 'Work is losing the gift it once had of joy', declared a solemn James Strachey Barnes.[71] In this idealised, aesthetic view of work, artistry, creativity and beauty were to be found only in the individual craftwork associated with the small workshop and the artisan. Complaining that the rise of the machine had 'ruined handicrafts and damaged artistry', the BUF's Raven-Thomson pledged that a future Fascist Britain would make work once again a 'natural' activity. Standards of craftsmanship in the tradition of the medieval artisan would be upheld and there would be renewed pride in handicrafts, all under the patronage of the Corporate State.[72]

On the second count, mass production apparently destroyed the artistic impulse within the work process because it churned out a standardised product thought to be lacking in beauty and artistic worth. Raven-Thomson dreamt of a day in the future when one would find 'beautiful decorated hand-made furniture of Chippendale and Adam' in the homes of the people, rather than the 'Birmingham-produced "presents from Margate"' that adorned their mantle-pieces in this age of mass production.[73] Cuthbert Reavely, a BUF member too, referred to the 'vulgarians who claim to produce passable imitations of beautiful things by means of mechanical mass-production'.[74] The IFL also complained of the prevailing tendency in modern industry towards 'the standardisation of the cheap and the shoddy'. Not surprisingly, the fanatically anti-semitic IFL saw the hidden hand of the Jew behind this development.[75]

Some British fascists feared the ultimate creation of the machine-man, or the machine-body. The drive towards ever-greater efficiency in the techniques of mass production implied in the Taylorised or 'Fordist' model of manufacturing industry would result inevitably in the mechanisation of humankind. In this nightmarish technophobic vision, people find themselves increasingly subjugated to the tyrannical reign of technology, where before long they would become mere appendages of the machine or worse be transformed into dehumanised technological automatons. The modern worker 'is feeling himself more and more a mere cog in the wheel of so many great anonymous machines', wrote James Strachey Barnes, while Henry Williamson, in his usual vivid prose, referred to the modern 'gold-civilisation' which 'mechanised men for its economic factory-jungle pavement existence'.[76] For another follower of the BUF, the worker engaged in industrial production in the modern era tends to become a 'dehumanised and stereotyped unit in the production of the commodity concerned'.[77]

The image of the worker coming to resemble a technological automaton acting unconsciously like a machine was not the stuff of pure fantasy. It had some grounding in empirical reality. Advanced capitalist industrialisation had ushered in mass production, a system of 'scientifically' organised production developed and pioneered by Frederick Taylor and applied to the work environment by Henry Ford. Taylor sought to apply scientific principles and measurement to the labour process in order to maximise worker efficiency.[78] In order to make factory workers as efficient as the machines they worked on, Taylor designed a system of standardised physical gestures which would provide a model for all workers and which could be imparted by habit. In seeking to regulate the human and mechanical elements of the factory so as to bring them into perfect harmony, scientific Taylorism was the rationalisation of the machine age. Thus with its highly regulated, disciplined and super-rational approach, Taylorism, and its progeny, the Fordist model of mass standardised production, represented an attempt to purge the irrational from the workplace. The effect of this strict regulatory regime and denial of emotion, of course, was the creation of the machine-body.

Neither was the fear of a Taylorised work process and the trend towards the machine-body confined to the fascists. Writing a century earlier, Thomas Carlyle, for example, feared the creation of the former. In the new materialist age, he complained, 'men are grown mechanical in head and in heart'.[79] These themes were brilliantly satirised, too, at a much later date, in Charlie Chaplin's film *Modern Times*, with its graphic imagery of frenetic industry and of the worker's eventual incorporation into the machine.[80] The notion of technology as being destructive is there also in Fritz Lang's *Metropolis*, where technology, in the form of a Moloch, literally devours its victims.[81] Similarly, anxiety about technology is present in Aldous Huxley's *Brave New World*, a dystopian vision of a world falling under the sway of Fordism and its ethos of mass production and mass standardisation.[82]

The fascists' disquiet about the machine and Fordist mass standardisation fuelled their dread of Soviet Bolshevism. J. F. C. Fuller of the BUF described Lenin as the 'Mahomet of the Industrial Revolution', a 'synthetic-iconoclast' and 'mechanical monotheist' who sought to establish 'the Machine as the one God with this world as his heaven'.[83] In another image, Fuller depicted Lenin as 'nothing more than Henry Ford multiplied a million-fold; until Detroit covered the whole earth'.[84] Lenin's ultimate dream, according to Fuller, was to turn Russia, and 'perhaps the entire world, into one vast mechanical contrivance, in which its parts were built not of steel but of the flesh of men'.[85] James Drennan remarked that the Bolshevik-doped Russian masses 'infuse their steel tractors with the same aura of divinity which formerly developed their wooden "wonder-working" icons'.[86] For some fascists, Marx and his materialist philosophy was the progenitor of the communist machine-cult. Marx was a 'machine-enthusiast' and a 'materialist with visions of a mechanised social organisation', wrote one Mosleyite.[87]

Fascist unease about the machine, industrialisation and mass production was not only shaped by perceptions of the Industrial Revolution, Fordist industrial capitalism and Bolshevik productivism. It was also informed by the memory of the impersonal mechanised slaughter of the Great War. According to J. F. C. Fuller, the Great War 'was the military apotheosis of the Industrial Revolution'.[88] The 1914–18 experience also generated the nightmare vision of technology careering out of control. In a graphic image, Henry Williamson referred to 'the machine of civilisation running backwards into chaos, called the Great War'.[89]

When the fascists turned their minds to the philosophical dimension, however, they tended to view the modern machine age as a logical offshoot of materialism and positivism. Eighteenth-century materialists, such as Julien de Lamettrie, had referred to the human body as a machine made up of a series of discrete, mechanically moving parts. Materialist thinkers suggested also that people's material needs and capabilities could be assessed according to abstract mathematical formulas. Materialism was accused by Britain's fascists, however, of presiding over a degradation of the spirit by reconstituting people as machines. The generic fascist hostility to positivism is evident here. Interwar fascists of all national persuasions believed that something vital had been lost in the positivist quest to establish science as the supreme arbiter in the field of knowledge and its desire to delineate a sharp division between the realms of fact and metaphysical speculation.[90] Positivists asserted confidently that it was only through direct observation and experimentation, rather than traditional metaphysical abstraction, that genuine knowledge could be disclosed. For positivists, propositions were valid only if they were open to verification and analysis. Thus the claims of traditional metaphysics, which failed to satisfy these criteria, were rendered worthless. Bolstered by an unwavering self-confidence and armed with its tools of enquiry, positivism set about seeking to discover the causal relationships underlying individual phenomena in both nature and social life, apparently ordered and consistent patterns of causality which were amenable to mathematical prediction and analysis.

For many fascists, however, the positivist obsession with science and scientific objectivity was both vulgar and reductionist. Positivists were accused of subjecting individuals to the tyranny of an iron determinism by reducing nature and society to the status of a mundane, cold, law-governed and thus predictable machine which provided limited scope for the application of free will. For James Strachey Barnes, the dreary, predictable future offered by positivism would signal the death of true creative activity and reduce the life experience to that akin to the passive pleasures of a sentient plant.[91] This trend towards the mechanisation of life and the modern age's 'grim fetish-worship of Science' served to brutalise life in another respect for native fascists. Little scope remained for the mind to contemplate the mystery of nature and human existence. The BUF's E. D. Randall reflected forlornly on such an arid existence, 'when there were no mysteries or miracles left to man'.[92] By insisting on the primacy of 'first principles' and denying the validity of metaphysical truths, positivism was also accused of failing to appreciate that truth and knowledge could be gained through the senses, feeling or intuition. Fascism would invariably reject positivist explanations of life and the workings of nature. Instead, drawing on the new intellectual ideas of the *fin de siècle*, it turned to deeper, irrational and more mysterious forces, such as vitalistic intuition and the *élan vital*, in its attempts to comprehend the sources of the creative energies behind life and nature.

As with their attitudes towards the metropolis, it is tempting to interpret the views of the British fascists on the machine and the technological age as evidence of a reactionary anti-modernist outlook. However, as in the example of the city, the case is not clear-cut, for in fascist discourse there are frequent declarations of unbridled faith in technological progress which are quintessentially modernist in tone. This characteristic is most evident amongst the Mosleyites. BUF spokespersons were clearly fascinated with the implements and outward manifestations of technological modernity, such as high-powered aeroplanes, speeding automobiles and superhighways. Oswald Mosley looked forward to the day when a future fascist government would drive 'great motor roads through the country to link up our main cities', build 'high-powered cars' to put on them, and develop the 'overhead and underground method' of transport in the cities.[93] Oswald Mosley was a firm disciple of technology's Faustian mission to subdue nature and 'carry man to the further shore'. Fascism's grand project, according to Mosley, was to seek to harness 'the power of modern science to the reconstruction of civilisation', to create 'a world re-born through science'.[94]

Thus, on closer examination, this hostility towards the machine reveals itself to be not a blanket condemnation of the machine age and modernity but a critique of particular variants of it, namely those models promoted by liberal capitalism and communism. As with the city, the BUF sought to exert mastery over the machine in economic life, and aimed to reconstitute it anew in accordance with the movement's wider mythic vision of a regenerated national community. James Drennan recognised, for example, that Italian Fascism and Nazism represented 'a dynamic and consciously controlled effort to master the Machine' in economic life, similar to the way that these movements sought mastery over the city in cultural life.[95] The Mosleyites would pursue a similar goal. 'Not until man has mastered the machine and the machine has mastered material limitations', proclaimed Oswald Mosley in 1934, 'will the soul of man be free to soar beyond the fetters of materialism.'[96] Mosley's lieutenant 'Bill' Risdon recognised, too, that to turn back the clock by destroying the machine was senseless. He admonished the Luddites of the early nineteenth century, describing their attempt at machine-wrecking and factory-burning as 'a blind and impractical revolt'.[97] The BUF, on the contrary, he asserted, were the custodians of the ideals of the practical early socialists, who 'realised that the machine age had arrived' and 'resolved to make mankind the master rather than the slave of the machine'.[98]

This alternative modernising project would commence once the machine had been 'liberated', set free as it were from the destructive grasp in which it was supposedly held by the forces of liberal capitalism and its materialist mirror-image, Bolshevik communism. If Mosleyite fascism did nurture an anti-technological agenda, it hoped to temper the modernisation process, rather than halt it altogether. We should be aware, however, that Britain's fascists, including the BUF, were not always able to reconcile the contradiction between the pro- and anti-technology elements in their ideology, which is reflected in the ambiguity of attitude that occasionally surfaces in their commentary on the machine age. Thus we have that advocate of technological modernism and scientific progress, Oswald Mosley, attacking the legacy of the Industrial Revolution, singing the praises of a bygone mythical age of Merrie England and waxing lyrical about the virtues of the countryside and the soil and the need to return to it.[99]

Finally, so as to inject a further note of caution, there existed an ideological strand within British fascism that found it difficult to accept the entire ethos of material progress. These individuals steadfastly refused to embrace modernity and instead sought spiritual salvation from its consequences. Even within the BUF, some members had not reconciled themselves to the dominant modernising impulse within the movement's programme which saw in technological progress a panacea for the nation's ills. One Mosleyite technophobe, for example, Michael Penty, even lambasted the motor car, blaming its invention on a host of modern evils that were conspiring to desecrate England's countryside and its 'charming' towns, villages and architecture.[100] The motor car, which afforded people greater mobility and allowed them to reside some distance from their place of work, brought in its wake 'theories of town planning', 'concrete roads' and '"ribbon and rash" development along these roads by the indiscriminate building of bungalows and villas'. Even the once pretty Richmond in Surrey was feeling the brunt of such 'development'. Gone were the 'charming Georgian houses dating from 1720', while a new Richmond was emerging, complete with a newly built 'wide motor road' driven unnecessarily through the town centre, widened streets, an 'ugly modern cinema' and 'shops with vulgar chromium and plate glass fittings'.[101] One suspects when one considers Penty's thoughts on the motor car and its effects, that he had no desire to redeem the machine, redefine its role in society as it were, but rather wished to eliminate it altogether from the nation's economic and cultural life.

Notes

1 J. Drennan, *BUF Oswald Mosley and British Fascism* (London, John Murray, 1934), p. 186.
2 *Action*, 7 May 1938, p. 13.
3 See H. Miller, 'Some Reflections on the Concept of Megalopolis and its Use by Patrick Geddes and Lewis Mumford', in T. Barker and A. Sutcliffe (eds), *Megalopolis. The Giant City in History* (London, Macmillan, 1993), pp. 116–29.
4 *Fascist Bulletin*, 24 October 1925, p. 1.
5 *Fascist Bulletin*, 25 July 1925, p. 2.
6 Ibid.
7 The strike began on 31 July 1919. *Liverpool Daily Post and Mercury*, 4 August 1919, p. 2.
8 PRO HO144/19069/133. I am indebted to my research student, Stephen Martin, for drawing my attention to this document.
9 S. Payne, *A History of Fascism 1914–1945* (London, UCL Press, 1995), p. 30. See also M. Nordau, *Degeneration* (Appleton, 1895, 4th edition).
10 *Fascist Bulletin*, 25 July 1925, p. 2.
11 Ibid.
12 *The Fascist*, August 1932, pp. 2–4.
13 *The Fascist*, August 1931, p. 3.
14 *The Fascist*, August 1932, pp. 2–4.
15 *The Fascist*, November 1937, p. 3.
16 J. S. Barnes, *Fascism* (London, Thornton Butterworth, 1931), p. 71.
17 Ibid.
18 Ibid., p. 156; J. S. Barnes, *Half a Life* (London, Eyre and Spottiswoode, 1933), pp. 42–3.
19 Barnes, *Fascism*, pp. 72–3.
20 R. Gardiner, *World Without End. British Politics and the Younger Generation* (London, Cobden-Sanderson, 1932), p. 31.
21 *Action*, 13 February 1937, p. 6.
22 *Blackshirt*, 13 March 1937, p. 2.
23 See J. W. Blench, 'Henry Williamson and the Romantic Appeal of Fascism', *Durham University Journal*, 81, 1 (1988), pp. 123–39.
24 H. Williamson, *The Lone Swallows and Other Essays of Boyhood and Youth* (London, Putnam, 1933), pp. 151, 159 and 194.
25 Ibid., p. 156.
26 *Blackshirt*, 13 July 1934, p. 6.
27 Ibid.
28 *Action*, 4 June 1936, p. 12.
29 See Jefferies' novel, *After London*, which was published in 1885, for example. The novel depicted a return to a medieval society in close contact with nature, and was thus unashamedly anti-urban.

30 P. Rich, 'The Quest for Englishness', in G. Marsden (ed.), *Victorian Values. Personalities and Perspectives in Nineteenth-Century Society* (London, Longman, 1990), p. 220.
31 M. J. Wiener, *English Culture and the Decline of the Industrial Spirit* (Cambridge, Cambridge University Press, 1981), pp. 56–7.
32 See J. Giles and T. Middleton (eds), *Writing Englishness 1900–1950* (London, Routledge, 1995), pp. 73–103. See also P. Wright, *On Living in an Old Country. The National Past in Contemporary Britain* (London, Verso, 1985).
33 Wiener, *English Culture*, pp. 42 and 46–54.
34 Ibid., p. 51.
35 See above, Chapter Eight, on this.
36 *BUQ*, 111, 4 (October–December 1939), p. 65.
37 Williamson, *The Lone Swallows*, p. 136.
38 *Action*, 24 April 1937, p. 9.
39 *BUQ*, 111, 4 (October–December 1939), p. 65.
40 *Action*, 17 September 1938, p. 4.
41 *Blackshirt*, 1 February 1935, p. 9; *Action*, 6 March 1936, p. 8.
42 *Action*, 12 November 1938, pp. 8–9.
43 H. Williamson, *Goodbye West Country* (London, Putnam, 1937), p. 157.
44 Drennan, *BUF Oswald Mosley*, pp. 190–1.
45 Ibid., p. 194.
46 O. Spengler, *The Decline of the West. Perspectives of World-History. Vol. Two* (London, Allen and Unwin, 1922), pp. 98–9.
47 Ibid., p. 107.
48 Ibid., p. 102.
49 *Action*, 22 April 1939, p. 13.
50 Ibid.
51 Spengler, *The Decline of the West*, p. 100.
52 *BUQ*, 111, 1 (January–April 1939), p. 33.
53 *Action*, 3 June 1939, p. 13.
54 On the suburbs, see R. Silverstone (ed.), *Visions of Suburbia* (London, Routledge, 1997).
55 C. L. Mowat, *Britain Between the Wars 1918–1940* (London, Methuen, 1955), p. 227.
56 See *BUQ*, 111, 1 (January–April 1939), pp. 30–7.
57 Ibid.
58 *Blackshirt*, 1 June 1934, p. 6.
59 Drennan, *BUF Oswald Mosley*, pp. 193–4.
60 *Action*, 4 June 1936, p. 6.
61 Drennan, *BUF Oswald Mosley*, p. 184.
62 A. Raven-Thomson, *The Coming Corporate State* (London, Great Britain Publications, 1935), p. 43, on Raven-Thomson. *Blackshirt*, 28 December 1934, p. 2, on Raynor.

63 Gardiner, *World Without End*, p. 33.
64 J. F. C. Fuller, *The Dragon's Teeth. A Study of War and Peace* (Constable, London, 1932), p. 23.
65 *Action*, 18 February 1939, p. 6.
66 *Action*, 24 April 1937, p. 9.
67 N. Yates, 'Pugin and the Medieval Dream', in Marsden (ed.), *Victorian Values*, pp. 59–70.
68 M. Girouard, *The Return to Camelot. Chivalry and the English Gentleman* (New Haven, Yale University Press, 1981).
69 In *News From Nowhere* (1890), for example, Morris's hero dreams of an England that has returned to a more wholesome medieval way of life. Rich, 'The Quest for Englishness', p. 216.
70 See R. Williams, *Culture and Society. Coleridge to Orwell* (London, Hogarth, 1990).
71 Barnes, *Fascism*, p. 147.
72 Raven-Thomson, *The Coming Corporate State*, pp. 42–3.
73 Ibid.
74 *Blackshirt*, 30 August 1935, p. 9.
75 *The Fascist*, July 1931, p. 2.
76 Barnes, *Fascism*, p. 146; Williamson, *Goodbye West Country*, p. 237.
77 *Action*, 14 August 1937, p. 15.
78 On 'Taylorism', see J. Knapp, *Literary Modernism and the Transformation of Work* (Evanston, Northwestern University Press, 1988), pp. 1–18.
79 Cited in Williams, *Culture and Society*, p. 73.
80 See P. Wollen, 'Cinema, Americanism, the Robot', in J. Naremore and P. Brantlinger (eds), *Modernity and Mass Culture* (Indianapolis, Indiana University Press, 1991), pp. 42–69. Interestingly, the BUF press reviewed Chaplin's *Modern Times*, the reviewer sympathising with its basic anti-time and motion message. See *Action*, 28 February 1936, p. 7.
81 A. Huyssen, *After the Great Divide. Modernism, Mass Culture and Postmodernism* (London, Macmillan, 1986), p. 67.
82 A. Huxley, *Brave New World* (London, Chatto and Windus, 1932).
83 Fuller, *The Dragon's Teeth*, p. 189.
84 Ibid.
85 Ibid.
86 Drennan, *BUF Oswald Mosley*, p. 199.
87 *BUQ*, 11, 3 (July–September 1938), p. 62.
88 Fuller, *The Dragon's Teeth*, p. 22.
89 Williamson, *Goodbye West Country*, p. 344.
90 On positivism, see H. Stuart Hughes, *Consciousness and Society. The Reorientation of European Social Thought, 1890–1930* (London, MacGibbon and Kee, 1959), pp. 34–66, and M. Biddiss,

'Intellectual and Cultural Revolution, 1890–1914', in P. Hayes (ed.), *Themes in Modern European History 1890–1945* (London, Routledge, 1992), pp. 85–90.
91 Barnes, *Half a Life*, pp. 80–2.
92 *Action*, 12 February 1938, p. 7.
93 *Action*, 18 June 1936, p. 9.
94 *Fascist Week*, 16–22 February 1934, p. 5; *FQ*, 1, 1 (January 1935), p. 46.
95 Drennan, *BUF Oswald Mosley*, pp. 193–4.
96 *Fascist Week*, 16–22 February 1934, p. 5.
97 *BUQ*, 1, 3 (July–September 1937), pp. 27–8.
98 Ibid.
99 *Action*, 24 April 1937, p. 9, on rural life, and 8 May 1937, p. 9, on Merrie England and the industrial legacy. Leslie Susser argued that it was simply not possible for the BUF in England's cultural climate to 'aestheticise' technology and view it as a projection of national spirit, unlike the German Nazis who were thus able to resolve the tension between the reactionary and modernist elements in their ideology. L. Susser, 'Fascism, Literary Modernism and Modernization: The British Case', *Tel Aviver Jahrbuch für Deutsche Geschichte*, Part 18 (1989), pp. 463–86.
100 *Action*, 7 August 1937, p. 3.
101 Ibid.

CHAPTER ELEVEN

RESPONDING TO THE VISUAL ARTS: BRITISH FASCISM AND ARTISTIC MODERNISM

As with other contemporary cultural forms in Britain, such as literature and music, the visual arts were caught in the throes of change during the interwar years, which was both profound and deeply unsettling to established mores and conventions. Although the impact of intellectual modernism and avant-gardism on the visual arts in Britain after 1918 was not nearly as momentous as in some continental countries like France and Germany, many modernist ideas and styles would be adopted at some point during the 1920s and 1930s by native artists.[1] This was a new generation of mostly young modernists, all of whom were deeply committed to extending the frontiers of imagination and technical innovation in the arts. The British public would also encounter modernism through a number of lively and contentious exhibitions of modern art which were held in Britain during the interwar period.[2] Britain's fascists would also encounter the new modernist and avant-garde art. Their response, as we shall see, would comprise a mixture of incomprehension, fear and loathing. Indeed, in their attitude to modernism in the visual arts, Britain's fascists were more unambiguously anti-modern than in any other area of their thinking.[3]

The first shock-waves of artistic modernism in fact were felt in Britain before the onset of the Great War, with a number of native painters who eventually collaborated in the Camden Town Group, notably Spencer Gore, Harold Gilman, Charles Ginner and the older painter Walter Sickart, producing work which was distinctly Post-Impressionist in flavour.[4] Vorticism also hit the British cultural scene in 1912. Vorticism was an authentic 'home-grown' modernist movement. The Vorticists were fascinated by technological innovation and the energy of the modern machine age and sought to relate these explosive new forces to art, a mission which in many respects paralleled that of Filippo Marinetti and Italian Futurism.[5] July 1914 saw the launch of *Blast*, the avant-garde magazine which announced Vorticism's arrival to the English art establishment. Prime movers in *Blast* included Percy Wyndham Lewis and Ezra Pound, later to become fascist fellow-travellers, and Edward Wadsworth, whose ongoing attachment to artistic modernism was reflected in his embrace of Surrealism during the 1930s.[6]

Another British painter who gravitated towards Surrealism was Edward Burra, an innovative and unorthodox Surrealist who produced work of considerable depth and imagination in the 1930s.[7] The paintings of Stanley Spencer, one of Britain's most prominent artists between the wars, also contained Surrealist elements. Spencer's work explored First World War, biblical, satirical and erotic themes. The creative use of distortion was another characteristic of Spencer's style, which again linked him, albeit tenuously, to the modernist current in British art. The British avant-garde's developing passion for abstract styles and the methods of the Parisian Surrealists was reconfirmed in June 1933 when the painter Paul Nash, another domestic artist prepared to experiment in a new style, launched Unit One. In Unit One, which only lasted for two years, Nash gathered around him a number of like-minded individuals, all of whom were committed to the consolidation and revitalisation of the modernist project in Britain.[8] Apart from Nash, the Unit One group included Wadsworth, Burra, the abstract artist Ben Nicholson, who produced some notable Cubist paintings in this period, and the sculptor Henry Moore.

Other notable early twentieth-century avant-garde British artists were David Bomberg, whose early work was influenced by Cubism and Futurism, and the sculptor Jacob Epstein. Epstein was a close friend and collaborator of the radical sculptor Eric Gill.[9] Epstein, a New York Jew who settled in London in 1905, was a restless, irreverent personality possessed of considerable imagination and modelling technique who determined to steer an independent course for his sculpture outside the Hellenic and Renaissance traditions.[10] His search for alternative sources of inspiration for his art led him to an appreciation of Egyptian and Oriental art. Epstein's rich output of portrait sculptures, carvings from around 1907 to 1939, the majority unveiled in Britain, stressed a range of themes. Religious and allegorical figures were much in evidence. The primal themes of procreation, fertility, maternity, sexuality and eroticism were also emphasised in Epstein's art, which revealed the influence of so-called 'primitive' art on his artistic sensibility. Like Wyndham Lewis, Epstein was fascinated by the machine age and its implication for art, which led him to a brief flirtation with Vorticism. During the interwar period Epstein would become the *bête noire* of British fascism, as we shall see.

If these various modernists and avant-garde artists, and the movements they represented, shared a common agenda, it was the desire to challenge the assumptions and stylistic canons of traditional artistic forms and the aesthetic code related to those forms.[11] There was a belief that art needed to be more receptive to a rapidly changing world. Some modernists, like the Vorticists for example, contended that art had to confront the implications of the machine age and technological change and perceive the aesthetic potential in technology. Traditional art forms were thought to be anachronistic, inappropriate vehicles for conveying the dynamic, complex and myriad experiences of twentieth-century life. Modernism and avant-gardism thus stressed the importance of experimentation in art, as well as the need to liberate the imagination of both the artist and the consumer of art. Modernism also endeavoured to forge a new set of aesthetic principles deemed more suitable for the modern period.

Other defining themes of the modern movement included the conviction that the artist should not be bound by a need to depict 'reality' in a representational way. In Cubism, for example, where representational art gave way to abstraction, the mode of treatment rather than the subject became the defining feature of the art work. A style developed by Pablo Picasso and Georges Braque in 1908, Cubism rejected the Renaissance tradition of perspective and aesthetics. Cubism challenged the notion of a single, fixed perspective and the idea that art should faithfully depict nature. Rather, Cubist art was characterised by abstraction and fragmentation of form, its geometric figures, intricate parallels and conjunctions and its collages expressing an independent reality and subverting the idea of a fixed perspective by enabling the viewer of the art work to perceive different features of the same object simultaneously. Cubism represented a strident endorsement, too, of the modernist notion that the individual artist should cultivate a more subjective or personal view, an ideal even more strikingly emphasised in Surrealist art. Having its origins in André Breton's Surrealist manifesto of 1924, and counting among its devotees such notables as Picasso, Giorgio de Chirico, Max Ernst and Salvador Dali, Surrealism was fascinated by the creative power supposedly inherent in the individual subconscious. Fantasy and the inner world of dreams, rather than rational thought, would generate poetic truths and thus more meaningful art for the Surrealists, whose work clearly bore the mark of Sigmund Freud.

The desire to challenge and undermine conventional artistic codes, to disturb the 'complacent' bourgeoisie's artistic sensibility, marked another feature of the modernist and avant-garde agenda, sometimes taken to extreme lengths in Surrealism's bizarre and often nightmarish images. Dada pursued a similar aim. Dada was similarly interested in harnessing the irrational to the cause of art. The random and bizarre arrangements of mundane everyday objects into a new aesthetic characterised much of its art. Dada's repudiation of 'bourgeois' aesthetic values and artistic conventions was expressed in this new aesthetic, as well as its provocative assertion that all subjects merited artistic consideration. In a similar way, Dada's championing of eclecticism, experimentation and absurdity in its art struck at artistic conventions. Situated at the outer, more radical fringes of the modernist movement, Dada engaged in a more overtly political project from its inception in Zurich in 1915, attracting many communist and other leftist activists to its banner in its formative years.[12]

Modernist and avant-garde art also explored the theme of individual isolation in the age of impersonal mass society. In a similar vein, modernism focused on the issues of personal suffering, anxiety and trauma, the human and psychological fall-out from an increasingly complicated and heartless modern world. Expressionism convincingly depicted this inner emotional experience through its art, courageously delving into the troubled regions of individual psychology and the human heart. Expressionism was the dominant force in German avant-garde painting during the early part of the twentieth century and included among its practitioners such notables as Max Ernst, Max Beckmann and the Norwegian Edvard Munch.[13] An appreciation of non-Western cultures and art was another defining feature of the new movement, an orientation forcefully demonstrated by the sculpture of Jacob Epstein in a British context.

As mentioned, the response of native fascists to modernism and avant-gardism in the visual arts represented a mixture of incomprehension, fear and loathing. This was an almost universal reaction, despite the fact that fascism and artistic modernism in many ways shared a common intellectual heritage in that both drew on the radical and explosive intellectual ideas of the *fin de siècle*. Although they were poles apart politically, there were some evident points of convergence between fascism's ideology and some of the underlying principles of artistic modernism. Both fascism and Surrealism, for example, stressed the importance of the irrational sources of creativity and 'poetic' truth. British fascism, though, unlike Italian fascism which incorporated aspects of modernism into its cultural and artistic programme, including Futurism and Cubist art, almost wholly repudiated intellectual modernism in the visual arts. The British fascist outlook, rather, paralleled that of the German Nazi attitude to modern art, and perhaps owed some of its thinking on modern art to that source. British fascism thus revealed itself to be just as reactionary with respect to the new artistic mood, and bland and conventional in its artistic taste, as its far-right sister movement in Germany.

For British fascists, art should celebrate life. According to A. K. Chesterton, art is 'the mighty propagandist of life'.[14] Man creates art in gratitude for life, he asserted.[15] It followed, therefore, to Chesterton's way of thinking, that art should always seek to express a positive notion of life. In the same vein, the fascists thought that art should express humanity's aspiration to immortality, and triumphantly affirm the utter repudiation of death. Art is 'the eternal of mankind', declared Theo Lang of the BUF.[16] Sculpture, for example, should express 'life itself' with the undying elements of the earth.[17] Again, in the same vein, the fascists proposed that art's role was to elevate, uplift and inspire. According to the Mosleyite E. D. Randall, a healthy society, where art is alive and culture flourishes, is one in which people may lift their gaze to something nobler than themselves.[18] Art should be healthy and clean, too, in the opinion of another fascist.[19]

Modern art would clash fundamentally with these fascist conceptions of art, because, to the fascist mentality, it appeared to renounce life and lacked the 'supreme gift' of inspiration. It offended the fascists because it was prepared to reach down into the darker crevices of the modern soul. The inner condition was a pre-eminent theme of the modernists' agenda. In their art, they would embark on searching voyages of exploration which would lay bare alienation and psychological traumas. In addition, in their quest to create an art which was more responsive to life, some modernists did not flinch from revealing modern physical disabilities, brought on by poverty, self-abuse and modern technological war. The dreadful effects of the Great War on the human body became a recurrent theme. Again, this tendency was highly evident in the modernist art of continental Europe, with artists such as George Grosz and Otto Dix making war-induced mutilation and deformity the focus of much of their work.[20] The awful physical and mental suffering of the war had an equally disturbing effect on the artistic consciousness of some British modernists, such as Paul Nash and Christopher Nevinson, with the theme of the futility of war becoming a major concern of their art.[21] Modern art, with its morbid imagery and obsessive attachment to life's darker side, was the art of putrefaction and ultimate death, to the fascists, and as such they believed it to be the antithesis of true art. The paintings of Chaim Soutine, the Russian-born French Expressionist and avant-gardist, for example, with their disturbing physical and psychological imagery, were stale with disease, decay and death, according to an Imperial Fascist League writer.[22] In the same vein, another IFL member remarked that the work of Jacob Epstein represented the 'Cult of the Diseased' in sculpture.[23] Indeed, the entire cultural output of the modern artist, according to the Mosleyite E. D. Randall, was 'inanimate', the bankrupt product of an imprisoned soul.[24]

Modern art offended the fascists in other ways. The modernists were accused of deliberately propagating immorality. Not only was this thought to have achieved the desired aim of sapping national vitality, but an art based on moral relativism was perceived to be a travesty of authentic art. Truth in art required a definite moral foundation, according to an IFL writer, because it was reliant on inspiration rather than mere technical expertise.[25] Debasement of anything 'depicts an immoral form' at all times, declared this fascist.[26] The Mosleyites were equally perturbed. The work of groups like Dada, with its aim to shock and offend, was guided by principles of moral anarchy in E. D. Randall's view.[27] Randall recalled a visit to '*Entartete Kunst*', the exhibition of so-called Degenerate Art which opened in Munich on 19 July 1937, a crude propagandist attempt by the Nazis to discredit the modern movement in art, and was appalled at the outrageously 'perverse and pornographic' paintings on display.[28] Another BUF member reacted in the same manner to an exhibition of Surrealist art held in London in 1936, which displayed the work of Max Ernst, Giorgio di Chirico and Salvador Dali amongst others.[29] With its 'revolting' misrepresentations of womanhood, erotic themes and generally disturbing imagery, the exhibition was condemned as 'disgusting' and lacking in all decency.[30]

Modern art apparently attacked society's moral foundations in other ways. There was a perception that the modernists were deriding traditional religious beliefs. Jacob Epstein's sculpture of 'Christ', for example, aroused a feeling of indescribable 'horror and revulsion' in the heart of one fascist.[31] Appalled at the 'desecration' of the Jesus Christ we know, he imagined an England of yesteryear rising up in 'righteous indignation' at this affront to its traditional beliefs.[32] Epstein's *Adam*, unveiled in 1939, a 'vulgar and blasphemous' monstrosity executed in stone, aroused similar emotions in another fascist.[33] The *Patriot* had earlier labelled one of Epstein's stone carvings which bore a religious motif, the *Madonna and Child*, as an 'atrocity' which provided an example of the 'ancient Jewish blasphemy on the parentage and life of Christ'.[34] J. F. C. Fuller of the BUF wondered whether Epstein's sculptures were the product of Satanism. Possessed of an indisputable evil, Epstein's work appeared to revel in the worship of corruption for Fuller.[35] With such denunciations the fascists endeavoured to appeal to traditional religious sensibility, assisted by the display of photographs of Epstein's sculptures accompanied by mocking criticisms of the sculptor in the fascist press.[36]

In another variation on this line of thought, there was a belief that much of the modernists' artistic output amounted to a blatant celebration of bestiality, a descent into depravity which debased both humankind and art. True art and thus cultural progress, on the other hand, thought the fascists, only derived from humanity's 'finer instincts'.[37] Fascists like J. F. C. Fuller were perturbed and perplexed, too, by the endorsement of so-called 'primitive' art by avant-gardists such as Epstein. Fuller saw little virtue in this trend. To him, art in the modern period had descended to the level of a 'gross animalism'.[38] At another level, the new art was viewed as a form of regression, a reversion to an almost primordial state of artistic expression. The *Patriot* picked up this theme in the 1920s when it attempted to comprehend the meaning of *Rima*, Epstein's memorial to the naturalist W. H. Hudson, an innovative stone carving which was unveiled in the bird sanctuary in Hyde Park in 1925. Epstein's allegorical figures recalled the crude sketchings of the cave-dwellers for the *Patriot*, which went on to enquire as to why the modern age was prepared to tolerate this 'relapse to the primitive performances of neolithic man ...?'.[39] Epstein's *Night*, an architectural sculpture commissioned for Charles Holden's London Underground Headquarters in 1929, triggered a similar response. An exercise in 'frightfulness', its coarseness of design could have been created by any 'elemental people' with little difficulty, derided the *Patriot*.[40] This would become a recurring theme. To a BUF member, writing in 1937, Jacob Epstein and his contemporaries were 'backward stone-chippers' who derived from 'primitive Asia'.[41]

To the bemused fascist mentality, the modernists appeared to be engaged in a deliberate effort to promote a 'cult of ugliness' in art. Ugliness was 'being deified' by the exponents of the new art, bemoaned J. F. C. Fuller, while his BUF comrade E. D. Randall condemned those artists who sought 'unlovely forms' and promised that fascism would sweep away the modern 'cult of ugliness' in art.[42] The racial-fascists of the IFL also held the view that there was a conspiracy to 'foster the cult of the ugly' in art, as did Oscar Boulton of the Unity Band.[43] Nesta Webster, the prominent British Fascisti activist and leading light in the *Patriot* journal, played a key role in propagating such notions on the far right. In a *Patriot* article of 1925, Webster attacked what she referred to as the 'modern cult of the ugly' in the arts. She feared that those who delight in ugliness were intent on abolishing the traditional conception of beauty.[44] In this attempt to destroy a standard of aesthetics which, in her view, found universal acceptance, she detected a diabolical conspiracy to destroy Christian civilisation and its system of moral values. Not surprisingly, given her conspiratorial frame of mind, Webster believed that such subversion found an echo in the period of the French Revolution when works of art throughout France were violently mutilated. In resisting those who apparently sought the abolition of 'real beauty as conceived by sane and normal minds trained to true aesthetic standards', Webster believed that she was upholding the values of Christian civilisation and thwarting those who plotted its destruction. Webster deliberated on the matter at some length in that classic work of far-right conspiracy theory, *Secret Societies and Subversive Movements*.[45] Webster's comrades in the *Patriot* were soon to pick up this theme. One *Patriot* writer was convinced that Epstein's *Night*, with its distorted forms and human figures and general 'negation of conventional prettiness', was a further 'insolent example of the cult of ugliness' in art.[46] Another *Patriot* contributor saw in the modernists' 'hideous perversion of beauty' a more general assault by diabolical internal enemies on 'everything worth cherishing' in postwar Britain. This included its long-established traditions of honour, virtue, morality and religious belief, and even its rural beauty.[47]

A supposedly universal ideal of beauty was central to the fascist notion of culture and art, as we have seen in a previous chapter.[48] The creation of beauty should be one of the artist's supreme goals, according to Oscar Boulton.[49] British fascists equated beauty with celestial attributes and divine inspiration. A Mosleyite endorsed the sentiment of Michelangelo that a true work of art 'is but a shadow of divine perfection'.[50] An emphasis on beauty would lift the spirit, it was thought. Beauty was also equated with ethical values such as truth and honesty. Modern art, by 'deifying ugliness', was the antithesis of all this in the eyes of the fascists. We also noted earlier in this book that British fascists attached great importance to form and clarity in art, which, in many respects, at a deeper psychological level, reflected a longing for certainty and order in the social and political world.[51] Form in art, as in social life, because of its apparent 'discipline', stood for certainty and permanence, providing people with an anchorage in a turbulent world, according to A. K. Chesterton.[52]

In a similar way, artistic modernism was accused of failing to respect the rules of harmony in art. Again, it is tempting to detect a sub-text of fascist ideology here and interpret this as a yearning for an ordered and harmonious social structure purged of the alleged discord created by class conflict. The modernists' apparently calculated disdain of form and harmony, as with their radical attempts to create a new aesthetic for art outside the classical Renaissance tradition, appalled the fascists. Oscar Boulton was convinced that a 'clique' of 'moderns' was definitely in the business of cultivating the direct negation of form, harmony and beauty in art.[53] A BUF member complained that the 'new school' in art had callously discarded the old rules of perspective, proportion, composition and colouring.[54] Indeed, in a general sense, there was a belief that modernist artists were indulging in experiments which irresponsibly disregarded conventional boundaries. Moreoever, to Britain's fascists, artistic modernism, with its creative use of distortion, disintegrative images and general disdain for the traditional discipline of the art form, made a virtue of deformity. A BUF member, for example, described the 'Surrealistic' sculpture and painting of the 1930s as an 'orgy of morbid and distorted imaginings', while for a *Patriot* contributor, the subjects of modern art assumed the 'proportions of a nightmare'.[55]

Nothing expressed form and harmony, for the fascists, more than the 'beautiful body', an ideal enshrined in the well-proportioned figurative sculptures of Classical Antiquity. The German Nazis' predilection for a bland, muscular Neoclassicism in sculpture, which sought to emulate the Greco-Roman model, has been well documented.[56] The ideological significance of the beautiful body for fascism operated on a number of planes. At an obvious level, it appeared to establish, for the fascists, an incontestable standard of physical beauty. At another level, the beautiful body conveyed health, virility, strength, power and, in the more muscular excesses of the 'armoured body', indestructibility. The fascist masculine aesthetic of the muscular, perfectly proportioned, armoured body, with its static posture and hard lines, seemed to express, too, the fascist fear and rejection of the 'flabbiness', 'softness' and fluidity of contemporary life, which they equated with overt 'femininity'. There are other ways to interpret this fascist aesthetic. H. Glaser has pointed out that the beautiful body had appeal in fascist and national socialist ideology because it was considered to be an affirmation of moral and spiritual purity.[57] This notion, in the German case, can be traced back through the nineteenth-century cult of physical beauty, German Classicism, the Enlightenment and down to Antiquity. In a perverted reworking of Schiller's equating of aestheticism with truth and thus freedom, the idea that beauty made humanity free, the beautiful body could also function as a metaphor for people's desire to attain personal freedom.[58]

Given this exaltation of physical perfection and the body beautiful, an ideal weighed down with ideological baggage, the distorted human subjects and predominantly non-representational approach of artistic modernism evoked a predictably irate response. Oscar Boulton was scandalised by the 'distortions of the human figure' contained in Stanley Spencer's paintings, and the 'horrible disfigurements' foisted on the British public as an integral part of the 'prevailing cult of ugliness and distortion' in sculpture.[59] A *Patriot* writer referred to the 'grotesque and revolting caricature of the human form' found in certain of Epstein's sculptures, in which proportion and anatomy are 'shamefully falsified'.[60] In sublime contrast, Greek and Roman sculpture was adjudged to be true to the human form, 'presenting it in rare perfection'.[61] Another *Patriot* contributor reflected sarcastically on the thought that if Epstein's idea of anatomy and beauty was right, then perhaps those of the great sculptors of the past, including Pheidias, Praxiteles, Canova and

Michelangelo, were wrong.[62] The so-called 'cult of ugliness and distortion' in art, then, functioned as a denial of a host of factors, ranging from health and virility to moral purity and personal freedom. Little wonder, therefore, that a fascist like Oscar Boulton believed that 'discord, ugliness, obscurity and distortion' in art were 'essentially Powers of darkness' that were being used 'to subserve the forces of evil'.[63] This fascist aesthetic merged into the sinister realm of eugenics, for during the interwar years, as we know only too well, some varieties of fascism and national socialism would actively seek to achieve the unthinkable, the eugenic elimination of perceived 'ugliness' in human life, as well as in art.[64]

The British fascist temperament, then, eschewed abstract and stylised art. Rather, it tended to favour the classical and representational, such as in the figurative sculpture of classical Antiquity or the genre paintings of native artists such as Allan Ramsay and David Wilkie. The ex-BUF activist Henry Gibbs, for example, then collaborating with Lord Lymington's right-wing *New Pioneer* group, recalled a visit to the Exhibition of Scottish Art at the Royal Academy in early 1939. On surveying the paintings, Gibbs felt uplifted by Wilkie's 'faithful canvases of quiet family life' and Ramsay's graceful portraits of women, particularly his picture of *Ann of McLeod* with 'its hint of the Mona Lisa'.[65] British fascists, such as Joan Morgan, another BUF dissident who became involved with the *New Pioneer*, were equally inspired by the great English Romantic landscape painters Turner and Constable, and the celebrated portraitist and landscape painter Thomas Gainsborough.[66] It comes as no surprise that landscape paintings appealed to the fascist outlook. Not only did they acclaim nature and people's apparently deep metaphysical affinity with it, they also expressed uncomplicated, reassuring images free of contradictions and conflict.

The principles of artistic modernism also clashed fundamentally with the fascist idea of art. Art's proper function, in the opinion of British fascists, as we have seen, was to inspire and elevate. All true art should possess that 'elusive and mysterious quality of inspiration', according to Oscar Boulton, writing in the British Fascisti press.[67] Fascist aesthetes like Boulton were of the view that art had a solemn undertaking to uplift taste, conduct, and the human spirit.[68] The emphasis on beauty, for example, would assist in this aim of elevating the spirit. Furthermore, art should aspire to personify noble and heroic values, which would equally aid the goal of lifting the human spirit. Art should also be an affirmation of life and, moreover, seek to express a positive notion of life. Fascists believed, too, that art should have a moral basis. True art, in the fascist scheme of things, should be virtuous, therefore. In the judgement of a *Patriot* writer, art should also be dignified and reverent, while another believed that it should always express vital truths.[69] It should have a high purpose, too, according to one Mosleyite, a view on the function of art shared by the BUF's Leader, Oswald Mosley.[70] In the same vein, art should always realise an ideal and noble conception, claimed Oscar Boulton.[71] True art also transcended time and history, an eternal canon which was not prey to the whims of what Oscar Boulton referred to as passing 'fads'.[72] Art should thus convey reassuring messages of stability and permanence.

Patriotism and a spirit of adventure were also crucial to a virile and aspiring art, according to a Mosleyite.[73] For some fascists, there was an inseparable relationship between art and a nation's identity and character. In the words of one BUF member, art is 'the expression of a country's spirit and of its soul'.[74] Thus the unrivalled glories of English art under the Elizabethans, exemplified in the drama and poetry of Shakespeare, reflected the health and vigour of the nation at that time, for this Mosleyite.[75] The apparent link between a creative, flourishing art and a healthy nation was a commonly held view amongst Mosleyites. Art is 'always a pointer to the state of the national health', declared A. K. Chesterton.[76] According to another BUF cultural writer, 'the greatness of a civilisation can be, and is, judged by its art'.[77] Closely connected to this perception was the belief that art flourishes, in a creative sense, at times of national regeneration.[78] Thus, in BUF ideology, the heights reached by English art during the Tudor period were intimately connected to the then prevailing spirit of national revival, a mood supposedly fostered by the Elizabethan vital spirit of endeavour and 'will-to-achievement'.

If British fascists thought art was an expression of the nation's spirit and soul, then, they believed modern art to be intimately connected to the perceived postwar atmosphere of 'decadence' and national decline. To the range of charges levelled at artistic modernism which we have looked at in this chapter, therefore, was added the more general accusation that it was contributing to the nation's postwar state of ill-health. Through modern art, a lethal injection of poison had apparently entered Britain's cultural bloodstream. Artistic modernism, for the fascists, conveyed weakness and self-doubt rather than strength and virility and was thus suggestive of a loss of national direction. It was accused of fostering feelings of hopelessness, spreading demoralisation, destroying the spiritual urge and sapping national vitality. To this was added the charge that the modernist ethos was promoting social division and fracturing national unity.

So, from the fascists' perspective, from what areas of postwar life did modern art emerge and how was it able to prosper and flourish? Apparently, a number of contemporary 'evils' gave rise to artistic modernism and nourished its subsequent growth. Most fascists linked modern art to the postwar mood, which, as we know, they were fond of labelling as decadent. The new art, so ran this argument, was able to thrive in a climate of spiritual sickness and national lethargy. In a similar way, the modern movement was believed to be a product of the intellectual 'disease' of Freudianism and the general postwar fascination with introspection. In this sense, modern art was defined as a form or symptom of neurosis, or even madness, the product of diseased minds or 'psychological deformity'. 'Neurotic postwar minds' created the 'cult of ugliness and distortion' in art, declared E. D. Randall of the BUF, while A. K. Chesterton condemned the Surrealists for sanctioning the mind to 'reject all discipline and move about amongst the uncoordinated phenomena and prowling phantoms of insanity'.[79] Oscar Boulton, too, could not resist equating modern pictorial art, which to him amounted to little more than 'splishy-splashy splodges', with a 'lunatic asylum'.[80]

The view that a spiritually barren 'intellectualism' was fostering and sustaining the new art was popular amongst the Mosleyites, in particular. In the fascist imagination this could take the form of Freudianism, as we have seen. The fascists' obsession with sexual impropriety and sexual 'deviancy' was never far away here. A. K. Chesterton was of the view that 'sexual maladjustment' was mainly at the root of the intellectuals' fascination with introspection and the 'decadent' art which appealed to them.[81] At another level, however, artistic modernism was believed to have emanated from a deracinated mentality and outlook. For Kenneth Duffield of the BUF, the art works of the 'Epstein school' are those of Oswald Spengler's '*Asphaltmensch*', the 'nature-divorced reflection of a super-rationalist intellect'.[82] A 'nature-divorced' intellect, severed from a healthy attachment to the soil, is incapable of producing culture, declared A. K. Chesterton. 'Art must have roots', he proclaimed, for when it is uprooted, it is no longer the 'trumpet' of man's spirit and becomes the 'gangrened emblem of his spirit's death'.[83] Given the BUF's antipathy towards the city, it comes as no surprise to discover that its spokesmen often traced the new trends in art to a 'megalopolitan' intellectual culture.[84] In the fascist imagination, the city was the quintessential 'nature-divorced' environment, a truly artificial place from which the hated 'sterilities' and 'perversions' of modern art emanated. The allegedly neurotic minds that produced modern art had been made ill by protracted incarceration in dark modern cities, claimed E. D. Randall.[85]

It was not only decadence, disturbed minds and artificial environments which apparently spawned the new artistic consciousness. Many of Britain's fascists detected the 'hidden hand' of 'cultural Bolshevism' behind the so-called 'decadent' art of the postwar period. The *Patriot* was an early propagator of this conspiratorial theory of the origins of modern art. As early as 1924, a lead article in the *Patriot* proclaimed that the 'cult of the depraved and the insane' in the postwar art world was being deliberately stimulated by the Bolsheviks and their allies on the left.[86] Nesta Webster of the British Fascisti, closely associated with the *Patriot* group as we know, was a keen advocate of this view. For her, the 'atrocities' committed in the name of art in the early postwar age were not the product of spontaneity, but were developed in accordance with a definite plan hatched by hidden forces directing the world revolutionary movement.[87] In the mind of fascists like Webster, it was the Bolshevik revolutionaries and the anti-establishment socialists who had much to gain from an atmosphere where traditional moral values and certainties were being openly challenged and undermined. Native fascists during the 1930s would also equate artistic modernism with revolutionary Marxism, though the extreme conspiratorial arguments promoted by the likes of Nesta Webster were less in evidence. One Mosleyite, for example, stated that Karl Marx's original teachings were 'hideously expressed in that hacked and disfigured block of stone which Epstein calls "Night"'.[88]

The arrival of the new artistic values also sparked an outburst of anti-semitism on the far right. The 'bastardisation' of Britain's national art 'reeks of the Jew', declared a BUF member, while for another Mosleyite, the 'shapeless statues and lopsided pictures' of much contemporary art were 'examples of a Jewish fostered culture'.[89] 'Who is responsible for this world-wide campaign of corruption [in the arts]?', screamed another follower of the BUF, George Baker, who answered his rhetorical question by casting the Jews unambiguously in the role of arch-villain.[90] This would become a tediously familiar refrain in the art commentary of the BUF. The theory of a Jewish conspiracy to debase British art is evident in much of this discourse. In the vivid imagination of some fascists, the moral, and ultimately political, instability supposedly engendered by a radical, iconoclastic, artistic modernism aided the 'grand design' of international Jewry in its alleged efforts to secure world domination. Individuals like J. F. C. Fuller of the BUF, for example, believed that Jews were deliberately spreading immorality through art in order to destroy Christian culture and advance their supposed agenda of world domination.[91] The IFL, not surprisingly, also gave credence to such fantasies, claiming that the Jews promoted the 'cult of the ugly' and 'degenerate' in art as part of a diabolical plan to establish 'world-rule over the Gentile'.[92] The myth of the Jewish world conspiracy was more prevalent on the far right in the 1920s, of course, with groups such as the *Patriot* seeing the 'hidden hand' of international Jewry clearly at work behind the new trends in art. Some *Patriot* writers even imagined that the 'Protocolists', members of that mythical secret government of world Jewry the 'Elders of Zion', were directing the forces of artistic 'decadence'.[93]

Anti-capitalist conspiracy theories were occasionally woven into this patchwork of anti-Jewish rhetoric. The debasement of the national culture through modern art apparently increased the opportunities for commercial exploitation which, many fascists believed, ultimately served to increase the wealth of Jews.[94] A variant on this theme was the view that international dealers, thought to be predominantly Jewish, were flooding the art market with these works at grossly inflated prices. A corollary to all this was the notion that artistic modernism was a sham movement in art and that works of little or no artistic merit were finding their way into the nation's artistic heritage. Essentially a product of artistic impoverishment or a lack of talent, it was thought that a gigantic 'hoax' was being played on the British art public. The modernists' alleged lack of artistic talent was a commonly held belief amongst Britain's fascists. When the mask of eccentricity in modernist painting is torn away, a BUF member stated, only mediocrity remains.[95] The 'formless splodges of colour depicting anything or nothing so far as the spectator could judge', declared the Unity Band's Oscar Boulton, saved the modern artist 'the necessity of learning to draw, since no "form" of any kind was required'.[96]

Continuing on the theme of commercial exploitation, a BUF

British fascism 1918–39

writer alleged that since 1918 there had been an attempt by dealers to buy up Britain's art treasures, including paintings by Thomas Gainsborough and George Romney, and that it was Jews who were primarily behind it.[97] These lost treasures eventually found their way to countries like the United States, claimed this Mosleyite. Anti-Jewish hostility in the realm of art and culture, however, was just as likely to be based on the spurious notion that Jews were incapable of creating or appreciating 'true' art owing to their 'arid soul'. This arid soul was apparently a consequence of a nomadic existence, which prevented them from establishing permanent roots in the soil. For the fascists, art must have deep roots in the soil of the nation, while the nation itself was idealised as unique and eternal, which contained within it all that was vital and genuine. Depicted as the ultimate 'deracinated' type, therefore, Jews were thought to be only capable of aspiring to an art based on a vulgar materialism. This was a myth most prevalent amongst the racial fascists of the IFL. Thus it was, according to one IFL writer, that the work of Jacob Epstein emanated from a 'crude and mechanical' mind.[98] Such a mind, it was claimed, was incapable of appreciating beauty and truth or having the capacity for inspiration, all principles on which the fascists believed a true art depends.

Notes

1 On the modernist revolution in art, see R. Hughes, *The Shock of the New. Art and the Century of Change* (London, Thames and Hudson, 1991).
2 An International Surrealist Exhibition was held in London in 1936. The modernists of 'Unit One', too, organised a series of travelling exhibitions in the mid-1930s. B. Ford (ed.), *The Cambridge Cultural History of Britain. Vol. 8: Early Twentieth-Century Britain* (Cambridge, Cambridge University Press, 1992), p. 170. On Unit One, see below.
3 On the modern/anti-modern dichotomy within British fascist thought, see Chapter Ten and Introduction.
4 Ford (ed.), *The Cambridge Cultural History*, pp. 157–60.
5 W. C. Wees, *Vorticism and the English Avant-Garde* (Toronto, University of Toronto Press, 1972); C. Tisdall and A. Bozzolla, *Futurism* (London, Thames and Hudson, 1977).
6 Ford, *The Cambridge Cultural History*, pp. 162 and 170.
7 S. Compton (ed.), *British Art in the Twentieth Century. The Modern Movement* (Munich, Prestel-Verlag, 1986) p. 217.

8   D. Mellor, 'British Art in the 1930s: Some Economic, Political and Cultural Structures', in F. Gloversmith (ed.), *Class, Culture and Social Change. A New View of the 1930s* (Sussex, Harvester Press, 1980), p. 188.
9   Compton (ed.), *British Art*, p. 32.
10 Ibid., p. 33.
11 See Hughes, *The Shock of the New*. See also B. Fer, D. Batchelor and P. Wood, *Realism, Rationalism, Surrealism. Art Between the Wars* (New Haven, Yale University Press, 1993).
12 These included George Grosz, Otto Dix and John Heartfield.
13 Hughes, *The Shock of the New*, pp. 276–92.
14 *Action*, 24 July 1937, pp. 10–11.
15 Ibid.
16 *Blackshirt*, 27 July 1934, p. 9.
17 Ibid.
18 *Blackshirt*, 23–29 March 1934, p. 1.
19 *Blackshirt*, 11 January 1935, p. 11.
20 J. Willett, *The Weimar Years. A Culture Cut Short* (London, Thames and Hudson, 1984), pp. 20–3. On the art and culture of Weimar, see also B. Schrader and J. Schebera, *The 'Golden' Twenties. Art and Literature in the Weimar Republic* (New Haven, Yale University Press, 1988) and P. Gay, *Weimar Culture. The Outsider as Insider* (London, Secker and Warburg, 1969).
21 A theme captured, for example, in Nevinson's depressingly bleak painting *Returning to the Trenches*. Compton (ed.), *British Art*, p. 68.
22 *The Fascist*, December 1934, p. 6.
23 *The Fascist*, May 1931, p. 3.
24 *Blackshirt*, 23–29 March 1934, p. 1.
25 *The Fascist*, July 1931, p. 2.
26 Ibid.
27 *Action*, 5 February 1938, p. 7.
28 Ibid.
29 *Action*, 2 July 1936, p. 11.
30 Ibid.
31 This fascist was probably alluding to Epstein's stone carving *Son of God* (1933).
32 *Action*, 13 November 1937, p. 9.
33 *Action*, 5 August 1939, p. 13.
34 *Patriot*, 3 November 1927, p. 414.
35 *FQ*, 1, 1 (January 1935), p. 77.
36 See, for example, *Blackshirt*, 30 October 1937, p. 1, and *Action*, 5 August 1939, p. 13.
37 *Action*, 31 July 1937, p. 11.
38 Ibid.

39 *Patriot*, 3 December 1925, p. 692.
40 *Patriot*, 30 May 1929, p. 523.
41 *Blackshirt*, 21 August 1937, p. 2.
42 *FQ*, 1, 1 (January 1935), p. 77, on Fuller; *Blackshirt*, 23–29 March 1934, p. 1, on Randall.
43 *The Fascist*, July 1931, p. 2, on the IFL; *British Lion*, November–December 1936, pp. 4–5, on Boulton.
44 *Patriot*, 4 June 1925, pp. 49–51.
45 N. Webster, *Secret Societies and Subversive Movements* (London, Boswell Publishing Company, 1928), pp. 343–4 and 392–3.
46 *Patriot*, 30 May 1929, p. 523.
47 *Patriot*, 23 January 1930, p. 87.
48 See above, Chapter Eight.
49 *British Lion*, May 1933, p. 7.
50 *Action*, 5 August 1939, p. 13.
51 See above, Chapter Eight.
52 *Action*, 20 January 1938, p. 3.
53 *British Lion*, February–March 1934, p. 9.
54 *Blackshirt*, 21 December 1934, p. 9.
55 *BUQ*, 11, 3 (July–September 1938), p. 15; *Patriot*, 16 August 1923, p. 26.
56 See, for example, B. Nicolai, 'Tectonic Sculpture', in *Art and Power. Europe Under the Dictators 1930–45* (London, Hayward Gallery, 1995), pp. 334–7.
57 H. Glaser, *The Cultural Roots of National Socialism* (London, Croom Helm, 1978), pp. 44–9.
58 Ibid., p. 47
59 *British Lion*, May–June 1935, pp. 5–6.
60 *Patriot*, 22 August 1929, pp. 180–1.
61 Ibid.
62 *Patriot*, 2 July 1925, p. 165.
63 *British Lion*, February–March 1934, p. 9.
64 Chapter One above discusses eugenics. A eugenic programme was carried through most forcefully by the German Nazis. See M. Burleigh and W. Wipperman, *The Racial State. Germany, 1933–1945* (Cambridge, Cambridge University Press, 1996), pp. 23–73, and L. V. Thompson, 'Lebensborn and the Eugenics Policy of the Reichsfuhrer-SS', *Central European History*, 4 (1971), pp. 57–71. Of Britain's fascist parties, the IFL was the one most closely associated with a eugenic policy. On the IFL's eugenics, see above, Chapter Three.
65 *New Pioneer*, January 1939, p. 84.
66 *New Pioneer*, December 1939, p. 313.
67 *British Fascism*, March 1931, p. 6.
68 Ibid.

69 *Patriot*, 25 October 1923, p. 179, and 11 June 1925, p. 75.
70 *Action*, 5 August 1939, p. 13; *Blackshirt*, 6 July 1934, p. 4, on Mosley's view of art.
71 *British Fascism*, March 1931, p. 6.
72 O. Boulton, *Fads and Phrases* (London, Boswell Publishing, 1930).
73 *Blackshirt*, 6 July 1934, p. 4.
74 *Fascist Week*, 13–19 April 1934, p. 8.
75 Ibid.
76 *New Pioneer*, February 1939, p. 73.
77 *Fascist Week*, 13–19 April 1934, p. 4.
78 Ibid.
79 *Blackshirt*, 23–29 March 1934, p. 1, on Randall; *New Pioneer*, February 1939, p. 73, on Chesterton.
80 *British Lion*, February–March 1934, p. 9.
81 *Fascist Week*, 5–11 January 1934, p. 8.
82 *BUQ*, III, 3 (July–September 1939), p. 58.
83 *Action*, 24 July 1937, pp. 10–11.
84 See above, Chapter Ten, on the city.
85 *Blackshirt*, 23–29 March 1934, p. 1.
86 *Patriot*, 20 November 1924, p. 1.
87 *Patriot*, 4 June 1925, pp. 49–51.
88 *Blackshirt*, 6 July 1934, p. 4.
89 *Action*, 28 January 1939, p. 17, and 31 July 1937, p. 11.
90 *Blackshirt*, 21 December 1934, p. 9.
91 *FQ*, 1, 1 (January 1935), pp. 66–7 and 76–7.
92 *The Fascist*, July 1931, p. 2.
93 See *Patriot*, 22 August 1929, pp. 180–1, for an example of such fantasies.
94 *Action*, 31 July 1937, p. 11.
95 *Blackshirt*, 30 August 1935, p. 9.
96 *British Lion*, May–June 1935, pp. 5–6.
97 *Action*, 6 November 1937, p. 15.
98 *The Fascist*, July 1931, p. 2

SELECT BIBLIOGRAPHY

Published primary sources

Allen, W. E. D., *Fascism in Relation to British History and Character* (London, BUF Publications, 1933)
Barnes, J. S., *Fascism* (London, Thornton Butterworth, 1931)
Barnes, J. S., *Half a Life* (London, Eyre and Spottiswoode, 1933)
Barnes, J. S., *Half a Life Left* (London, Eyre and Spottiswoode, 1937)
Barnes, J. S., *The Universal Aspects of Fascism* (London, Williams and Norgate, 1929; first published 1928)
Bell, C., *Civilisation* (London, Chatto and Windus, 1928)
Blakeney, R. B. D., 'British Fascism', *The Nineteenth Century* (January 1925), pp. 132–41.
Boulton, O., *Fads and Phrases* (London, Boswell Publishing, 1930)
Boulton, O., *The Way Out* (London, Boswell Publishing, 1934)
Charnley, J., *Blackshirts and Roses* (London, Brockingday, 1990)
Chesterton, A. K., *Oswald Mosley. Portrait of a Leader* (London, Action Press, 1937)
Clarke, J. H., *The Call of the Sword* (London, The Financial News, 1917)
Clarke, J. H., *England Under the Heel of the Jew. A Tale of Two Books* (London, Judaic Publishing Company, 1921)
Drennan, J., *BUF Oswald Mosley and British Fascism* (London, John Murray, 1934)
Dutt, R. P., *Fascism and Social Revolution* (London, Lawrence, 1934)
Eliot, T. S., *The Idea of a Christian Society* (London, Faber and Faber, 1938)
Fuller, J. F. C., *The Dragon's Teeth. A Study of War and Peace* (London, Constable, 1932)
Fuller, J. F. C., *War and Western Civilisation 1832–1932. A Study of War as a Political Instrument and the Expression of Mass Democracy* (London, Duckworth, 1932)
Gardiner, R., *World Without End. British Politics and the Younger Generation* (London, Cobden-Sanderson, 1932)

Select bibliography

Gordon-Canning, R., *The Inward Strength of a National Socialist* (London, Greater Britain Publications, c. 1938)
Huxley, A., *Brave New World* (London, Chatto and Windus, 1932)
Jacobs, J., *Out of the Ghetto* (London, Simon, 1978)
Jenks, J., *Spring Comes Again. A Farmer's Philosophy* (London, The Bookshelf, 1939)
Joyce, W., *Twilight Over England* (Metairie, Sons, n.d.)
Kidd, B., *Social Evolution* (London, Macmillan, 1894)
Leavis, F. R., *Mass Civilisation and Minority Culture* (Cambridge, Minority Press, 1930)
Le Bon, G., *The Crowd. A Study of the Popular Mind* (London, Fisher Unwin, 1896)
Lewis, P. W., *Hitler* (London, Chatto and Windus, 1931)
Lewis, P. W., *The Mysterious Mr Bull* (London, Robert Hale, 1938)
Mosley's Blackshirts. The Inside story of the British Union of Fascists 1932–40 (London, Sanctuary Press, 1986)
Mosley, O., *The Greater Britain* (London, Greater Britain Publications, 1932)
Mosley, O., *My Life* (London, Thomas Nelson, 1968)
Mosley, O. and J. Strachey, *Revolution by Reason* (Birmingham, Birmingham Labour Party, 1925)
Nordau, M., *Degeneration* (Appleton, 1895, 4th edition)
Powys, J. C., *The Meaning of Culture* (London, Cape, 1930)
Priestley, J. B., *English Journey* (Harmondsworth, Penguin, 1934)
Raven, A., *Civilisation as Divine Superman. A Super-organic Philosophy of History* (London, Williams and Norgate, 1932)
Raven-Thomson, A., *The Coming Corporate State* (London, Great Britain Publications, 1935)
Raven-Thomson, A., *The Economics of British Fascism* (London, Bonner Company, 1935)
Reich, W., *The Mass Psychology of Fascism* (London, Souvenir Press, 1972; first German edition published in 1933)
Sanderson, W., *Statecraft. A Treatise on the Concerns of our Sovereign Lord the King* (London, Constable, 1932 edition)
Scanlon, J., *Pillars of Cloud* (London, Chapman and Hall, 1936)
Spencer, H. S., *Democracy or Shylocracy?* (London, The Britons, 1922)
Spengler, O., *The Decline of the West. Perspectives of World-History. Vols One and Two* (London, Allen and Unwin, 1918, 1922)
Strachey, J., *The Menace of Fascism* (London, Gollancz, 1933)
Wallop, G. V., *Famine in England* (London, H. F. and G. Witherby, 1938)
Webster, N., *Secret Societies and Subversive Movements* (London, Boswell Publishing Company, 1928)
Webster, N., *Spacious Days. An Autobiography* (London, Hutchinson, 1950)

Select bibliography

Webster, N., *The Surrender of an Empire* (London, Boswell Printing and Publishing Co. Ltd., 1931)
Williamson, H., *Goodbye West Country* (London, Putnam, 1937)
Williamson, H., *The Lone Swallows and Other Essays of Boyhood and Youth* (London, Putnam, 1933)

Unpublished primary sources

In public repositories

Board of Deputies of British Jews, Woburn House, London, C6, C15, E3
National Council for Civil Liberties Archive, Brynmor Jones Library, University of Hull, DCL 8, 37, 47
Mocatta Library, University College, London, Neville Laski Papers, AJ
Public Record Office, London, HO 45, 144, MEPOL 2

Newspapers

Action
Blackshirt
British Fascism
British Lion
British Lion. The Official Organ of the Unity Band
Daily Express
Daily Herald
Daily Sketch
Evening News
The Fascist
Fascist Bulletin
Fascist Gazette
Fascist Week
Free Press
Hackney Gazette
John Bull
Liverpool Daily Post and Mercury
Liverpool Post
Morning Post
New Pioneer
The Patriot
Sunday Referee
The Times

Periodicals

British Union Quarterly
Fascist Quarterly

Select bibliography

Secondary sources

Books

Alderman, G., *Modern British Jewry* (Oxford, Oxford University Press, 1992)

Anderson, G. D., *Fascists, Communists and the National Government. Civil Liberties in Great Britain, 1931–1937* (Columbia, University of Missouri Press, 1983)

Baker, D., *Ideology of Obsession. A. K. Chesterton and British Fascism* (London, I. B. Tauris, 1996)

Barkan, E., *The Retreat of Scientific Racism. Changing Concepts of Race in Britain and America Between the Wars* (Cambridge, Cambridge University Press, 1992)

Barker, T. and A. Sutcliffe (eds), *Megalopolis: The Giant City in History* (London, Macmillan, 1993)

Beetham, D., *Marxists in the Face of Fascism. Writings by Marxists on Fascism From the Inter-War Period* (Manchester, Manchester University Press, 1983)

Benewick, R., *Political Violence and Public Order* (London, Allen Lane, 1969)

Biddiss, M., *The Age of the Masses. Ideas and Society in Europe Since 1870* (Harmondsworth, Penguin, 1977)

Boyes, G., *The Imagined Village. Culture, Ideology and the English Folk Revival* (Manchester, Manchester University Press, 1993)

Brewer, J. D., *Mosley's Men. The BUF in the West Midlands* (Aldershot, Gower Publishing, 1984)

Brooks, D., *The Age of Upheaval. Edwardian Politics 1899–1914* (Manchester, Manchester University Press, 1995)

Carey, J., *The Intellectuals and the Masses. Pride and Prejudice Among the Literary Intelligentsia, 1880–1939* (London, Faber and Faber, 1992)

Coetzee, F., *For Party or Country. Nationalism and the Dilemmas of Popular Conservatism in Edwardian England* (Oxford, Oxford University Press, 1990)

Cohn, N., *Warrant for Genocide. The Myth of the Jewish World Conspiracy and the Protocols of the Elders of Zion* (Chico, CA, Scholars Press, 1981)

Cronin, M. (ed.), *The Failure of British Fascism. The Far Right and the Fight for Political Recognition* (London, Macmillan, 1996)

Cross, C., *The Fascists in Britain* (London, Barrie and Rockliff, 1961)

De Felice, R., *Interpretations of Fascism* (Cambridge, MA, Harvard University Press, 1977)

Durham, M., *Women and Fascism* (London, Routledge, 1998)

Eatwell, R., *Fascism. A History* (London, Vintage, 1996)

Farr, B. S., *The Development and Impact of Right-Wing Politics in Britain, 1903–1932* (New York, Garland Publishing, 1987)

Select bibliography

Fer, B., D. Batchelor and P. Wood, *Realism, Rationalism, Surrealism. Art Between the Wars* (New Haven, Yale University Press, 1993)
Ford, B. (ed.), *The Cambridge Cultural History of Britain. Vol. 8: Early Twentieth-Century Britain* (Cambridge, Cambridge University Press, 1992)
Giles, J. and T. Middleton (eds), *Writing Englishness 1900–1950* (London, Routledge, 1995)
Gloversmith, F. (ed.), *Class, Culture and Social Change. A New View of the 1930s* (Sussex, Harvester Press, 1980)
Graves, R. and A. Hodge, *The Long Weekend. A Social History of Great Britain 1918–1939* (London, Abacus, 1995 edition)
Green, M., *Children of the Sun. A Narrative of Decadence in England After 1918* (London, Pimlico, 1992)
Gregor, A. J., *The Fascist Persuasion in Radical Politics* (Princeton, Princeton University Press, 1974)
Griffin, R., *The Nature of Fascism* (London, Routledge, 1991 and 1993)
Griffin, R. (ed.), *Fascism. A Reader* (Oxford, Oxford University Press, 1995)
Griffin, R. (ed.), *International Fascism. Theories, Causes and the New Consensus* (London, Arnold, 1998)
Griffiths, R., *Fellow Travellers of the Right. British Enthusiasts for Nazi Germany 1933–39* (Oxford, Oxford University Press, 1983)
Griffiths, R., *Patriotism Perverted. Captain Ramsay, the Right Club and British Anti-Semitism 1939–40* (London, Constable, 1998)
Harrison, J., *The Reactionaries* (London, Victor Gollancz, 1966)
Higginbottom, M. D., *Intellectuals and British Fascism. A Study of Henry Williamson* (London, Janus, 1992)
Holmes, C., *Antisemitism in British Society, 1876–1939* (London, Arnold, 1979)
Holmes, C., *John Bull's Island. Immigration and British Society 1871–1971* (London, Macmillan, 1988)
Holmes, C. (ed.), *Immigrants and Minorities in British Society* (London, Allen and Unwin, 1978)
Hughes, H. S., *Consciousness and Society. The Reorientation of European Social Thought, 1890–1930* (London, MacGibbon and Kee, 1959)
Hughes, R., *The Shock of the New. Art and the Century of Change* (London, Thames and Hudson, 1991)
Huyssen, A., *After the Great Divide. Modernism, Mass Culture and Postmodernism* (London, Macmillan, 1986)
Hynes, S., *A War Imagined. The First World War and English Culture* (London, Bodley Head, 1990)
Kennedy, P. and A. Nicholls (eds), *Nationalist and Racialist Movements in Britain and Germany Before 1914* (London, Macmillan, 1981)
Kushner, T. and K. Lunn (eds), *The Politics of Marginality. Race, the*

Select bibliography

Radical Right and Minorities in Twentieth Century Britain (London, Frank Cass, 1990)

Kushner, T. and K. Lunn (eds), *Traditions of Intolerance. Historical Perspectives on Fascism and Race Discourse in Britain* (Manchester, Manchester University Press, 1989)

Kushner, T. and N. Valman (eds), *Remembering Cable Street. Fascism and Anti-Fascism in British Society* (London, Valentine Mitchell, 2000)

Lebzelter, G., *Political Anti-Semitism in England, 1918–1939* (London, Macmillan, 1978)

Lewis, D. S., *Illusions of Grandeur. Mosley, Fascism and British Society, 1931–1981* (Manchester, Manchester University Press, 1987)

Linehan, T., *East London for Mosley. The British Union of Fascists in East London and South-West Essex, 1933–40* (London, Frank Cass, 1996)

Lunn, K. (ed.), *Hosts, Immigrants and Minorities* (Folkestone, Dawson, 1980)

Lunn, K. and R. Thurlow (eds), *British Fascism* (London, Croom Helm, 1980)

Mandle, W. F., *Antisemitism and the British Union of Fascists* (London, Longman, 1968)

Mangan, J. A. (ed.), *Shaping the Superman. Fascist Body as Political Icon – Aryan Fascism* (Frank Cass, London, 1999)

Milfull, J. (ed.), *The Attractions of Fascism. Social Psychology and Aesthetics of the 'Triumph of the Right'* (Oxford, Berg, 1990)

Mosse, G., *Nazi Culture. Intellectual, Cultural and Social Life in the Third Reich* (London, W. H. Allen, 1966)

Mowat, C. L., *Britain Between the Wars 1918–1940* (London, Methuen, 1955)

Naremore, J. and P. Brantlinger (eds), *Modernity and Mass Culture* (Indianapolis, Indiana University Press, 1991)

Nolte, E., *Three Faces of Fascism* (New York, Mentor, 1969)

Nugent, N. and R. King, *The British Right. Conservative and Right Wing Politics in Britain* (Farnborough, Saxon, 1977)

Payne, S. G., *A History of Fascism 1914–45* (London, UCL Press, 1995)

Pollard, S., *The Wasting of the British Economy. British Economic Policy 1947 to the Present* (New York, St Martin's Press, 1982)

Pugh, M., *The Making of Modern British Politics 1867–1939* (Oxford, Blackwell, 1982)

Semmel, B., *Imperialism and Social Reform. English Social-Imperial Thought* (London, Allen and Unwin, 1960)

Silverstone, R. (ed.), *Visions of Surburbia* (London, Routledge, 1997)

Simpson, A. W., *In the Highest Degree Odious. Detention Without Trial in Wartime Britain* (Oxford, Oxford University Press, 1992)

Skidelsky, R., *Oswald Mosley* (London, Macmillan, 1981)

Sternhell, Z., *The Birth of Fascist Ideology* (Princeton, Princeton

University Press, 1994)
Stevenson, J. and C. Cook, *The Slump. Society and Politics During the Depression* (London, Quartet Books, 1979)
Stuart Hughes, H., *Consciousness and Society. The Reorientation of European Social Thought, 1890–1930* (Brighton, John Spiers, 1979; first published by MacGibbon and Kee Ltd, 1959)
Theweleit, K., *Male Fantasies. Vol. 1: Women, Floods, Bodies, History* (Cambridge, Polity Press, 1987)
Theweleit, K., *Male Fantasies. Vol. 2: Male Bodies: Psychoanalysing the White Terror* (Cambridge, Polity Press, 1989)
Thurlow, R., *Fascism* (Cambridge, Cambridge University Press, 1999)
Thurlow, R., *Fascism in Britain. A History, 1918–1985* (Oxford, Blackwell, 1987), revised and updated as *Fascism in Britain: From Oswald Mosley's Blackshirts to the National Front* (London, I. B. Tauris, 1998)
Turner, D., *Fascism and Anti-Fascism in the Medway Towns 1927–1940* (Rochester, Kent Anti-Fascist Action Committee, 1993)
Turner Jnr, H. A. (ed.), *Reappraisals of Fascism* (New York, Franklin Watts, 1975)
Webber, G. C.,*The Ideology of the British Right, 1918–1939* (London, Croom Helm, 1986)
Weber, E., *Varieties of Fascism* (New York, D. Van Nostrand, 1964)
Wees, W. C., *Vorticism and the English Avant-Garde* (Toronto, University of Toronto Press, 1972)
Wiener, M. J., *English Culture and the Decline of the Industrial Spirit* (Cambridge, Cambridge University Press, 1981)
Williams, R., *Culture and Society. Coleridge to Orwell* (London, Hogarth, 1990)
Witherell, L., *Rebel on the Right. Henry Page Croft and the Crisis of British Conservatism, 1903–1914* (Delaware, University of Delaware Press, 1998),
Wright, P., *On Living in an Old Country. The National Past in Contemporary Britain* (London, Verso, 1985)

Chapters in books

Biddiss, M., 'Intellectual and Cultural Revolution, 1890–1914', in P. Hayes (ed.), *Themes in Modern European History, 1890–1945* (London, Routledge, 1992)
Cassels, A., 'Janus: The Two Faces of Fascism', in H. A. Turner Jnr (ed.), *Reappraisals of Fascism* (New York, Franklin Watts, 1975)
Gottlieb, J., 'Suffrage Experience Through the Filter of Fascism', in C. Eustace, J. Ryan and L. Ugolini (eds), *A Suffrage Reader. Charting Directions in British Suffrage History* (London, Leicester University Press, 2000)

Select bibliography

Hagtvet, B. and R. Kuhnl, 'Contemporary Approaches to Fascism: A Survey of Paradigms', in S. U. Larsen, B. Hagtvet and J. P. Myklebust (eds), *Who Were the Fascists? Social Roots of European Fascism* (Oslo, Universitetsforlaget, 1980)
Lebzelter, G., 'Antisemitism – A Focal Point for the Radical Right', in P. Kennedy and A. Nicholls (eds), *Nationalist and Racialist Movements in Britain and Germany Before 1914* (London, Macmillan, 1981)
Nugent, N., 'The Ideas of the British Union of Fascists', in N. Nugent and R. King, *The British Right. Conservative and Right Wing Politics in Britain* (Farnborough, Saxon, 1977)
Rawnsley, S. J., 'The Membership of the British Union of Fascists', in K. Lunn and R. Thurlow (eds), *British Fascism* (London, Croom Helm, 1980)
Wheelwright, J., '"Colonel" Barker: A Case Study in the Contradictions of Fascism', in T. Kushner and K. Lunn (eds), *The Politics of Marginality. Race, the Radical Right and Minorities in Twentieth-Century Britain* (London, Frank Cass, 1990)

Articles
Blench, J. W., 'Henry Williamson and the Romantic Appeal of Fascism', *Durham University Journal*, 81, 1 (1988), pp. 123–39
Cammett, J. M., 'Communist Theories of Fascism, 1920–1935', *Science and Society*, 31 (Winter 1967), pp. 149–63
Coupland, P. M., 'The Blackshirted Utopians', *Journal of Contemporary History*, 33 (April 1998), pp. 255–72
Cullen, S., 'The Development of the Ideas and Policy of the British Union of Fascists, 1932–40', *Journal of Contemporary History*, 22 (1987), pp. 115–36
Cullen, S., 'Leaders and Martyrs: Codreanu, Mosley and Jose Antonio', *History*, 71, 4 (October 1986), pp. 408–30
Cullen, S., 'Political Violence: The Case of the British Union of Fascists', *Journal of Contemporary History*, 28 (1993), pp. 245–67
Feldman, D., 'There was an Englishman, an Irishman and a Jew: Immigrants and Minorities in Britain', *Historical Journal*, 26, 1 (1983), pp. 185–99
Gregor, A. J., 'Fascism and Modernization: Some Addenda', *World Politics*, 26 (1974), pp. 370–84
Griffin, R., 'Totalitarian Art and the Nemesis of Modernity', *Oxford Art Journal*, 19, 2 (1996), pp. 122–4
Hewitt, A., 'Wyndham Lewis: Fascism, Modernism and the Politics of Homosexuality', *English Literary History*, 60, 2 (1993), pp. 527–44
Hoffman, L., 'Psychoanalytical Interpretations of Political Movements, 1900–1950', *Psychohistory Review*, 13 (1984), pp. 16–29
Hope, J., 'British Fascism and the State 1917–1927: A Re-Examination of

the Documentary Evidence', *Labour History Review*, 57, 3 (Winter 1992), pp. 72–83

Howard, W., 'Nietzsche and Fascism', *History of European Ideas*, 11 (1989), pp. 893–9

Killin, K., 'Women and British Fascism', *Modern History Review*, 4, 4 (April 1993), pp. 21–3

Laqueur, W., 'Fin-de-siècle: Once More with Feeling', *Journal of Contemporary History*, 31 (1996), pp. 5–47

Linehan, T., 'Fascist Perceptions of Cable Street', *Jewish Culture and History*, 1, 2 (Winter 1998), pp. 23–30

Lipkis, J. M., 'The Odd Couple: Oswald Mosley and John Strachey', *Continuity*, 13 (1989), pp. 31–57

Mandle, W. F., 'The Leadership of the British Union of Fascists', *Australian Journal of Politics and History*, 12 (December 1966), pp. 360–83

Mandle, W. F., 'The New Party', *Historical Studies*, 12 (October 1966), pp. 343–55

Mandle, W. F., 'Sir Oswald Mosley's Resignation from the Labour Government', *Historical Studies*, 10 (May 1963), pp. 493–510

Mitchell, A., 'Mosely and the BUF: British Fascism in the 1930s', *Modern History Review*, 4, 4 (April 1993), pp. 18–21

Mosse, G. L., 'Introduction: The Genesis of Fascism', *Journal of Contemporary History*, 1, 1 (1966), pp. 14–26

Pinto, A. C., 'Fascist Ideology Revisited: Zeev Sternhell and His Critics', *European History Quarterly*, 16 (1986), pp. 465–83

Sternhell, Z., 'The "Anti-materialist" Revision of Marxism as an Aspect of the Rise of Fascist Ideology', *Journal of Contemporary History*, 22 (1987), pp. 379–400

Susser, L., 'Fascism, Literary Modernism and Modernization: The British Case', *Tel Aviver Jahrbuch für Deutsche Geschichte*, Part 18 (1989), pp. 463–86

Webber, G. C., 'Patterns of Membership and Support for the British Union of Fascists', *Journal of Contemporary History*, 19, 4 (October 1984), pp. 575–606

Unpublished material

Blume, H. S. B., 'A Study of Anti-Semitic Groups in Britain, 1918–40' (M.Phil. thesis, University of Sussex, 1971)

Cullen, S., 'The BUF, 1932–1940: Ideology, Membership and Meetings' (M.Litt. thesis, University of Oxford, 1987)

Geiger, D. M., 'British Fascism as Revealed in the British Union of Fascists' Press' (Ph.D. thesis, New York University, 1963)

Gottlieb, J., 'Women and Fascism in Inter-war Britain' (Ph.D. thesis, University of Cambridge, 1998; to be published shortly as *Feminine Fascism. Women in Britain's Fascist Movement, 1923–1945* by I. B. Tauris)

Select bibliography

Mitchell, A., 'Fascism in East Anglia: The British Union of Fascists in Norfolk, Suffolk and Essex, 1933–1940' (Ph.D. thesis, University of Sheffield, 1999)

Rawnsley, S. J., 'Fascism and Fascists in the North of England in the 1930s' (Ph.D. thesis, University of Bradford, 1983)

Susser, L., 'Fascist and Anti-Fascist Attitudes in Britain Between the Wars' (Ph.D. thesis, University of Oxford, 1988)

Woodbridge, S., 'The Nature and Development of the Concept of National Synthesis in British Fascist Ideology, 1920–1940' (Ph.D. thesis, University of Kingston, 1997)

INDEX

Note: literary works can be found under authors' names.

abdication crisis (December 1936) 105
Allen, W. E. D. ('James Drennan') 15, 88, 225, 233, 245, 252, 256, 257, 261, 263
Amery, Leopold 19
Anderson, G. D. 77
Angles 143
Anglo-German Fellowship 46
Anglo-Irish Treaty (1921) 39
Anglo-Irish War (1919–21) see Irish 'Troubles'
anti-Americanism 222–3, 231, 234, 237
anti-Bolshevism 43–5, 47–9, 54, 64, 66, 142, 154, 235, 246, 261, 264, 282
anti-capitalism 16, 32, 256, 263–4, 283
anti-city 8, 28–30, 32, 233, 239, 245–7, 282
anti-communism see anti-Bolshevism
anti-conservatism 5
anti-decadence 5, 29, 223–40, 245, 280–2
anti-democracy 15–16, 20–1, 29, 75, 90–1, 124, 127, 135–6, 206
anti-fascism 103, 106–7
Anti-German Union 44
anti-Germanism 47–9
anti-intellectualism 10, 239–40, 245, 281
anti-liberalism 5, 14, 16, 223, 234
anti-machine 31–2, 42, 203, 257–64
anti-Marxism 5, 133

anti-materialism 5, 10, 32, 129–30, 229, 237, 261
anti-modernity 8–10, 31–3, 76–7, 93–4, 249–50, 255–6, 262–4, 269, 272–3
anti-positivism 5, 10, 33, 261–2
anti-psychoanalysis 193, 233, 236–7, 281
  see also Freud, Sigmund
anti-rationalism 5, 10, 33–4, 240
anti-semitism 27, 45–54, 67, 74, 78, 79, 99, 103, 109, 111, 127, 133, 135, 137, 138, 143–4, 176–96, 235–6, 282–4
  anthropological roots of fascist anti-semitism 183–4
  discourse theory of anti-semitism 190
  genetic roots of fascist anti-semitism 182–3
  'interactionist' theory of anti-semitism 188–90
  psychological interpretations of anti-semitism 188
anti-socialism 21–2, 42–6, 61, 131
Anti-Socialist Union (ASU) 45–6
Arkell-Smith, Valerie 126
Armstrong, (Rear-Admiral) A. E. 62, 65, 156
Arnold, Matthew 32, 204–5, 258
artistic modernism, fascist attitudes to 208, 216, 269–84
Aryan racial myth see Nordic racial myth
Ashley, William 46

298

Index

Attwood, Thomas 16

Bailey, James 'Bill' 193
Baker, David 53, 193, 207
Ballie, (Major) J. 72
Banister, Joseph 52, 53, 144, 195
Barker, (Colonel) Victor *see* Arkell-Smith, Valerie
Barnes, James Strachey 29, 128–9, 134, 194, 196, 203, 205, 207, 211, 212, 234, 239, 248, 249, 259–60, 262
Beamish, Henry Hamilton 47, 51–2, 53–4, 73, 131, 143, 180
Beckett, John 99–100, 111, 138–9, 141, 195
Beckmann, Max 272
Bell, Clive 204–5
Belloc, Hilaire 20–1
Benewick, Robert 65, 69, 92–3, 126, 152–4, 161, 187–8
Berdyaev, Nicholas 212
Bergson, Henri 33, 95, 201, 211
'Birmingham Proposals' 87
Blakeney, (Brigadier-General) Robert B. D. 53, 54, 61–2, 63, 65, 73, 143, 155, 156, 234, 235
Blast 270
Blatchford, Robert 31, 258
Blume, Hilary 50, 53, 69, 77, 79, 131, 144, 152–4, 158–9, 160
Blumenfeld, Ralph D. 46
Board of Deputies of British Jews 106, 152
body, the 30, 56, 91, 207, 214, 215, 224, 261, 274, 278
Boer War 19, 51
Bolshevik Revolution (1917) 38, 47, 48, 177, 178
Bomberg, David 270
Boswell Printing and Publishing Company 48–9, 54, 133, 179
Boulton, (Lieutenant-Colonel) Oscar 133–6, 196, 204, 206, 208, 231–2, 234, 238, 276, 277, 279, 280, 281, 283
Box, F. M. 99–103 *passim*
Braque, Georges 271
Brecker, Arno 207

Breton, André 271
Brewer, John D. 163–4, 169
'bright young things' 224–7, 234
British Brothers' League (BBL) 53, 189
British Commonwealth Union (BCU) 43, 44, 55, 156
British Council for Christian Settlement in Europe (BCCSE) 140
British Democratic Association 106
British Empire Fascist Party (BEFP) 132–3, 194
British Empire Fascists 130
British Empire Union (BEU) 44, 45, 55
British Fascists (Fascisti) (BF) 6, 43–6 *passim*, 50, 61–71, 74, 76, 77, 93, 124–5, 128, 130–5 *passim*, 166, 227, 228, 246
  anti-semitism 176, 177–8
  ideology 63–5, 66–7
  impact of General Strike 65–6
  membership 151–8
  organisational and administrative profile 62–3
British Lion 68, 133
British Loyalists 65
British Movement 79
British National Fascisti *see* National Fascisti
British National Party 79
British People's Party (BPP) 139–40, 142, 196
  see also British Council for Christian Settlement in Europe (BCCSE)
British Union 131
British Union of Democrats 106
British Union of Fascists (BUF) 5, 6, 9, 31, 46, 62, 67, 69, 84–114, 131, 134, 137, 138, 139, 176, 202, 230, 281, 283
  Abyssinian peace campaign 102
  anti-fascist opposition 103, 106–9
  anti-semitism 186–94
  anti-war campaign (1938–40) 113–14, 167

299

Index

economic policy 85–7, 89–90
European philosophical influences 94–7
London County Council elections (1937) 109–10, 112
March retrenchment (1937) 109–12
membership 151–2, 159–70
organisational and administrative profile 97–106 *passim*, 109–13 *passim*
origins in New Party 87–9
relations with the Imperial Fascist League (IFL) 77–8, 79
views on the city 248–51, 253–7
views on the Industrial Revolution 257–8
views on the machine 260, 261, 262, 263–4
British United Fascists 131
British Workers' League (BWL) 44
Britons Society and Publishing Company 45, 46, 50–4, 73, 76, 78, 79, 131, 137, 194
Burn, (Colonel Sir) Charles 45, 62, 155
Burra, Edward 270

'Cable Street' disturbances 107
Camden Town Group 269
Carlyle, Thomas 16, 32, 203, 204–5, 258, 260
Carlyle Club 139
Carpenter, Edward 250
Cassels, Alan 7
Centre International d'Études sur la Fascisme (CINEF) 46, 74, 128, 194
Centre Party 31
Chadwick, (Sir) Burton 45, 155
Chamberlain, Houston Stewart 181
Chamberlain, Joseph 18, 91
Chamberlain, Neville 87, 113
Chesterton, A. K. 99–100, 113, 141, 144, 169, 193, 195, 205, 207–8, 212, 224, 225, 229–30, 233, 238, 256, 273, 277, 281
Chesterton, Cecil 47

Cheyette, Bryan 177, 190
Chirico, Giorgio de 271, 274
Churchill, (Sir) Winston 48
Clarion, The 31
Clarke, E. G. 'Mick' 193
Clarke (Dr) John Henry 52
Coefficients 31
Cole, (Commander) E. H. 136
Coleridge, Samuel Taylor 32, 203
Collier, Vincent 138
Communist Party of Great Britain (CPGB) 39, 103, 106
  see also anti-Bolshevism
Comrades of the Great War 43
Conservative Party 68, 87, 130
Corporate State *see* corporatism
corporatism 66–7, 74–5, 90–1, 139, 212–13
Council of Economic Leagues 46
'Councils of Action' (1920) 41
countryside *see* rural nostalgia
Coupon Election (14 December 1918) 41
Croce, Benedetto 1
Croft, Henry Page 19, 43, 55
Cross, Colin 126, 158–9, 160–1, 177, 187
Cubist art 270, 271, 273
Cullen, Stephen 92–3
'cultural Bolshevism' 235, 282
  see also anti-Bolshevism

Dada 272, 274
Dali, Salvadore 271, 274
Darwin, Charles 24, 183
  see also Social-Darwinism
Deans, Leonard James 'Dixie' 193
Decie, (General) Prescott 126, 127, 131
Defence Regulation 18b (1A) 78, 114, 150
Defence Regulation 18b (AA) 114
Derrida, Jacques 190
Dix, Otto 274
Domvile, (Admiral Sir) Barry 143, 157
Donovan, B. D. E. 104
Dopolavoro recreation scheme 213
Douglas, (Lord) Alfred 47, 48, 177

Index

Downe, (Viscountess) Dorothy 154
'Drennan, James' *see* Allen, W. E. D.
Durham, Martin 97, 167
Duty and Discipline Movement 46

Earls Court peace meeting (16 July 1939) 114
Eatwell, Roger 68, 77, 160
economic conservatism *see* laissez-faire economics
economic crisis (1929–31) 84–5
Economic League (EL) 44–5, 55
economic radicalism 85–9
Edwardian radical right *see* social-imperialism
élan vital 33, 94–5, 262
Eliot, T. S. 205, 237, 238, 245
  The Waste Land (1923) 245
Elizabethan age of achievement 15, 210, 280
  see also Tudor State
Empire Fascist League 133
Empire Fascist Movement 130
English Array 140, 141–2
English literature 231, 238
  see also literary modernism (Bloomsbury)
Englishman 47
English Mistery 73, 137, 140, 141
  see also English Array
Entartete Kunst (July 1937) 274
Epstein, Jacob 270–1, 272, 274, 275–6, 278, 282, 284
Ernst, Max 271, 272, 274
eugenics 24–30, 54, 76, 141, 182, 218, 247, 279
Expressionist art 272, 274
Ex-Servicemen's Movement Against Fascism 106
Eyre, Giles Edward 126

Fabian socialists 30–1
Farr, Barbara 43, 54, 61, 64, 65–6, 70, 89, 93, 130–1, 134, 152–3, 155, 156,157
Fascist Children's Clubs 64, 154
'fascist feminism' 66–7, 70, 135
Fascist Gazette, The 126
Fascist League 71, 130

Fascist Movement 130
Fascist Quarterly 138
Faustian mission 9, 94–5, 168, 214–15, 263
Feldman, David 189
fin-de-siècle cultural revolt 3, 10, 33–4, 95, 201, 211, 262, 273
First World War 10, 38–43 *passim*, 47–8, 61, 129, 169, 224, 261
'flapper', the 136, 224–6
folk culture 201–2, 213
'Fordism' *see* Taylorism
Forgan, Robert 88
Forster, E. M. 250
  Howard's End (1910) 250
Francis-Hawkins, Neil L. M. 62, 69, 104, 109–10, 111, 113, 156
Freikorps 4
Freud, Sigmund 236, 272
  see also psychological interpretations of fascism
Fromm, Erich 3
Fuller, J. F. C. 28, 29, 42, 50, 99, 100–3 *passim*, 141, 193, 206, 236, 257, 261, 275, 283
Futurism 8, 270, 273

Gainsborough, Thomas 279, 284
Galton, Francis 25–6
Gardiner, Rolf 73, 141, 248, 249, 257
Garvagh, (Lord) 61
Geddes, Patrick 245
Geiger, D. M. 69, 77, 92
gender basis of fascism 67, 70, 97, 157, 166–7
General Strike 61, 65–6
'generational revolt', fascism as a 166
generic interpretations of fascism 4–6
  see also Weismann, August
German National Socialism *see* Nazism
Gibbs, Henry 141, 279
Gill, Eric 270
Gilligan, Arthur E. R. 158
Gittens, Anthony 53, 73
Glaser, H. 278

301

Index

Glasgow (8th Earl of) 62, 65
Gordon-Canning, (Captain) R. 140, 212, 229
Gore, Spencer 269
Gottlieb, Julie 69–70, 97, 157, 167, 169
Government of India Act (1919) 39
Greene, Ben 139, 141
Gregor, A. J. 6, 8, 9,
Griffin, Roger 4, 5, 7, 9, 55, 223
Griffiths, Richard 66, 137, 152
Grosz, George 274

Hannon, Patrick 43, 155, 158
Hardinge, (Sir) Arthur 62
Hardy, Thomas 250
  Far From the Madding Crowd (1874) 250
Harnett, D. G. 157
Harvey, John Hooper 73, 160
Hegel, G. W. 95–6, 214
Hegelianism 6, 96
Herf, Jeffrey 94
'heroic vitalist' vision 16, 30, 95, 168
'hidden hand' myth 47–9, 51, 142, 144, 177–8, 189, 195, 235–6, 259, 282–3
Hidden Hand, The 51
'high' art 206, 208
  see also 'high culture'
'high culture' 204–9
Hitler, Adolf 52, 113, 137
Hobson, J. A. 89
Holden, Charles 276
Hollywood motion picture 225–6, 231–2
Holmes, Colin 54, 177, 186, 188–9, 195
Hope, John 44, 45, 68
Houston, 'Jock' 103, 143, 193
Howard, L. A. 125
Huxley, Aldous 237, 260
  Brave New World (1932) 260
  Eyeless in Gaza (1936) 237

Ibsen, Henrik 252
  A Doll's House (1879) 252
'idle rich' 226–8

Illuminati 49
Imperial Fascist League (IFL) 27, 52, 53, 71–9, 130, 131–2, 136, 151, 176, 192, 217, 227, 232, 234, 236, 247–8, 276, 283–4
  anti-semitism 178–86
  ideology 74–7
  membership 158–60
  organisational and administrative profile 72–3
Imperial Maritime League 22–3
Imperial Mission 43
Independent Labour Party (ILP) 32, 88, 89, 139
Industrialisation *see* anti-machine
Industrial Revolution, reaction to 257–8
Irish 'Troubles' 17, 39, 87, 163
'I' Squad division (BUF) 100
Italian Fascism 8, 50, 61, 65, 74, 93, 105, 124–5, 126, 128, 129, 133, 137, 208, 213, 263

January Club 139
Jazz 225, 232
Jeffries, Richard 250, 258
Jenks, Jorian 226, 257
Jewish People's Council Against Fascism and Anti-Semitism 106
Joad, C. E. M. 88
Joyce, James 238
Joyce, William 16, 62, 69, 99–100, 109–10, 111, 126, 138–9, 143, 144, 192, 195, 205, 236, 237
Judaic Publishing Company 51

Kant, Immanuel 211, 216
Kensington Fascist Party 131
Keynes, John Maynard 86
Kidd, Benjamin 23, 24–5
Kipling, Rudyard 19, 22, 250
Kitson, Arthur 52, 71, 73, 77
Knight, Maxwell 44, 158
Ku-Klux-Klan 49, 143, 195

Labour government (1929–31) 84–5
Labour Party 41, 44, 46, 49

laissez-faire economics 13, 15–16, 18, 20, 21, 22, 32
Lamarckian model of evolution 25–6, 27, 192
Lane, (Lieutenant-Colonel) A. H. 45, 52, 53, 73, 134, 144
Lang, (Lieutenant-Colonel) A. G. B. 131, 156
Lang, Fritz 260
  Metropolis 260
Laski, Neville 112
Lawrence, D. H. 237, 238
Leaper, W. J. 88
Leavis, F. R. 204–5
Le Bon, Gustave 33, 34, 201
Lebzelter, Gisela 51, 53, 74, 76, 79, 186
Leese, Arnold 27, 53, 54, 62, 68, 69, 71–9 *passim*, 124, 126, 128, 130, 143, 158, 159, 179–86 *passim*, 188, 192, 236
Left-Book Club 239
Legion of Blue and White Shirts 106
Legion of Loyalists 131
Lenin, Vladimir Ilich Ulyanov 261
Lewis, D. S. 6, 68, 92, 93
Lewis, Percy Wyndham 226, 232, 233, 237, 270, 271
liberal interpretation of fascism 2, 4, 162
Liberty League 46
'life-force' 30, 95
Link 143, 157
Lintorn-Orman, Rotha 48, 61, 63, 65–6, 70, 77, 134, 135, 152, 156, 157
Lipset, Seymour 7, 162
literary modernism (Bloomsbury) 237–9
Lloyd George, David 47
Loyalty League 130–1
Ludovici, (Captain) Anthony 140, 141
Lunn, Kenneth 70–1, 153, 157
Lymington, (Viscount) Gerard Wallop 140–1

MacDonald, Ramsay 86
MacKinder, Halford J. 20

MacNab, Angus 138, 195
Mairet, Philip 140, 141
Mallon, J. J. 107
Mandeville Roe, E. G. 62, 67, 69, 156
Mandle, W. F. 88, 162–3, 166, 187, 188
Marconi scandal 189
Marinetti, Filippo 270
Marsden, Victor 52
Marxist interpretation of fascism 1–2, 3, 4, 7, 162–3
mass culture 42, 205–6, 213, 226, 237
Maxse, Leopold James 19, 20, 47, 48, 177, 179
Megalopolis *see* anti-city; Spengler, Oswald
Meinecke, Friedrich 1
membership *see* motivation (fascist 'joiners'); social basis of fascism
Mendel, Gregor 183
'Merrie England' myth 258, 264
Metropolis *see* anti-city
Middle Ages, nostalgia for 31, 129, 212, 248, 258
'middle class fascism' thesis 6–7, 162–3, 165
  see also social basis of fascism
Middle Class Union 45
  see also National Citizens' Union
Militant Christian Patriots (MCP) 45, 144, 195
Milner, (Viscount) Alfred 19, 20, 21, 22, 44
modern art *see* artistic modernism, fascist attitudes to
modernism, intellectual 41, 135, 191, 208, 216, 222
  in the visual arts 269–84
Modern Times 260
Mond, (Sir) Alfred 51–2
Moore, Henry 270
Moran, T. P. 'Tommy' 112
Morell, John 78
Morgan, Joan 141, 279
Morris, William 31–2, 203, 258
Mosley Memorandum 86–7

303

Index

Mosley, (Sir) Oswald 14, 17, 20, 30, 32, 34, 50, 68, 77, 78, 85–98 *passim*, 102, 103, 105–7, 109–14 *passim*, 137, 139, 142, 161, 163, 166–9 *passim*, 187–8, 191–2, 203, 227, 228, 251, 263–4, 280
  Revolution by Reason (1925) 87
  The Greater Britain (1932) 89, 168
Mosse, George 34, 202, 208
motivation (fascist 'joiners') 167–70
  see also social basis of fascism
Mudge, George 46, 54, 131
Mullally, Frederick 162–3
Mumford, Lewis 245
Munch, Edvard 272
Mussolini, Benito 74, 128

Nash, Paul 270, 274
National Citizens' Union (NCU) 45
National Council for Civil Liberties (NCCL) 106–7
National Defence Association 22
National Democratic Party 44
National Fascisti (NF) 50, 65, 71, 124–8, 130, 158–60, 194
National Front 53, 79
National Maritime League 22
National Party (NP) 42–3
National Policy, A 88
National Political League (NPL) 46
National Propaganda Movement Central 46
National Review 47, 48, 177, 179
National Security Union 46
National Service League (NSL) 22
Nationalsozialistische Deutsche Arbeiterpartei (National Socialist German Workers' Party) (NSDAP) *see* Nazism
National Socialist League (NSL) 111, 138–9, 140, 194
National Socialist Workers' Party *see* National Workers' Party (NWP)
National Workers' Movement *see* National Workers' Party (NWP)

National Workers' Party (NWP) 136–7, 140, 194
Navy League 22
Nazism 2, 8, 9, 52, 74, 93–4, 105, 106, 132, 137–8, 166, 181, 186, 194, 208, 217, 233, 256, 263, 273, 274, 278
Nevinson, Christopher 274
new fascist man 211–12
New Movement 131
New Party 20, 31, 87–9, 91, 133
New Pioneer group 139–42, 279
New Witness, The 47
Nicholson, Ben 270
Nicholson, Harold 88
Nietzsche, Friedrich 33, 95, 96–7, 168, 201, 211, 222
Nolte, Ernst 4
Nordau, Max 247
  Degeneration (1892) 247
Nordic League (NL) 132, 143–4, 195
  see also Angles
Nordic racial myth 27, 32, 74–6, 78, 180–1, 184, 206, 217–18, 234
Nordics 78, 136, 179, 180, 184, 206, 217–18
Northumberland (8th Duke of) 48–9, 50, 134, 177
Nugent, N. 92–3
Nutt MacKenzie, M. I. 144

Olympia meeting (7 June 1934) 98, 103, 187
Order of the Red Rose 46
organic model of culture 209–10, 212–14, 216
Oxford Movement 258

palingenetic myth 5, 55, 129, 168, 191, 223–4, 229
palingenetic ultra-nationalism *see* palingenetic myth
Partito Nazionale Fascista (PNF) *see* Italian Fascism
Patriot, The 49–50, 177, 179, 230, 231, 235, 275, 276, 277, 278, 282
Payne, Stanley 4, 5, 7, 8–9, 29

304

Index

Pearson, Karl 23–7 *passim*, 30, 54
Penty, Michael 264
People's Defence League 55
Peto, Basil 43
Philby, H. St John 140
Picasso, Pablo 271
Pilcher, (Major-General) T. D. 43, 155
Plain English 47, 48, 177
Plain Speech 47
Pollitt, Harry 69
Portsmouth, F. G. 126, 131
Pound, Ezra 237, 270
Pownall, Capel 73, 225
Powys, John Cowper 205
Primrose League 69
pro-modernity 8–10, 255–7, 263–4
Protocols of the Elders of Zion 47, 48, 51, 52, 131, 137, 142, 177, 178, 179, 194, 195, 235, 283
psychological interpretations of fascism 3–4
Public Order Act (1936) 78, 107–9, 113, 152
Pugin, Augustus 258
Pullen-Burry, Betsy 52

racial notion of culture 217–18
Ramsay, Allan 279
Ramsay, (Captain) Archibald Henry Maule 142, 143, 144, 195
Randall, E. D. 223, 255, 257, 274, 281, 282
Raven-Thomson, Alexander 90, 99, 201, 209–10, 212–15, 227, 257, 259
Rawnsley, Stuart 92, 163, 164, 165, 169
Reavely, Cuthbert 144, 259
'Red' Sunday Schools 44, 45, 64
Reich, Wilhelm 3
Reveille movement 43
Right Club 142–3, 195
Rippon-Seymour, (Lieutenant-Colonel) Henry 125, 126, 127
Risdon, William 88, 99, 263
ritual murder myth 78, 179–80
Roberts, D. D. 6

romantic notion of work 31–2, 202–3, 258–61
see also anti-machine
Romney, George 284
Rothermere press group 98, 160, 187
Round Table group 20
rural nostalgia 8, 9, 29, 32, 94, 129, 141–2, 170, 203, 249, 250–1, 257, 264
Ruskin, John 32, 203, 258

Salomon, Sidney 106
Sanderson, William 46, 73–4, 141, 160
Sauer, Wolfgang 8
Scanlon, John 139, 141
Scottish Fascist Democratic Party 133
Scrimgeour, A. C. 139
sculpture 207, 270–9 *passim*, 282
Secret Societies and Subversive Movements (1928) 276
see also Webster, Nesta
Seton-Hutchison, (Lieutenant-Colonel) G. 132, 136–7, 194
sexual revolution (post-war), attitudes to 28, 135, 193, 224–5, 229–30, 252, 281
Shakespeare, William 204, 210, 280
Shaw, George Bernard 30–1, 95
Shelley, Percy Bysshe 204
Sherrard, Leslie H. 72
Shop Stewards' Movement 41
Sickhart, Walter 269
Silver Badge Party of Ex-Servicemen 46
Simpson, Henry 71
Skeels, Serocold 131–2, 196
Skidelsky, Robert 31, 86, 160, 161, 165, 189
Snowden, Philip 87
social basis of fascism 6–7, 66, 154–67
'social credit' idea 89, 140
Social-Darwinism 23–7, 29–30, 181–2, 214
social-imperialism 18–23, 91
socialist tradition and British fascism 30–2

Index

socio-psychological interpretations of fascism *see* psychological interpretations of fascism
Sorel, Georges 33–4, 201, 211
Sorelian revolutionary syndicalism 6
Soucy, R. 6
Soutine, Chaim 274
Spanish Civil War 105, 142, 166
Spencer, Stanley 270, 278
Spengler, Oswald 33, 94, 191, 214–15, 253–6
  Decline of the West (1918, 1922) 214
'spiritual' dimension of fascist revolt 129–30, 168, 211–12, 222, 229, 240, 251, 282
Stamford Fascists 71, 130
Sternhell, Zeev 2, 7, 9–10, 176
Stopes, (Dr) Marie 230
Strachey, John 2, 87, 88
suburbs 254–5, 264
suffragette agitation 17
sun-worship, fascist 251
Surrealist art 270–4 *passim*, 277, 281
Susser, Leslie 93–4, 238
Sydenham of Combe, (Lord) 46, 48, 50, 52, 54, 128, 154
synthetic definitions of fascism 5, 7

Tariff Reform League 18, 43
Tavistock, Lord (12th Duke of Bedford) 139
Taylorism 259–61
Theweleit, K. 4
Third Reich 94, 137
  see also Nazism
Thorak, Josef 207
Thurlow, Richard 27, 49, 53, 54, 63, 66, 68, 69, 72, 73, 79, 142, 161, 166, 192
trade union militancy (post 1918) 40–1
Tudor State 14–15, 17
  see also Elizabethan age of achievement
Tulloch, (Brigadier-General) D. Erskine 72
Turner, H. A. (Jnr) 8

under-consumptionist theory 89
United British Party (UBP) 132, 196
United Empire Fascist Party 131–2, 195
  see also United British Party (UBP)
Unit One 270
Unity Band 68, 131, 133–4, 176, 196, 230

Veteran, The 47
Victory Corps 46
Vigilantes Society 46
Vorticism 269–70, 271

Wadsworth, Edward 270
Wall Street Crash 84
Waring, Dorothy G. *see* Harnett, D. G.
Washington Conference (1921–22) 39
Waugh, Evelyn 225
Webb, Beatrice 31
Webb, Sydney 30, 31
Webber, G. C. 68–9, 144, 152–3, 160, 161
Weber, Eugen 6
Webster, Nesta 46, 48–9, 50, 62, 156, 157, 178, 179, 206, 235, 276, 282
Weimar 'decadence' 233–4
Weismann, August 25–6, 183
Wells, H. G. 30
Wheatley, Frank 134
White, John Baker 45
White Knights of Britain 143, 195
Wilkie, David 279
Williams, Raymond 204
Williamson, Henry 169, 211, 233, 239, 245, 249, 251, 252, 257, 260, 261
'will-to-power' 96–7
Winter, (Brigadier-General Sir) Ormonde 62, 155
Wodehouse-Temple, C. G. 131–2, 196

Yorkshire Fascists 130

EU authorised representative for GPSR:
Easy Access System Europe, Mustamäe tee 50,
10621 Tallinn, Estonia
gpsr.requests@easproject.com